BETWEEN DIGNITY AND DESPAIR

STUDIES IN JEWISH HISTORY

Jehuda Reinharz, General Editor

OTHER VOLUMES
ARE IN PREPARATION

BETWEEN DIGNITY AND DESPAIR

Jewish Life in Nazi Germany

Marion A. Kaplan

New York   Oxford
Oxford University Press
1998

Oxford University Press

Oxford   New York

Athens   Auckland   Bangkok   Bogotá   Bombay
Buenos Aires   Calcutta   Cape Town   Dar es Salaam
Delhi   Florence   Hong Kong   Istanbul   Karachi
Kuala Lumpur   Madras   Madrid   Melbourne
Mexico City   Nairobi   Paris   Singapore
Taipei   Tokyo   Toronto   Warsaw

and associated companies in

Berlin   Ibadan

Published by Oxford University Press
198 Madison Avenue, New York, New York 10016

Oxford is a registered trademark of Oxford University Press

Library of Congress Cataloging-in-Publication Data

Kaplan, Marion A.
Between dignity and despair : Jewish life in Nazi Germany / Marion A. Kaplan.
p.   cm.
Includes bibliographical references and index.
ISBN 0-19-511531-7 (cloth)
1. Jews—Germany—History—1933–1945.   2. Jews—Germany—Social conditions.
3. Holocaust, Jewish (1933–1945)—Germany.   4. Germany—Ethnic relations.   I. Title.
DS135.G3315K37   1998
943.086'09424—dc21   97-46721

3 5 7 9 8 6 4 2
Printed in the United States of America
on acid-free paper

Contents

Preface and Dedication

I have often been told that historians practice their craft because they love to uncover the past and to tell a good story. Certainly, this was true for me in my prior work. I experienced the excitement of revealing hidden stories, of bringing women's history to the fore and challenging old paradigms. Writing this book, however, provoked different feelings, so different that it is important to me to write about them. This book is one I had to write, but, of all my work, it was the hardest book to write. And this, of course, has everything to do with its topic, the genocide of the Jewish people.

More personally, it has to do with my own background. I was born in January 1946. This means that my parents, refugees from Nazi Germany, waited to start a family until they were experiencing the relief of Germany's defeat, until Russian tanks were winning the Battle of Berlin. My mother had emigrated from Germany in 1936, a twenty-two-year-old with no possibility of pursuing her teaching career after the Nuremberg Laws. My father, who worked as a manager in a store owned by a Jewish family, fled to Holland in 1939 upon being summoned by the police in his hometown. My parents met in America. They counted themselves among the "lucky" ones: my mother rescued her parents, my father's siblings escaped Germany, and his parents died natural deaths. Still, they lost all of their uncles and aunts, as well as cousins and friends. Moreover, those who remained—the German-Jewish diaspora—scattered to the ends of the earth. Our family had relatives in Australia, Canada, England, Israel, Latin America, the Netherlands, South Africa, and even West Germany. Wherever they settled, though, the cloud of Nazi Germany's murderous rejection of them remained, even as they and my parents created new lives.

It was precisely their silence, interspersed with occasional references to Hitler, that intrigued me. I wanted to fill in the missing stories, to try to understand how Jews like my parents grasped the meaning of Nazism. How did they react? How did they negotiate the ever-building tensions? What were their options? This is the focus of my book, not the politics or ideology of the Nazis or the causes of fascism and genocide. Instead, I ask how creeping fascism and blatant antisemitism affected Jews in their daily lives, how Jews coped with the loss of their friends, careers, and businesses, the defeat of their hopes, dreams, and futures. What combination of energy, foresight, and luck did it take to get out in time? What role did gender play in assessing Nazism or reacting to it? Personal incidents and unfolding realizations set against a backdrop of social disintegration may, I believe, give us insight into later startling and cataclysmic events.

In coming to this subject, I took a circuitous route (but one which, it seems, led to the Nazi era), studying German literature as an undergraduate and German history as a graduate student. I wrote a dissertation on the Jewish feminist movement in Germany, as well as a later book on Jewish middle-class life in Imperial Germany. Until this project, I avoided the genocide of the Jews. Writing this book brought me to the greatest tragedy of modern Jewish history and one of the central defining milestones of the twentieth century. Moreover, it brought me face-to-face with the very personal nature of this catastrophe. I cried as I finished reading many memoirs. Sometimes, I could not continue my research for the day. I was overwhelmed with relief when one of my friends read a chapter in which I described the deportation of Polish Jews in October 1938 and she marked in the margin: "My family got out just in time, *September*!" Some of the letters I used were written by another friend's grandmother, trapped in Berlin. Sometimes I could only numb myself to the intense pain of the memoirs or letters and to my own connections with them in order to get myself through them.

Thus, this has been an emotionally draining task, but it has also been a labor of love. I am deeply moved by the people I have studied. My respect for them has grown profoundly even when I see—in hindsight—their misreading of Nazi intentions or their self-delusions. One of my friends wondered whether I hadn't constructed women who were too "plucky." I wondered, too, as I reread my manuscript. But the interpretation arises from these women's actions, not from how they framed them in later memoirs or interviews. Despite their inner fears and the acutely depressing nature of the brutality they suffered, they showed enormous outward resolution and energy as they attempted to sustain their families or rescue their men. Although Jewish women were only partially successful—since all too many Jews were caught in the Nazi genocide—they managed, for the most part, to resist their own despair and to remain the "women of valor" so often acclaimed in Jewish prayer and mythology. I dedicate this book to them.

Acknowledgments

The reward of finishing a book is the opportunity to thank the people without whom, literally, the book would not have been written. I have looked forward to expressing my gratitude to many friends and colleagues, as well as to the organizations, libraries, and archives, that have fostered my work. In the first instance, I would like to turn, once again, to my German women's history study group. We have been meeting in each other's homes for fifteen years, sharing our insights about German history and women's history with devotion and an absolutely indispensable sense of humor. This group has provided kind but rigorous criticisms. We have jelled into caring friends who make the pursuit of historical inquiry a collective, rather than a lonely, experience. My admiration and appreciation go out to Bonnie Anderson, Dolores Augustine, Maria Baader, Rebecca Boehling, Renate Bridenthal, Jane Caplan, Belinda Davis, Atina Grossmann, Amy Hackett, Young Sun Hong, Jan Lambertz, Molly Nolan, Nancy Reagin, and Heidrun Suhr. To Renate Bridenthal go my special thanks for reading and rereading, for being there at all times. I am also grateful to my supportive editors Nancy Lane and Thomas LeBien, to Trude Maurer for her meticulous review of the book, to Mark Anderson, Werner T. Angress, and Volker Berghahn for providing help with certain chapters that troubled me, to Amy Hackett and Belinda Cooper for assisting me with translations, and to my agent Sydelle Kramer for her enthusiasm and wise counsel.

I am particularly indebted to Paula Hyman, Rose Kavo, Claudia Koonz, Hanna Schissler, and Frank Stern, who made time for my revised and expanded manuscript in the midst of their overcrowded lives. Good friends, they provided generous critiques and much comfort over coffee, by letter and phone, and in cyberspace.

The aid given by the following institutions and individuals was of major importance: the American Council of Learned Societies, the City University of New York (PSC-CUNY grants, as well as a Scholar Incentive grant), the Leo Baeck Institute, the Littauer Foundation, the National Endowment for the Humanities, and Queens College (Presidential Research Award). I also extend appreciation to the archives and libraries I used in Coswig, Düsseldorf, Hamburg, Koblenz, and Potsdam, as well as to Harvard University's Houghton Library and Yad Vashem Archives in Jerusalem. In particular, I want to thank my colleagues at the Leo Baeck Institute, especially Wendy Henry, Frank Mecklenburg, Diane Spielmann, and Renata Stein, for making my visits there productive and enjoyable.

Finally, I want to thank my family. Writing about the plight of Jewish children and youth in the 1930s with my own (now) seven-year-old and nineteen-year-old in the background and imagining their reactions and their grief made my project deeply personal and even more painful. At the same time, watching them grow and thrive made me grateful and happy to return to their world. So, Joshua and Ruth, thank you for forcing me to switch gears from the 1930s to the 1990s and for being a source of so much love and joy. And Ruth, many thanks for your scrupulous reading of this manuscript during your summer vacation and for sharing your impressions with me. To Douglas Morris, my friend and husband, whose intense interest in and knowledge about the subject have encouraged me and enriched my thinking, goes my deepest appreciation. Your painstaking editing and thoughtful comments have been of utmost importance to me, and your caring and good nature have sustained me through this project.

BETWEEN DIGNITY AND DESPAIR

Introduction

At the advent of danger there are always two voices that speak . . . in the human heart: one . . . invites [consideration] of the nature of the peril and the means of escaping it; the other . . . argues that . . . it is not in man's power to foresee everything. . . .   —LEO TOLSTOY

How did Jews endure the living nightmare of Nazism? This chronicle of how their living space narrowed step by step focuses on the everyday tyranny Jews experienced and the dignity and despair with which they encountered oppression. It examines how Jews assessed the dangers they confronted when the Nazis came to power in 1933 and how they reacted thereafter, when the Nazis attacked their political rights, economic livelihoods, and social relationships. In exploring the most basic and quotidian aspects of Jewish lives—their homes, families, and communities—we can begin to answer the complex questions that have not paled in the past fifty years: What did it feel like to be a Jew in Nazi Germany? What kind of Jewish life was there in Germany after 1933? Why did German Jews not leave sooner? What did non-Jewish Germans do, and what did they know?

Unlike the cataclysm that engulfed Jews trapped by the Nazi invasion of Eastern Europe after 1939, German Jews confronted a growing menace bewilderingly embedded in life as they had known it. For almost six years, they suffered the agonizing double bind of preserving the sanity and normality of their lives while assessing the mounting danger around them, helpless to stop it. Their dilemma was magnified by their ties to Germany—their friends, culture, and identities—and by Nazi policy, which vacillated enough to keep its victims off guard. By the late 1930s, more and more Jews were fleeing Germany. Those left behind faced the harrowing cruelties of ghettoization, forced labor, deportation, and ultimately the atrocities of the "Final Solution to the Jewish Question."

Although the history of Germany's annihilation of its Jewish population has been written and rewritten, the emphasis has been on the killers, on Nazi policies toward the Jews, and, to a lesser extent, on Jewish organizational responses. A plethora of memoirs has also appeared as individuals try to come to terms with their experiences. Yet there is no general history of Jews at the grass-roots level. To fill this gap, I have presented the "little picture" of Jewish daily life to cast new light on the big picture. Combining women's, Jewish, and German history, I hope to reveal how Jews contended with deteriorating and then barbarous circumstances. A focus on Jewish women illuminates the ways in which Jews coped privately; it emphasizes their feelings and personal accommodations. And, just as women's history allows us to investigate the inner sanctums of Jewish life, the history of Jewish everyday life highlights how the German "racial community" (*Volksgemeinschaft*) increasingly cast out the Jews in its midst and what it did on a daily basis to tyrannize Jews.

Historians who study the Nazis tend to argue that their Jewish policy was either part of a methodical plan (the intentionalist approach) or haphazard, contradictory, and the result of internal bureaucratic dynamics (the functionalist approach). Most recently, the debate has focused around the peculiar character of German antisemitism: its wish to "eliminate" Jews, which led to their extermination by "willing executioners," akin to the old cliché that German antisemitism followed a straight path from Luther to Hitler. These debates stem from the bias of looking at the killers. When one examines the hapless *victims* of these policies, the debates pale; they are not something the victims lived. What is striking in the victims' accounts is not whether the Nazis intended the destruction of the Jews due to their unmitigated and unparalleled hatred or whether they backed into it, but the speed *and* the ambiguities of the attack against Jewish life, and the speed *and* the ambivalences with which Jews reacted in the years before 1938. In 1933, a Jewish ten-year-old observed Nazis marching with placards reading "Germans, Don't Buy from Jews. World Jewry Wants to Destroy Germany. Germans, Defend Yourselves." But in 1935, her father was still decorated for active service in the past war, receiving a citation signed by Berlin's chief of police. Jews read these mixed messages with fear and hope. They thought about and prepared for emigration, all the while wishing they would not have to leave their homeland.[1]

The history of Jewish daily life shows how the Nazi government— through indoctrination, bribery, and coercion—turned antisemitic prejudices into a mass movement. Despite the confusing, momentary lulls in persecution and the shifts in some policies at the top, the daily experiences of Jews underline how deeply implicated most Germans were in the gradual yet dramatic process that led Jews toward "social death"—their subjection, their excommunication from the "legitimate social or moral community," and their relegation to a perpetual state of dishonor.[2] As the regime disenfranchised Jews, robbing them of their economic livelihoods and social integration, many Germans approved and more looked on, bolstering, and sometimes preempting, the regime's cruelties. Well before the physical death of German Jews, the German "racial community"—the man and woman on the street, the real "ordinary Germans"—made Jews suffer social death every day. This social death was the prerequisite for deportation and genocide.

Jewish daily life also shows that, despite the abundant deprivations and humiliations, until November 1938 the majority of Jews attempted to adjust to the new circumstances. At home in Germany for many generations, they were aware of antisemitism but distinguished between its varieties and thought they understood its nuances. Even if their dreams of complete acceptance had never been fully realized, they were patriots who had entered German culture. They had achieved amazing success amid antisemitism and in spite of it. Thus, as they continued to maintain their families and communities, they clung to mixed signals from the government as well as from non-Jewish friends and strangers—a lull in antisemitic boycotts here, a friendly greeting there. They hoped the regime would fall or its antisemitic policies would ease.

At the center of Jewish family life, holding it together and attempting to keep the effects of Nazism at bay, women's stories provide a history not of mere victims but of active people attempting to sustain their families and community, to fend off increasingly nightmarish dilemmas. Additionally, these stories offer a more intimate history of the Jewish victims of Nazism than has previously been written. These women's memoirs, interviews, letters, and diaries explore the unfolding Nazi horror through their own eyes, humanizing otherwise impenetrable events of the past and personalizing an otherwise incomprehensible tragedy. These eloquent stories chronicle inner terrors and resourceful reactions and "bring home" the destruction of Germany's Jewish population.

DAILY LIFE AND WOMEN'S HISTORY

"We were so German," "we were so assimilated," "we were so middle class"—these are the refrains we read over and over again in the words of German Jews who try to explain to us (and to themselves) what their lives were like before Nazi savagery overpowered them. They stress how normal and varied their lives were—from small-town cattle dealers to wealthy business people, from religious stalwarts to atheistic communists—and how "German" their habits and attitudes. German Jews—a predominantly middle-class group constituting less than 1 percent of the German population—had welcomed their legal emancipation in the second half of the nineteenth century. Until 1933, they lived in a relatively comfortable and secure environment. Between 1933 and 1939, however, they saw their livelihoods destroyed and their social integration dissolved.

In order to understand what it felt like as the noose slowly tightened, this book emphasizes the stages of persecution and the pace at which conditions for Jews deteriorated. The years before the November Pogrom of 1938—when few dreamed that developments would end in anything like Auschwitz—are often overshadowed by the later, shocking years of genocide. Yet these earlier years shed light on the incremental nature of Nazi persecution. They illustrate how Jews and other Germans adjusted—how victims learned to cope while others looked on or took part—as Nazism penetrated daily life. Even in mid-1938, as Jews endured second-class citizenship and privation, the situation looked unclear to many. Hindsight may make everything seem inevitable, but at the time even the November Pogrom did not provide a clear indicator of the genocide to come. After 1939, however, the rapid escalation of persecution by both the government and German society left German Jews scrambling to flee.

Since the experiences of German Jews varied by gender, age, class, and geography—in urban or rural settings, Catholic or Protestant villages, middle- or working-class[3] neighborhoods—there is no single story of Jewish daily life. Instead, I have aimed to make some sense out of a multiplicity of experiences while acknowledging their diversity. Looking not only at daily events but at subjective experiences helps us understand historical ambiguities and casts light on the varied and sometimes conflicting Jewish recollections of the Nazi era.

A history of daily life shows how mundane issues matter—and often dominate—even in extreme situations. Children must attend school, even as their teachers and classmates become more antisemitic; women must serve dinner, even if grocery stores display "Jews Unwelcome" signs. A history of daily life also illuminates how and why the victims—and also the aggressors—adapted to their roles by showing how abuse, insidiously and incrementally, became "normal" to some and familiar to all. For many Germans, awareness of the regime's cruel intentions came "drip by drip, rather like an anesthetic.... It was only when it hit you personally that you realized what was going on."[4] A Jewish refugee to the United States echoed this sentiment: "I don't think one can ever see if something is on a steady acceleration . . . the terror is steady and you live with it and you go right along with it. And you really crack only if it suddenly increases."[5] By addressing the perceptions of Jews, their coping behavior, and their hopes —as well as the obstacles the Nazis threw in their paths—I want to offer a balanced rejoinder to the oft-repeated accusation that German Jews should have known better, should have left Germany sooner.

Women's history asks the kinds of questions that are central to an understanding of daily life. Women's memoirs illuminate the critical issues of daily life, revealing crucial private thoughts and emotions. Moreover, a focus on women uncovers women's distinctive perspectives on public life, which often differed from those of men. But such a focus shows more than how gender—the culturally and hierarchically constructed differences between the sexes—made a difference in the way people perceived and reacted to daily events. It also shows how gender made a difference, ultimately, in matters of life and death. For example, the Nazis murdered a disproportionate number of elderly women, suggesting that age and gender were a fatal combination. Thus, there were times when gender was of critical significance. At other times, however, its impact was more muted. When was it a matter of life and death, and when was it an ordinary backdrop to the way people perceived and reacted to events? To stress women's history, however, is not to exclude men—quite the contrary. To understand how gender operated, men's history is also required; their memoirs and diaries are also essential. In addition, the memoirs and interviews of Jewish women provide an inclusive viewpoint. Men and children, as well as extended family and friendship networks were central to women's recollections and hence are visible and active at every turn.

Although the calamity that hit German Jews affected them as Jews first, they also suffered based on gender. First of all, racism and sexism were intertwined in the minds of the torturers. The Nazis attacked Jewish men first, demolishing their careers and businesses and leaving women to carry the burden of maintaining their homes and families, of keeping their households and communities together. Jewish men were far more vulnerable to physical assault and arrest until the deportations began. Even if ultimately Jewish women, seen as procreators, were also enemies in the Nazi's "race war," at the beginning Jewish women saw their men arrested —whether for political affiliations or on trumped-up charges—and tried to rescue them.

Not only did racism and persecution mean something different for women and men, so did survival strategies in both practical and psychological terms. The victims reacted not always and not only simply as Jews but as Jewish women and men. For example, gender made a difference in deciding between fight and flight. In the early years, Jewish women were more sensitive to discrimination, more eager to leave Germany, more willing to face uncertainty abroad than discrimination and ostracism at home. In what has been described as communities of "men without power and women without support," we find, for the most part, active women who, early on, expanded their traditional roles. We see anxious but highly energetic women, taking note of the political and social environment and strategizing ways of responding. Many experimented with new behaviors rarely before attempted by *any* German women: interceding for their men with the authorities, seeking paid employment for the first time, selling their homes on their own, and deciding on countries of refuge by themselves. Often taking on "male" roles both within and outside the family, they absorbed much of the domestic stress caused by such accommodations and transformed their own female identities, at least for the duration of the crisis.Even though women transcended certain gender roles, gender as such continued to have consequences in the later years as well, in emigrating, in doing forced labor, and in hiding: in short, "being male or female mattered during the Holocaust."[6]

Afterward, too, gender mattered as people reflected upon their lives. This is important because memoirs are among my most vital sources. They have guided and influenced me as I wrote this book. There is a relationship between gender and memory. Women and men concentrate on different recollections. As one might expect, women's memories tend to center on family and friends, schools and neighborhoods, while men's tend to focus on their business or the political environment. Do they remember differently, or did their original experiences, gendered as they were, provide for the different perspectives they offer? Memoirs raise other issues as well. They are, for example, exceptionally self-selective. Only those women whose sense of self or history was strong enough wrote memoirs. Certainly, many wrote to tell their children of the horrors they and their loved ones had experienced, to express the fears and uncertainties they had felt, but we rarely find women who were paralyzed into inaction or made the wrong decisions, since they would not have survived to write their memoirs. Many women, particularly young women, remained silent (although their voices can be found in later interviews). Gender, then, is both an enriching challenge to memory and another warning sign about the limits of memory.[7]

A history of the daily lives of Jewish women and families necessarily confronts the ways in which German history is remembered and told. It challenges the myth of political innocence that informs some of the most widely known accounts of German "daily life." Mainly oral histories, these accounts leave out Jews almost entirely: the victims are silent, anti-semitism is only rarely addressed.[8] Relying on the memories of bystanders and perpetrators for their part in the crime-saturated Nazi period is morally and historically untenable and gives the impression of the "mor-ally neutral ordinariness of the average German's experience." It leaves us with the question: "Where did all the Nazis go?"[9]

Other questions are equally pressing: How could Germans let Jews be persecuted? Did the "normality" of German daily life stand in opposition to the "abnormality" of Jewish life, or did they actually coexist? Were they even deeply connected?[10] That some kind of "normality" characterized German daily life, even in a terrorist state, may help us understand why so few resisted and so many either acquiesced to or supported the regime. Some framed their lives to avoid looking at what was happening to the Jews. For others, imbued with traditional antisemitism and highly sup-portive of the early antisemitic legislation, the task of normalizing their lives under Hitler was simple. As "racism permeated every aspect of life," they lived with "Jews Not Wanted" signs and remained indifferent to what happened to the Jews. Still others believed that persecution of the "racial enemy" was normal and necessary, actively applauding the undoing of the Jews. It is not surprising that Germans tried to normalize their lives; even Jews tried to normalize their increasingly abnormal lives. It is essen-tial to see Nazism's double character of normality and terror—the effects of both a normal bureaucratic state and a radical racial state on both "Aryans" and Jews.[11]

Re-creating the experiences and consciousness of everyday Germans demands the inclusion of Jews; otherwise we empower and legitimize the perpetrators and silence (once again) the victims. Focusing on the daily lives of *Jews* helps us discover how *German* "normalcy" actually func-tioned. In tracing the innumerable daily interactions of Jews with other Germans and the stages in the social death of the Jews, we see the extreme power that Germans, from Nazi officials to strangers on a tram, had over Jews. It is no wonder that these divided experiences left such "antagonis-tic" memories among Jewish and non-Jewish Germans. What many Germans insisted on classifying as "normal" did not look that way to Jews. Nor did it look normal to a few Germans then or to those of us who look back now. Of course, the regime perversely attempted to make the abnor-mal seem normal, matter-of-fact, even sensible—for example, by labeling its cruel anti-Jewish measures with names like the "Law for the Protection of German Blood and Honor" or the "Social Compensation Tax" and, later, announcing that Jews would be "evacuated" to the East. What is normal when the government behaves abnormally? Those Germans who approved of antisemitic measures could assure themselves that all was "legal," that the Jews deserved to be "brought down a notch," or that the Führer himself did not know about the anti-Jewish "excesses." Such rationalizations notwithstanding, the loss of daily normality for Jews was echoed at many points for non-Jews—from individuals who dropped a Jewish friend, denounced a Jewish neighbor, or refused to serve a Jewish customer to the government officials who used euphemisms to hide their intentions. Life was actually far from normal for those who witnessed vandalism against Jews, worked near Jewish forced laborers, or helped a Jew in dire need. Normal life amid the subjugation and humiliation of others is not so normal after all.[12]

The tension between the normal and the abnormal, the ordinary and the extraordinary, the daily and the long range pervaded Jewish life in Nazi Germany and is critical to our understanding of why some Jews remained while others fled. This tension can be seen most clearly in Jewish women's everyday lives. As they shopped, kept house, cooked, and cared for children and relatives, their everyday life in Nazi Germany resembled an abnormal normality, but one to which they became accustomed. Their success in maintaining the household, in celebrating holidays or birthdays, and in holding family and friends together illustrates their will and their need to structure daily survival. The satisfaction they derived from their efforts also gave some false hope and allowed their families the dangerous assumption of some normalcy amid the hostility of Nazi Germany.

"Daily life" came to a standstill on November 9, 1938, during the state-organized pogrom against Jews, Jewish property, and synagogues. Thereafter, daily life consisted of the unexpected. The unprecedented brutally overshadowed all else as mothers, wives, and daughters sought to free their men from concentration camps and to escape from Germany, as Jews coped with forced labor, cramped housing, and, after September 1939, war, ghettoization, and deportation. It was only when their expectations for daily life and life itself were cruelly limited, when the unprecedented predominated, that Jews understood their true dilemma.

OVERVIEW OF THE JEWISH COMMUNITY

Jewish Life Before 1933

In 1933, about 525,000 people, or less than 1 percent of the German population, were registered as Jews. Seventy percent lived in large cities with populations over 100,000 (while half of non-Jews lived in places with under 10,000 inhabitants), and a third (144,000) lived in Berlin, where they made up close to 4 percent of the population.[13] Like every minority, the Jewish minority had a career profile that differed significantly from that of the general population. Historically prohibited from participating in a variety of economic endeavors, almost 62 percent of Jews (compared with 18 percent of non-Jews) worked in business and commerce. They were underrepresented in agricultural jobs, in which less than 2 percent of Jews (but 29 percent of other Germans) were employed. The employment of Jewish women had increased from 18 percent in 1907 to 27 percent by 1933, but it was still less than that of non-Jewish women (34 percent). Of those employed, over one-third were salaried (white-collar workers in offices or retail shops); about one-fifth were assistants in family enterprises; and another one-fifth were self-employed.[14]

German Jews belonged overwhelmingly to the middle classes. They had achieved legal equality and financial success, although not complete acceptance, by the late nineteenth century. The inflation of the early 1920s and the Great Depression hurt them, and more and more women had to assist or support their families. Their economic decline intensified in the Nazi period, when greater numbers of Jews than ever before had to rely on financial aid from their own Jewish communities. In addition, almost one in five Jews in Germany was a refugee from Eastern Europe (about 70 percent of these from Poland), eking out humble existences as industrial workers, minor artisans, or peddlers. A larger proportion of Eastern European Jewish women than German-Jewish women worked outside the home.[15]

Jewish women were a diverse group, from respectable middle-class housewives to a tiny but noticeable contingent of "new women" who lived independent lives in the exciting and disturbing cities of Weimar Germany. In comparison with non-Jewish women, Jewish women generally had smaller families and more education and were more likely to have household help. Although married Jewish women devoted themselves to their families, parents expected their unmarried daughters to study for a career or, if necessary, to work in a shop until marriage. Many attended a university. By 1932, 7 percent of all women students were Jewish.[16]

Strictly religious observance and practices declined and intermarriages increased during World War I and the Weimar Republic. By 1927, 25 percent of Jewish men and 16 percent of Jewish women were marrying outside their religion. Most of the children of intermarriage were raised as Christians, some learning of their Jewish lineage only after 1933. In the large cities, marriage to Christians was becoming so common—especially among Jewish men—that some Jewish leaders actually feared the complete fusion of their community into German society by the end of the twentieth century.[17]

Jewish women and men eagerly joined nonsectarian organizations. For example, the League of Jewish Women, with its 50,000 members, belonged to the German bourgeois feminist movement from 1908 until 1933, and individual Jewish women were prominent members of German women's organizations. Jews felt a deep allegiance to the ideals of German culture as they understood them: the liberal values of the German Enlightenment, tolerance, humanism, and reason. They enjoyed general acceptance, even acclaim, in the worlds of art and culture, participated in center and moderate left politics, and excelled in the professions of medicine and law. A significant proportion of women doctors and some of the leading women parliamentarians in Weimar Germany were Jewish.[18]

While most Jews adapted enthusiastically to the social, political, or cultural styles of their surroundings, proclaiming their German patriotism and "[quoting] Goethe [at] every meal," the vast majority also preserved a sense of ethnic solidarity and religious cohesion. They did so by organizing religious or secular Jewish groups and creating new forms of German-Jewish culture in literature, music, fine arts, education, and scholarship. Most also maintained traditional holiday celebrations in the family. Most German Jews were religious "liberals" (similar to the contemporary American Jewish Conservative movement), with about 10 percent remaining Orthodox. Secular Jewish organizations fostered a sense of Jewish identity—including religious identity—throughout the Weimar years. The League of Jewish Women, for example, combined feminist with Jewish aims. Its members' interest in their Jewish heritage during the Nazi period was, therefore, not a sudden shift; it was an intensification of a trend already well under way. Before 1933, a growing segment of Jewish youth in urban centers, too, experienced the rebirth of a Jewish milieu via newly organized Jewish schools and a Jewish youth movement. A small Zionist movement, while failing to make significant inroads, also sharpened Jewish self-consciousness.[19] Still, it was the April 1933 boycott that caused the sharpest reevaluation of "Jewishness" and "Germanness" among this population. The boycott forced many to see the impossibility of integrationist aspirations, of laying claim to "Germanness" in Nazi Germany.

Growing Jewish cohesiveness and consciousness notwithstanding, memoirs about the 1930s do not concentrate on "Jewishness," that is, the practice of Jewish rituals or religious behavior and the Jewish milieu. This does not mean that Jews were less religious—the opposite seems to be true. It does mean that these sources do not dwell on the Jewish side of private life for the Nazi years, even among intensely observant people, but focus instead on coping and, later, on survival.[20] They describe Jewish friends and family networks as vital safeguards rather than as the preferred ethnic social milieu of earlier years. As Jews were forced into a social and psychological ghetto, they were preoccupied not with their "Jewishness" but with the world outside.

Jewish cohesion had always been one response to pervasive antisemitism. With roots in Christianity, an increasingly racist variant spread in Imperial Germany (1871–1918). This does not mean, as has recently been argued, that German antisemitism was unusually violent in its imagery or more deeply embedded in German culture than elsewhere.[21] In fact, when German Jews looked toward France, they saw the startling antisemitism unleashed by the Dreyfus Affair; when they looked eastward, they saw pogroms and thousands of Jews fleeing toward Germany's safer political climate. Germany, even with its antisemitism, appeared—and was—a safe haven in late-nineteenth-century Europe. Still, German Jews were neither blindly loyal nor politically foolish. To secure their rights in the face of antisemitic attacks, they banded together to create a dynamic defense organization, the Central Union of German Citizens of the Jewish Faith, in 1893.

Germany's defeat in World War I and postwar political and economic instability magnified anti-Jewish passions. To the radical right, Jews became the scapegoats for all social and economic ills. Even more common and widespread was what has been called "moderate antisemitism, that vague sense of unease about Jews that stopped far short of wanting to harm them but that may have helped to neutralize whatever aversion Germans might otherwise have felt for the Nazis." This atmosphere could be found in churches, universities, political parties, and the government, as well as in relationships between Jews and other Germans. Even those, like Rahel Straus, who worked closely with other German women during the Weimar Republic, commented on the distance between the groups: "We lived among each other, sat together in the same schoolroom, attended university together, met each other at social events—and were complete strangers."[22] There were significant exceptions, such as intermarriages and close friendships that extended until deportation, or even until today. But for the vast majority of Jews, their tenuous friendships with other Germans dissolved as the Nazi terror grew.

Establishing the Racial State

Before their seizure of power, the Nazis had pledged to pursue more aggressive foreign policy aims, to counter "Jewish influence," to attack the political left, and to promote a "racial community" (*Volksgemeinschaft*). This romanticized vision of a racially based *Volk* as one happy family without class conflict rested on a darker premise. It would exclude "traitors," such as socialists and communists; "asocials," such as those with police records or on welfare; homosexuals; "useless eaters," such as the mentally retarded and physically handicapped; and "racial aliens," such as Jews or the Roma or Sinti people (called Gypsies). The Nazis' anti-Bolshevism endorsed the brutal dismemberment of the parties on the left, while their biological politics promised a racial cleansing and reorganization of Germany and Europe that would be implemented through large-scale eugenic schemes. Nazi Germany was hardly the first state hostile to the left, but it became "the first state in world history whose dogma and practice was racism."[23]

Nazi antisemitism was both an instrumental strategy—pulled out at the appropriate moment in front of receptive audiences in election campaigns—and a deeply held conviction. The Nazis dubbed the "Aryan" race the highest of all races, claiming its chief representative was the German people. The label "Aryan" is found throughout this book in quotation marks to remind the reader of its Nazi usage; it was a much-coveted asset in the Third Reich, much as "non-Aryan" (referring mostly to those with "Jewish blood" but also to the Roma and Sinti communities and to other non-Nordic peoples) was a term of disgrace. In memoirs written by Jews, one finds the term "Aryan" with and without quotation marks. Some simply adopted widespread usage, without the ironic or angry distancing quotation marks. The term "race" is more complicated and I have used several approaches in order to recognize it both as part of Nazi policy (without quotation marks, as in racial segregation or racial laws) and as a socially constructed, dangerous fiction (from which I want to distance myself with quotation marks). The Nazis' own terminology (e.g., "racial defilement"), of course, appears in quotation marks.[24]

Along with "non-Aryans," Hitler and the Nazis despised communism, socialism, pluralism, liberalism, and democracy, claiming they were all inspired by Jews. Hence Jews were an amalgam of evils. Hitler and many of his early followers were convinced that there was a Jewish conspiracy to dominate the world. They saw Jews as all-powerful and the cause of Germany's predicament. Although the vast majority of antisemitic caricatures and Nazi propaganda attacked Jewish men, portraying them with hideous facial features and distorted bodies, all Jews, including women and children, were implicated. The Nazis argued that Germany was locked in a life-and-death struggle with a powerful enemy they called "Jewry," a racial struggle in which only one side would emerge victorious. Against Jews, all "defensive" measures were justified. This vitriol succeeded in instilling non-Jews with both hatred and fear, allowing them to see their own aggression as defensive.

From the start, then, Nazi antisemitism was marked by a pathological hatred against Jews similar to that used against political enemies on the Left. In contrast to the immediate, brutal Nazi crackdown on parties of the Left, however, in the 1930s there was a tension between Hitler's desire to give a legal face to his anti-Jewish measures and his storm troopers', the SA's (*Sturmabteilung's*), activism. This tension between propriety and violence played itself out in confusing, sometimes contradictory, decrees and events, as well as in lulls in persecution, such as the months before the 1936 Olympics. Also, in the prewar years, local and regional practices differed slightly from each other and from national directives. At the grass roots, then, Jews experienced mixed signals not only from the government but also from loyal or sympathetic "Aryans," giving some Jews a glimmer of hope. The direction and speed of Nazi policies in the 1930s—legal disenfranchisement, social ostracism, economic collapse and forced emigration within a few short years—appeared obvious to those who had suffered it only in retrospect.

A tiny minority, helpless in the face of massive state persecution, Jews were vulnerable to, and ultimately trapped by, Nazi ruthlessness. Jewish social and cultural life did not cease in 1933. At the onset, many read encouraging signs in their continued economic existence and in the confusion of Nazi decrees. As loyal Germans, they anticipated hanging on to their lives in Germany, hoping the Nazis would weaken after the initial victories. Their daily lives continued—with limitations—at school, work, and play. Religious and cultural life flourished—under communal auspices. Jews rescued some normalcy from increasingly difficult times by assuaging their constant *Angst* in the family and community and making do with less. They endured the increasing onslaught by struggling to maintain their dignity and their daily survival. By the late 1930s, they tried desperately to emigrate but faced onerous, and sometimes insurmountable, barriers.

Jews also organized politically. Before 1933, Jews had resisted appearing as a separate political entity in German society. Anti-Jewish laws, propaganda, and actions in the spring of 1933 provided the impetus for Jewish organizations to come together. In September they formed the Central Organization of German Jews (*Reichsvertretung der deutschen Juden*), a federation of major Jewish organizations that attempted to represent Germany's Jews to the state and the Nazi Party, to influence the regime, and to aid the Jewish community.[25]

Jews were careful, if flawed, observers of an unprecedented situation. They had voted for predominantly liberal parties and the left during the Weimar Republic, political groups that included Jews and opposed antisemitic fanaticism. After 1933, they were neither obtuse nor stubbornly German. Many, especially Jewish women, saw early warning signs. Hindsight that condemns them for not having left in time fails to acknowledge how unimaginable Nazism was to most contemporary observers or how earnestly Jews tried to emigrate once the danger was apparent. Jewish behavior has to be understood within the context of their political understanding, their hopes, and their abandonment by potential countries of immigration.

In describing Jewish life at the grass roots, I want to offer respectful testimony to the struggles of German Jews. I also hope to enrich the fields of women's, Jewish, and German history with evidence and questions from each other. Still, there are many unanswered questions. For example, how did wealth, location (from urban to rural settings), Jewishness (the spectrum from Orthodox to secular), or Zionist versus integrationist beliefs influence one's appreciation of danger and ability to flee or hide? Which contacts with non-Jewish Germans (friendly, neighborly, professional, business, coincidental) proved helpful, and which lethal? In the end, however, this book will be successful if readers begin to visualize how confusing the so-called writing on the wall really was before 1938 and to recognize the frequently gendered ways in which the victims of massive oppression attempted to save their families, their communities, and ultimately—though often unsuccessfully—their lives.

1

In Public: Jews Are Turned into Pariahs, 1933–1938

The problem ... after all, was not what our enemies did, but what our friends did.
                                                        — HANNAH ARENDT

From the outset, the Nazi government used legislation, administrative decrees, and propaganda to defame and ostracize Jews and to lower their social, economic, and legal standing. The April boycott of 1933 attempted to expose German Jews to public opprobrium and to destroy Jewish businesses, and the laws of that month limited Jewish participation in the economy. In September 1935, the Nuremberg Laws formally deprived Jews of their rights as citizens and established racial segregation. It took less than two years to destroy the foundations upon which Jewish life had existed in Germany since the country's unification in 1871.

Jewish women shared the predicament of Jewish men: economic decline, social ostracism, and the loss of trust in their children's economic and social futures. Jewish women also shared the reactions of Jewish men: disbelief, outrage, and fear. Still, their experiences were gendered. In their public tirades and actions, the Nazis focused on Jewish males. Moreover, at first they spared Jewish women physical abuse. Therefore, women took on new roles—interceding for their men with the police, the tax offices, and the landlord—while continuing older patterns of mediating for their families in the neighborhood, at the grocery, or in the schools. They took their cues and considered their alternatives from their vantage point as Jews and as women.

POLITICAL LAWLESSNESS AND ECONOMIC OPPRESSION

The Nazis celebrated January 30, 1933, with torchlight parades and what they called the "restoration of law and order"—instantaneous and cruel assaults on their political opponents. Hitler's SA broke up socialist and communist headquarters—arresting, imprisoning, torturing, and murdering members of these parties and labor unionists. The violence worsened after February 28 when Hitler, using the Reichstag fire as a pretext, abolished basic civil liberties, raised penalties for many crimes from imprisonment to death, and increased the powers of the central government over those of the states. Almost 10,000 communists were arrested and incarcerated in rapidly built concentration camps. The infamous "Enabling Act," officially labeled the "Law for the Relief of the Distress of Nation and State," sanctioned Hitler's assumption of dictatorial power. By March 23, legality had given way to "national will" as represented by Hitler and the Nazi Party.

The Nazis did not immediately single out Jews for attack, busy as they were coordinating the states with the central regime, abolishing all other political parties, and destroying the trade unions. Still, Jews could not always escape violence.[1] And, when a communist, socialist, or pacifist happened also to be Jewish, he or she had far more to fear than a non-Jewish political colleague. Jews were treated even more ruthlessly. Because of their double risk, some Jews fled Germany immediately. The Nazis often "taught a lesson" to those who remained. For example, right after the election of 1933, a Jewish father and daughter were arrested as suspected leftists. The young woman had taken photos of socialist and Nazi demonstrations and of working-class children at play. Officials confiscated her camera and jailed her. She recounted: "The women were put in the same room as female criminals. They were not beaten, they could read books and write letters, but they heard the screams of men being tortured." After three weeks both she and her father were freed. The father had been tortured to such an extent that the cleaners asked if the man whose suit they were cleaning had been hit by a car.[2]

Politically affiliated or even politically interested Jews realized immediately the severity of the Nazi threat. They feared house searches and the possibility that the Gestapo (the Secret State Police) would find—or plant—evidence that would incriminate them. While the Nazis burned books in public, many Jews burned portions of their libraries and their papers in private. In Berlin, the Jewish wife of a non-Jewish political prisoner arrested for "anti-Nazi" behavior was terrified of every move she made. She had been active in the cooperative movement, in tenants' leagues, and,

since 1932, in anti-Nazi activities. Although she "looked Aryan" and therefore met few antisemitic threats on the street, she adjusted to using only
public phone booths, fearing that her own phone was tapped, and burned
her "compromising documents."[3] Journalist Inge Deutschkron also
described how her mother insisted on burning the leftist material in their
library: "Every time my mother consigned another pamphlet to the scrap
heap, Father would protest mildly. 'Are you sure?' he'd ask, and Mother,
who'd always been the more practical of the two and had developed a nose
for danger, would respond almost gruffly."[4]

Fear of house searches caused one couple to spend many evenings looking through books and letters to rid themselves of:

> everything which could be interpreted as doubtful. . . . I . . . fed to the
> flames many papers which might have been of interest to children and
> grandchildren; for example, excerpts of various newspapers and periodi-
> cals, . . . papers of the "World Peace Association of Women and Mothers."
> . . . The Minister of Culture for Bavaria had stated: "Every pacifist deserves
> to be whipped out of the country."[5]

The Nazis were brutal toward politically affiliated women, both Jewish
and non-Jewish, and a number of female Reichstag deputies and female
state parliamentarians suffered beatings and death at their hands. Of the
five most prominent Jewish women in politics—all members of socialist
parties—everyone escaped. Four left the country immediately, presuming
that their politics would bring the wrath of the Nazis down on them. The
fifth left in 1938 after her mother had died.[6]

Jews jailed as communists—whether the charge was true or false—had
the most to dread. They were accused of "preparing for high treason."
Recha Rothschild, a member of the Communist Party, quickly destroyed
her files in February 1933. She fled her apartment, returning to it (at the
end of March) after the SA had stormed in, stolen her belongings, and
shredded all of her books and papers. She hid but was caught and charged
with being a courier for the Communist Party, even though there was no
hard evidence against her. The Reich court declared the evidence too
flimsy, but the Prussian court, under Nazi control, sentenced Rothschild to
two years in prison. There, among political prisoners, criminals, and pros-
titutes, her health deteriorated dangerously. Spitting up blood, she still
refused "to drop dead for the Nazis."[7] The Nazis treated Jewish women
caught in the act of resistance even more brutally. Käthe Baronowitz was an
active communist who led a cell of ten people. Her landlord, who was in the

SA, spied on her, and in 1936 she and eighty-three other communists were arrested. First, she was tortured: "The cruelties and perversities of the interrogation can hardly be described. [She] had to undress completely. A howling pack goaded on by alcohol surrounded her. They stuck pens in her vagina and paper flags which they burned so that they could gloat over the tortured woman's screams of pain." They called her "Jew whore" as they tormented her. Ultimately, she was sentenced to twelve years of hard labor.[8]

As was the case for non-Jews, the Nazis frequently took Jewish wives hostage in order to force politically active husbands who had fled or hidden —often at the urging of their wives—to give themselves up. Also, the police or Gestapo interrogated wives or mothers about the whereabouts of men. Sometimes these women suffered punishment for their sons' or husbands' escapes. After Isaak Plaut fled the small town of Rauschenberg in 1935, the police arrested his wife, Therese. Luckily she and the mayor had been classmates. She called him from jail and asked, "Aren't you ashamed to leave me sitting here?" He freed her, and she left Germany in early 1936. Early Nazi terror was capricious. Although Therese Plaut managed to turn to an old friend, most women hostages had no such recourse. At the end of 1935, 75 percent of all women in the Hohenstein jail, one of six women's penal institutions, were hostages for their male relatives. Hostages' memoirs give a sense of the extraordinary violence that started even in the very first weeks of the regime. When the Jewish wife of a Leipzig Jewish communist was arrested as a hostage after he had fled for his life, their five-year-old son—atypically—was also imprisoned with his mother. Fearful, he refused to separate from her, hugging her tightly when the guard came to take her for interrogation. The guard tore him away from his mother, throwing him backward brutally. He died when his head hit the metal edge of a prison bed.[9]

More frequently than official arrest, Jewish families confronted sudden lawlessness: "Naked brutality, breach of law, the most dreadful hypocrisy, unmitigated barbarism pose[d] as law." The law also became a source of persecution. As bourgeois champions of the *Rechtsstaat*, or rule of law, which had bolstered Jewish claims to equal citizenship in the nineteenth century, German Jews found the perversion of law difficult to bear. And individual Germans took advantage of the legal defenselessness of Jews. A Jewish woman, living in Nuremberg, reported: "The most frightening fact at this moment was being deprived of the protection of the law. Anybody could accuse you of anything—and you were lost." The worst was reserved for Jewish men. One woman described how her husband had been badly beaten by one of his tenants. When he asked the police for support (something some Jews still tried to do in 1933), they refused. Another man was arrested because a neighbor complained of his behavior toward her dog. Leaving a note explaining that he "could no longer stand the unjust and defenseless life of a Jew in Germany," he killed himself in prison.[10]

In general, Jews navigated increasingly menacing public spaces. Even a trip to the post office could have dire consequences. After Hilde Sichel muttered about the unreliability of the post, a postal clerk threatened to denounce her: "Every evening I thought about the day that just passed and asked myself if I had done or said anything that could endanger my husband or myself." Jews even feared being the recipients of occasional grumbling by non-Jews. Lily Krug described her reaction when an "Aryan" neighbor complained to her about the price of butter in front of others: "I did not answer and hurried away without buying anything. I was frightened. Fear, fear, fear—morning, noon and night. Fear followed us into our dreams, racking on nerves. How imprudent, how inconsiderate of the woman to speak like that in public."[11]

For Jews, daily fear was accompanied by economic strangulation. Long before forced "Aryanization"—the complete takeover of Jewish assets—occurred, families began to lose their businesses, could no longer pay for their properties, and were often subjected to extortion. Although some larger Jewish business and manufacturing establishments maintained their economic position somewhat longer, as did Jews in certain sectors of the economy (such as the fur trade),[12] small "mom-and-pop shops" (*"Tante Emma" Läden*) declined precipitously. Many individuals of "Aryan" ancestry benefited from the demise of Jewish businesses, purchasing them at greatly reduced prices.

Governments, courts, and storm troopers urged customers and clients of Jews to do business elsewhere. Almost immediately the SA began a series of economic boycotts against Jewish shops and professionals. Boycotts created a climate of fear that affected Jews and non-Jews, intimidating the latter and frightening and hurting the former. On April 1, 1933, "on one of the best business days of the year, on the Saturday before Easter," the regime declared a national boycott of Jewish businesses. In announcing this first national boycott, Hitler called it a "defensive measure" against anti-Nazi propaganda abroad for which he blamed the Jews. The boycott generally lacked public enthusiasm. It was uneven, with little support displayed in Berlin but excesses, including injury to and even murder of Jews, reported elsewhere.[13] SA and Nazi Party circles were joyful, but apathy, even resistance, was widespread. While SA men stood in front of businesses owned by Jews, threatening and taunting those who dared to enter, some Germans chose precisely that day to visit a Jewish doctor or grocer. Moreover, the stock market fell, in part because many Jewish stores were in foreign creditors' or German banking hands. And, the boycott once again raised a vexing question: Who, after all, was a Jew? These problems forced cancellation of the boycott on the same day it had begun. Still, the Nazis claimed "success" despite their own disappointment at "Aryan" responses. To some extent, their claims were right. The boycott had taken a large toll among Jews in fear and intimidation.

Since the boycott was the first major public event turned specifically against them, many Jews left memoirs describing that day. A few shut their businesses to avoid trouble, but most remained open deliberately. Some commented on the loyalty of their customers during this first, early test. One man recalled that his small department store in Hanau did far more business the week before the boycott than it had in years. His customers stocked up in case the boycott dragged on, declaring their solidarity with his family. In Dortmund, observers noted the disgust with which many Germans approached the boycott and the courage with which they entered Jewish stores while the SA hurled insults and abuse their way.[14]

Jews also described their own resistance. Some resisted silently, as in the case of World War I veterans who stood in front of their own stores wearing their uniforms and medals. Others resisted verbally. When a young ruffian, determined to cause damage, aggressively barged into Dr. Herta Nathorff's office shouting, "Is this a Jewish enterprise?" she responded: "This is not an enterprise at all, these are doctor's office hours. . . . Are you sick?" With that, the boy left. Nathorff made a point of buying in stores owned by Jewish people on that day and told the SA sentry, "For my money, I'll buy where I want!" Erna Albersheim, who had been born "half Jewish" in New York and had married a German-Jewish man, displayed great personal courage in confronting Nazis in Frankfurt, where the boycott was relatively effective. When the Nazis picketed her store, she confronted them as an "American" and told them to leave. They did. "I walked into my store with head erect, but I was glad that no one could see my knees—they had the firmness of jello." In Stettin, Olga Eisenstädt tried education rather than confrontation. She stood outside her small shop arguing her personal case to passersby, in the hope that they might generalize to other Jews:

> I pointed out that I was a soldier's widow, that I had received the Emperor's Service Cross in the First World War and the Cross of Honor for soldiers' widows from Hindenburg. . . . I had also received a diploma from . . . Stettin in recognition of my social work during the . . . war. I had

taught hundreds of soldiers' wives and widows [how] to make supplies for the army.[15]

As measured by Nazi expectations, the official boycott day failed. Jewish businesses were given a brief—official—lease on life because the precarious German economy could not then stand further destabilizing measures. Moreover, Jewish big businesses remained relatively intact, since they employed many "Aryans" and their failure could hurt the overall economy.

Unofficial boycotts, however, whether spontaneous or instigated by local officials, persisted. Many Germans who had been angered or embarrassed by the boycott on April 1 and had shown courage on that day tended to retreat into privacy thereafter. They gradually submitted to the pressures of the "racial community," remaining silent rather than defending Jews. In rural areas, for example, Jewish dealerships of cattle, horses, and grain declined as a result of long-term boycotts. Although at first some peasants remained loyal to business relationships that had occasionally spanned generations, arguing that they got good prices and products from Jewish dealers, they gradually succumbed to pressure. Also, the Nazis disrupted long-term working relationships in the countryside between Jews and non-Jews. Jewish cattle dealers often had to fire their non-Jewish helpers in order to protect them from abuse.[16] But in the cities, too, customers who were loyal at first began to dwindle as the government increased its attack on Jewish businesses.

Boycotts were only one among many strategies used by the government and mercenary individuals to attack Jews in the economy. Jews were physically brutalized by the regime: in Breslau, for example, the SA beat up Jewish jurists, chasing them from their offices. The Nazis also pressured Jews to liquidate their businesses or sell out to "Aryans." Restrictions and official and unofficial harassment increased in frequency and fervor. As a result, many Jewish businesses, particularly small ones, were forced to shut down or sell out. Alice Baerwald, who lived in Danzig in the early 1930s, described how the Nazis ruined the livelihoods of Jewish families. She wrote about a couple who had built up a large clientele as hairdressers to support themselves and two children. After the Nazi takeover, a German asked to buy the store for a ludicrously low price. Surprised, they turned him down. Soon thereafter, local authorities accused the couple of tax evasion, arrested the man, and confiscated their valuable equipment. The family suffered ruin within a few days. Another couple owned a small drugstore, which they put up for sale when the wife suddenly went blind. An interested buyer exploited the situation by accusing the couple of tax evasion. The husband was arrested and forced to sell for a pittance. The government arrested another head of household for allegedly transferring money abroad, although it was clear that he had legally purchased a delivery car abroad. His business and home furnishings were confiscated. A variety of "Aryans" used the beleaguered position of Jews to their own financial advantage. One cattle dealer recalled: "Blackmail occurred every day. Debtors demanded receipts for bills that they never paid. There was no point in bringing legal action against them in court." Tenants could refuse to pay rent with impunity, and in some cases they accused the landlord of being an "enemy of the state" in order to be temporarily freed of their obligations. By 1936, many areas of small business, particularly those associated with agriculture, were declared *judenrein*, "free of Jews."[17]

Jewish businesses in which non-Jews held significant shares were relatively safe at first. Some Jewish owners could continue their businesses if they found an "Aryan" partner. But this was a short-term solution at best. Ultimately, Jews had to sell out to their "Aryan" partners, and Jews whose "Aryan" partners had died or disassociated themselves had to give up their businesses. For example, a Jewish woman, no longer protected by her deceased husband's "Aryan" status, had to give up her business at the weekly market in 1939. She became a cleaning woman. Of the approximately 50,000 Jewish small businesses operating at the end of 1932, only 9,000 still existed by July 1938. The bulk had failed to attract "Aryanizers" and had simply collapsed. By November 1938, no more than 20 to 25 percent of all Jewish businesses remained.[18]

While some Jews lost businesses, others lost their jobs or realized the futility of finding jobs as a result of laws passed in April 1933. Feigning strict legality, the Nazis passed the "Law for the Restoration of the Professional Civil Service" and others like it. The Nazis used these "laws" to exclude opponents of the regime and "non-Aryans," defined as people who had one "non-Aryan" parent or grandparent. The so-called Aryan Paragraph of the April laws forced the dismissal or early retirement of Jewish doctors, lawyers, judges, and civil servants (along with political "undesirables"), with the exception, insisted upon by the aging President Hindenburg, of those who had fought in World War I or had been in their jobs before August 1914. About half of Jewish judges and prosecutors and almost a third of Jewish lawyers lost their jobs. A significant proportion of Jewish doctors lost their German National Health Insurance affiliation (severely limiting or ruining their practices). Since the civil service in Germany encompassed far more jobs than, for example, in the United States, the April laws meant that even lower-status jobs such as civil service messengers, city street cleaners, and train, postal, or Reichsbank employees had to be filled by "Aryans." A further set of decrees put a quota on Jewish students in schools and universities. These decrees affected up to 867,000 people, Jews as well as other "non-Aryan" Christian Germans.[19]

Hereafter, the jobs of millions of Germans—Jews, "Aryans," and those caught in the middle—depended on the Nazi definition of their racial status. A scramble for proof of "Aryan" lineage ensued. The journalist Bella Fromm noted in her diary that "genealogists are doing a grand business. There are advertisements ... daily.... 'We provide you with every kind of document and evidence.'"[20] They located birth, parish, or synagogue records, acquired declarations from Vital Statistics Offices, or unearthed old family trees.

The field of teaching illustrates the changes that occurred. In 1933 in Prussia, 1 percent of male teachers and 4.5 percent of female teachers were discharged (at least two-thirds of the women who were fired were "non-Aryan," as were almost all the women student teachers who were fired). In early April 1933, Hanna Bergas entered the school in which she taught for the last time:

> When I arrived at the school building,... the principal, saying "Good morning" in his customary, friendly way, stopped me, and asked me to come to his room.... When we were seated, he said, in a serious, embarrassed tone of voice, he had orders to ask me not to go into my classroom. I probably knew, he said, that I was not permitted to teach anymore at a German school. I did know, but was it to happen so abruptly? ... Mr. B. was extremely sorry.... I collected myself [and] my belongings.... There was nobody ... to say goodbye to, because everybody else had gone to the classroom.... In the afternoon ... colleagues, pupils, their mothers came, some in a sad mood, others angry with their country, lovely bouquets of flowers, large and small, in their arms. In the evening, the little house was full of fragrance and colors, like for a funeral, I thought; and indeed, this was the funeral of my time teaching at a German public school.

Bergas's pain at losing her position reflected the loss not only of a job but also of a community and profession. Like Jewish men, professional women suffered economic adversity and the anguish of seeing their social status diminished and their professional reputation rendered meaningless.[21]

Dismissing Jewish teachers conveniently allowed the government to find teaching assignments for 60 percent of 1,320 "Aryan" job applicants in 1933. Here were opportunities for the unemployed and upward mobility during

the Great Depression. Similarly, the dismissal of Jews in the Prussian administration affected between 12.5 and 15 percent of positions, and in other
states between 4.5 and 5 percent. There seems to have been little public
complaint—and silent endorsement—about the ousting of Jews.[22] When
the Nazis purged the courts, even as staunch an anti-Nazi as Thomas Mann
approved. Married to a Jewish woman, he nevertheless confided to his
diary: "It is no great misfortune . . . that . . . the Jewish presence in the judiciary has been ended," although he worried about his "secret, troubling"
thoughts regarding the Jews. He evinced satisfaction when Alfred Kerr, a
well-known Berlin critic who had often attacked Mann's work, lost his position. Selfish motives played an important role with Mann as with others. In
Hamburg, Lotte Popper's friendly non-Jewish neighbor told her that her
daughter had chosen one of two suitors, the assistant judge: " 'Now he has
the best prospects . . . in court, where they are firing so many . . . people.'
Mrs. Hansen stifled the word 'Jews' and . . . expounded at great length upon
her daughter's happy future."[23]

Non-Jewish doctors, too, profited from the removal of Jewish doctors,
accepting positions that had "become free" and patients who no longer
patronized Jewish doctors. In June 1933, there were about 5,500 Jewish
doctors in Germany, or 11 percent of all physicians (although the percentage is higher if one includes all "non-Aryan," that is, partly Jewish, doctors).
They were concentrated in large cities, where most Jews lived. The early
1930s had seen vicious competition among doctors, resulting from the
depression and from the increasing numbers of doctors who either
belonged to or wanted to join the National Health Insurance organizations.
While some doctors demanded the removal of their Jewish colleagues from
the National Health Insurance, others pushed for their total ruin. Dr.
Henriette Necheles-Magnus described the crude tactics of a non-Jewish
doctor who was so eager to absorb her practice that he told her patients she
had killed herself.[24]

In June 1933, about 13 percent of women doctors were Jewish, with the
proportion much higher in big cities. A few weeks after the German
Doctors' League (*Verband der Ärzte Deutschlands*) expelled Jews, the League
of German Women Doctors (*Deutscher Ärztinnenbund*) ousted its Jewish
members. Herta Nathorff described this exclusion in her diary:

> April 16, 1933: Meeting of the League of German Women Doctors. As
> usual, I went today, after all this is where the most respected and best
> known women colleagues in Berlin gather. "Strange atmosphere today, I
> thought, and so many strange faces." A colleague whom I did not know

said to me, "You must also be one of us?" and showed me the swastika on the lapel of her coat. Before I could answer, she stood up and fetched a gentleman into our meeting, who said that he had to demand the *Gleichschaltung* [the Nazi takeover or Nazification] of the League in the name of the government.... Another colleague ... my predecessor in the Red Cross ... who had been dismissed ... because of unfitness and other not very nice human qualities ... stood up and said, "Now I ask the German colleagues to go into the next room for a discussion." Colleague S., a good Catholic, ... asked: "What does that mean—German colleagues?" "All who are not Jews, of course," was the answer. Now it had been said. Silently, we "Jewish and half-Jewish" doctors stood up and with us some "German" doctors—silently we left the room—pale, outraged to our innermost selves. We then went ... to discuss what we should do now. "We should quit the League as a united group," some said. I was opposed. I will gladly allow them the honor of throwing us out, but I will at least not voluntarily abandon my claim to membership.... I am so agitated, so sad and confused, and I am ashamed for my "German" colleagues![25]

Either on their own or because of government pressure, patients, too, turned away from Jewish doctors. The National Health Insurance organizations scolded and later threatened them for continuing to go to Jewish doctors (and this was only to those remaining Jewish doctors who had not been dropped from the insurance system in April 1933). Moreover, racial enthusiasts accused patients who continued to go to Jewish doctors of being traitors to the *Volk*.[26]

Late to enter what Germans called the "free" professions—notably medicine and law—Jewish women suffered severe job losses. Whereas some Jewish men could claim exceptional status as veterans or because they had been in their jobs since before 1914, Jewish women could hardly profess to have fought at the front. Furthermore, because of the late admission of women to German universities, most female Jewish professionals had taken their positions only after 1914. The result in the medical field was that the vast majority of Jewish women doctors lost their health insurance affiliation, compared with about 40 percent of Jewish males. In a letter about her sister's loss of most of her medical practice, Betty Scholem concluded that Jews "are being destroyed in this bloodless way just as certainly as if their necks had been wrung."[27]

In September 1933, Goebbels took over the Chamber of Culture and excluded Jews from German cultural life, film, theater, music, fine arts, literature, and journalism—areas in which Jews had been disproportionately active. Simultaneously, many private businesses and state licensing boards demanded that their employees be "Aryans."[28]

Unemployment began to plague the Jewish community. In 1933, about two-thirds of Jewish salaried employees worked in Jewish businesses and firms. With the disappearance of many Jewish firms, joblessness soared. By the spring of 1933, nearly one-third of Jewish clerks—compared with one-fifth of the non-Jewish ones—were looking for jobs. In Berlin alone, where the general unemployment rate hovered at 16 percent, more than a third of Jewish salaried employees and half of Jewish workers were jobless. Even as the German economy improved, with unemployment dropping from 6 million in January 1933 to 2.5 million in January 1936, Jews took no part in the general recovery.[29]

Because more than half (53 percent) of employed Jewish women worked in business and commerce, largely as family assistants (22 percent) and salaried employees (40 percent), they lost their jobs as family businesses and Jewish shops closed down. Jewish sources estimated that three-quarters of Jewish women in business and trade were hurt by the discriminatory laws and the early anti-Jewish boycotts. Jewish Employment Bureau statistics for 1934 and 1936 show that, although women seemed to find employment more readily than men (except in the free professions), only a minority of job seekers of either sex actually found placements.[30] By April 1938, over 60 percent of all businesses that Jews had owned before 1933 no longer existed, and Jewish social workers were trying to help 60,000 unemployed Jews. Furthermore, those businesses that lingered on tended to be either at the very top (a few banks and financial institutions) or the bottom (independent artisans). Women rarely worked in either.

Despite limited job options, many Jewish women who had never worked outside the home suddenly needed employment. While some sought jobs with strangers, others began to work for their husbands who could no longer afford to pay employees. The hope was that "work for married women [was] only ... an expedient in an emergency." By proclaiming the crisis nature of women's new position, Jews, both male and female, could dream of better times and ignore the even more unsettling issue of changing gender roles in the midst of turmoil. Contrary to their hopes, by 1938 there were "relatively few families in which the wife [did] not work in some way to earn a living." Finding a job under new and hostile circumstances, particularly for women who had never worked outside the home, could be deeply demoralizing. Women had to assess their abilities in midlife—often with little more than a typical girl's education and no marketable skills. Job ads, employment offices, friends, and acquaintances held out little hope.[31]

Still, in spite of discouragement, both memoirs and statistics show that women eagerly sought opportunities either to train for a job for the first time or, in many cases, to retrain for new jobs. Some prepared for new work in Germany, many for jobs they hoped to fill abroad. Ruth Abraham took a speed course in becoming a corsetiere while on a three-month visit to her sister in Palestine. Although Jews could no longer be licensed by the time she returned to Germany, she quickly developed a private circle of customers. Some women prepared for several jobs and studied several different languages at once, assuming that they needed to be versatile should they emigrate. One woman studied English and took lessons in sewing furs, making chocolate, and doing industrial ironing. A mother and her daughter took courses in Spanish, English, baking, and fine cookery. Then they asked their laundress to accept them as apprentices. This role was not only new for them but was also a reversal of their previous class position.[32]

Whereas most women understood their behavior within the context of an emergency, some may have taken advantage of dire circumstances to fulfill ambitions that would have languished in better times. One woman not only took cooking classes because she would soon need to handle the household herself but also began training as a psychotherapist to support her family when they emigrated. She had to leave her husband and children for an entire year in order to study at Jung's institute in Zurich. In normal times, she probably would have remained simply a doctor's wife.[33]

The Jewish communities in various towns and cities also offered courses in which women eagerly enrolled. In Hamburg, such courses included cooking and baking, sewing and tailoring, hat making, glove making, artificial flower arranging, and smocking. Communities also offered typing, shorthand, bookkeeping, photography, and languages classes. By 1935, Jewish organizations needed more home economics teachers. While many financed their training (and, in many cases, retraining) themselves, the Jewish community's Central Bureau for Economic Relief supported the instruction of 20,000 men and women until the end of 1937. Moreover, by 1938 there were ninety-four retraining collectives for agriculture, handicraft, home economics, and nursing. Zionist organizations played a large role in these collectives through their *Hachsharah* centers, which taught practical skills needed in Palestine. About 23,000 young people—about one-third of them females—learned how to raise chickens or to work as locksmiths, tailors, or baby nurses. Ultimately, by 1941, 17,000 Jews readied in these centers entered Palestine under its quota for "workers."[34]

Cooks at the Jewish Winter Relief kitchen, Berlin. (Courtesy of the Leo Baeck Institute, New York)

According to Jewish observers, women seemed "more accommodating and adaptable" and had "fewer inhibitions" than men; were willing to enter retraining programs at older ages than men; and were more amenable to changing their lives to fit the times. The number of women who successfully retrained in these years was almost evenly distributed between the ages of twenty and fifty, whereas men most frequently retrained between the ages of twenty and thirty, and usually stopped seeking retraining by forty. Leaders of the Berlin Jewish Community noted that retraining for women was less costly and took less time than for men (three to six months for women, compared with about one year for men). Presumably, women were taught less skilled jobs than men. Also, although most had worked as sales clerks or office help, they already knew many of the skills necessary for jobs as seamstresses, milliners, or domestic workers.[35]

Younger women under age thirty-five were the most likely to still find work. They took jobs in Jewish concerns as other Jews began to emigrate. Also, the demand for help picked up in the expanding Jewish social service sector and—after the Nuremberg Laws—in Jewish households. In 1936, 52 percent of the female applicants for commercial jobs in Berlin could be placed, compared with 22 percent of the male applicants. That same year the demand for Jewish female household personnel in Berlin exceeded the

Used clothing exchange of the Jewish Winter Relief Agency. (Courtesy of the Leo Baeck Institute, New York)

supply. There was a general shortage of female household helpers, particularly in small towns, and an even more serious shortage of nurses in Jewish hospitals and convalescent homes.[36]

Job availability in some sectors notwithstanding, the employment and economic prospects of all Jews was bleak. Whereas only 8 percent of Jews were manual workers in 1933, 56 percent fell into that category by 1939. As unemployment increased, so too did poverty. The highest percentages of needy Jews were found in areas with the largest proportion of Eastern European Jewish immigrants. In 1937 the Berlin Jewish Community supported fifteen soup kitchens and provided used clothing for thousands of Jewish Berliners.[37]

Legally, Jews had rights to public assistance until 1939. In practice, however, the Nazis found ways of denying all forms of state and quasi-state benefits to Jews. Although the total number of Jews receiving every form of public welfare during the 1930s is not available, as early as the winter of 1935–36 the Jewish Winter Relief Agency subsidized 20 percent of the Jewish population; another 20 to 25 percent were living off the capital they had received from the sale of their businesses.[38] In 1936, nearly 60,000 Berlin Jews received clothing from such used-clothing storerooms. Men's suits, in particular, were in great demand, whereas women's clothing, easier to repair by experienced housewives, could be replaced more readily. Winter Relief Agency workers remarked that the social descent of Jews could be seen "most clearly by their depleted clothing. To remedy [this] means not only material, but also psychological relief."[39]

As early as April 1933 (a few months before the founding of the Central Organization of German Jews), leading Jewish organizations had founded the Central Committee for Help and Construction (*Zentralausschuss für Hilfe und Aufbau*) to prepare for possible emergencies. The Central Committee broadened the scope of social welfare work, joining the Central Organization of German Jews in early 1935. The Central Organization spent its budget for 1936 (of about 4.3 million marks) on migration and emigration, economic aid, and welfare work. Its revenues came only in part (1.6 million marks) from the German-Jewish community; grants from abroad provided about 2.1 million marks, and the rest was pure deficit. Sadly , as early as 1937 the Central Organization recognized that it could no longer meet the requirements of its constituencies. It had received monetary requests "from all regions . . . because poverty had soared. All of these petitions had to be turned down with a heavy heart."[40]

DAILY LIFE, DAILY DEPRIVATIONS: FOOD, SHELTER, AND RELATIONSHIPS WITH OTHER GERMANS

On the national policy level, the status of Jews substantially deteriorated between 1933 and 1938. On the individual, experiential level, the lives of individuals and families were affected unevenly. Many assessed their situation by how much they suffered while doing daily tasks. They wondered how to sort out the truly menacing from the merely annoying or disappointing and how to react—by ignoring? warding off? fighting back? Despite the routine nature of their tasks, and often amid the apparent ordinariness with which Jews continued their daily existence, many began to fear the arbitrary, and often surprising, callousness and hostility of their neighbors, colleagues, and fellow citizens. This want of compassion and growing animosity toward Jews was part of a widespread attitude toward other purported "enemies," such as communists or Jehovah's Witnesses. It was characteristic of the everyday interactions of many non-Jewish Germans toward each other, since the Nazi state destroyed "bonds of solidarity . . . and [applauded] as strong and healthy those 'who have no sympathy for any but themselves.'" Rabbi Joachim Prinz summarized the situation: "The

Jew's plight is to be neighborless. . . . Who knows how long one can stand a life without neighbors."[41]

Renting and Shopping

Vigilant in public, Jews no longer felt safe even in their homes. Aside from ever-threatening police searches, Jewish families had to face the arbitrary decisions of their landlords, since their rental contracts were no longer secure. In early 1936 in Berlin, for example, a number of municipal rental agencies canceled rental contracts because of "non-Aryan" status and evicted Jewish occupants. Private landlords acted similarly. Elizabeth Bab recalled that although their landlady had promised her family that they could live in their apartment forever, she "found an Aryan doctor who seemed more secure as a tenant than a Jewish writer." Bab's family had to look for a new apartment, even though they assumed no one would rent to Jews. And, even if the landlords respected leases, they often harassed their Jewish tenants.[42]

Food purchases were also limited, either by decree or through the hostility of shopkeepers. The early prohibition against kosher butchering (April 21, 1933) caused great hardship for the Orthodox community but also affected other Jews who had continued to purchase kosher meats. At first, the Orthodox community imported more expensive substitutes from Denmark and the Netherlands, but many could not afford these. Even this practice stopped well before the official prohibition against importing in 1938, creating difficulties for religious Jews and even malnutrition. In spite of state directives and potentially severe punishment, some successful resistance to these decrees continued in Orthodox communities throughout the 1930s. Schlomo Wahrmann, who grew up in an Orthodox family in Leipzig, wrote: "I soon discovered that in spite of the ban on *shechitah* [kosher slaughtering], we continued to eat chicken at regular intervals. . . . When I presented this . . . to my parents, I was not granted a satisfactory answer despite my obstinacy and persistence. . . . I was simply told that I was too young to understand this." He learned that a small group of kosher slaughterers continued to perform their work in secret, slaughtering thousands of chickens every week. Hundreds of Jews knew this was happening, as well as over thirty of the children in his Jewish school. The boy marveled that no one informed the police. His father, who owned a small shop but had been trained as a kosher butcher, also slaughtered meat for the community at great personal risk. Wahrmann's mother "lived in . . . constant fear. . . . My father, of course, took every precaution. . . . Often, my younger sister would carry the [koshering knife] to the chicken market because we were confident the Gestapo would not apprehend such a young girl. Nonetheless, my mother remained tense."

Despite its rather startling incidence in Leipzig and its occasional occurrence in small towns, illegal kosher slaughtering was an exception.[43] Many religious Jews had to learn to live with meatless dishes. In an attempt to solve the dilemma for Jews who had difficulty buying kosher meat, the League of Jewish Women published a cookbook with many vegetarian dishes; the book went through four editions in its first year (1935). The League's newsletter, as well as other Jewish papers, also suggested vegetarian recipes. By November 1937, the League's winter menus placed a heavy emphasis on apples, potatoes, and cabbage. A typical day's menu included oatmeal, cabbage stuffed with rice, and steamed apples for the main meal, and salad, a hard-boiled egg, and cooked plums for the lighter one.[44]

Increasingly, Jews encountered difficulty in buying basic goods. Well before the Nazis forbade the purchase of various essentials, Jews faced hostile store owners. More and more signs reminded them that they were "not desired." Even schoolchildren had to be wary of where they purchased their supplies. Ann Lewis received a list of "friendly" bookstores from her Jewish school but wandered into one closer to home. The storekeeper tried to ascertain the name of her school: "I think he strongly suspected that I was Jewish but was not absolutely sure. . . . He kept on asking for the name of the school and I continued to withhold it, and eventually I went out without the book and ordered it from our friendly Jewish-owned shop." Friendly shop owners, or those who did not want to turn any customers away, continued to serve Jews. But this was unusual enough that some Jews commented upon it in their memoirs.[45]

Strangers

As troublesome as renting or shopping had become, the most important indicator of how the Nazi takeover affected Jewish life was the daily interaction that Jews had with non-Jewish strangers, neighbors, household helpers, and friends. Well before Jews were forced to wear a star in order to facilitate their identification, popular responses, cruelly anticipatory of later Nazi policies, made their lives miserable. Strangers on trams, in stores, and even on the street targeted those who "looked" Jewish and mortified their victims by pronouncing their suspicions loudly. In a small town tram, a woman insulted a Jewish man who got up to give her his seat, refusing to sit where a Jew had sat. Some Germans claimed such keen olfactory senses that they could identify Jews by their "garlic" smell. In these cases, Germans drew on their long-standing aversion to garlic, really an antipathy to things foreign, to torment German Jews, a group whose own aversion to garlic was just as strong as that of other Germans. The Jewish victims of these verbal assaults met with shrill complaints on streetcars: "It smells like garlic" or "It smells like Jews." Sensitive eyes and noses prevailed in restaurants as well, where some Germans complained about "a terrible smell of garlic" when Jews walked in. German patrons also caused commotions in restaurants if they identified Jews eating there. One Jewish woman from a small town dined with colleagues from work. The next day, her friends told her that patrons at a table close by had seen her laugh and had warned "if they saw that Jew woman laugh one more time, they would throw her out into the street."[46]

Germans often believed Jews resembled the antisemitic caricatures in Nazi newspapers. This had two results. The first was that non-Jews frequently mistook Jewish people for "Aryans" and vice versa. Such faulty "expertise" could lead to altercations, as when a man commented about a "fat Jewish woman," provoking a punch from her husband. The couple was "Aryan." The second result of confusing Jews and "Aryans" was that for Jews there was indeed less need to conform, less fear of intimidation, and more freedom of movement if one's light skin color, blond hair, and blue eyes corresponded to Nazi stereotypes and allowed one to "pass." Not only, for example, did such Jewish teenagers roam the city, visiting movie houses forbidden to Jews, but they even hitchhiked with unsuspecting "Aryans."[47]

Accounts of mistaken identity are legion and are told with a certain relish by Jewish witnesses. In one case, a woman remarked upon three children seated across from her in a train compartment. She admired the two "Aryan" types and denigrated the darker girl. The father of the two finally told her that the two blonds had a Jewish mother and the darker one was "Aryan." A favorite anecdote describes a Nazi "race hygiene" expert visiting a school who would unwittingly invite a Jewish child to come to the head of the class in order to point out the characteristics of "Aryans" on the Jewish child's body—to the general hilarity of the rest of the class.[48] In part, the narrators tell these stories to "prove" how stupid many Germans were, how so many believed the nonsense their government spewed forth. The narrators also reveal a sense of pride, a way of identifying *with* Germans, that is, "We really looked 'German'!" (During the deportations, "looking German" could indeed save lives for those who hid from the Nazis or passed with false identification.)

Jewish women may have been the subject of mistaken identity more often than men because the Nazis' caricature of "the Jew" was most often male. In Nazi propaganda, a strangely distorted Jewish male might be accompanied by an obese, jewelry-bedecked woman and her grotesque children, but usually it was the male whom the Nazis vilified. Generally, Jewish men and "Jews" were conflated. For example, at a dinner party in late 1933 the vice mayor of Berlin, Oskar Maretzky, assured the Jewish journalist Bella Fromm that "I am only against Jews, not against Jewish women. Especially not against charming Jewesses."[49]

Since Jews were not typically as dark, nor "Aryans" as light, as the Nazis' bizarre imaginations conceived, color stereotypes misled those who hoped to detect Jews. So did gender stereotypes. For example, women's identities were less easily ascertained by their profession, since fewer Jewish women than men worked outside the home. And women could escape detection by avoiding unfriendly storekeepers who knew them to be Jewish. Two cases from Danzig during the early years of the Nazi regime show situations in which Nazis mistook Jewish women as "Aryan" (and in which these women courageously denied that identity). In one incident, an SA man stopped a blond Jewish woman walking down the street with the reprimand "A German woman does not wear make-up." Affably, she responded: "Luckily I am a Jew and can do as I wish with my face." When an SA member came to the home of another woman and asked if she would like to buy a German fashion magazine, she answered: "Jewish women have concerns other than German fashions." When he showed surprise at her statement, she replied: "I'm an absolutely Jewish type, dark, small, lively.... In any case, the way they depict us in the *Stürmer,* we certainly don't look like that." There were even some Nazis who, steeped in their ignorance and inflated in their arrogance, refused to believe that Jews who "didn't look Jewish" were so. At a ball in May 1933, Ernst (Putzi) Hanfstaengl, Hitler's close friend (and a Harvard graduate), told Bella Fromm, "You should go to the Anthropological Institute for a consultation. I think it is absurd that you should be Jewish. Your skull has the perfect Aryan formation."[50]

Neighbors, Acquaintances, and Employees

Insults by strangers, as offensive and intimidating as they were, had less impact upon Jews than the behavior of people they actually knew. It was likely that adult Jews had a wide circle of non-Jewish acquaintances through work and Jewish children through school. The reverse also seems to be true: many Germans knew some Jews. One postwar survey determined that about 66 percent of respondents had some Jewish acquaintances up until 1939.[51]

Jews commented on the new silence of neighbors and associates—not only toward Jews but also toward each other. A Jewish dentist in a working-class district of Hamburg observed that his patients no longer discussed politics. His wife, Lotte Popper, wrote: "They had all become quieter." She also noticed that non-Jewish women, who used to grumble about price increases or discuss politics while shopping, "mutely bought their cabbage and their potatoes," and the grocers served them without a word.[52]

As Germans began to treat each other with reserve, they broke decisively with Jews. Neighbors and acquaintances turned away most abruptly in small towns and villages, where about 17 percent of the Jewish population lived. In one southern town a Jewish woman and her non-Jewish neighbor had spent the previous twenty years gardening in their adjoining plots, chatting as they worked. As a result of Germany's new mood, they no longer spoke. Two other sets of neighbors—friends for generations—stopped seeing each other when the non-Jewish neighbor's daughters became Nazis; the mother cut all contact with the Jewish family. Former employees also deserted Jews. For example, Jewish cattle dealers found that their aides refused to milk their cows on the Sabbath. This refusal left the Orthodox Jewish owners in a predicament, since Jewish law forbade work on the Sabbath. In 1936, rabbinic authorities gave permission to milk the cows, declaring the situation in Germany a "time of great emergency."[53] Finally, among the peasant population, where stereotypes that Jews belonged in Palestine, had certain physical characteristics, or engaged in strange rites were present well before 1933, these beliefs became rampant.

In villages and small towns, where everyone knew each other, Jews stood exposed to planned and random attacks, and they often either knew or recognized the culprits. Hitler Youth processions, in which boys sang blood-curdling antisemitic songs as they purposely marched past Jewish homes, were particularly intimidating. And even early on, personal physical attacks and stone throwing were commonplace. Although Jewish men received the brunt of abuse, women and children were not spared entirely. In Ihringen (south Baden), several Jewish women feared leaving their homes because villagers had thrown stones at them. In Fulda, not far from Frankfurt, an "Aryan" child attacked a Jewish boy by smashing into his bike, spitting at him, and shouting, "Damned Jew, aren't you in Palestine yet?" The Jewish boy's father observed two women standing in front of the *Stürmer* reading Nazi allegations of Jewish involvement in "ritual murder." He heard: "Isn't that horrible. . . . And it must be true otherwise the Jews wouldn't stand for it!"[54] By attributing power to Jews, Germans rationalized their own vile prejudices even as Jews felt more and more impotent.

It was in such towns that Jews regularly found their windows smashed and their homes smeared with tar. In the tiny town of Gladenbach (in

Hesse), 108 of the 1,756 residents (a relatively high percentage) were Jewish. In March 1933, a mob raided the home of one family twice, destroying its contents and intimidating the residents. A few days later, rowdies beat a Jewish man and taunted and threatened other Jews. The next day, another Jewish man was forced to "recant" his alleged defamations of Hitler in a public spectacle. In June, authorities arrested several Jewish men. In August 1935, ruffians assaulted Jews in their homes, stoning and ransacking their apartments. One Jewish woman, who no longer slept at home for fear of being attacked, returned from a neighboring town one morning to find her house completely flooded. In September another band of masked men invaded three homes, assaulting the Jewish inhabitants.[55]

Funerals were a time and place where small-town meanness was particularly conspicuous, since funerals had previously been a time of general neighborliness, sympathy, and piety. In one town, a Jewish man saw a corpse being removed from a house and asked a stranger who had died. The response was, "A Jew just kicked off. Thank God. Now we have one Jew less!" In 1937, a Jewish man, well-known and liked by his neighbors, died. Even at this late date, some non-Jews intended to come to the funeral but were intimidated by threats that their photos would appear in the *Völkischer Beobachter*, the slanderous Nazi publication posted in every town. Only two peasants from a neighboring village came to the funeral, saying they were not going to let threats stop them from paying their final respects. As Jewish guests arrived at the house, local children mocked them with loud laughter and nasty comments. By the end of 1938, harassment at Jewish funerals had become widespread. Small groups of Germans would shout antisemitic insults at the mourners gathered at the cemetery, whether in cities, like Leipzig, or in small villages.[56]

Big city neighbors, too, could make life upsetting for Jews. Jews feared the male and female "block wardens" assigned by the Nazis to spy on neighborhood affairs, as well as the superintendents of their own buildings. Too often, neighboring housewives, well positioned to watch everyone, anointed themselves as guardians of the locality and zealously tormented Jews. In Leipzig, a woman insisted that the baker stop delivering rolls to her Jewish neighbors. "Jews don't need fresh rolls!" she protested. The baker apologized to the distressed Jewish family but stopped making deliveries. In another city, an overzealous neighbor put a warning sign on her door: "Do Not Leave Packages or Messages Next Door. THEY ARE JEWS." The last three words were underlined in red. Other neighbors took it upon themselves to spy on Jewish tenants and to report them to the Gestapo.[57]

Surprising acts of simple neighborly decency—as little as a good-morning greeting—came as a great relief but also served as a false basis for optimism. They meant that Germans weren't all "that way," that there were "good Germans." Lisa Brauer recalled: "There were days when we were overwhelmed by desperation, but an understanding word from an Aryan neighbor, a kind inquiry from a Gentile acquaintance, gave us always . . . new hope and confidence." Neighborly solicitude could also save some Jews from danger. A neighbor warned Brauer to break up a birthday party when he heard that she was suspected of holding a secret meeting and would be arrested. Although Brauer's physician husband had often treated this man's ten children for free, she believed that gratitude alone did not explain the concern he had shown. It was such ambiguity—small kindnesses on the one hand, meanness on the other—that made the assessment of danger so complicated for many Jews. Furthermore, in the early years, Jews experienced mostly isolated local ostracism or attacks, often based on personal resentments or economic rivalries rather than on racism pure and simple. Thus, despite the pain or shock these caused, Jews could hope that the animosity might diminish.[58]

In memoirs and interviews, the decline of sociability in the neighborhood is remarked upon more by Jewish women than men, for most women spent more time at home and in the neighborhood than did men. Women's lives bridged the gap between family and community; they were more integrated into and dependent upon the neighborhood and more accustomed to neighborly exchanges and courtesies. Those who had been active in communal, volunteer, or women's organizations suffered when they were ostracized. Moreover, women probably had more frequent contacts with local government officials than did men. Since fewer women than men worked full-time, they did the family chores, which included more meetings with such state agents as post office and railroad clerks, social workers, and, for mothers in particular, teachers. They could observe clearly, on a local level, the changing mood toward them of such government personnel. Men saw less of neighbors and had less time to engage in communal or volunteer activities or to approach local officials. Also, although men now suffered the loss of courtesy at work, they were used to competition and a certain degree of conflict in their everyday work life and may have made more allowance for unfriendly, or even hostile, behavior.[59]

Many Jewish families worried not only about their neighbors but also about their own hired household help. They began to fear that non-Jewish employees would be disloyal or, worse, would denounce them. Memoirs describe how a maid's boyfriend became an SA or Nazi Party member and, to her employers' dismay, continued to visit his girlfriend in their home. That this was the situation not only for Jews but for anti-Nazi "Aryans" as well is illustrated by Maria Kahle, who noted ruefully, "My servant's fiancé, who had been repeatedly jailed for theft and counterfeiting, was the first party comrade I came to know." Although there are no studies of how hired help reacted to Jewish employers, one can read stories of touching fidelity as well as the opposite. Hostile employees rarely betrayed Jews but, instead, continued to work for them while expressing antisemitic beliefs, breaking the house rules, or stealing. Lotte Popper recalled that the maid she had employed for six years became a Nazi. The maid suddenly slept with her boyfriend in the house and stole linens and tableware. Such robbery was yet another example of popular reactions, "significantly predating the massive thefts of the November Pogrom." Popper was not only upset about the house rules and thefts; she and many others were also experiencing a strange phenomenon occurring within their homes: the disruption of former class relations. Just as in society at large, many "upstarts" and formerly déclassé rose to the top, so, too, in the home, the maids got the upper hand. Afraid to fire these employees, some Jewish families found new positions for them and were relieved when they departed.[60]

It is the allegiance of female household help, however, that stands out in most narratives. Older women, in particular, seem to have remained loyal, a good number even after they were forced to leave the employ of Jewish families. Often, women who had worked for Jewish families for many years, sometimes for generations, felt part of the family and were treated as such. In Munich, Charlotte Stein-Pick's former domestic rushed to her side when she heard that Stein-Pick's husband had been arrested. There the older woman confronted an SA man stationed in front of the house to ward off visitors. She admonished him and dashed inside. In Berlin, Elisabeth Freund, disappointed in "some of our so-called friends," described the devotion of "old Hedwig," who had worked for the Jewish family for over forty years (first in Freund's parents' home). Knowing that her husband could lose his job if she were caught, she still brought food from her own family's allotment until the Freunds emigrated in 1941: "Despite . . . fear and nervous tension she comes anyway and hauls groceries."[61]

Friends

Former friends provided the most painful evidence of a "new era." As early as 1933, a woman from Nuremberg noticed that "it had become a great guessing game as to which of your friends would have the courage to stand by you and which ones would suddenly abandon you." Marta Appel's experience illustrates the texture of some of these friendships, as well as the responses of many Jews to them. She had regularly enjoyed coffee with non-Jewish friends in a Dortmund café, but after the Nazi takeover she decided to avoid them: "I was afraid to go to the meetings. I did not want the presence of a Jewess to bring any trouble." One day she met one of her friends:

> She begged me: "Come again to us; we miss you; we feel ashamed that you must think we do not want you anymore." . . . She tried to convince me that they were still my friends. . . . I decided to go to the next meeting. . . . I had not slept the night before. I was afraid for my gentile friends . . . and I was also afraid for myself. . . . I knew I would watch them, noticing the slightest expression of embarrassment in their eyes when I came.

On the appointed day, she entered the café, but:

> It was not necessary for me to read their eyes or listen to the change in their voices. The empty table in the little alcove which always had been reserved for us spoke the clearest language. . . . I could not blame them. Why should they have risked losing a position only to prove to me that we still had friends in Germany?

Appel came to understand the processes at work. In early April 1933, she had expressed delight at the constancy of her non-Jewish friends, many of whom purposely came to her home to voice their dismay:

> But after some months of a regime of terror, fidelity and friendship had lost their meaning, and fear and treachery had replaced them. . . . With each day of the Nazi regime, the abyss between us and our fellow citizens grew larger. Friends whom we had loved for years did not know us any-more. They suddenly saw that we were different from themselves. Of course we were different, since we were bearing the stigma of Nazi hatred, since we were hunted like deer.[62]

Sometimes Jews tried to protect their non-Jewish friends and themselves by avoiding contact. In Dortmund, the Appels began to look away when they saw Christian friends on the street, "for we did not want to bring upon them the danger of imprisonment for being considered a friend of Jews." In a small Rhineland town, in late 1933, a Christian woman went to visit her

Jewish friend. When she arrived at the door, her friend looked at her in horror: "For God's sake, Frieda, leave, don't come in, we are already being watched." With tears in their eyes, they turned away from each other.[63] There may also have been Jews who avoided non-Jewish friends to protect themselves from the anguish of eventual disloyalty by the "Aryan" side, although memoirs and interviews are silent on this subject.

Despite the pain they felt, or perhaps to assuage it, some Jewish women tried to redefine their own understanding of "friendship" to include friends who were no longer willing—or, as they saw it, able—to be seen with Jews in public. One Jewish woman from a small university town in southern Germany, for example, claimed she had not been disappointed by her "gentile" friends. She gave the example of a "very good gentile friend" who had apologized that she could no longer be seen with her Jewish friend because her own husband's position would be jeopardized. She continued to visit the Jewish woman at night.[64]

The strangest situations occurred in friendships with "half Jews" or Jews in mixed marriages. Erna Albersheim, considered a "half Jew" by the Nazis but protected by her U.S. passport, tried to maintain a social life with Jewish and non-Jewish friends. By the mid-1930s, she noted: "This Aryan business was getting on my nerves. Jews were afraid to associate with me and Aryans also. I sometimes felt like a leper. . . . My intimate friends still came. I was very careful for their sakes and never invited Jews and Aryans at the same time." Erna Becker-Kohen, a Jewish convert married to a Catholic, described how her pharmacist's wife tried to befriend her. Resigned and sad, Becker-Kohen informed the woman that she was Jewish, adding that within three days the woman would no longer greet her on the street. The pharmacist's wife argued with her but shortly thereafter avoided her, following threats that she would be reported to the Gestapo. Becker-Kohen concluded: "I understand the steadfastness of people."[65]

Friendships between Jewish and non-Jewish members of the opposite sex—not necessarily lovers—could be dangerous to both parties. In September 1935, the Nuremberg Laws defined in detail who was a "Jew," limited the rights of Jewish and non-Jewish Germans to have sexual relations with or to marry the partners of their choice (the "Law for the Protection of German Blood and Honor"), and revoked Jewish legal rights to full citizenship ("Reichs Citizenship Law"). Since the anti-mixing laws forbade sexual intercourse between "Aryans" and "non-Aryans" (including "Jews, gypsies and negroes"), any friendship between a woman and man of different "race" could be, and often was, construed as sexual. These relationships were not just illegal but challenged the basis of the Nazi state, its vaunted "racial hygiene." The danger of false accusations made most Jews and non-Jews of the opposite sex avoid each other.[66]

Germans, in general, avoided Jews anyway. Although I have found no memoir of a German admitting this, Christabel Bielenberg, an English woman married to a German and living in Germany, acknowledged her personal failure to maintain relationships with Jewish friends:

> I could pinpoint no exact date when normal ... association with Jewish friends became an act of defiance and then petered out.... When was it that credulity turned to doubt, doubt to resignation, and to the unhappy, rather shamefaced admission that you were sorry, you could not help it, you happened to have been labelled an Aryan ... and truth to tell you'd be mighty relieved to know that the good friend was safely off your conscience overseas?[67]

While most Germans avoided Jews, many barred them outright from previous social gatherings. A good number of organizations swiftly "Nazified"—even before they were forced to do so. Like the German doctors described earlier, the German Chess League, the Association of the Blind, the Teacher's Association, the German Association of Pharmacists, and the German Automobile Club, to name only a few, swam ahead of the tide, eagerly banning Jews from their midst. And if an organization lagged in its racial enthusiasm, individual members eagerly expelled Jews. In Bad Dürkheim, for example, a Jewish woman attended a reading society until a hostile neighbor expressed her surprise that Jews could still belong. The Jewish woman took the hint and, fearful of denunciation, never showed up again. This kind of incident repeated itself innumerable times: a zealous member of the *Volk* apprised a Jewish associate that she or he no longer belonged to a particular group, and, fearing further embarrassment, pain, or denunciation, the Jewish person withdrew—without a word from former colleagues or friends. Well before national laws prohibited or limited Jewish and "Aryan" interactions, individuals and organizations began to spurn Jews. After the war, Hannah Arendt summed up this situation: "Our friends Nazified (*gleichschalteten*) themselves! The problem ... after all, was not what our enemies did, but what our friends did."[68]

Not all Germans abandoned their Jewish friends. It was often precisely an experience of loyalty—the friend who came by ostentatiously, the former classmate who went out of her way to shake hands with a Jewish woman in a crowded store, or the "sympathy purchases" after the April boycott—that gave Jews mixed messages, letting some deceive themselves into staying on.[69] Jews clung gratefully to the smallest kindnesses—often only common courtesies—and recalled these instances in their memoirs. A non-Jewish German had to be exceptionally strong to sustain friendships with Jews or to help them. Maria Kahle and her grown sons, living in Bonn, helped a number of Jewish families. As a result, her husband lost his job as a professor and the family was persecuted by Nazis during the November Pogrom. When her name appeared in the *Westdeutsche Beobachter* as a "traitor to the *Volk*," none of her former friends stood by her. Ultimately the Kahle family emigrated to England.[70]

Touching cases of loyalty notwithstanding, the Nazis could generally count on grass-roots acceptance of, or even enthusiasm for, isolating Jews: "It was not a matter of SA brutality or SS terror, it was the organized strength of the *Volksgemeinschaft* which step-by-step transformed Jews into impotent pariahs." The process of isolating Jews resulted not only from Nazi propaganda or venal motives, but also from deep-seated prejudices that approved of racial segregation and the removal of Jews from their career posts. Not only fear of state terror but also the zealous, self-imposed restrictions by Germans themselves isolated Jews. Well before the Nazis prohibited contacts with Jews (not officially a crime for nonparty members until November 1941), gossip and denunciations inhibited such associations. Denunciations abounded, with about one-fourth coming from women. False accusations, most invariably based on corrupt reasons, mushroomed.[71] "Mistrust was everywhere," wrote a Quaker woman in 1940, describing situations in families and neighborhoods. Moreover, at work she sat in the same room with thirty women for one and one half years without becoming acquainted with *any* of them. Commenting on non-Jewish Germans, a Jewish woman wrote in 1940: "The worst thing in the Fatherland today is that spies are so protected and sponsored that no one is sure that his best friend, or his nearest relative will not betray him. No one can be trusted. Traitors are everywhere."[72] For Jews, companionship with non-Jews became the rare exception. Officials, neighbors, even the mail carrier looked past or through Jews as they crossed paths.

Long before widespread physical violence began, the regime transformed Jews into the object of a general, hateful taboo. Hanna Bergas recalled that when she traveled on the tram, on the day of the April 1933 boycott, she felt self-conscious about being Jewish and feared that the people next to her might move away from her if they guessed her true identity. Marta Appel wrote:

I hated to go out, since on every corner I saw signs that the Jews were the misfortune of the people. Wherever I went, when I had to speak to people in a store I imagined how they would turn against me if they knew I was Jewish. When I was waiting for a streetcar I always thought that the driver would not stop if he knew I was Jewish.... I did not go into a theater or a movie for a long time before we were forbidden to, since I could not bear to be among people who hated me so much.[73]

A series of practices and policies to Nazify public spaces and segregate Jews compounded fear and social ostracism. While many Germans already shied away from Jews, in 1934 Nazi Party members were forbidden from appearing in public with Jews and by 1935 they were prohibited from having personal contact of any sort. As early as 1933, many municipalities withdrew special transportation funds from Jewish youth groups, and, in Prussia, "race studies" were introduced into the schools. Increasingly, localities posted "Jews undesired" signs at the entrances to swimming pools and beaches, some officials noting by 1935, "The public is beginning to feel [that] togetherness with Jews, especially integrated bathing, is disgusting (*ekelhaft*)."[74] Jewish children were harassed in public playgrounds, and by 1935 Jewish youth groups could no longer camp on public sites or use public youth hostels. Frequently, private business practices against Jews preceded official decrees. Private tennis courts began to shut their doors to Jews; growing numbers of hotels refused to accommodate Jews; and restaurants and movie theaters started to hang signs on their windows requesting only non-Jewish clientele.

The café, or *Konditorei*, a favorite location of respite for bourgeois Germans of all faiths, became "off-limits" as well. Jews avoided such cafés, with one man noting that "the owners were doubtlessly happy, because they did not want unpleasantness.... We encapsulated ourselves and spared ourselves personal hurt." Those Jews who "tried to go on with our lives" gathered in the few cafés owned by—or newly opened by—Jews or in the train stations of larger cities. There, the signs banning Jews were not displayed for the sake of Germany's international reputation. By the middle of the 1930s, even an eight-year-old could notice the Nazification of public space: Ann Lewis observed the Nazi flags and the showcases where the scurrilous, antisemitic *Stürmer* tabloid was displayed. She could not enter her favorite café because "the proprietors ... no longer wished to serve Jews," and a "nearby cinema put up a card ... saying 'Jews are not wanted here.'"[75]

The Nazi government largely succeeded in its endeavor to isolate Jews completely by the mid-1930s. Between 1933 and 1938, "people's moral insensibility to the fate of the Jews became more profound and wide-spread." The government bureaucrats, Gestapo, and courts worked "to discipline (or 'educate') society at large about the importance of the race issue [and] to adjust all opinions to bring them into line with Nazi teachings." Charges of "friendship with Jews" and, more seriously, "race defilement," were used to scare Jews and non-Jews away from each other. The Nuremberg Laws led to the final destruction of many relationships, as well as to arrests of Jews and non-Jews who had close friendships. By 1936, the Nazis had "achieved a deepening of the gap" between Jews and other Germans; "the belief that Jews were another race was widespread."[76]

JEWISH REACTIONS IN PUBLIC:
JEWISH SOCIAL LIFE AND JEWISHNESS

Banned from "German" culture, theater, film, music, and art, Jews were unwelcome even as audiences (although officially permitted until 1938). Loath to accept cultural deprivation, they created their own events, continuing to appreciate German music and the Enlightenment classics in their own theaters and auditoriums (to the extent that the ubiquitous Nazi censors allowed). They also promoted Jewish education, opening two Jewish continuing education institutions in 1934.[77]

Individual Jewish communities and organizations attempted to replace the camaraderie and leisure activities from which Jews had been excluded. In Düsseldorf, for example, when tennis clubs excluded Jews, the Organization of Jewish War Veterans opened its own court. Non-Orthodox synagogues opened their doors to secular lectures and concerts. Even Orthodox synagogues offered cultural programs in surroundings normally reserved for sacred purposes. In small towns, however, some synagogues shut down because of the abuse Jews experienced en route to Sabbath services.[78]

The Jewish Cultural Association (*Jüdischer Kulturbund*) is the most famous example of Jewish creativity in response to cultural exclusion. Founded in the spring of 1933 at the initiative of Jewish civic leaders, it endured under Nazi auspices and censorship until the Nazis dissolved it in 1941. The Jewish Cultural Association offered entertainment to Jewish audiences, employed Jewish artists who had been fired as a result of racial decrees, and provided a semblance of leisure for its almost 70,000 members in forty-nine locales. Of course, the Nazi regime permitted the association solely for its own advantage, to hide the oppression of Jews. Moreover, the association could not perform works forbidden by the Nazis: at first, for example, Germanic legends and, later, the works of Schiller,

Goethe, Beethoven, or Wagner. In hindsight, Elizabeth Bab, whose husband worked for the Jewish Cultural Association, was critical, believing the organization gave Jews a chance to earn an income, the illusion of life as normal, and the "fantasy that they could do themselves and their companions some good." The psychological denial inherent in the association's activities may have gone too far for some. Nevertheless, it offered an important "window to the world." In "its stubborn refusal to give up its bond to Europe and to deny its intellectual tradition," it provided some momentary psychological relief from and a sense of fleeting dignity to daily life under Nazism: "People emerged from their loneliness and fear to laugh together for a few hours."[79]

The Jewish Cultural Association was particularly important to Jews in small towns who could not hope to slip into a performance and remain unrecognized as they might in larger cities. But after the brief diversion of a concert or a theater performance, Jews periodically confronted Nazis waiting for them in the streets. In a small university town one such event was interrupted by a mob shouting "Jewish traitors." The frightened Jews cut the meeting short and hurried away, all too aware that the police would not protect them. Antisemites also harassed Jewish performers and speakers as they traveled to small Jewish communities to present lectures or cultural events. Speakers needed Gestapo permission for every event, and a Gestapo agent usually sat in the audience.[80]

Jewish women's organizations, the League of Jewish Women in particular, tried to alleviate the worsening conditions of all Jews, with special attention to women. From its inception in 1904, the League had focused on feminist issues relevant to observant, but not Orthodox, Jews. In 1933 the League resigned from the Federation of German Women's Associations, the umbrella organization of the German women's movement. The Federation dissolved itself rather than face *Gleichschaltung*, although many of its members and affiliates quickly agreed to Nazi principles, immediately ousting Jewish members.

Like other Jewish organizations, the League of Jewish Women took part in a battle for survival, endeavoring to keep communal organizations intact, to maintain Jewish traditions, to help needy Jews, and to prepare people for emigration. As the Jewish community drew together under outside pressure, it began to work closely with the Central Organization of German Jews and its welfare bureau. The League also intensified its ties to other Jewish women's organizations and to the Jewish youth movement. Consisting of about 50,000 members with 34 local and 430 affiliated groups, it founded new chapters and welcomed new members. Even in

1935, when it needed Gestapo authorization to expand, 2 more locals and 20 new affiliates joined the League. In Berlin, the League's Professional Women's Group grew so large that it divided into nine subgroups: welfare workers, technical assistants, kindergarten teachers, nursery school teachers, youth group leaders, doctors, gym teachers, arts and crafts instructors, and groups interested in pedagogy. In 1935 a member wrote: "As everything crumbled around us, . . . as we lost our jobs, the League invited all professional women. Soon, various groups were formed to give everyone the opportunity to meet with professional colleagues and to attend professionally interesting lectures."[81] New topics, such as "What Does the Émigré Have to Know about Diseases in Other Countries?" and "Women and Employment Today," suggest the needs of the women in attendance.

Concerned that economic insecurity and cultural deprivation could disrupt "emotional balance," the League looked after members' morale. It instituted neighborhood evenings, "so that women of different professions living in one neighborhood could meet . . . to come together both intellectually and spiritually in a small circle." One woman reported on a meeting that took place in 1935: "The first evening was unforgettable. Everyone introduced themselves by name and profession, skimmed over their education, hiring and job, and—the disintegration. . . . Then we spoke of our adjustment to our current lives." For many, the study of Jewish traditions also enhanced morale. Accordingly, the League sponsored cultural activities, such as reading circles, lectures, and a newsletter, that focused on Jewish custom, history, and religion. Local League groups arranged traveling libraries, concerts, and exhibits of work by Jewish women artists. For several years, the League also organized a one-week summer school. In 1935, Martin Buber lectured there, in a small synagogue in Bad Nauheim, where he spoke about Talmudic literature. But, "in the middle of a lecture a burst of stones shattered the windows. . . . Buber continued as if nothing had happened. Thanks to his presence of mind and self-discipline, the violent interruption was completely ignored."[82]

Local sections of the League also, but more rarely, discussed general topics relating to German culture and feminism. At first, Jewish women, like Jewish men, refused to give up their dual identities as Germans and Jews. Even as the League increasingly turned to Jewish topics, it upheld its own version of German culture—enlightened and liberal. The leaders of the League of Jewish Women reaffirmed their allegiance to the women's movement, seeing themselves as "trustees of the German women's movement in its purest, most spiritual, social-ethical, unpolitical form." Bertha Pappenheim, the founder of the League, insisted that "being a German, a woman and a Jew are three duties that can strain an individual to the utmost, but also three sources of . . . vitality. They do not extinguish each other, in fact they strengthen and enrich each other."[83]

The League of Jewish Women encouraged its members to do volunteer work within the Jewish communities. When the Nuremberg Laws of 1935 excluded Jews from the German Winter Relief, the League participated in a Jewish Winter Relief program. Its members collected money, clothing, and fuel. In Berlin, the League's eighteen depositories sent about 30,000 care packages as well as special diet packages to needy families every month. As more Jews lost their jobs or businesses, the League helped women and families adjust to lower living standards. Its local chapters offered courses in cooking, baking, darning, ironing, knitting, tailoring, sewing, first aid instruction, and household repairs. The League also set up communal kitchens, small play groups for children whose mothers needed to do part-time work, and discussion sessions at which women could talk about their problems and receive practical and moral support. In addition, the League expanded its child care facilities, its rest home for working women, and its support of retired women and widows' groups. Repeatedly, the League's newsletter underlined the essential role of women in providing persecuted families with a peaceful home environment. Its leaders took for granted the notion that women preserved the family's equilibrium and optimism.

At first, the organization did not support emigration, but after the Nuremberg Laws it intensified its efforts to train girls for agriculture, domestic service, and crafts—skills in demand abroad. By 1936, the League's newsletter and counseling centers focused extensively on the question of emigration. They described practical problems, cultural differences, and the legal status of women in such faraway places as Paraguay, Shanghai, or New York. But the League remained dissatisfied with the rate at which women emigrated.[84] The League's efforts to help women emigrate, like its attempts to alleviate poverty and suffering, were stymied by overwhelming state persecution. The League and other Jewish organizations could only begin to ameliorate the pain Jews felt as they reeled from defamation and ostracism at the hands of strangers, former friends, and the state.

2

In Private: The Daily Lives
of Jewish Women and Families, 1933–1938

As the prisoners in Dostoyevsky's House of the Dead *speak only of
the freedom that they might enjoy in perhaps 20 years, perhaps never,
so the people in our circle spoke only of freedom beyond Germany,
which they hoped to reach one day.*   — MAX REINER

As never before in their lives, Jewish women and families faced new and
mounting social, economic, and psychological hardships. The family
became a refuge even as the Nazis challenged its basic security. To salvage
peace of mind and accommodate to a dire situation, women took on traditional as well as novel roles. They remained the ones to calm the family, to
keep up the normal rhythms of life. Yet gender roles were dramatically
reversed when women, rather than men, interceded for their families with
state officials and when women, rather than men, pushed their families to
flee Germany.

ACCOMMODATION AND CONFORMITY IN PRIVATE LIFE

As we have seen, Jewish organizations strove to counteract the constrictions
on freedom experienced by Jews as a group. Individual Jews, however, did
not feel the full weight of the Nazis' comprehensive antisemitic policies,
instead experiencing the weight of particular decrees or humiliations.
Thus, individuals reacted to the increasing frustrations in daily life in a
variety of ways depending on their political awareness and the extent to
which particular Nazi policies affected them. In 1941, Harvard psychologists analyzed the coping strategies used by ninety émigrés whose memoirs

they had collected in an essay contest. These included flight into the family and into one's self; the increased importance of Jewish friendships; "an endless procession of petty conformities to the harrowing demands of the Nazi persecutors"; the lowering of ambitions; increased planning and action; and a change in life philosophy.[1]

"Most dramatic are the many instances of return to the healing intimacy of the family after bitter experiences of persecution," the Harvard study observed. Memoirs and interviews later corroborated these findings: "Life centered more around the family then." Memoirs by men, too—which in normal times tend to focus on career and public activities, often to the exclusion of family matters—pay some attention to the importance of family. This emphasis on the family was both comforting and isolating. As one survivor put it: "If I search for the special element associated with . . . existence as an outcast, then what I think of first is a positive gain . . . the increase in the intensity of family life. . . . Yet there was a loss here too: in that entire period of ten years . . . I only made two new friendships."[2]

Jews turned to each other for friendship and comfort. This was usually not difficult, since most Jews, even those who had made genuine friendships with non-Jewish Germans, lived in a Jewish milieu, maintaining a circle of Jewish friends and colleagues. Given the atmosphere outside, Jews often limited their social life to their own homes or organizations, staying away from public theaters, concerts, and museums but still, occasionally, frequenting movie houses. Many turned with new zest to their remaining friends. Mally Dienemann, the wife of Rabbi Max Dienemann of Offenbach am Main, marveled at the close friendships she witnessed: "Those who remained behind, whose circle got increasingly smaller, closed ranks all the more tightly. Friendship once again became the essence of life."[3]

Yet in the strained circumstances affecting the entire Jewish community, tension hovered over social evenings: "When one met in Jewish company, it meant mostly that there was not the slightest relaxation, because every last person had either his own unpleasant experience or some sort of ill tidings to report from somewhere else." The topic of conversation inevitably turned to the worsening situation for Jews, the emigration of friends and children, and details about visas, foreign lands, and foreign climates, "of an existence where they would no longer be frightened to death when the doorbell rang in the morning, because they would be certain: it is only the milkman!" In small towns, where unemployment hit faster, unemployed Jewish men gathered to seek comfort from each other. The men had lost their businesses, their children had left for other cities or countries, and they sat around and talked, played cards, and visited one another's homes. Commenting on this strange situation for men, one wrote: "The women had their daily work, but the men—to see idle men loitering about —horrible!"[4]

When groups of Jews gathered in private homes, they feared that they were being watched by suspicious neighbors or, worse, the Gestapo. All Jewish gatherings, even in private homes, were suspect. This situation deteriorated so much by the war that a participant described the sheer panic that broke out at a birthday party when the police showed up to check on why the light was on during a blackout: "The eyes of the women . . . showed how cruelly one was once again torn from the illusion of a normal middle-class existence. . . . That more and more each day the Jew was becoming fair game was the devastating realization that underscored every experience of this kind."[5]

For single people, social life outside of the family network became increasingly difficult from 1933 through 1938 unless they were young enough and interested enough to join a Jewish youth organization. One young woman without family connections sought human contact after a hard day's work. Lonely, she went to cafés in the evening and sat in a corner, reading. "I would have loved to join in" the dancing, she wrote, but she feared the possible repercussions. She lived in a rooming house and had to eat her meals in a separate room: "I . . . tried to avoid meeting anyone, stuffed my lunch down in ten minutes and disappeared." Even if some Germans behaved decently toward her, others caused trouble: on her birthday she invited some coworkers to her room only to have the *Völkischer Beobachter* excoriate her the next day.[6]

Only wealthier Jews had the options that allowed them to maintain the illusion of normalcy. They could, for example, hire non-Jews to represent them in legal matters at first. They also could take vacations outside of Germany. When fewer hotels accepted Jewish clientele, Ruth Glaser's parents sent her to Switzerland for a vacation. Others traveled to Italy, France, and Eastern Europe. Financial means also alleviated daily strains. Non-Jewish domestic help could be asked to shop in markets that no longer welcomed Jews. Those willing to pay the costs could even order food by telephone and pay delivery charges to avoid aggravation.[7]

Religion provided solace to many Jews. Observant Jews continued their adherence to Jewish laws and their celebration of Jewish holy days, even risking attention and possible eviction when they built a *sukkah* in their backyards and ate in it. A substantial number of Jews even became more religious or began to take religious traditions more seriously. Ruth Glaser described her confirmation in 1935—the first time in Düsseldorf that girls had ever been confirmed. She reflected on how identities had shifted: "First one was a German and then a Jew. Now that we were reminded every day that we were Jewish, we became more aware of it. It became a comfort and something to hold onto." Also, religion offered a realm in which one could feel at home, safe from outside enmity. Synagogue attendance increased dramatically as Jews, depicted as evil and inferior by the government and the media, sought balm for their raw nerves and affirmation of their identity. Rabbi Joachim Prinz called his sermon in Berlin on the night before the boycott of April 1, 1933, an "attempt at collective therapy."[8]

Other Jews turned to Zionism, which had been a minority position within German-Jewish circles. In 1933 "a mass movement emerged out of the elite movement of German Zionism." New subscribers purchased the Zionists' *Jüdischer Rundschau* looking for moral support. In the first few months of 1933, thousands of people streamed into the Palestine Office of the Zionist Organization in search of a new homeland. Between April 1933 and September 1934, the Haluz societies, or the German branch of the worldwide Zionist worker-pioneer organization, grew from 500 to over 15,000 members.[9]

Many Jews gradually accommodated to the hostility, hoping the Nazis would go no further, feeling grateful for small loopholes or exceptions. The mother of four children who had emigrated recalled how the children urged her and her husband to leave: "But we within the borders of Germany had once more adjusted ourselves to the prevailing conditions." A recurrent theme in Victor Klemperer's diary was his and others' attempts to deaden their feelings. He remarked upon the "unbelievable human capacity to endure and get accustomed" to the increasing cruelties of daily life. This adjustment may have exhausted some, distorting their perspective and harming their ability to make sound judgments about the overall situation. Still others may have pretended to dismiss hostility in order to maintain their own or their loved ones' calm. Mally Dienemann recalled hearing "Jew-pig, Jew-pig!" resounding from the windows of the Offenbach am Main *Gymnasium*: "Max said it didn't bother him. It shocked me terribly."[10]

Sometimes an outsider, someone who had been out of the country for several years, could detect the increasing danger that those within the country no longer saw as clearly. Bella Fromm's daughter, returning from the United States for the 1936 summer Olympics, told her mother: "I could not breathe here anymore." In 1937, a seventeen-year-old, whose parents had insisted that he flee while they stay, came back for a visit:

It was 1937 and my parents wanted me back home for my summer vacation! This decision shows the supreme trust my parents ... had in their government, despite what they saw happening around them. It showed how they had somehow accepted and adjusted themselves to the new conditions. Evidently they felt little risk in having their child return to a land ... about to explode.[11]

THE "DUTY" OF THE JEWISH WOMAN: THE HOUSEHOLD

In the face of progressively worsening living conditions, women were supposed to "make things work" in the family and household. Jewish housewives tried, where possible, to prepare less expensive meals, to repair their homes and clothing themselves, and to make do with less help around the house. The Nuremberg Laws (which forbade Jews from hiring female "Aryan" household help under the age of forty-five), left most middle-class Jewish women entirely to their own devices in running a household with greater problems, shopping for food in stores staffed by increasingly hostile personnel, and performing all these tasks with ever-shrinking resources. Moreover, women attempted to comfort frightened children and encourage family members who faced frustrations and harassment.

Women's organizations urged women to preserve the "moral strength to survive" and pointed to biblical heroines for role models. But it became increasingly apparent that biblical role models could not provide Jewish women with the courage or the help they needed. Jewish newspapers began to deal more openly (and perhaps more honestly) with the issues plaguing families, particularly women. For example, as families moved into smaller apartments or took in boarders in order to make ends meet, tighter living quarters caused strain. The League of Jewish Women acknowledged this but, characteristically, urged women to put up with it:

> It is the duty ... of the Jewish woman to regulate ... the household so that everyone is satisfied. She has to give ... the head of the household the necessary time ... to relax.... She has to adjust without being subordinate. This is more necessary than ever, given today's living arrangements. Then, living together, even with many people in tight circumstances, will bring about that kind of communal feeling that will bring peace to the household.[12]

Cooking played a prominent role among issues causing stress because of tight budgets, limited household help, and the difficulties for religious

Jews in acquiring kosher meat. Jewish newspapers advised housewives to consider vegetarian menus because they were cheaper and healthier, and avoided the kosher meat problem. Although preparing meat might be easier and far less time-consuming, women were told that their "good will [was] an important assistant in a vegetarian kitchen," and newspapers printed vegetarian menus and recipes for their readers. After the Nuremberg Laws, the *Central Verein Zeitung* ran articles entitled "Everyone Learns to Cook" and "Even Peter Cooks." [13]

These articles emphasized how children, particularly daughters, could help their mothers. They suggested introducing work as fun, giving children, especially small ones, *permission* to help out and warned against demanding too much. They also frowned upon authoritarian behavior—even by the "head of the family"—as detrimental to the entire family. "Daughter exchanges," another alternative to help overworked mothers, provided a half year's training without pay to two young women who switched households. Some Jewish families hired young female relatives to help out, usually in exchange for pocket money and room and board. [14]

In the household, husbands were expected to pitch in—but only minimally. Despite women's new responsibilities, the "domestication" of men felt illegitimate to women and men alike. When Erna Becker-Kohen found grocery shopping distressing because of the hostility of neighbors and government regulations against Jewish shoppers, her non-Jewish husband took over. She was especially grateful to him for this because he had hated shopping, considering it "unmanly." The League of Jewish Women timidly suggested that since women had more to do for their families, often becoming the sole support, men should begin to do some housework, "as is customary in North American homes. It is necessary to ... talk about our resistance to this—a resistance found more in women than in men ... in order to overcome it." But this resistance continued. Moreover, some League members had little faith in men's competence even if they tried to help: "Jewish women cannot count on the practical support of husbands (Jewish men are not as handy as Aryan husbands)." Most commonly, husbands were asked only to limit their expectations. For example, female commentators urged husbands to restrain their criticisms if the meals were not what they used to be; to try praising their wives once in a while; to close their eyes to some imperfections: "We demand no sacrifices from husbands —only some consideration and ... adjustment to the changed circumstances!" Thus, they urged a complete reevaluation of the class privilege formerly permitted the middle-class housewife and daughter but stopped short of assailing the gender hierarchy within the family. [15]

To lighten women's load, the League of Jewish Women preached "Spartan simplicity," and Jewish newspapers proclaimed the "gospel of scientific management," urging women to rationalize their households by organizing, streamlining, and cutting back on their tasks. Household rationalization had been introduced into Germany during the Weimar Republic, but for bourgeois Jewish women the ideology—and necessity—first arose in the Nazi era.[16] The *Central Verein Zeitung* promoted the suggestions of American efficiency experts as to how to make a smaller kitchen into a practical work space, how to save steps and hand motions, and how to complete two tasks at once (like watching children and cooking). One such article maintained that even though it might be hard to imagine a man in the kitchen, "group work" (which included men) completed tasks more quickly and was often a source of "merriment and inspiration."[17]

Advice columns counseled women to hire daily or hourly help where possible. In what must have been desperation, they urged hiring young men to help in the household. While leaving gender roles intact within the family, male helpers solved two simultaneous problems: relieving housewives and reducing male unemployment. Some housewives did hire such men—Jewish and non-Jewish—but these new helpers may have added to, rather than relieved, household stress. Some young men complained that they could not be expected to do as much as female housekeepers had always done. Elizabeth Bab hired Jewish men from a group called the "Maccabees" (named after Jews who engaged in a seemingly hopeless yet successful struggle against Greek rule in 168 B.C.): "One spent most of his time in bed, another disappeared with a few valuable books and pieces of jewelry. One . . . didn't rush with his work, . . . he could be found in the corner of the kitchen with a book." A busy composer recalled hiring a whole series of people after the Nuremberg Laws, including two non-Jewish men to replace her one female housekeeper. Worse yet was the predicament of one woman who hired a man who turned out to be a Nazi.[18]

Rationalizing the household or hiring unconventional helpers provided, at best, only a partial answer to family stress. After the Nuremberg Laws took effect, articles in Jewish newspapers addressed overworked, overwrought mothers. Written in the language of the psychoanalytic discourse of the 1920s and reworked by Jews in the dismal 1930s, these articles focused on mother-child relationships. With titles like "Mommy, Do You Have Time for Me?" they pleaded with mothers not to neglect their small children in their overcrowded day. After cooking and cleaning, mothers ought to repair torn clothing or help their older children with schoolwork, the articles suggested. But no matter how little time was left over, mothers should not overlook their youngest. A half year later, stories featured even more tension and strain. One article entitled "Mommy Is So Nervous!" depicted a tense housewife who scolded her small children for small misdemeanors, leaving them anxious and depressed. Her husband, also overtired and overworked, tried to smooth things out when he came home. Eventually she discussed her overreactions with him, and he suggested that she should try to "pull [herself] together if at all possible." This story concluded with forced cheeriness: "Although, she, like many of our mothers today has a huge amount of unaccustomed work to complete every day and actually has every reason to be nervous," she forced herself to make the necessary psychological accommodations. After a few weeks her appreciative child noted: "mother you haven't been sooooo nervous in a while."[19]

In offering "solutions" to crises—from streamlining work to repressing nervousness—these newspapers actually document the enormous stress weighing on Jewish families, particularly housewives. They are echoed by many restrospective accounts. Memoirs and interviews accentuate coping behavior far more than feelings. Although feelings are not absent in memoirs, they are the backdrop to a frenzy of activity intended to relieve mounting stress. While it is hard to imagine that exertion and repression made life any easier, maybe they *did* help Jews to carry on and to survive (and also to be able, in later years, to write a memoir of such anguishing times). Letters to a Jewish newspaper in August 1938 by women who worked both outside and inside the home recognized the strain and despair women experienced, but focused on action: "'You have to do it' is the eleventh commandment for all of us now."[20]

THE "DUTY" OF THE JEWISH WOMAN: THE CHALLENGES OF NEW ROLES AND THE TENACITY OF OLD ONES

Fighting Gloom

The psychological blow of Nazism affected all Jews deeply. In December 1935, Dora Edinger, a leader of the Jewish women's movement, acknowledged in a letter: "It is hard to bear, even though I had long anticipated it rationally. Again and again, it is something entirely different to know something and to experience it." Despite their dejection, women added the task of raising their families' spirits to their double burden of employment and housework. This could mean trying to wrest some lighthearted moments from the surrounding gloom or celebrating Jewish holidays and

family events with feigned cheer. It could also mean restraining or repressing their anger in order to maintain family peace when they desperately
wanted to emigrate but their husbands insisted on staying. The League of
Jewish Women urged that all new hardships should be met as "duties . . .
with calm and presence of mind." It called on Jewish women to maintain
the home and family. Other leaders reminded Jewish women that they traditionally lit the Sabbath candles and urged them once again to brighten
their homes. These expectations even affected Jewish women whose husbands were "Aryan": Erna Becker-Kohen, who lived in constant dread of
what could happen to her mother (before she admitted to herself that she,
too, was in danger), restrained herself from sharing her worries with her
husband. She confided to her diary: "I can't burden my husband . . . with
my family problems."[21]

Even when women could no longer "light candles" of joy, they often
engaged in denial of their immediate hardships. Women adopted what psychologists then called "temporary frames of security," for example, by
engaging in practical efforts, or even taking solace in additional housework.[22] Although occasionally their efforts to distract themselves and their
families may have kept all involved from realizing just how significant the
increasing deprivations were, some denial was necessary to preserve personal and family stability. Moreover, most people function on several levels
at the same time. Women could occupy themselves with the details of daily
life while still studying a language useful for emigration, pushing a reluctant spouse to consider emigration, or filling out the mountains of forms
necessary to apply to emigrate.

Finding safety in the routines of housework was generally a female form
of escapism. This usually lasted longer than the male version of escape by
submerging into occupational activities, since many men lost their jobs and
businesses. Women also joined voluntary organizations, studied foreign
languages, or learned new skills in an effort to help the community and to
"drown [their] worries." In retrospect, many women realized what they had
been doing. Alice Baerwald became so involved in setting up a Zionist
youth emigration program in Danzig that she "forgot to dismantle my own
life." But these activities were not only distractions or practical necessities;
they "set our mind and spirit free."[23]

Gallows humor may have helped Jews as well. Mally Dienemann remarked upon the frustrations of language training. If one studied Spanish
or Portuguese in preparation for going to Latin America, sudden barriers to
entry arose and one had to prepare for another country. If one turned to
Hebrew, obstacles to acquiring the necessary certificates were certain to

develop and one had to change to yet another language. Thus, a joke made the rounds of her small town: "'What language are you learning?' 'The wrong one, of course.'" Children, too, turned to humor. A twelve-year-old in a home for "non-Aryan" children, where lunch consisted of potatoes and vegetables, called to his friends: "Now we're all becoming vegetarians, so, from behind, we'll be 'arians'!"[24]

Later, humor expressed more serious defiance. In her memoirs, Edith Wolff recalled that graffiti scribbled in unexpected places helped Jewish morale and may have even been written by Jews. On a sign near a swimming pool in Berlin declaring "Jews and Dogs Prohibited," for example, someone scrawled, "What if the dogs can't read this?" One of Wolff's favorite "whispered jokes" (*Flüsterwitze*) heard in Berlin was a complaint by the SA that "now we want the Jews to march and we'll do the joking!" In 1941, one way Wolff opposed the regime was by writing postcards to Nazi headquarters and bureaucrats echoing a joke making the rounds of Berlin: "Germany is now called Braunschweig [a city in Germany]: one half is brown [*Braun* = Nazi uniforms], and the other half is silent [*schweig* = silence]."[25]

Role Reversals Among Jewish Women and Men

At a time when Nazi ideology shrilly reaffirmed male privilege, relegating "Aryan" women to "*Kinder, Küche, Kirche*" (children, kitchen, church), Jewish women took on new roles as breadwinners, family protectors, and defenders of businesses or practices. Gender roles in Jewish families shifted because devastating economic, social, and emotional realities forced families to embrace strategies that they would never have entertained in ordinary times. The Nazis essentially destroyed the patriarchal structure of the Jewish family, leaving a void to be filled by women.

Increasingly, women found themselves representing or defending their men—whether husbands, fathers, or brothers. As early as 1933, a non-Jewish colleague suggested to Dr. Ernst Mueller and his wife, Liselotte, that because Ernst "had such a Jewish nose," she should appeal to a prominent non-Jewish doctor, Dr. Kleine at the Robert Koch Institute, on behalf of her husband. Discouraged by political events, Ernst agreed that his wife should represent him. When Dr. Kleine interviewed Liselotte, he asked why her husband had not come himself, and she began to cry, explaining the circumstances. Dr. Kleine thereupon invited them both to dinner. "When I told Ernst about the dinner invitation, he felt as if a miracle had happened. How quickly one's outlook changes! A short time before he would not have considered it a miracle to be invited by a non-Jewish doctor."[26]

Many tales have been recorded of women who saved family members from the arbitrary demands of the state or from the Gestapo. In these cases, it was always assumed that the Nazis would not disrupt gender norms: they might arrest or torture Jewish men but would not harm women. Thus traditional gender norms afforded women greater freedom, at first, so they took on more assertive roles in public. Some took responsibility for the entire family's safety. Liselotte Müller traveled to Palestine to assess the situation. Her husband, who could not leave his practice, simply told her: "If you decide you would like to live in Palestine, I will like it too." She chose Greece. Her husband, older and more educated than she, who previously had been the decision maker, agreed. Ann Lewis's mother, who had always been "reserved with strangers," went to England to apply for residence and work permits. She was the one fluent in English, and, as a psychoanalyst, she was welcomed in England, while her husband, a medical doctor, was not.[27]

Women drew upon tenacity they did not know they possessed. After traveling to the United States to convince reluctant and distant relatives to give her family an affidavit, one woman had to confront the American consulate in Stuttgart, which insisted that it had no record of her. She showed her receipts, but the secretary just shrugged. At closing time she refused to leave, insisting that her husband's, mother's, and children's lives depended on their chance to go to the United States. She would spend as many days and nights in the waiting room as necessary until they found her documents. After much discussion, the consul ordered a search of the files and the documents were discovered. Today, her daughter refers to her mother as the "first sit in."[28]

Women often faced routine danger and dramatic situations, requiring both bravery and luck. Twenty-year-old Ruth Abraham urged her parents to move to Berlin to escape the hostility in their small town. The Nazis permitted this move only if the father promised to appear at Gestapo headquarters weekly. Ruth always accompanied her father to these perilous interrogations. When her uncle was arrested in Düsseldorf, she hurried from jail to jail until she found out where he was. Then she appealed to a judge who seemed attracted to her. He requested that she come to his home in the evening, where he would give her a release form. Knowing that she risked a sexual demand or worse, she entered his home. The judge treated her politely and signed the release. She commented in her memoir: "I must add, that I look absolutely 'Aryan,' that I have blond hair and blue eyes, a straight nose and am tall." Later, these traits would save her life in hiding; now she was able to gain the interest or sympathy of men who did not want to believe that she was Jewish.[29]

The judge's treatment of Abraham notwithstanding, sexual conventions could be quite menacing. Despite increasing propaganda about "racial pollution" or "race defilement" (*Rassenschande*), Jewish women recorded frightening incidents in which "Aryans," Nazis included, made advances toward them. In one small town, a young single woman became troubled about her safety on the streets at night. "In daylight they reviled me as a Jewish woman and at night they wanted to kiss me. The whole society disgusted me." Another woman wrote of the perils of sexual encounters: "During the Hitler era I had the immense burden of rejecting brazen advances from SS and SA men. They often pestered me and asked for dates. Each time I answered: 'I'm sorry, that I can't accept, I'm married....' If I had said I was Jewish, they would have turned the tables and insisted that I had approached them."[30]

Other gender conventions also angered and hindered women. A social worker from Breslau attempted to have her new husband released from prison in June 1938. Convinced of his innocence, she appealed to his friend, a lawyer, for help. The lawyer warned her that "when a woman is married for six weeks only, she does not know anything of the previous life of her husband." She wrote: "All these shocks undermine your self-confidence and ... confidence in the world and in the goodness of men."[31] She doggedly held to her opinion that the wrong man had been arrested, proved it, and was able to save her husband.

Women's new roles may have increased stress in some cases, but in general both women and men appreciated the importance of the women's initiatives. Edith Bick summed up the situation: "In the Hitler times ... I had to take over, which I never did before. Never." Her husband "didn't like it [but] he not only accepted it, he was thankful." As conditions worsened, role reversals became ever more common, with some women putting up a strong front when men could no longer cope. One woman struggled to retain her self-control as her husband sank into a deep depression. "He stopped eating, as he said no one had the right to eat when he did not work and became ... despondent.... He feared we would all starve ... and all his self-assurance was gone.... These were terrible days for me, added to all the other troubles, and forever trying to keep my chin up for the childrens' sake." An extreme case of this kind occurred when Frieda Cohn discovered a double suicide. She wanted to share her grief with her husband but could not "because of his own depressions." Instead, she confided in her girlfriend.[32]

Many women strove to maintain their self-control as a way of preserving the families' dignity and equilibrium in the face of dishonor and persecution. Men rarely describe this kind of behavior, probably because they took it for granted, while women, previously allowed and encouraged to be the more "emotional" sex, were particularly conscious of their own efforts at self-control and their husbands' fragility.

THE EMIGRATION QUANDARY

Migration and the Desire to Emigrate

Jews fled the personal hostility of villages and smaller towns by seeking the anonymity, and hence relative safety, of large cities. A teenager noted that by 1935 Jews in his small town could no longer go to cafés, the pool, or parks, not to mention the "Hitlerplatz," which no Jew could enter because of its name. After moving to Berlin in 1935, he enjoyed the freedom of not being recognized among the larger population. Ann Lewis also remarked that she was glad to be a Berliner, grateful—like many of her elders—for her relative freedom. Economic strangulation, occurring most quickly in small towns, also provoked migration. By 1935–36, in some small towns over 80 percent of the Jewish population was destitute. As people migrated in search of work, local Jewish communities dwindled in number and in resources. By 1937, 200 of the 1,600 communities had dissolved and over 600 of those remaining required outside subsidies. A large proportion of the migrants were women. Many sought jobs as domestics and would later become the sole support of families left behind.[33]

For those left behind, the loneliness was of "such a degree and so sudden ... as had never before been experienced even in Jewish history." Family and friendship circles shrank. In 1936, one woman described the feeling of leaving a woman friend as "dying a little."

> Female friendships.... There is something sisterly.... Parting from a friend! Last hour together. Suitcases ... are packed, the furniture stored, the apartment ... stands empty and ... appears almost hostile.... Will we elderly people ever see each other again? ... Will friendship last ...? ... A personal story from an individual fate but also a community fate for us Jews; for who does not feel ... this tear, this shock ... during separation, emigration, departure! *Partir c'est mourir un peu!*

By 1938, Jewish newspapers had concluded: "We must learn to endure loneliness."[34]

In the families that migrated, women had to adjust their household to a new urban environment: crowded apartments, unskilled jobs, and public constraints, not to mention deteriorating political circumstances. Women who stayed in big cities participated as never before in social welfare work within Jewish communities and Jewish women's organizations to integrate the steady stream of newcomers. Jewish communities and organizations worked to provide the new arrivals with shelters, soup kitchens, and used clothing and furniture centers. They also expanded orphanages, old-age homes, and meal and transportation subsidies. Often women volunteered in such endeavors while prodding their own families to emigrate.

As emigration became more and more crucial, women usually saw the danger signals first and urged their husbands to flee Germany. Among rural Jews, "the role of women in the decision to emigrate was decisive.... The women were the prescient ones ... the ones ready to make the decision, the ones who urged their husbands to emigrate." Urban Jewish women had similar reactions. Marta Appel described a discussion among friends in Dortmund about a doctor who had just fled in the spring of 1935. The men in the room, including her husband, a rabbi, condemned him.

> The women ... found that it took more courage to go than to stay.... "Why should we stay here and wait for our eventual ruin? Isn't it better to go and to build up a new existence somewhere else, before our strength is exhausted by the constant physical and psychic pressure? Isn't the future of our children more important than a completely senseless holding out ... ?" All the women shared this opinion ... while the men, more or less passionately, spoke against it. I discussed this with my husband on the way home. Like all other men, he ... couldn't imagine leaving one's beloved homeland and the duties that fill a man's life. "Could you really leave all this behind you to enter nothingness?" ... "I could," I said, without out a moment's hesitation.

The different attitudes of men and women described here suggest that gender significantly determined the decision between flight and fight.[35]

Women were more inclined to emigrate because they were not as integrated into the public world. For example, they rarely saw themselves as indispensable to the Jewish public. One man declared in his memoirs that he could not leave Germany because he thought of himself as a "good democrat" whose emigration would "leave others in the lurch" and would be a "betrayal of the entire Jewish community."[36] Rabbi Leo Baeck, the official leader of German Jewry, evinced similar feelings. Offered safe permanent passage by two Britons in 1939, he responded: "I will go, when I am the last Jew alive in Germany."[37]

Women were also less involved than men in the economy, even though some had been in the job market their entire adult lives. This had several effects. First, Jewish men had a great deal more to lose. Only when they could no longer make a living were some men willing to leave. To emigrate before they had lost their positions or before their businesses or professional practices had collapsed would have required men to tear themselves away from their lifework, their clients, and colleagues. There were other considerations as well. The daughter of a wealthy businessman commented: "When the Nazis appeared on the scene, he was too reluctant to consolidate everything and leave Germany. He may have been a bit too attached to his status, as well as his possessions." But even businesswomen appeared less reluctant than their spouses to emigrate. One wealthy female manufacturer, whose husband managed her inherited business, wanted to flee in 1933. He refused. She insisted that at least they both learn a trade (which later served them well in Shanghai).[38] In short, the family could be moved more easily than a business or profession. In light of men's close identification with their occupation, they often felt trapped into staying. Women, whose identity was more family-oriented than men's, struggled to preserve what was central to them by fleeing with those they loved.

Women's subordinate status in the economy probably eased their decision to flee, since they were familiar with the kinds of work, generally domestic, they would have to perform in places of refuge. Lore Segal described how her mother, formerly a housewife and pianist, cheerfully and successfully took on the role of maid in England, whereas her father, formerly a chief accountant in a bank, experienced his loss of status as a butler and gardner with great bitterness.[39] Even when both sexes fulfilled their refugee roles well, women seemed less status-conscious than men. Perhaps women did not experience the descent from employing a servant to becoming one as intensely as men, since their status had always been determined by that of their father or husband anyway.

Finally, women's lesser involvement in the economy allowed them more time for greater contact with a variety of non-Jews, from neighbors to schoolteachers. Jewish men worked mostly with other Jews in traditional Jewish occupations (in specific branches of retail trades, in the cattle trade, or in independent practices as physicians and attorneys). They may have been more isolated than women from non-Jewish peers (though not from non-Jewish customers). This spared them direct interactions with hostile peers but also prevented the awareness of deteriorating circumstances garnered from such associations. Many Jewish men were isolated further as the boycotts of Jewish concerns grew, for the clientele of Jewish businesses that survived turned predominantly Jewish. And discriminatory hiring meant that Jewish blue- and white-collar workers found opportunities only within the Jewish economic sector. In 1936, some Jews decried a "Jewish economic ghetto," and in 1937 the Council for German Jewry in London reported that the German-Jewish community lived in a "new type of ghetto . . . cut off from economic as well as social and intellectual contact with the surrounding world."[40] In contrast, Jewish women (even those who worked in the same "Jewish ghetto") picked up other warning signals from their neighborhoods and children.

Men and women led relatively distinct lives, and they often interpreted daily events differently. Although women were less involved than men in the work world, they were more integrated into their immediate community. Raised to be sensitive to interpersonal behavior and social situations, women had social antennae that not only were more finely tuned than their husbands' but also were directed toward more unconventional—what men might have considered more trivial—sources of information. For example, an American Jewish couple who resided in Hamburg during the 1930s were alerted to danger by household help. The wife wrote: "Any woman knows . . . her best source of information are the servants. . . . I received more information from Harold . . . than I could have received at the best . . . intelligence office."[41] Women registered the increasing hostility of their immediate surroundings unmitigated by a promising business prospect, a loyal employee or patient, or a kind customer. Their constant contacts with their own and other people's children probably provided them with further warning signals—and they took those signals seriously.

Men, on the other hand, felt more at home with culture and politics. Generally more educated than their wives, they cherished what they regarded as German culture—the culture of the German Enlightenment. This love for their German liberal intellectual heritage gave men something to hold on to even as it "blunted their sense of impending danger." When Else Gerstel argued with her husband about emigrating, he, a former judge, insisted that "the German people, the German judges, would not stand for much more of this madness."[42]

One could argue that men were more "German" than women not only with regard to their education but also with regard to their sense of patriotism. Even in a situation gone awry, there were war veterans who refused to take their wives' warnings seriously. These men had received reprieves in

1933 because of President Hindenburg's intervention after the exclusionary April laws (although the reprieves proved to be temporary). Their wives typically could not convince them that they, too, were in danger. One woman, who pressed her husband to leave Germany, noted that he "constantly fell back on the argument that he had been at the front in World War I."[43] Most men expressed their arguments in terms of having served their country and, hence, having certain rights. Nevertheless, the "front" argument had a deep emotional core, for the war experience had aroused strong feelings of patriotism.

A widespread assumption that women lacked political acumen—stemming from their primary role in the domestic sphere—gave women's warnings less credibility. One woman's prophecies of doom met with her husband's amusement: "He laughed at me and argued that such an insane dictatorship could not last long." Even after their seven-year-old son was beaten up at school, he was still optimistic. Many men also pulled rank on their wives, insisting that they were more attuned to political realities: "You're a child" said one husband. "You mustn't take everything so seriously. Hitler used the Jews . . . as propaganda to gain power—now . . . you'll hear nothing more about the Jews."[44] Often the anxious partner heard the old German adage: "Nothing is ever eaten as hot as it's cooked."

Men, therefore, attempted to see the "broader" picture, to maintain an "objective" stance, to scrutinize and analyze the confusing legal and economic decrees and the often contradictory public utterances of the Nazis. Men mediated their experiences through newspapers and broadcasts. Politics remained more abstract to them, whereas women's "narrower" picture—the minutiae (and significance) of everyday contacts—brought politics home. Summing up, Peter Wyden recalled the debates within his own family and those of other Berlin Jews:

> It was not a bit unusual in these go-or-no-go family dilemmas for the women to display more energy and enterprise than the men. . . . Almost no women had a business, a law office, or a medical practice to lose. They were less status-conscious, less money-oriented than the men. They seemed to be less rigid, less cautious, more confident of their ability to flourish on new turf.

The Berlin artist Charlotte Salomon, who painted a stunning exploration of her life while awaiting her fate in southern France in 1941–42, depicted this dilemma. She portrayed her short grandmother looking up to her tall grandfather, whose head is above the frame of the painting. The caption reads: "Grossmama in 1933: 'Not a minute longer will I stay here. I'm telling you let's leave this country as fast as we can; my judgment says so.' Her husband almost loses his head."[45]

Even given the gender differences in picking up warning signals and yearning to leave, it is crucial to recognize that these signals occurred in stages. Alice Nauen and her friends "saw it was getting worse. But until 1939 nobody in our circles believed it would lead to an end" for German Jewry. Interspersed with personal, daily observations, women's assessments were often more on target than men's, but obviously women could also be confused by Nazi policies and events. When Hanna Bernheim's sister, who had emigrated to France, returned for a visit in the mid-1930s, the sister wanted to know why the Bernheims remained in their south German town. Hanna Bernheim replied:

> First of all it is so awfully hard for our old, sick father to be left by all his four children. Second there are so many dissatisfied people in all classes, professions and trades. Third there was the Roehm Purge and an army shake up. And that makes me believe that people are right who told us "Wait for one year longer and the Nazi government will be blown up!"

Moreover, these signals were often profoundly mixed. As we have seen, random kindnesses, the most obvious "mixed signals," gave some Jews cause for hope. One woman wrote that every Jewish person "knew a decent German" and recalled that many Jews thought "the radical Nazi laws would never be carried out because they did not match the moderate character of the German people."[46] Ultimately, confusing signals, often interpreted differently by women and men, as well as attempts by the government to rob Jews of all their assets, impeded many Jews from making timely decisions to leave Germany.

Decision Making

Women and men often *assessed* danger differently, reflecting their different contacts and frames of reference. But *decisions* regarding emigration seem to have been made by husbands. Despite important role reversals, both men and women generally held fast to traditional gender roles in responding to the political situation—unless they were overwhelmed by events.

The common prejudice that women were "hysterical" in the face of danger worked to everyone's disadvantage. Charlotte Stein-Pick begged her father to flee in March 1933. Her husband brought her father to the train station only moments before the SS arrived to arrest the older man. Not knowing about the SS visit, her husband said upon returning home: "Actually, it was entirely unnecessary that your parents left, but I supported you because you were worrying yourself so much." Stein-Pick also overheard a private conversation in a train on November 6, 1938, two days before the November Pogrom, in which the participants discussed what was about to happen to Jewish men. "When I arrived home I implored my husband and a friend who lived with us to leave . . . immediately. . . . But my counsel was in vain. They believed my nerves had given way: how should these people have known anything and one could not have built camps big enough." Another husband believed his wife to be completely overwrought when she suggested—in 1932—that he deposit money in a Swiss bank. While cabaret artists were already joking about people taking trips to visit their money in Switzerland, her husband refused. In this case, the belief that women should keep out of business matters made it even less likely that her suggestions would be heeded. If women's appraisals were considered too emotional in general, pregnancy discredited them completely, since men considered pregnant women especially high-strung. A month before the Germans annexed Austria, a Viennese Catholic wife told her Jewish husband that Hitler meant trouble for him and packed all of his things. But she could not persuade him to depart; he attributed her worries to her pregnancy.[47]

Men's role and status as breadwinners made them hesitant to emigrate and gave them the authority to say no. Else Gerstel fought "desperately" with her husband of twenty-three years to emigrate. A judge, he refused to leave, insisting: "There is as much demand for Roman law over there as the eskimos have for freezers." Describing their dispute as a great strain on their marriage, she wrote, "I was in constant fury." Another wife recalled her attempt to convince her husband to flee: "A woman sometimes has a sixth feeling. . . . I said to my husband, '. . . we will have to leave.' He said, 'No, you won't have a six-room apartment and two servants if we do that.' . . . I said, 'OK, then I'll have a one-room flat . . . but I want to be safe.'" Despite his reluctance, she studied English and learned practical trades. His arrest forced their emigration to Australia, where she supported the family.[48]

In the rare cases in which husbands followed their wives' assessment and emigrated, the wives either recruited other male friends to help convince the husbands or were themselves professionals whose acumen in the public world was difficult to deny. Marie Bloch had read Hitler's *Mein Kampf* in 1929 and insisted on sending her children out of the country in 1933. Her husband refused to leave his factory and could not "give up the thought that the Germans would see in time what kind of a man Hitler was." After the Nuremberg Laws she knelt in front of his bed, begging him to leave. Distraught, she asked him whose opinion he would respect and invited that friend to their home. The friend told them to flee to the United States where he, himself, was heading. Only then did her husband agree to go. A woman lawyer had an easier time convincing her spouse, since she had been politically aware and active. It was her decision to flee: "My husband saw that I was consumed with anxiety. Despite his good job, he decided to leave Germany with me." They fled only as far as France, where he was later caught by the Nazis and murdered in Auschwitz, while she managed to join the Resistance. In retrospect, she wished she had thanked him—which she never did—"for his selfless decision . . . for this most ardent proof of his love that he had ever given me."[49]

In the late 1930s, events often jolted families into leaving, with women sometimes taking the lead. In early 1938, one daughter reported that her mother "applied to the American authorities for a quota number without my father's knowledge; the hopeless number of 33,243 was allocated. It was a last desperate act and Papa did not even choke with anger anymore." Her parents and young brother were deported and murdered. After narrowly escaping battering by a Nazi mob in her small hometown, another woman convinced her husband to "pack their things throughout the night and leave this hell just the next day." After the November Pogrom, some wives broke all family conventions by taking over the decision making when it became clear that their husbands' reluctance to flee would result in even worse horrors. Else Gerstel's husband had been arrested but not imprisoned, and he still "had no intention of leaving Germany, but I sent a telegram to my brother Hans in New York. . . . 'Please send affidavit.'"[50]

Sometimes the "Aryan" wives of Jewish men took the lead. Verena Hellwig, for example, feared for her two "mixed" (*Mischling*) children even as her husband, also of "mixed blood," insisted on remaining in Germany until his approaching retirement. When her teenage son could not find an apprenticeship, she spoke to a Nazi official. He told her that people of "mixed blood" were "our greatest danger. They should either return to Judaism . . . and suffer the fate of the Jews or they should be prevented from procreating, like retarded people." She had reached her turning point: "Her homeland was lost"; "Germany was dead" for her. She soon emigrated to England with her son, followed by her daughter. This meant a temporary separation from "her husband, [her] best friend," but she had to find a future for her children.[51]

Emigration: Facing Closed Doors and Poverty

One of the chief objectives of Nazi policies toward the Jews between 1935 and September 1939 was to foster emigration, once called "the territorial final solution." The Nazis devised a series of plans with such titles as Syrian Project, Madagascar Plan, Ecuador Project, and the Haavara Transfer to deposit Germany's unwanted Jews around the globe. The government urged individual emigration as well. Jewish agencies, in particular the Aid Society of Jews in Germany, the Central Office for Jewish Emigration Relief, and the Palestine Office, advised Jews on emigration matters, obtaining visas, and financial aid, and the Jewish press ran articles detailing emigration possibilities. Jews had to confront a bewildering array of countries, requirements, and details. Peter Wyden remembered that the language around his house changed between 1935 and 1937:

> Our future had come to depend on three new guideposts: "the quota"—
> the total number of German refugees permitted to enter the United States
> under the miserly immigration laws; "the affidavit"—the document from
> an obscure umpteenth cousin . . . guaranteeing that he would support us if
> we became destitute; and "the visa" . . . our stamped admission ticket into
> the promised land. . . . Beyond [these words] everyone learned about the
> *"Zertifikat"* from the British authorities to enter Palestine; the Reich Flight
> Tax that had to be paid to the Nazis as an exit fine . . . and the "certificate of
> harmlessness" required before one could cross the border.[52]

Profound barriers to emigration existed. During the worldwide depression of the 1930s, foreign countries restricted immigration. In July 1938, the thirty-two nations assembled at the Evian Conference "regretted" they could not take in more Jews. Those few countries with open doors needed farmers, not middle-class professionals or business people. Also, German Jews were disproportionately old, and no country wanted middle-aged and elderly people.[53] Fearing that they would become burdens on their children or relatives abroad, many of the elderly stayed behind.

The Nazis created another major obstacle by restricting the amount of currency and property Jews could take with them. The plunder of Jewish property was part and parcel of all emigration proceedings. The Nazis "pressured Jews to leave the country, but the privilege of leaving was expensive." The Reich Flight Tax (*Reichsfluchtsteuer*), a stringent property tax on émigrés, threatened to impoverish prospective emigrants. First passed by the Brüning government in 1931 to prevent capital flight, the Nazis raised it to punitive heights for emigrating Jews. In all, the German treasury may have collected as much as 900 million marks from the Reich Flight Tax alone. Many people had to sell all their belongings simply to pay this one tax. Gerdy Stoppleman, for example, sent her husband, recently released from Sachsenhausen concentration camp, ahead to England while she stayed behind to pay the tax: "To be able to pay the . . . tax I sold our furniture, valuable paintings and carpets . . . dirt cheap. Many a home of true Aryans, SA and SS became exceedingly well furnished."[54]

From the very beginning, blocked bank accounts (made even stricter in 1938) proved to be serious impediments for Jewish emigrants. Even after paying exorbitant taxes, emigrants could not transfer their after-tax money abroad but had to deposit it in "blocked accounts in marks for prospective emigrants." From these accounts, they could buy foreign currency—at very unfavorable exchange rates, in essence a further punitive tax. Until 1935 the exchange rate stood at half the official market rate of the mark; thereafter, the government steadily pushed it downward. By 1939 Jews could buy foreign currency worth only 4 percent of the value of their blocked German money. When war broke out, the Nazis forbade all money transfers. Thus, emigrating Jews lost 30 to 50 percent of their capital in the years 1933–37 and 60 to 100 percent between 1937 and 1939. For many, it became harder and harder to leave because new laws robbed them of the means to start a life elsewhere. While these conditions forced individuals and families to hesitate before emigrating, the more they hesitated, the more conditions deteriorated.[55]

What these laws meant in terms of everyday reality can be seen in the memoirs of Ann Lewis, whose parents tried to leave in 1937. By then,

> the sum my parents received in sterling was less than a quarter of what it would have been at the official rate. When the transfer to their English bank had been completed, their 27,000 marks had become only £450 instead of the £2,160 which they would have obtained if their funds had been exchanged at what was then the normal rate.

Due to this poor exchange rate, her parents decided to buy everything they could in Germany, because they would barely have the means for subsistence once they arrived in England: "Nothing would be bought in England that could possibly be brought from Germany, and that applied not only to furniture and other household goods but also to items such as soap, . . . stationery, medical supplies, and of course enough clothes to last us for the next few years." Some Jews were even taxed in advance. Bella Fromm reported that she had to pay taxes for one year in advance, although she would not even be in the country, as part of the emigration scam.[56]

Jews also faced plunder by individuals. Gestapo agents, civil servants, packers, and even people in foreign consulates demanded bribes and tributes of every sort.[57] The story of how individual Germans enriched themselves from the theft of Jewish property still needs to be told. It would be a worthwhile project for historians of daily life in Nazi Germany. The memoirs and interviews of the Jewish victims provide rich documentation. "We have come to see what you may take with you when you leave," said two Gestapo agents, transparent in their greed. Lola Blonder responded: "Feel free to look around." She added in her later memoirs: "They . . . took whatever little objects they liked—from the wall, . . . from the tables. . . . I was used to this by now. Whenever a group of Nazis visited, they helped themselves to . . . valuables. Robbing, robbing! Every day robbing me!" Later, they took her to the bank, where they forced her to withdraw her money and give it to them. Hardly the banal bureaucrats who were just "taking orders," many government officials were highly corrupt, relishing their new roles.

While many exploited the situation financially, some exploited it sexually. One bureaucrat, eyeing a Jewish woman who had come to his office several times for emigration visas for her husband and family, told her, "We know each other very well by now, don't we. I can see, you are wearing a different blouse today. You really look very attractive in it." She could not respond to him, but she told her daughter: "It is written all over his face. . . . How appetizing she [looks]. How good she will taste." Another woman is still thankful today that her mother saved their lives by having sex with a bureaucrat who then provided their exit papers.[58]

Plunder was still not the worst of it. A major barrier to emigration for most was not having relatives or friends abroad who could sponsor admission into a country of refuge. Another obstacle to emigration arose in 1937 with the issuance of passports for emigration only. The regime forbade exploratory trips intended to assess the possibilities available in another country, and only people who were ill or visiting children studying abroad could leave and return. For those with no contacts, applying abroad for positions as domestic servants became an important escape route—especially, but not only, for women. The committees in charge of these matters sternly demanded "qualifications."[59] Then, after acceptance by a potential employer, Jews had to complete mountains of paperwork.

Despite all obstacles, Jewish emigration was far from negligible, although it took an uneven course. About 37,000 Jews left Germany in 1933. More discrimination, however, was not matched by more emigration. In 1934, 23,000 fled. By early 1935, about 10,000 had returned because Jewish émigrés abroad were increasingly sliding into poverty. Jews stopped returning in early 1935 when the Nazis threatened internment in a concentration camp for returnees. By the end of that year (after the Nuremberg Laws), about 21,000 had emigrated, followed by another 25,000 in 1936 and 23,000 in 1937. With increasing persecution in 1938, another 40,000 emigrated. The first wave of refugees fled to neighboring countries, some hoping to return home when the situation improved. The proportion of emigrants who fled overseas grew dramatically as conditions in Europe worsened.[60]

Statistics may give the false impression that Jews smoothly managed to leave Germany and enter the country of their choice. They cover up the individual stories, which show complicated emigration attempts, failures, and new attempts. For example, one family in Leipzig first decided to go to Palestine. The father, who had owned a silverware shop, trained to become a painter. By the time he received his diploma from the Leipzig League of Painters, there were too many applications to Palestine. The family next considered Chile and the Dominican Republic, but these did not work out either. Finally, the father wrote to a sister in Brooklyn, and his family received a U.S. affidavit in 1937. Often attempts to emigrate failed as the doors to the country of refuge closed—hence, the joke about Jews having to switch languages several times in the middle of their studies.[61] Still, before 1938 about one quarter of German Jews fled their homeland, showing that a substantial number could "really leave all this behind . . . to enter nothingness."

3

Jewish and "Mixed" Families

We will be surrounded by . . . hatred and contempt because I am
Jewish and my husband is a race defiler.

— ERNA BECKER-KOHEN

The racial state[1] defined "Jews," limited their marital options, and tried to destroy their relationships, both casual and intimate, with all non-Jews. The regime intruded in the daily lives not only of Jews but also of non-Jews married to Jews, their children and grandchildren. Mixed couples, those with a Jewish and a non-Jewish partner, saw their extramarital relationships criminalized, their prospective marriages prohibited, and their old marriages stigmatized. In already existing mixed marriages (*Mischehen*), gender played a crucial role. Nazi sexism privileged those couples with "Aryan" men over those with Jewish men. Hence a Jewish person's fate often hung not only on the "race" but also the sex of the "Aryan" spouse.

ENGAGEMENT, MARRIAGE, AND THE DECISION TO BUILD A FAMILY

Nazism touched every decision Jews made about their most intimate relationships: whether to marry under straitened circumstances, whether to have children who would be ostracized by their non-Jewish peers, whether to adopt non-Jewish children into their families, and even whether to file for a divorce. But Nazism caused particular upheaval in mixed families, in which one partner was "racially" Jewish (even if a convert) and one "Aryan." The "Law for the Protection of German Blood and Honor," one of the Nuremberg Laws of September 1935, prohibited intermarriages and sexual intercourse between Jews and "Aryans." It was the first in a series of decrees and court decisions affecting family life and defining more precisely who was a "Jew." Children of unions between Jews and "Aryans" were labeled *"Mischlinge"* ("of mixed blood" or "hybrid"—but with a derogatory connotation, as in "mongrel," "mixed breed," or "crossbreed"). By the 1930s, only about 11 percent of such children had remained religiously Jewish. These children, as well as *"Mischlinge"* who had married Jews, were called *"Geltungsjuden"* (literally, people who "counted as Jews") and were treated as full Jews.[2] According to some estimates, there may have been as many as 300,000 *"Mischlinge"* and another 100,000 persons who "in one degree or another counted Jews among their immediate ancestry" and were thus affected by racial laws.[3]

Mixed couples, accused of "race defilement" and "contaminating German blood," also had to decide whether to marry (before the Nuremberg Laws made this impossible), whether to have children, and whether to divorce. Unlike Jewish couples, mixed couples had to scrutinize their relationships with relatives on both sides of the perceived "racial" divide, to define their identities to themselves and society, and to face severe familial, state, and societal pressure to separate.

The Great Depression had caused a sharp drop in the overall rate of marriage in Germany. The beginning of economic recovery and Nazi marriage loans to the politically and eugenically reliable, that is, not to Jews, *"Mischlinge,"* or other "foreign races," helped reverse the drop. The number of marriages increased to 516,800 in 1932, to 638,600 in 1933, and to 740,200 in 1934. Thereafter, although the number of marriages failed to meet Nazi expectations, declining until the marriage frenzy of war-anxious 1939, the marriage rate remained well above the average for the 1920s.[4] Considering the risks of setting up a new life in the Third Reich, one might expect Jewish marriage rates to have dropped. Surprisingly, this was not the case. Although the events of 1933 made some Jewish couples pause, Jewish marriages increased appreciably after 1933, dropping only in 1939 with mass emigration. Despite adversity, Jewish couples still hoped to build a future together, either in Germany or abroad. When Lisa Grubel married in July 1935, she wore a white bridal gown and carried a bouquet of lilies of the valley. Three musicians played as the guests ate the "sumptuous meal. . . . Everybody was in a good mood. . . . We did not foresee that in a short while all of us would be dispersed . . . or would perish. . . . Our wedding feast was . . . without our knowing it . . . the farewell to generations of a good life and happy community."[5]

Conditions created by the regime influenced Jewish couples' decisions about when to marry or whether to marry at all. A social worker in Breslau had to postpone her marriage until her fiancé had paid off a former employee who was blackmailing him. Other Jewish couples devised unusual engagement celebrations and marriage preparations. When twenty-year-old Ruth Sass, studying in Switzerland, accepted her fiancé's proposal, the engagement party was held in Düsseldorf—without her. She feared confiscation of her passport if she returned to Germany and spent a lonely day in Geneva while friends and family drank a toast to her future happiness. Not only did the family celebrate without the future bride, but her mother and fiancé bought the items necessary to set up a new household, packed them, and had them stored in Belgium until the couple knew where they would emigrate.[6]

Sometimes the actual marriage did not occur in Germany at all, with couples waiting until they had emigrated. Ruth Sass, who could not return to Germany to marry, decided to go to Palestine with her fiancé: "My mother's reaction was that she could not understand how I could leave with Eric not being married to him yet [but there was] no choice." Much later, she reflected: "At that time to leave with your fiancé for a new country overseas was not such common practice and took a bit of determination." Other couples dispensed with all formal engagement proceedings, simply announcing their "engagement" before emigrating, "in order to please the family."[7] Still others may have married just to go abroad. Social workers worried about what they called "certificate marriages," which were enacted only so that two people could enter Palestine on one certificate.

Marriage was complicated enough when both partners were Jewish, but the complications multiplied when only one partner was Jewish or partly Jewish. From the nineteenth century until 1933, intermarriages between Jewish and non-Jewish partners had steadily increased. By 1930–33, the percentage of intermarriages among all Jews marrying had reached 24 percent in Prussia, 27 percent in Berlin, and 39 percent in Hamburg. In 1933, approximately 35,000 confessionally mixed marriages existed in Germany. As these couples fled, the figure declined to 20,000 by May 1939, to 16,760 in December 1942, and to 12,487 in September 1944.[8] Of mixed marriages, the large majority were between Jewish men and non-Jewish women, since Jewish men—for reasons of careerism, greater opportunities to meet non-Jews, and more secular attitudes—married "out" more often than Jewish women.[9] As more Jews emigrated, the percentage of Jews in Germany in mixed marriages grew. Some claim that by 1939 about 25 percent of all existing marriages involving Jews were mixed.[10] By the end of the war, the vast majority of registered "full" Jews left in Germany lived in intermarriages.

Until the Nuremberg Laws, the Nazis had faced the problem of defining who was a "Jew," even as "racial mixing" continued to infuriate them. The Nuremberg Laws and subsequent addenda set forth a classification system for defining Jews and rules regulating such "mixing." The most dramatic anti-Jewish legislation to date, the laws elevated "Aryans" to "citizens of the Reich" (*Reichsbürger*) while labeling Jews "state subjects" (*Staatsangehörige*). The laws also invalidated the exceptions made for Jewish World War I veterans or officials who had held their posts since before 1914. Most infamously, the laws instituted an intricate pseudoscientific classification system that labeled people according to the amount of their "Jewish blood" in order to revoke their citizens' rights and prohibit certain categories of "racial mixing." To inhibit extramarital relations, the laws created the category of *Rassenschande*, the Nazi term for miscegenation. Literally, it meant "racial disgrace" but more colloquially it suggested "racial pollution" or "race defilement" bordering on "racial treason." The laws also prohibited marriages between certain combinations of partners.

The Nuremberg Laws defined "full Jews" as people with at least three Jewish grandparents or, if fewer than three, a person belonging to the Jewish community or married to a Jew. (Thus, ultimately, even the Nazis relied on religious affiliation.) "First-degree *Mischlinge*" were defined as people who did not belong to the Jewish religion and were not married to a Jewish spouse but had two Jewish grandparents; "second-degree *Mischlinge*" as people with one Jewish grandparent;[11] and "Aryans" as people with no Jewish grandparents. The Nuremberg Laws permitted "full Jews" to marry other "full Jews," as well as "first-degree *Mischlinge*," but forbade "Aryans" from marrying "full Jews" or "first degree *Mischlinge*." They permitted "second-degree *Mischlinge*" to marry "Aryans," forbade them from marrying "full Jews" or even others like themselves, but allowed special dispensation for them to marry "first-degree *Mischlinge*." In effect, the Nuremberg Laws split "non-Aryans" roughly into two groups: *"Mischlinge"* and Jews. Both groups had to observe strict marriage restrictions, but in general the *"Mischlinge"* would be spared the expropriation, ghettoization, and destruction reserved for Jews.

Now there was danger in marrying "down." For example, by marrying a "full Jew," a Christian half Jew became "Jewish" and suffered all the disabilities of "full Jews." To find "suitable" spouses, the *"Mischlinge"* advertised for mates in their own news bulletin. Further intricacies of these laws confused and intimidated marriage applicants. In short, the Nazis created four categories of people and decreed which group could marry the other, insisting that the government (the Ministry of the Interior and the Führer's deputy) be the final arbiter in about one-fourth of the possible instances.[12]

While the April laws and boycotts had attempted to reverse economic integration, the Nuremberg Laws intended to reverse assimilation—the merging of Jewish with non-Jewish society through marriage and conversion. The complications in the provisions are significant. The Nazis could not and did not simply and clearly define Jews and encapsulate them. Instead, they created an elaborate system, inherent with ambiguities. The references to parents and grandparents had a historical dimension, first recreating a chronology of assimilation and then intending its rollback in layers. This historical/chronological dimension shows how seriously the Nazis took the "problem" of assimilation and how deeply Jewish Germans had actually blended into non-Jewish German society over several generations.

In fact, some individuals and families, registered as Christians, discovered—to their dismay—that by Nazi definitions they were still "Jews." They faced discrimination, but without Jewish organizations, friends, or relatives to console them. The Reich Association of Non-Aryan Christians, formed in 1933 to provide support for "partially Jewish" people, claimed that by 1935 one-third of its members had lost their jobs. Letters to government ministries from baffled "Jews" attest to their surprise and alarm— and their hope of rectifying their situation. Some tried to prove they were not Jews. Some tried to change their names (although the Nazis eventually forbade name changes in 1938). Still others asked for special dispensation, that is, to be included in the *Volk*, since they had not known they were Jews.[13] Nazi racial obsessions and laws were wreaking havoc with generations of assimilation.

If the number of half Jews, quarter Jews, intermarried Jews, and Christian "Jews" approached 1 million, then the number of "Aryan" relatives who had close or distant contact with them was significant, and the Nuremberg Laws affected broad kinship networks throughout German society. "Aryan" relatives might worry about their Jewish relatives, which could turn them against the system, although there were many, as with racists in general, who believed that their own relatives were "exceptions" and that most Jews deserved the harsh treatment meted out to them. "Aryan" relatives, however, would also worry intensely about themselves. Did they also have Jewish "blood"? Would they be suspected of helping Jews? Would they be penalized because of their Jewish relatives? Thus the Nuremberg Laws and the government's vicious antisemitism divided the populace into those unrelated to Jews and those related to Jews, putting "Aryan" family members in fear of being treated as Jews. To avoid possible punishment, some distanced themselves from Jews, accentuating their "Aryan" origins or their

Nazi activities. Many saw good reason to maintain a low profile. Hence, by defining the Jewish "danger" as central, the Nuremberg Laws probably helped the Nazis obtain greater compliance from a large number of "Aryan" relatives and increased social control over a large population either intimately or distantly tied to Jews.

The Nuremberg Laws also had very specific consequences, criminalizing sexual relations as well as certain marriages between Jews and "Aryans." Even before the laws, such relations had been openly condemned and sometimes punished. Only months after the Nazi takeover, "Aryan" women in Nuremberg were forced to walk through the streets with shaven heads and self-deprecating placards for their real or alleged sexual relations with Jews. In the two months before the passage of the Nuremberg Laws, a group of émigrés in Paris collected an incomplete list of 293 cases of "race defilement" from announcements in the foreign press, as well as Berlin and Frankfurt newspapers.[14]

Well before Nuremberg, families and communities attempted successfully to halt many intermarriages. Frequently, marriage registrars refused to allow intermarriage, and these decisions—based not on law but on the "official and unofficial writings of the state and the National Socialist Party"—were often upheld by the courts. In one case, a Berlin Catholic priest was condemned to three months in prison for officiating at a wedding of a couple who had already been turned down by the marriage registrar on racial grounds. Although the wedding took place in March 1935, the priest was convicted of abetting "racial defilement." Cities sometimes introduced their own racial laws. As of June 1934, for example, Berlin schools fired "Aryan" teachers who had married Jewish spouses after July 1933 or still intended to marry Jews. Even when couples could still intermarry, they often faced harassment from local SA who demonstrated in front of their homes. In October 1935, for example, the antisemitic *Stürmer* newspaper listed the names, birth dates, professions, and addresses of "recent mixed marriages" and suggested that local party cadres in charge of housing should look into the situation of these "race defilers."[15]

After the Nuremberg Laws, the punishments were far more severe, and many relationships suffered. One "Aryan" lover abruptly cut off his affair with a Jewish woman when his brother, who "did not want trouble in the family," threatened to denounce him to the Gestapo. Moreover, many courts construed the language of the laws broadly—for example, interpreting "race defilement" to include *any* contact, not just physical contact. Any friendly ties between the sexes became hazardous as the regime politicized these relationships as "attempted race defilement" or actions that violated

"German honor." People were reported to the Gestapo for having been friends with Jews even before 1933.[16]

The Nazis punished men more harshly than women, believing that "in adulterous relationships men were the determining component." In fact, Hitler had originally insisted that women ("Aryan" or Jewish) would not be subject to prosecution for violating the Nuremberg Laws, although after 1937 the Gestapo took women, too, into custody. In contrast to men, however, "Aryan" women were more likely to be humiliated in public rather than being imprisoned. In the case of "Aryan" women, male "Aryan" pride was at issue. In 1938 a state superior court allowed a man to divorce his wife because in 1932 she had had a relationship with a Jewish man. A woman who "did not have enough feeling for her race or pride of race to avoid an erotic relationship with a Jew," even before the Nazi seizure of power, was fair game for divorce.[17] This and other such cases suggest that by the late 1930s many Germans were well informed about the plight of Jews and knew how to manipulate that plight for personal advantage, even against other "Aryans."

The judiciary viewed "race defilement" as seriously as "high treason" (*Hochverrat* and *Landesverrat*)—the other major crimes to the "body of the Volk" (*Volkskörper*)—and handed down severe penitentiary sentences to male offenders. By the end of 1938, the average sentence was four to five years, with Jewish men receiving longer and harsher sentences than "Aryan" men. Jewish women were taken into "protective custody" as soon as their "Aryan" lovers were convicted. During the war, alleged Jewish transgressors —male and female—were deported to their deaths, frequently without trial. Others, as in the case of a Jewish man from Nuremberg, were executed after rigged trials even during the deportations. Such executions were probably intended as lessons to the "Aryan" population, since the Jews were to be murdered anyway.[18]

Characteristic of the Nazi view of Jews—although not always consistent with their view of women as sexually passive—the courts accused Jewish men and women alike of seducing "innocent German-blooded" sexual partners. In one case the Jewish woman was accused of being a "sex-craved, morally degenerate Jew-woman, who with her unrestrained sexual desire and ruthless determination had the defendant under her strong influence." In what must have been mass psychological projection, probably inflamed by the lewd caricatures of Jewish men as sexual predators in the *Stürmer*, the authorities arrested Jewish men for "race defilement" on the slightest suspicion. Worse, individuals used "race defilement" to intimidate Jews and officials to arrest them even if no relationship with an "Aryan" existed. In

1938 a young Jewish man was arrested for being in the same department store elevator with an "Aryan" woman, even though she entered when he was already there. Another elderly Jewish man, who stopped on the street when a non-Jewish female friend greeted him, was later arrested and investigated. False accusations also abounded.[19] Even when the trials and investigations revealed nothing, they fortified the stereotype of evil and lustful Jews, threw Jewish families into turmoil, and reinforced the distance between Jews and other Germans.

In such a climate of intimidation, intermarriage between those of "German blood" and the various categories of *"Mischlinge"* created hazards. Individuals and families had to appeal to the government when a marriage candidate conceded even a hint of "Jewish blood." Often these petitions came from the "Aryan" side, begging for special permission to marry someone who was, according to the plea, only minimally "Jewish." For example, one "Aryan" woman wrote to the Ministry of the Interior because her nephew wished to marry a woman who was a "second-degree *Mischling*," but whose grandmother had recently converted to Judaism. Thus, the young woman's "racial" identity had worsened by Nazi standards to that of a "first-degree *Mischling*." This case was unusual, for a bureaucrat decided in favor of the young couple. Another case involved a woman who had only recently discovered that she was Jewish and whose son did not know his status (as a half Jew). Her letters begging that he be allowed to marry an "Aryan" went unanswered. Bella Fromm recorded the suicide of a wealthy and prominent "half-Aryan" man and the attempted suicide of his fiancée after the failure of their efforts to get special permission for their marriage — including appeals to Hitler via well-placed friends.[20]

Some couples tried getting around these laws by marrying outside Germany, but they often faced prosecution when they returned. For example, an "Aryan" man who traveled to Leningrad to marry a Soviet Jewish woman in February 1936 was sentenced to two years in a penitentiary because he had undermined the "spirit" of the law. Other couples who were turned down by state officials, or knew they would be turned down, lived in common-law marriages. If caught, the "Aryan" partner could be imprisoned and the Jewish or part-Jewish partner sentenced to death. In 1937 Reinhard Heydrich, head of the security police, noted that couples who had been denied permission to marry would probably resent the authorities and should be "inconspicuously, but thoroughly" observed, especially for the possibility of such unauthorized unions. The police received names of such couples and exercised surveillance accordingly.[21]

If couples planning marriage faced impediments, their decision to have children was even more fraught. The Nazis encouraged procreation among "Aryans" by making contraception more difficult, punishing abortion more severely than ever, and providing new financial incentives for large families through the Reich Marriage Loan Program. This pronatalist policy went hand in hand with a complementary antinatalist policy. The Nazis discouraged procreation among those deemed biologically "inferior" and "asocial," and among Jews, *"Mischlinge,"* and intermarried couples, by excluding them from the Reich Marriage Loan Program. More cruelly, the government pressed a ruthless sterilization program that victimized over 320,000 Germans in the prewar years, including an unknown number of Jews. The victims of sterilization were doomed by diagnoses such as "feebleminded," "depressive," "schizophrenic," or "inferior" (*Minderwertigkeit*). Rumors also spread within Jewish circles that *"Mischlinge"* would be forcibly sterilized. Even before 1933, Arthur Gütt (later of the Ministry of the Interior) had pushed for the sterilization of all Jews, particularly Eastern European Jews, and by 1935 Reich Medical "Führer" Gerhard Wagner concurred. Mass sterilizations were not carried out, however, because the Nazis devised more radical solutions.[22]

Such political machinations, in combination with the emigration of young Jews, resulted in a slight rise in the birth rates among "Aryans"—the rate had reached 1924 levels again by 1939—and plummeting birth rates among German Jews.[23] Jewish couples who chose to have a baby faced an unpredictable future, one in which they, as outcasts, would be able to offer their children far less than they themselves had received or achieved. At best, they could hope for a change of regime or emigration. Sometimes a baby's birth could even delay emigration. Less fortunate parents had to struggle with their new responsibility under the dictatorship's intensifying repression. Erna Becker-Kohen, a Catholic of Jewish ancestry married to an "Aryan," experienced terrible foreboding regarding the hostility that awaited her baby. "We will be surrounded by ... hatred and contempt because I am Jewish and my husband is a race defiler. Although he is loyal to me, because he loves me very much, he won't be able to change [the situation] that one scorns not just me, but also his child."[24]

Anxiety about the future prompted some Jewish women to abort pregnancies. Although statistics are unreliable, since abortions (even for Jewish women) were illegal, anecdotal evidence, interviews, and special requests to public health officials for permission to abort indicate that some pregnant women saw no alternative to an abortion. Some managed to find a doctor or abortionist who would end the pregnancy. Ruth Klüger recalled how her father, a gynecologist and pediatrician, had been arrested for performing abortions. Her mother told her that a poor young woman had begged him for an abortion and he had taken pity on her. Then someone denounced him. Klüger continued: "At that time he stopped a number of pregnancies. Who wanted children in such times? Also my mother's, that is, his own child. She said it would have been a boy and 'he was sad for days.'" Extreme uncertainty and adversity notwithstanding, there were those whose desire for children actually increased. Eva Wysbar, the Jewish wife of an "Aryan" film director, was delighted with her second pregnancy. Because of pressures on her husband, she and he had been living apart, both under surveillance: "The more danger I saw, . . . the more strongly I [wanted to] fortify the family and to support the tiny being who already existed with a second one."[25]

"MIXED" MARRIAGES AND "MIXED" FAMILIES

Families of mixed marriages confronted both external and internal challenges. The disapproval of neighbors, employers, and the state weighed on them from outside. From within their own families, they faced rejection by "Aryan" relatives who had previously either welcomed or, at least, tolerated the Jewish partner or by relatives who had always opposed the Jewish partner and now felt that the couple had brought bad times "upon themselves." Moreover, the situation of children in mixed marriages was complicated, both legally and socially. Most mixed couples had registered their children as Christians. Some, whose children had been registered as Jewish, tried to have them baptized to save them from categorization as "Jews." Also, in obvious terror, some mothers tried to prove that children whose fathers-of-record were Jewish or partly Jewish had actually been conceived in an adulterous affair with an "Aryan." Such desperate attempts rarely met with success any more than did baptism.[26]

Aware that mixed marriages and *"Mischlinge"* had wide-ranging familial and friendship networks, reaching even into high Nazi ranks, the government proceeded against them in uneven stages. In the first phase, between 1933 and 1935, Jews in mixed marriages, their children, and their grandchildren could not avoid the legal discrimination against all Jews in the professions or in schools. In the second phase, from 1935 until 1938, the Nazis hoped to separate Jews from non-Jews completely. They created the separate legal category of *"Mischlinge,"* who were given some rights beyond those of ("full") Jews who had married "Aryans." For a very short time, the lot of these *"Mischlinge"* slightly improved. The third phase began in late 1938 (although officially in April 1939) with the invention of the category of "privileged" mixed marriage. At that time, Jews were to be physically isolated, except for those in "privileged" mixed marriages. Although such Jews would suffer fierce discrimination and the destruction of their economic existence, they would not be physically annihilated *as a group* because of their "Aryan" relatives (at least until 1945; see chapter 7). Still, they justifiably feared for their lives, since the Nazis could always change the rules, as they regularly did—for example, pulling some in when the number of Jewish deportees was insufficient. Moreover, the Nazis had decreed that "*Mischlinge*" and Jews in mixed marriages could be deported if they displayed "a hostile attitude" toward the German government. More monstrously, the Gestapo frequently extorted "confessions" of "misconduct" from terrorized Jewish men and women and then deported them. Jewish women married to "Aryans" were viciously taunted as "Jew whores" by Gestapo agents and sometimes brutally assaulted. During the deportations, agents snarled, "Do what you want with [these women], it doesn't matter whether they croak here or in Auschwitz."[27]

Government regulations tormented the daily lives of these mixed families, jeopardizing their livelihoods and futures. Helmut Krüger's family was treated as "mixed." His father was a civil servant, and his Jewish mother had converted to Christianity, hoping to help her husband keep his job. After 1933 their lives became a nightmare. His father lost his job, and his fifteen-year-old brother was ousted from his Pathfinders troop, a group similar to the Boy Scouts, to which he had belonged for eight years. The children's schooling suffered as well. His brother dropped out of school in 1937, a year before his final exams. Legally he did not have to leave, but the teachers made life miserable for him, and his family's financial problems prevented him from continuing anyway. Krüger noted: "We lived permanently between fear and hope. Our situation could really not have been more absurd." Even relatively trivial problems caused bewilderment, for example, whether or not to display the swastika flag: "Should we . . . display the hated banner . . . ? Should we demonstrate contempt publicly by not displaying the banner?" All citizens had to display the flag, but the Nuremberg Laws forbade Jews from doing so. Jews were no longer citizens, but "*Mischlinge*" were. In the end, Krüger thought his mother made the decision to hang the flag on their railing "out of a sense of guilt for everything. . . . The feeling was indescribable, just thinking that we had in our apartment the banner which, in earlier years, we had found loathsome."[28] Nostalgically, Krüger recalled a school essay he had written prior to 1933 in which he had happily described himself as "a *Mischling* of many nations and races."[29]

"Aryan" relatives provided both relief and additional pain. Jewish partners might have felt some relief from seeing that not all Germans believed
Nazi racial mythology and from expecting an extra layer of protection
around their own exposed families (since, ultimately, "Aryan" relatives
could try to use their influence or their resources to protect Jews or provide
them refuge). But even in such families, one could not take for granted that
the "Aryan" relatives were automatically opposed to Hitler. Even those well
disposed to their Jewish in-laws might have considered them "exceptions"
to their own antisemitism or might, for other reasons, have been avid sup-
porters of Hitler. One Jewish woman recalled how her mother-in-law, a
"pure Aryan," had voted for Hitler even though she lived in the Jewish
woman's home.[30]

Some Nazi enthusiasts had a change of heart when they realized their
own Jewish relatives were endangered. When one party member was told
to dissociate from her *"Mischling"* grandchildren: "She threw away her
... membership ... and said: 'My grandchildren are the dearest thing I
have, and you could all learn a thing or two from my Jewish daughter-
in-law!' Then she was cured." Other "Aryan" relatives, however, chose to cut
off ties with a Jewish in-law or even with their own kin who had intermarried. Still others simply ignored the pain of their Jewish relatives.
Erna Becker-Kohen wrote: "As a good German, my mother-in-law feels
entitled to ignore my misery."[31] The political mistrust that lurked within
many, perhaps most, German families was particularly palpable in these
families.

Nazi regulations also caused divisions among Jews. Victor Klemperer, in
a "nonprivileged" mixed marriage, commented in his diary on the jealousy
and hatred the Nazis caused among Jews by dividing them into "privileged"
and "nonprivileged." Bruno Blau noted that "privileged" Jews were exempt
from all degrading regulations that made the lives of other Jews miserable:
"They ... received the same foodstuffs as non-Jews, got ration coupons for
clothes ... were permitted to make unlimited use of public transportation.
[They] experienced none of the torments that were devised for Jews with
genuine sadism." He believed that "privileged" Jews "felt superior to other
Jews," tending to avoid contact with other Jews, especially in public.[32]

Children of intermarriages faced pressures in school and from peers.
Some parents had never told their children of their origins, and the children were staggered—and probably furious—to learn of them (see chapter 4). In a few cases, Nazi teachers and peers succeeded in turning children
against their Jewish parent. One boy blamed his Jewish mother "for the fact
that I am being discriminated against in school" and rejected his own

"Jewish part" to the point of supporting the Nazis. Singing bloodthirsty songs about killing Jews with the Hitler Youth, he "identified with this aggressive tendency against the Jewish people." Still, he felt, "I am related somewhat to these Jewish people who are to be killed."[33]

Often, the existence of *"Mischlinge"*—if still young and baptized—later saved the life of a divorced or widowed Jewish parent. *"Mischling"* sons, in particular, could help a Jewish parent as long as they served in the military —as did the two (baptized) Krüger brothers. Six months after *"Mischlinge"* were banned from the army, Helmut Krüger, still undiscovered, received the Iron Cross: "How can I explain what a decoration meant for me at that time? I believed I had saved myself and my mother for good."[34] While her sons were in the army, their Jewish mother, divorced from her "Aryan" husband, was not deported. She was deported to Theresienstadt after their dismissal and survived, possibly because of the delay caused by her sons' military participation.

The Nazis attacked not only the offspring of intermarriages but also ties between parents and foster or adopted children. "Aryan" foster children could be removed from families where even one parent was Jewish. The courts declared that "it was unacceptable from a National Socialist viewpoint" for a "non-Aryan" child to be brought up among "Aryan" foster parents "in an environment in which it does not racially belong." Further, after the Nuremberg Laws, adoptions of "racially" different children were forbidden. Worse yet, a family law of April 1938 allowed removing adopted children from their adoptive parents if the "parties belonged to different races." In some cases, children voluntarily left their parents as a result of this pressure.[35]

The state interfered directly in mixed families. More and more frequently, courts decided in favor of the "Aryan" partner in custody disputes. After mid-1936, whenever the courts awarded custody to the "Aryan" father, the children were forbidden from visiting their Jewish mothers in their homes. The mothers had to apply for permission to meet the children elsewhere. On occasion, the government forced a mixed couple to separate from its children, taking custody of an "Aryan" child away from her or his "Aryan" mother who had married a Jewish man. In one instance, the government informed an eighteen-year-old that her Jewish father was not her biological father but had adopted her. As an "Aryan" she could not live with her "mixed" parents after they had moved to a *Judenhaus* (see chapter 6) but had to stay with her maternal "Aryan" grandparents. In another case, the government admonished an adopted son to separate from his Jewish (though converted) parents. He refused. However, when he came to visit his parents in his army uniform and went for a walk with his mother, she, who had to wear a Star of David, was ordered to remove it: "A soldier's uniform and a Star of David next to each other—that was out of the question!"[36]

Other bizarre familial interactions occurred even without direct state intervention. When his mother—a convert to Christianity—died, a young baptized *"Mischling"* saw his "Aryan" father marry another "Aryan" and his own status in the family decline. His father told him that his previous marriage and the boy's presence would ruin his career as a civil servant. Accordingly, the son emigrated to his mother's relatives in the United States in 1934. Such a "happy end" was not to be for the "three-quarters" Jewish child Cordelia Edvardson. Her father had been a Jew and her mother a "first-degree *Mischling*." Her mother later married an "Aryan" and had Christian children with him, securing herself in a "privileged" mixed marriage. After September 1941, Cordelia, the "Jew," could no longer live in the new "Aryan" family, even though she had been raised Catholic and her stepfather had adopted her. Ultimately, she was deported (see chapter 7). In an even stranger case, an "Aryan" family rejected its own child. According to the daughter, her parents had to prove their "Aryan" status when she was a teenager: "And in this situation my mother put me in great danger: as a 'good German' she acknowledged that I was the illegitimate child of a Jew!" The Nazis classified her a "first-degree *Mischling*," after which she left her parents and worked for Jewish families as a nanny or housekeeper. Other "Aryan" parents refused to protect their Jewish children, leading to the children's deportations from the Jewish Hospital in Berlin.[37] Severe government pressure, human fear, and wickedness tore at the fabric of family life.

DIVORCE

Jewish Marriages

In the 1920s, Jewish marriages ended in divorce proportionately more often than non-Jewish marriages as a whole but less often than marriages in Berlin or Hamburg. Intermarriages generally fared worse than Jewish marriages. Although more statistical research is necessary to trace the rate of Jewish divorce in the 1930s, we do know that marriages suffered under intense new strains. Ruth Klüger's parents did not seek a divorce, but their relationship was tense:

> When I explain to people ... that the two quarreled during their last year together, ... people act astonished and say that under conditions such as those you had to endure in the Hitler years the persecuted should have

come closer together.... That is sentimental nonsense and rests on fatal notions of purification through suffering.... From experience we know that during an earthquake more porcelain breaks than usual.[38]

Although Jews got divorced after 1933, it seems that a combination of loyalty, habit, and unsettling circumstances may have made people less willing than usual to radically break with their spouses. Moreover, as circumstances worsened, individuals in unhappy relationships may have made their private peace in order to help the family escape or survive. Perhaps, as in the case of a Hamburg couple, the partners helped each other through bad times and postponed their divorce until both arrived in another country. Peter Wyden's parents made this decision openly.

> My parents' marriage had, in effect, broken up. Both wanted a divorce, but wait! According to rumor ... the pious Pilgrims of America frowned on divorce. Divorced persons were said to be guilty of "moral turpitude," and moral turpitude was a capital cause for visa rejection. So my parents postponed their formal separation. They would not even proceed with it in the United States until after they had secured their "first papers" toward permanent citizenship. Moral turpitude lived.[39]

"Mixed" Marriages

How did mixed marriages fare in this environment? Beyond the general tensions generated by the Nazis, the regime also advised, bribed, and threatened "Aryans" to divorce their Jewish spouses. In 1933, civil service candidates had to prove the German ancestry of their spouses. The German Railroad refused to hire "Aryans" married to Jews and fired such "Aryans" already working there. In 1936, the pressure on mixed marriages increased as the civil service refused to promote state and federal employees married to Jews. Shortly thereafter, it required their resignation. By the winter of 1936–37, the government expelled mixed families from the German Winter Relief. They had to seek assistance from the Jewish Winter Relief Agency: in Hamburg alone, of 535 new applicants, 457 (or 85 percent) came from mixed families in which the wife was "Aryan."[40]

The courts helped to disband marriages as well. As of late 1933, some judges granted divorces based on racial differences. As one woman summarized the situation: "My mother could have got a divorce with the stroke of a pen." Her mother endured an unhappy marriage "especially ... after she knew [a divorce] would be [her Jewish husband's] downfall."[41] The Civil

Code had long allowed marriages to be disbanded within six months if one spouse had been unaware of "personal qualities" in the other that would have prevented the marriage. Courts construed the relevant paragraph loosely interpreting "personal qualities" as Jewishness and "six months" as from Hitler's seizure of power—or even later. After 1938, when a new marriage and divorce law established the legality of annulling mixed marriages —and after Reich Marshal Göring had announced that German women who divorced their Jewish husbands could rejoin the "racial community" —the Gestapo and employers treated "Aryan" spouses harshly if they still resisted divorce, and, late in the war, the government exacted hard labor from the men.[42]

Whether or not a "mixed" couple intended to be political, the mere continuation of their marriage was a form of defiance and was seen as such by the government. Since the government insisted on racial purity and total fealty, it saw "Aryans" in intermarriages as siding with the enemy, and thus standing in opposition to the "racial community." Moreover, these couples faced enormous social pressure in a society conforming rapidly to government visions. Thus, an actress who still refused to divorce her Jewish husband even after he had emigrated lost her job at a radio station and faced disparagement from her family and insults from officials.[43]

Government belligerence and chicanery notwithstanding, most intermarriages endured—although estimates of 93 percent seem too high. This was no small accomplishment, since Nazi intimidation caused grave tensions and anxieties in these marriages and the divorce rate in the general population was on the rise. Almost immediately after 1933, intermarriages resulted in impoverishment and ostracism by former friends and colleagues. Either the "Aryan" husband lost his position and the family had to scrape by or the "Aryan" wife suffered the privation resulting from the radically diminished status of her Jewish husband, often losing her own job as well.[44] Moreover, just as in Jewish marriages, mixed marriages experienced new gender roles. "Aryan" wives, many of whom had married "up" economically, often found it necessary to support their families. Also, they had to represent and protect their Jewish husbands, a role formerly played by the man of the house. Finally, keeping a marriage together sometimes implied long periods of separation as one spouse went abroad in search of either emigration possibilities or work.

Some couples pretended to go along with the "system" in order to maintain their marriages. For instance, one man, married to a Jewish woman, displayed his SA uniform prominently, to the dismay of his anti-Nazi relatives. "I'm doing this for my wife, so that nothing happens to her," he assured them. The Nazis did not allow such a charade for long: he was rejected from the SA when his wife's identity became known. Others tried to dupe the regime but met with rigorous scrutiny. The Wysbars, for example, attempted to save the "Aryan" husband's career as a film director by suing for what both considered a phony divorce based on "insurmountable aversion." Eva Wysbar, the Jewish wife, demanded the usual one-year period of reconciliation. When the year was up, each partner delayed signing the final papers. By this time, they were hoping to emigrate, since the Nazis, probably seeing through the ruse, had barred the husband from work. Eva Wysbar lived in their home with their children. Her husband, whose passport had been confiscated, lived in a hotel, where Gestapo agents watched him closely, pressing for the divorce. She traveled to Zurich, Prague, Paris, London, Rome, and the United States in an unsuccessful effort to help the family emigrate, facing prejudice against mixed marriages even outside Germany. Undeterred—and lucky—she and her children were ultimately invited to the United States. They left in June 1938. The divorce took place in September. In October the Gestapo returned her husband's passport, and he joined his family the following month.[45]

While some tried to skirt restrictions, others faced their friends and colleagues with courage. When the suggestion was made to one man that he divorce his Jewish wife based on "insurmountable aversion," he replied that that would be impossible due to an "insurmountable attraction." Still others made their own, private peace with the racial laws. A doctor withstood the unrelenting pressure of the League of German Doctors to divorce his Jewish wife and lost his large practice as a result. But in 1934 (*before* the Nuremberg Laws) he informed her that as a steadfast German Nationalist (*not* a Nazi) he could no longer live with her "as husband and wife." He would stay with her and their child but no longer have sex. His personal allegiance remained unwavering throughout the regime, saving her life.[46]

Sexual abstinence on racial grounds echoed the fanatical views of the German legal press and courts. A German legal journal argued that, in view of the "deep change in the racial sensitivity of the German *Volk*," it was not a dereliction of marital duty if an "Aryan" partner refused sex with a Jewish spouse. Courts frequently reasoned that sexual relations with someone of a different "race" could lead to an aversion for which the "Aryan" spouse was blameless: "It would contradict healthy *Volk* sentiment to declare the spouse guilty for the divorce because of this refusal."[47]

Driven to despair by the viciousness of the regime and the hopelessness of their situation, an increasing proportion of Jews turned to suicide.

Although there are no separate suicide statistics for Jews within mixed marriages, memoirs mention suicide attempts by Jewish partners whose spouses wanted to separate. When one husband demanded a divorce at the end of 1938, his terrified and despondent Jewish wife tried suicide. She survived to see her husband acquire custody of their children and marry another woman. Her three *"Mischling"* children had to learn to live with a stepmother who was, according to one daughter, "an absolute Nazi! One example: After work, I went [and] washed my hands with warm water. But, we were supposed to save electricity and gas for the *Endsieg* [the final victory of the war]! She came into the bathroom and spat at me: 'You lackey of Stalin!'" In some suicides, the "Aryan" partner may have actually pressured the Jewish spouse. One woman took her life in 1938 because her husband, a dedicated Nazi, "suffered so much" when he could not display the Nazi flag. He entertained while she was banished to a side room. Their daughter, the writer Anja Lundholm, suspects that her father, a doctor, gave her mother the poison with which to kill herself and also gave poison to her aunt—which she took—after refusing to give her 300 marks to help her escape Germany.[48]

The (misplaced) guilt Jews felt toward their loyal "Aryan" spouses and the belief that their families would survive better without them caused some Jewish partners to end their own lives. One Jewish woman killed herself so that her "Aryan" husband could continue to support their family as a lawyer. A Jewish man, married to an "Aryan" woman and the father of their two children, could no longer support his family and moved with them to the home of his parents-in-law. He wanted to emigrate, but the grandparents wanted the children to stay with them until the parents had settled down. The wife was torn between her husband and her parents. Since the grandparents were very wealthy and would be able to take care of his wife and children, the man decided it would be best for the family if he killed himself.[49]

Contemporary observers and anecdotal evidence suggest that it was more likely for an "Aryan" man to divorce his Jewish wife than for an "Aryan" woman to divorce her Jewish husband. An émigré wrote: "My younger brother-in-law has a gentile wife, who is a very good support to him in these difficult situations, as most of them are, they don't leave their Jewish husbands, though urged and threatened." "Aryan" wives were less likely to work for a living, especially in organizations such as the civil service, which could exert enormous pressure, and some continued to depend on their Jewish husbands for support. In contrast, lack of loyalty by "Aryan" men probably resulted from job or career pressure. Such tensions convinced "The Jewish Wife," in Bertolt Brecht's play, to leave her husband before he would leave her. She rehearses what she will say to him:

> I'm packing because otherwise they'll take away your position as chief surgeon at the clinic. And because they already cut you there to your face and because already you can't sleep at night. I don't want you to tell me not to go. I'm going in a hurry because I don't want to have you tell me I *should* go. It's a question of time. Character is a question of time.

Upon entering, her husband lamely tries to stop her. Lying to each other, they agree it will only be "for a couple of weeks." Then he hands her a winter coat—in springtime.[50]

Some "Aryan" men may have viewed divorce as the only way to protect their families. For example, one woman from Dresden wrote: "For years men have had to divorce their Jewish wives or lose their jobs. I know of many such cases. Some men did it in order to be able to give alimony to the wives they loved, otherwise, jobless, the entire family would have starved." Other divorces were complicated not only by Nazi cruelty but by the enigmas of love. According to Helmut Krüger, his parents decided to divorce at the end of 1937 so that his father could find a job again and his Jewish mother might gain protection by regaining her Dutch citizenship. After the divorce, his father was able to support her and the children. When his mother's apartment was bombed, his father hurried to her and offered her his quarters; when she was deported to Theresienstadt, he tried, unsuccessfully, to gain her release. After the war they did not reunite. After the Nuremberg Laws, the Jewish wife in a Hamburg couple suggested divorce in the hope of protecting their business. The "Aryan" husband quickly remarried. Nevertheless, he always protected his former spouse and their son. Even when he was imprisoned for criticizing Hitler, he arranged for a friend to pass money on to his former wife. After the war they lived together until he died.[51]

Of course, there were also "Aryan" men who simply, or eagerly, bowed to expediency. The writer Erich Kästner quoted one such individual whom he encountered after the liberation: "'I divorced my wife, but the separation would have been unavoidable even in normal times. After all, unhappy marriages don't only occur just under a dictatorship. Besides, I sent her money as long as that was possible.'" The last line revealed her fate, and Kästner commented: "The man is standing between high trees, as though they were the High Court of Justice. He defends himself without being asked. He practices. Practices his alibi. He looks for people to listen to him. So he can check how convincing his arguments are." Gershom Scholem recounted the story of his aunt, a physician, who married a non-Jewish colleague in 1911: "The big test came in 1933. After a while my uncle discovered, following a marriage of more than twenty years, that he was an "Aryan" and asked my aunt Käthe to release him so he could marry a German. Thus my aunt was . . . taken to . . . Theresienstadt, where she died." A handful of these craven or heartless "Aryan" men were prosecuted after the war for divorcing their Jewish wives and thus causing their deportation and death.

More research on mixed marriages and divorce is needed before we draw final conclusions. It is possible that divorces occurred in spurts, for example, directly after the Nuremberg Laws and the November Pogrom, or when couples in "nonprivileged" mixed marriages had to move into a *Judenhaus*. It is also important to analyze why the divorces took place, in an attempt to save the Jewish partner, for example, or under Gestapo lies and threats. Finally, if we consider that mixed marriages always had higher divorce rates than marriages within the same religion, and if we recall the divorce rates for the non-Jewish population—33 per 10,000 in 1935—it seems that mixed marriages remained quite steadfast.[52] Despite the contemptible deeds of those "Aryans" who divorced their Jewish spouses—and the ghastly consequences—most "mixed" couples withstood enormous pressure to divorce in a nation that had gradually excommunicated Jews and their spouses, socially, morally, and physically.

4

The Daily Lives of Jewish Children and
Youth in the "Third Reich"

Death, not sex, was the secret about which the grown-ups whispered,
about which one wanted to hear more.   — RUTH KLÜGER

In 1933, approximately 117,000 Jewish children and youth between the
ages of six and twenty-five lived in Germany. Compared with their elders,
whose loss of jobs and businesses proceeded erratically, the younger generation faced a more drastic deterioration in conditions at public schools and
among non-Jewish friends, often finding their first safe haven in a Jewish
school. They also experienced a drastic reduction in their aspirations and
lived in tense homes with families on edge. Gender played an important
role in children's and young people's lives. Parents and Jewish communal
organizations held different expectations for girls and boys, and gender
framed the ways in which children envisioned their futures. But from 1933
on, both girls and boys had to make unprecedented adjustments in their
lives while facing unrelenting assaults on their self-esteem.

SCHOOL

Jewish Children in "Aryanized" Schools

Nazi legislation of April 1933, euphemistically entitled the "Law Against the
Overcrowding of German Schools," established a quota of 1.5 percent total
enrollment for Jews. Where Jews made up more than 5 percent of the population, schools could allow up to 5 percent of their pupils[1] to be Jewish.
Exemptions included Jewish pupils whose fathers had served during World

War I, children of mixed marriages (with no more than two Jewish grand-parents), and Jewish children with foreign citizenship. Elementary school (the *Volksschule*) attendance remained, for the time being, required for all. Like the other April laws, the actual number of exemptions surprised the Nazis. But for Jews, the exemptions were, at best, a Pyrrhic victory. The massive hostility they faced and practical concerns with learning a vocation forced many to leave school.

Because children spend so much time in school, unprotected by family, Jewish children continually met with the blatant repercussions of Nazism there. Well before Jewish children were expelled from German public schools, the majority lost the rights of non-Jews. They often had to sit apart from classmates. The curriculum isolated them further. In German class, one Jewish teenager had to study literature on the need for German expansion. Titles varied, including the bestseller *Volk without Space*. In English class, the same girl read news articles from a British pro-Nazi tabloid. Teachers often required essays on Nazi themes. Jews, however, were prohibited from addressing these topics and, instead, were given arbitrary topics that had never been discussed in class. No matter how well an essay was written, a Jewish child seldom received a top grade.[2]

School administrators and teachers barred Jewish children from school events, whether inside or outside school. When Nazi movies were shown, Jewish children could not attend but afterward had to listen while other children discussed the film. Denied school subsidies, they were forbidden from going to swimming pools or sleeping in dormitories on class trips. A mother described her daughter's unhappiness about missing special events: "It was not because she was denied going to the show that my little girl was weeping ... but because she had to stay apart, as if she were not good enough to associate with her comrades any longer." On Mother's Day, Jewish children had to take part in the school festivities but were not allowed to sing along. When they protested, their teacher responded haughtily: "I know you have a mother ... but she is only a Jewish mother." On the rare occasion when Jewish children could take part, the "Aryan" children would show up in their Nazi youth group outfits, making it clear who did not belong.[3]

The extent of persecution depended on various factors: whether Jewish children attended urban or rural schools, whether they lived in areas where the Nazis were particularly popular, and what political attitudes their teachers held. Children were more likely to be victimized in small town and village schools. There, non-Jewish children, even if they had wanted to, did not dare to be seen with Jews. Between 1933 and 1935, in a small town in the Mark Brandenburg, no one wanted to sit near a Jewish boy or play with him during breaks. In a small town near Aachen, a Jewish child suffered the abrupt rupture of her closest friendship—the other child even stopped greeting her—and had to listen to her female teacher make nasty remarks about Jews in class. For many children, public events were not nearly as upsetting as the situation at school, which grew worse and worse.[4]

Even in cities, Jewish children experienced at least some animosity. At best, Jewish children retained some of their non-Jewish friends for a short time, while self-identified "Aryan" teachers or classmates were unfriendly. There were segregated Jewish classes in some schools, Jewish benches in "mixed" classrooms in others. In a Berlin elementary school, which was not known for antisemitism and in which almost half the pupils were Jewish, non-Jewish children brought "pails full of soap and water ... in order to wash the seats clean where the Jewish children had sat." In a notably rare situation, "Aryans" in a Berlin *Gymnasium* defended their Jewish friends, resisted singing the bloodthirsty Nazi anthem, and as late as 1936 refused to hail the reoccupation of the Rhineland. Nonetheless, some teachers there insulted Jewish pupils or mumbled Nazi eugenics.[5]

Helmut Kallmann's description of his Berlin high school between 1932 and 1938 manifests both his clear awareness of the political leanings of his teachers and the contradictions confronting Jews. The chemistry teacher, for example, was not an overt antisemite but still told his classes not to purchase their supplies from a Jewish woman's store. Some teachers simply wore their SA or SS uniforms to class, while others were ideologues who harassed the Jewish teenagers. The biology teacher taught "racial education," insisting that "the Jew is the Master of the Lie, the King of Crime." This rhetoric backfired at first, embarrassing the non-Jewish pupils who could not imagine that these insults fit the fathers of their Jewish friends. Ultimately, however, such tirades intimidated Jews and non-Jews alike. By 1937, another Nazi teacher regularly alternated between long-standing antisemitic stereotypes, such as, "What kind of whispering and Yiddish-sounding dialect [*Gemauschele*] is going on? We're not in a Jew-school here, you know," and more novel approaches, such as "Shut your non-Aryan trap." Strangely enough, there were teachers who missed no opportunity to make sarcastic remarks about Jews but seemed to grade pupils impartially.[6] The behavior of these teachers was replicated all over Germany: official hostility toward "the Jew" but personal tolerance or regard for a particular Jewish person.

Berlin may have provided the best experience for which Jewish children could hope. In Magdeburg, one Jewish girl, only a half year away from achieving the *Abitur* (final school exam and certification), quit school because some girls refused to go on a class trip if she, the only Jew, came along. Moreover, she had to sit all alone on a bench separate from the rest of the class. In Düsseldorf, school became increasingly unpleasant for Ruth Sass as her friends buckled under to the pressures of antisemitism: "For the first time in my life, I felt left-out, not wanted, a second-class human being." Worse, "New, younger teachers [were] hired and started to preach the philosophy of the Third Reich." In 1934, when Sass was fifteen years old, her history teacher taught that the Jews were second-class citizens. She asked to be excused from these lessons because she was Jewish. Presumably still believing in her "rights," and attempting polite resistance, she "made a point of always being in front of the classroom door when he came out after his lesson to remind him of my protest." When he told her she had to return to class so he could grade her, she asked that he warn her in advance before making comments about Jews, to allow her to leave the class. They both adhered to this compromise. In biology class, however, the torment continued as the teacher taught about the superiority of the "Aryan" race. One of these lessons, at least, was interspersed with comic relief when the teacher taught the children how to recognize an "Aryan" name. She asked the pupils to state their last names. When it came to the Jewish girl, the teacher declared "Sass," her last name, to come from good "Aryan" stock: "I smiled at her and told her that I was non-Aryan."[7]

Some children more directly resisted the indignities and abuse foisted upon them in the early years. In 1934, Annemarie Scherman, a Berlin "Mischling," confronted a teacher who continually gave her grades of "unsatisfactory." Despite his animosity, she achieved her Abitur a year later. In 1934, in a small town in Ostwestfalen-Lippe, a thirteen-year-old girl attending a school assembly found herself sitting through a Nazi song. When she heard its words,

> I was blind with rage and fear. . . . I got up and decided . . . I'm not listen-
> ing to this. I was pretty certain that they would kill me, grab me and break
> my bones. . . . But no one touched me. Somehow, the teachers as well as
> the pupils must have respected . . . my courage. In a German school where
> discipline was stressed, to get up . . . in the midst of a ceremony and simply
> leave without permission, that was incredible.[8]

This kind of opposition took a great deal of courage, because German teachers did not brook disobedience from pupils, especially Jewish pupils. Indeed, such protest was short-lived and was ultimately useless against the power of the state.

Well before legislation forced them out, Jewish adolescents over the age of fourteen (after which attendance was no longer compulsory) left school in droves. While some pupils had to consider nonacademic career alternatives and others emigrated, most fled the insufferable atmosphere there. In Württemberg, only 10 percent of Jews attending higher schools were affected by the April laws of 1933, yet shortly thereafter 58 percent left school because of massive hostility. In Berlin, 5,931 Jewish youths attended higher schools in May 1933; two years later, only 1,172 remained. Statistics for Prussia indicate that there were 8,609 Jewish boys and 6,317 Jewish girls in public higher schools in May 1932, and that only 28 percent of boys and 26 percent of girls remained by May 1936, with girls dropping out at a slightly greater rate. Jewish university students also suffered discrimination, whether by having to sit on separate "Jewish" benches or in the back of the lecture hall or, as at the Friedrich Wilhelm University of Berlin, by having a yellow stripe stamped in their matriculation books. The result was that while 3,950 Jewish students (2,698 men and 1,252 women) matriculated at German universities in the summer of 1932, by the summer of 1934 only 656 (486 men and 170 women) were left.[9]

School was not only a daily trial but also the site where some children learned of their "Jewish" identity according to Nazi law. Five-year-old Rita Kuhn, whose father was Jewish and mother Christian, was uncertain of her own religion. In school "the teacher had to ask the whole class who's Jewish. I looked around the classroom and nobody raised [a] hand.... I wasn't really *sure* whether I was Jewish.... I raised my hand, because ... I knew I had *some*thing to do with being Jewish." After that, of course, she had no chance of joining the League of German Girls (Bund deutscher Mädel, or BDM). When her teacher asked who wanted to join, "I raised my hand. I mean, who doesn't want to be part of a group?" Her teacher explained, gently, that she could not belong. "I couldn't understand what was the matter with me," she recalled. In the fall of 1933, a ten-year-old in her first year of a girls' upper school was given a homework assignment to find out the "racial" background of her grandparents. Although she had been baptized, her family had not observed any religion. At this point her parents acknowledged her mother's Jewish origins, attempting to sweeten the blow by assuring the girl that she was a descendant of King Solomon and the Queen of Sheba.[10]

Discovering a Jewish "racial" identity was a shock for children, just as it was for adults. But children also felt betrayed by their parents. A Protestant born in 1923, for example, recalled the anguish she felt at this discovery at age thirteen: "My parents had outright lied to me.... They didn't tell me until the day my school [required] an 'Aryan certificate.'" Another child, born in 1929, found out that she was "Jewish" from the taunts of a classmate. When she announced to her father that he would have to come to defend her at school the next day: "My parents glanced at each other . . . and my mother (who had converted to Protestantism . . .) said: 'And what if that were the case?' At that I began to scream and was sick for four weeks. . . . I could not cope with it!"[11]

Although Jewish children received the brunt of abuse from their peers, half-Jewish children were not exempt. In Hamburg, a "half-Aryan" boy raised as a Protestant had to be hospitalized for two months because of the constant physical and emotional persecution he experienced in school. Thereafter his parents saw no alternative but to enroll him in an Orthodox Jewish school. For a few children, their Jewishness and the hostile school atmosphere ended in tragedy. One Hamburg woman described her nephew's tormented reaction to the new conditions at school:

> [He] used to greet us when he came home from school with "Heil Hitler." He [declared] he did not want to be a Jew and that he did not believe in being one. He wanted to march with the other boys . . . and join the Hitler Youth. . . . One day he came home from school complaining of having been struck on the head by his chum who [had] called him "dirty Jew!" He had a severe headache and his father gave him aspirin which did not relieve him. Trying to help himself to more aspirin, he picked up the veronal bottle by mistake, and overdosed himself with the sedative. . . . [H]e became delirious. He kept shouting "Heil Hitler," which were the last words we heard him say.[12]

The Effects of School on the Family

The pain of children—who often faced antisemitism from classmates and teachers—disturbed both women and men profoundly as parents, but women coped with their children's distress more directly than did the men. Children told their mothers the latest incidents. Principals summoned mothers to pick up their children when they were expelled from school— often more than once—and mothers then searched for new schools. Mothers were usually the ones whom teachers phoned when children were excluded from class events or received grades beneath their actual achievement level. In a small city in Baden, a female teacher sent Verena Hellwig a letter regarding her daughter's grades:

> Today we were informed at a teachers' meeting that Jews or *Mischlinge* could no longer receive prizes for their achievements. Because your little daughter is the best pupil in the class, she will be affected by these measures. I'm informing you in order that you can tell Irene, so that she won't be surprised and too hurt during tomorrow's awards ceremony. You know how close your little daughter and I are, but, unfortunately, there is no way that I can counter this hurtful and unjust policy.

Her daughter was upset but insisted on going to the prize ceremony anyway because it was not her fault "if they make such mean laws." Even Nazi teachers might phone a child's mother when the child was to be excluded. One mother wrote: "I believe that the Nazi teacher was ashamed of herself now and then, when she looked into the sad eyes of my little daughter, because she phoned me several times and asked that I not send the child to school on the days when something enjoyable had been planned for the children."[13]

Sympathetic teachers were not uncommon in the early years. Yet the threat to job security made those who had earlier shown sympathy more careful later on—behavior that was multiplied a thousandfold in the German population. When a Jewish girl had to leave public school in Wiesbaden, she asked her teacher to write a few lines in her autograph album. The teacher happily complied for her favorite pupil, but a few days later the principal asked to see the girl's mother. He feared that the teacher's affection for a Jewish child could endanger her career if the authorities found out. Clearly ashamed of himself, he asked that the girl remove the page from her album and give it to him.[14]

Mothers also supervised their children's homework. One can imagine the contradictory emotions of a Jewish mother who was reassured to learn that her son had sung patriotic songs, said "Heil Hitler" to the teacher, and received praise for his laudatory essay about Hitler: "[His] gross political miseducation at school would keep [him] out of trouble." About a year later the same child, now enrolled in a Jewish school, wrote a story about Jewish resistance as a Mother's Day gift for his mother. Upon reading it, she was frightened: "[His] political awakening . . . could lead to trouble for the whole family." Another mother, in a small southern German town, commented on the lies that her children were expected to echo in their homework assignments:

> There were . . . compositions with delicate subjects, and they were not allowed to put down a contradictory opinion. Sometimes a judicious teacher gave a selection of subjects . . . but . . . all the children knew what

they were expected to write. It was bad enough that this kind of state's
education taught them to hate, to despise, to be suspicious, to denounce,
but worst of all perhaps was this . . . lying.[15]

Young children often shared their bewilderment openly with parents.
Little ones found it agonizing not to be part of the group. When asked in
late 1933 what he would wish for, a seven-year-old answered "To be a Nazi."
When his father asked what would happen to the rest of the family, he
responded that he wished they could be Nazis too. This is the same child
whose teacher noted that he flinched every time the Nazi flag was raised.
Another little boy, referring to his circumcision, confided to his father that
he wished he were a girl. Then the other children would not know immediately that he was a Jew.[16]

Older children kept more of their pain to themselves, hiding their feelings and some of the more troubling events in their daily school lives from
their already overburdened parents, who had "no time and too much
angst." In a small town in Ostwestfalen-Lippe, the only Jewish girl in the
school had enthusiastically participated in swimming exercises in the gym
all winter long. When spring came, the class was to go to the public pool to
actually swim. With sadness, her female teacher told her she could not join
the class. "'You know why you cannot go with us to the park swimming
pool?' And I said, 'yes, I know.' I did not cry. For a minute, I believe, I
wanted to die. . . . Curiously, I was hurt more for my parents than for
myself." Children's attempts to spare their parents notwithstanding, mothers, and probably fathers too (to the extent their wives did not shelter
them), surmised what was happening. The Protestant mother of two
"Mischling" children noticed that many of her daughter's friends no longer
came to their home: "Loneliness enveloped us more and more each day."[17]

Often, children had to walk a tightrope between the demands of parents
and school. In one small town, the elementary school teacher insisted that
Jewish children give the Nazi salute. The parents advised the children not to
do so. The teacher threatened the Jewish children with the wrath of their
"Aryan" schoolmates: "'I am not responsible if the children turn against
you.' . . . And then, after a short time, we went along, cooperated, and
didn't mention it at home." Another Jewish child whose parents had forbidden him from giving the Nazi salute was simply delighted when he was
forced to do so in school.[18]

Unlike Jewish teens, Jewish children younger than fourteen could not
simply leave school. Why did they remain in public schools as long as they
did, when, as early as 1934, the Central Organization of German Jews

reported that many Jewish children were showing signs of psychological disturbance?[19] Clearly, there were practical reasons: the Jewish community could not build Jewish schools as quickly as they were needed, and the public schools had acquired reputations for educational competence. Moreover, some Jews still lived in towns in which the population of Jews was too small to support a Jewish school.

A gender-specific dimension also appears to be involved: while mothers had grave trepidations, fathers exhorted the children to remain in school. Toni Lessler, the founder and director of a Montessori school in Berlin, which became a Jewish school when the government forbade "Aryan" children from attending it, described the attitudes of Jewish families:

> The . . . city schools became ever more difficult for the Jewish children and ever more unbearable. But there were still many parents who wanted to give children the advantage of a city school. If the parents had only guessed what the children had to go through there. . . . And it must probably have been a false pride which caused the fathers in particular to keep their children in city schools. . . .[20]

Lessler pointed not only to fathers' aspirations to give their children a quality education but also to their "stand-tough" approach.

Memoirs also attest to fathers' unrealistic hopes that their children would not suffer and to their insistence that their children "tough it out" and develop "thicker skin." When a sixteen-year-old, the only Jewish girl in her class, balked at participating in a class trip, aware that the class would eat at a hotel that displayed a "Jews Undesired" placard, her mother supported her. The mother dreaded the anxiety and pain her daughter might experience— "she'll worry about what might happen during the entire trip"—but her father insisted that she participate. Another father knew the horrid details of his son's school experience but did not seem to fathom the child's emotional state. When this father finally agreed to remove the child from the school, the ten-year-old proclaimed: "Father . . . had you continued to force me to go to a school—I would have thrown myself under a train." The father confessed: "My hair stood on end with fear, cold chills ran down my spine. What must have been going on in the soul of a small, innocent child?"[21]

These gender-specific reactions in which men wished to stand firm were often exacerbated by a division of roles in which husbands made ultimate family decisions even though their wives were more aware of their children's emotional states. In fact, fathers may have been making crucial decisions in the dark, since wives frequently kept the worst from them, knowing the men's lives outside the home were bitter enough. Also, boys, taught to be "manly," may have remained more silent than did the girls. One boy remembered coming home often to his mother's admonition, "Don't talk to your father," who was very upset.[22]

Jewish Schools

Harassment, as well as expulsions from public schools, provoked many families to enroll their children in Jewish schools. In 1933, there were about 60,000 school-aged Jewish children (between the ages of six and fourteen) in Germany. As a result of the Nazi takeover, the proportion of Jewish children attending Jewish schools leaped from 14 percent in 1932, to 23 percent in 1934, and to 52 percent in 1936. To keep up with demand, the communities provided 130 schools by 1935 and 160 (with over 1,200 teachers) by 1936. In 1937, Jewish schools peaked at 167, serving about 60 percent of Jewish children (23,670). Still, a significant proportion of Jewish children between the ages of six and fourteen remained in the public elementary schools, subject to torment by teachers and other children, until the Nazis barred their attendance in November 1938.[23]

The Central Organization of German Jews, parents, and Jewish communities supported Jewish schools with ever-smaller means, trying to maintain a sizeable pool of teachers while more and more teachers emigrated. In small towns, school accommodations were meager. In Pforzheim, near the Black Forest, the Jewish "school," located within the public school building, consisted of two classrooms with children of different ages; the Jewish children had to use a separate entrance. Large cities offered more educational variety, with Berlin providing the most. Berlin had one Jewish *Oberschule* (upper grades), one *Mittelschule* (fifth through tenth grades), eight *Volksschulen* (elementary grades), a school for the hearing- and speech-impaired, and a school for disabled children. Also, the Reform and Orthodox communities had their own schools.[24]

Private Jewish schools—not subsidized by the Jewish communities or organizations—grew considerably. Toni Lessler's "Private Jewish School Grunewald," for example, grew from 140 to 425 children as Jews fled the public schools. She rented a bigger building and, in 1938, added a Home Economics School. She also received permission to add higher grades (*Oberschule*) so that pupils could study for the *Abitur* and the Oxford English exam. All Jewish schools were under the direct supervision of the Nazi school bureaucracy. Thus, a graduate of the Jewish *Gymnasium* in Breslau received a diploma that displayed "under the logo of the school—a Star of David—the official seal of the board of education—a swastika."

And, even in Jewish schools children on occasion had to listen to Hitler's speeches, which, according to one participant, could be "real torture." Moreover, the authorities, ever respectful of the comfort of "Aryan" neighbors, compelled Jewish schools to follow strict regulations about outdoor activities, and sometimes, without notice, required Jewish administrators to decrease the number of children in attendance.[25]

Along with a traditional German curriculum, Jewish schools taught Judaism and Jewish history and culture. Sometimes Jewish children learned about Judaism or celebrated the holidays for the first time at these schools. As Lotte Kaliski, founder of the (private) Kaliski School in Berlin, noted: "Most of us came from very assimilated families and so did the children, but we understood that in order to give children a more positive attitude, they had to know something about their background." Some private schools offered unconventional curricula: they prepared children for both the British matriculation exams and the American College Board exams; because Palestine, too, was a likely destination, they also gave courses in gardening and Hebrew.[26]

Although some Jewish observers regretted that Jewish schools further segregated Jews—"this way, the antisemites had achieved their goal, alienation and separation from the surrounding Christian world"—the Jewish schools also provided immediate relief for most children. Toni Lessler wrote about a nine-year-old girl who asked her "whether we used special pens for our written work, because with us she could write every word so easily, it seemed to her as if the words flowed from the pen, and in the other school they had always remained stuck in the pen because of fear." Recalling his relief at entering a Jewish school as a fifteen-year-old, one man later wrote: "There was no longer a picture of the *Führer* . . . no unfair brawls and no Nazi fighting songs. Liberated, I was allowed to breathe freely." This sense of safety could lead to anti-Nazi pranks. Arnold Paucker recalled how two friends regularly imitated Hitler and Goebbels to uproarious laughter from their schoolmates. Although the teachers objected to such dangerous antics, these same teachers discreetly celebrated the world championship of the Jewish boxer Max Baer over the German Max Schmeling by canceling school for one day.[27]

Their happiness among other Jews notwithstanding, Jewish children learned to expect radical change at any time: new teachers, new classmates, and new curricula; occasionally, the arrest of one of their fathers; and the disappearance of classmates as families emigrated without notice. About two-thirds of Jewish children and youth left Germany between 1933 and September 1939. One Jewish school in Berlin exemplifies the enormous changes Jewish children had to face. At the end of 1932–33, 470 children attended the Jewish middle school on Grosse Hamburgerstrasse. Two weeks later, at the beginning of the new school year, the enrollment burgeoned to 840, and one year later it rose to 1,025. Then a rapid decline set in. As families fled, attendance dropped to 380 by the spring of 1939.[28]

Emigration became a recurrent theme in Jewish schools. In 1934, a teacher at the Theodor Herzl School in Berlin asked her class how many families planned to leave Germany. Seven years old at the time, Ann Lewis later reported:

> Nearly every hand went up. What amazes me now . . . is not the fact that apparently as early as the middle of 1934 so many families were planning to leave Germany, but that a whole class of seven-year-olds was aware of the situation and that our teacher expected us to be aware of it. We all knew what "auswandern" meant, and I cannot help wondering how many children in a class of similar age in an ordinary German elementary school would at that time have known the meaning of the word "emigration."

Shlomo Wahrman reported that in his Jewish school in 1936 "only one of the more than thirty pupils questioned responded that his family planned to remain in Leipzig for the time being."

Jewish children in public schools where teachers did not discuss emigration were also aware of Jewish flight. Daily, they watched their Jewish classmates' and neighbors depart. In Berlin, children saw large moving vans in their neighborhoods, particularly in the Jewish areas: "The vans were labeled . . . with the destinations: Shanghai, Sydney and many cities in North and South America." Ruth Klüger's experience in Vienna was typical of many children. Born in 1931, she attended eight different schools between the ages of six and ten. The decreased enrollments as children and teachers emigrated forced Jewish schools to merge. She recalled that what most interested her when she arrived at school each morning was how many other pupils had vanished. Then the remaining pupils would be transferred to another school and would have to get used to new teachers, as they, too, emigrated.[29]

Jewish children who attended Jewish schools lived a dual existence: safety in school and danger outside. But, on occasion, Nazis did not hesitate from threatening Jewish children even within the confines of Jewish schools. The Home Economics School of the League of Jewish Women, for example, a boarding school that had expanded from fifty to eighty girls immediately after the Nazi seizure of power, was situated in a relatively secluded area. Its low profile notwithstanding, one night a car stopped in front of the school and men threw rocks through the bedroom windows. Although none of the residents were hurt, all were badly frightened.[30] Similarly, children in a Jewish camp found that in 1934 local Nazis had painted the slogans "Jews Are Our Misfortune" and "Death to Jewish Race Defilers" directly across from the camp's entrance. In 1935, a group of forty to fifty Nazis gathered in front of the main camp building shouting racist slogans.

> Inside the building, we felt that we were under siege. We were convinced that the Nazis would break into the camp grounds at any moment. . . . The thirty minutes we had spent in a state of terror affected many of the young campers emotionally. Some were too fearful . . . to leave the camp premises. . . . It was not much of a vacation for them.[31]

HOSTILE ENVIRONMENT BEYOND SCHOOL

Although Jewish schools maintained a veneer of normalcy, Jewish children faced hardship elsewhere. Toni Lessler described several incidents that exemplify the psychological stress children regularly faced en route to school. In one case, a little boy got up for an elderly woman in the tram. She thanked him by saying: "So, my good boy, that's the way a true Hitler Youth behaves. That was nice of you." Frightened, the little boy responded, "But I'm not a Hitler Youth, I'm a Jewish boy," and then quickly stepped off the tram. In a more alarming incident, a man dressed in Nazi uniform angrily demanded that a Jewish boy get off a bus. The driver, however, argued that no laws forbade Jews from riding the buses, and others agreed. Enraged, the Nazi departed. The boy was left worrying about future confrontations. Girls were not protected by their sex any more than young children were by their age. One woman recalled how adolescents on the streets of Berlin jeered "Jewish cow" at her and pressed "tickets to Jerusalem" into her hands. In Berlin, a gang of boys attacked even a six-year-old Jewish girl. Jewish teachers constantly reminded children to be quiet and unobtrusive on the streets; to walk in twos, not groups; and to avoid lingering in front of the school.[32]

Parental debates about emigration must have increased strain among beleaguered children, those who hoped to leave, as well as those who hoped to stay. They faced hostility in Germany if they stayed, and strange surroundings, foreign languages, and new faces if they fled. Some children, especially teenagers, realized the dangers from incidents they confronted in and out of school and implored their parents to emigrate. Ruth Sass told

her parents of her experiences in school and pressed them to leave
Germany. She was frustrated with their response:

> They looked bewildered. How could they pack up and leave everything
> that was . . . dear to them, and where to? How could they start a new busi-
> ness in a strange country, not knowing the language, and which country
> was willing to let them immigrate? Uppermost in my mother's mind was
> that she would not leave her mother behind alone.

Sadly, she admitted defeat: "It became more and more clear to me that I
had to leave Germany, my home, my parents, the nice secure life that I
knew." She left Germany on her own to finish her schooling in Geneva.[33]

Children also internalized tensions from home. In Leipzig, the children of
Orthodox Jews, aware that their father was still engaged in the ritual slaughter of animals long after the Nazis had forbidden it, registered the anxiety on
their mother's face and worried about the family's safety if their father got
caught. Ann Lewis recalled the Hebrew classes in her home that her parents
took with other potential émigrés. When her parents decided against going
to Palestine, the lessons suddenly switched to English, with the accompanying anxiety over whether that would be the right language after all.[34]

Children listened carefully and read their parents' worried faces. If they
came from politically aware families, they immediately understood the
meaning of Hitler. Born in 1922, Inge Deutschkron recalled that in light of
her socialist upbringing she knew how dangerous Hitler was as soon as he
came to power. Others noticed the sudden changes in their families' financial condition as they were drafted to work in family shops. Some children
picked up more unusual clues. When a religious boy observed his mother
breaking the Sabbath in order to help those in acute need, he understood:
"My mother had always been a scrupulous Shabbos observer. Therefore,
watching her . . . cooking and baking on Shabbos, had a profound effect on
me. . . . The dangers and uncertainties of our own existence became crystal
clear to me."[35]

Children not only were aware of the political and social situation of their
families but also experienced rejection directly from other children. They
were perhaps even more deeply hurt than their parents. A thirteen-year-old
who had had many girlfriends "was forced to be alone. When I got home, I
turned to my homework immediately." Some of these wounds lasted a lifetime. Marion Gardner, born in 1931, wrote: "I was lonely, and until today
. . . it is hard for me to make friends. . . . It didn't take long until one got
used to not being allowed to be together with other Germans." When

Gardner's Jewish cousin from England visited her and decided she did not have to avoid Germans because she was from abroad, the two Jewish girls played with German girls. Local boys discovered this transgression and threw stones at them. When the cousin entered an ice cream parlor with the German girls, Gardner was afraid to follow them. Teased by her cousin, she finally joined them; to her surprise, nothing happened. The memory of her fear, however, endured.[36]

As the stone-throwing incident shows, the lawlessness that oppressed adults also extended to children. When a young girl was beaten up by her former girlfriend, she fought back. The "Aryan" girl told her: " 'You're a Jew, you can't fight back.' So I went to my father and asked him, and he said he didn't think so either—and then I understood." Boys, who were more likely to get into frays, found such warnings even more painful. One boy, "the strongest in the class," "got into a scrap the first day that I was confronted with my new name, *Saujude* [Jewish swine]." He was hurt to meet with his family's reproach, even that of his uncle, a boxer: "His father could be a big Nazi. This could bring ruin to all of us. Don't ever do that again!" Sometimes this kind of frustration resulted in children turning their anger against their parents. One person wrote of hating the swastika and the Nazi flag and "everything connected with it. . . . I could not look at it without becoming furious. I became incensed and would take it out even upon my poor mother in rudeness."[38]

Perhaps only sleep provided a respite, as the dream of an eight-year-old illustrates. In the dream, classmates showed her their Nazi swastika pins, taunting her that she could not have any. She replied that she could and produced an armband full of swastikas. The children protested, and the teacher tore it away from her and said she could not wear it. Triumphantly, she announced that Hitler had met her, had said she was a good child, and had given her all the swastikas. Thereafter, the teacher and children were kind to her.[38]

Older children paid closer attention to the media than they might normally have done: one wrote that he read the newspapers carefully at the age of thirteen and worried about the plight of Jews in Germany. Those who did not experience acute dread at least felt diffuse anxiety. One woman remembered: "The adults had been acting differently for some time. All were full of anxiety, seemed to be afraid of something that threatened their existence. And wherever two persons met, they became lost in endless discussions." Thus, Jewish children grew up quickly. Recalling her fear of the Nazis as early as 1932, a woman remembered: "I stood . . . with my ten years and thought, 'Now your childhood is over.'" By 1936, fourteen-year-old

Miriam Carlebach had regularly noticed antisemitic signs and newspapers, parades of the Hitler Youth, and boycotts of Jewish shops. Her favorite non-Jewish neighbors had grown distant, and an antisemitic landlord had forced her family to relocate. Many of her relatives were fleeing. In early 1938, at sixteen, she decided on her own that the time had come to leave Germany for Palestine.[39]

JEWISH TEENS

In 1933, about 58,000 Jewish "youth," between the ages of sixteen and twenty-four, lived in Germany. Adolescents and young adults needed and had more freedom than children but faced new challenges. In Düsseldorf, Ruth Sass noted: "Every few months a new situation presented itself and had to be overcome like another hurdle." Still, in 1933 and 1934 she was "able to lead a normal life. I could go ice skating in the winter and . . . swimming in the . . . indoor pools of the city. And a group of girls and boys got together and had dancing lessons. I also had my first boyfriend." In big cities, the more fearless could still go to a café or see a movie, at least until November 1938. However, a relaxing excursion with Jewish friends could turn into a confrontation. In Danzig, for example, when a group of young Jews in their early twenties went to a beer garden, they were threatened by German patrons, who accused one of them, a blond Jewish woman, of being a whore because she associated with Jews. One of their mothers reported: "I trembled when my son left the house, you could never be certain that something [terrible] wouldn't happen."[40]

Increasingly, Jewish youth groups became an important source of comaraderie, distraction, and hope for young people. Before 1933, many Jewish children and youth had belonged to nonsectarian groups, with Jewish organizations appealing only to a minority. In 1932 about 26,000 people, or 25 to 30 percent of Jewish youth, belonged to Jewish associations. These groups were divided among those interested in German culture (for example, the non-Zionist Kameraden, founded in 1916); those with a religious orientation (the orthodox Esra, also founded in 1916); and those with a Zionist affiliation (such as the Blau-Weiss, founded in 1912). There were also Jewish sports clubs and Jewish student fraternities, although no Jewish sororities. In 1933, ninety-seven Jewish youth groups registered in Germany.[41]

Thereafter, Jewish groups expanded significantly. By 1936, 50,000 youths between twelve and twenty-five, about 60 percent of the total, had joined. From early on, their realm of action was limited: members could no longer

Jewish children at a sports festival, Berlin, 1937. (Courtesy of the Leo Baeck Institute, New York)

camp in public places, wear uniforms, or appear in group formation. In addition, the groups were in constant flux as members emigrated or left for apprenticeships and agricultural training centers. Nevertheless, they played an important role, providing teens with a haven from work, school, or tense families. They also helped some teens question the political judgments of parents who hoped to remain in Germany, making the younger people more eager to flee. And they helped others challenge the bourgeois illusions of parents who still aspired to good careers for their children, focusing the teens on careers useful for emigration.

An example of an organization for those who preferred a Jewish, but not Zionist, orientation was the Association of German-Jewish Youth (Bund deutsch-jüdischer Jugend, renamed Bund der jüdischen Jugend in 1936). The association included about 5,000 members in sixteen provincial organizations. Its members, mostly in their teens, included students, apprentices, employees, and the unemployed. Most were from the middle or lower middle class, with some from the working class. Many had come from German organizations and had little in common with the others, except their rejection by former friends. They "resolved to go back to our roots, to Jewish history" and met in private homes, offices, and camps to study with teachers. Open to a Jewish identity, theirs was not a rejection of Germany as such: "We loved the idyllic lakes, romantic rivers and picturesque towns," the "other Germany" of "Goethe, Schiller and Lessing."[42] Their loyalty to an enlightened Germany notwithstanding, many sought retraining by the organization for skills useful in countries of emigration. In 1936, a farm, Gross-Breesen, in Silesia, became the site for some of these non-Zionist youth to prepare for a life of manual labor until it, too, was overrun by the SS in November 1938.

One of the largest groups before the Nazi takeover had been the Jewish Pathfinders, with sixty-five locals in 1931–32. After fusing with the Zionist Maccabi Hazair in 1934, the JPF-MH became the largest Jewish youth group in Germany. The following year the Zionists claimed membership by over 60 percent of all Jewish youth in ten major organizations.[43] Zionist organizations provided *Hachsharah* centers—agricultural training to ready young people for Palestine. Zionists also educated Jewish youth about Judaism—subjects they had never known, had been poorly taught, or had forgotten. Some teens, under the pressure of wildly erratic times, rapidly changed allegiances, swinging within one year from secular Jewish nationalism to German antifascism, and even to Jewish religiosity.[44]

This coming together of Jewish youth both reflected and intensified a generation gap with parents. Young people saw no future for themselves in Germany, whereas many parents clung to whatever they still had. The generation gap—this difference in outlook—was brought into sharp relief upon the death of Hindenburg in 1934. Arnold Paucker, a member of the Jewish youth movement in these years, reported that most youths laughed at the sadness with which their parents—from all positions on the political spectrum—greeted the president's death. Young Jews felt no loss. Moreover, he added that most insisted on having some fun. They clung to the hopes and dreams of youth: even in the darkest times there was a will to live, a lust for life, and silliness and humor among Jewish boys and girls.[45]

The generation gap was particularly apparent between acculturated parents and newly Zionist children. Young people crystallized their hopes and also found solace in joining a new culture and preparing, mentally at least, to leave. However, since well before the 1930s, many parents had opposed Zionism politically and philosophically. In Bielefeld, for example, the Zionist Pathfinders "defined themselves as an internal Jewish opposition and understood their oppositional behavior as a conscious answer (even before 1933) to the process of societal exclusion." Their official Zionism notwithstanding, in 1934 the Bielefeld group still "acted ... 'covertly Zionist.' An open affirmation of a Zionist youth movement would have provoked an incalculable negative reaction among parents." Other parents, less politically engaged, simply feared that their children would emigrate to distant Palestine. Ruth Sass, born in 1919, was attracted to Zionist youth groups, but her mother "did not want me to get the idea in my head to leave and go far away."[46]

The transformation of Margot Spiegel is typical of many Jewish youth. She felt strongly attached to her German heritage, which she described as a love of nature and a romantic feeling for the ideals of Schiller and Goethe. As a teenager, she belonged to a German hiking and singing club. When she once expressed reservations about continuing with this group, her "Aryan" friend urged her to remain, adding that she did not look Jewish and that, therefore, the others "won't know." This remark badly hurt her feelings, and she withdrew immediately. Instead, she sought out Jewish teens who were organizing for the first time. They had lived in the same town, Constance, for nineteen years without having felt the need to know each other. Suddenly they thirsted for knowledge about Judaism, the Bible, and Jewish history, "in order to find consolation and an understandable reason for everything that happened." Step-by-step they approached Zionism. Her attachment to this new creed infuriated her father, a veteran of World War I, and he refused to speak with her for weeks.[47]

Regardless of parental disapproval, Jewish youth thrived on the activities and institutions set up by private or community groups. For example, when it became clear that Jews were either unwelcome in or prohibited from using German youth hostels, "Haus Bertha" was founded in July 1934 in cooperation with the League of Jewish War Veterans for use by Jewish groups. In the midst of forests and heaths twelve miles outside of Gelsenkirchen, it lasted until 1937, when the Nazis closed it. The visiting teenagers played sports, took hikes, and attended lectures on Jewish themes. According to the lodgers, the hostel was "a ray of hope . . . if only for a short time." Another sixteen-year-old boy believed his training there gave him the "backbone" to overcome the enormous adjustments of emigration. One visitor summed up the short three-year existence of the hostel by commenting that it gave "many hundreds of Jewish boys and girls" vacations which they could not have had anywhere else in Germany.[48]

Half-Jewish teens, or *"Mischlinge,"* often had a harder time finding a circle of friends than did Jewish teens. Excluded from most "Aryan" clubs and activities, they were also isolated from Jewish activities. At first, many children and young people of mixed background attempted to deny their part-Jewish origins. They could no longer hide their origins by the age of ten, however, when most "Aryans" entered Nazi youth groups. Christian groups had the same requirements as the Nazi groups. A young Protestant woman, considered a Jew because she had three Jewish grandparents, could not find a place to live with Christians or Jews. Training to be a nurse, she was not allowed to live at the Jewish Hospital in Hanover because she was Christian, and she was also thrown out of the room she had rented by "Aryans" who refused to live with a "non-Aryan." She ultimately found refuge in a Christian shelter for what were then called "fallen women." Cordelia Edvardson, a Catholic with three Jewish grandparents, was asked to leave her Catholic girls' group. The leader told her that the club would suffer if she continued to belong, adding: "You know our slogan: One for all and all for one." Cordelia sadly acquiesced, wondering why this was not the moment to stress the "all for one."[49] Discouraged and isolated, she did not join Jewish groups either.

A handful of half-Jewish teens were lucky enough to join Quaker youth groups, which were few and far between. There, one young woman met "*Mischlinge* like me, 'first-or even second-degree,' or children of parents in concentration camps or otherwise politically persecuted." These Quaker-led teens sang German folk songs, played games, went on hikes, and "behaved like German youth generally behaved. Of course, we did not have to—or were not allowed to, depending on one's perspective—join the Hitler Youth or the BDM." Most teens of mixed parentage, however, stood exposed, unsuitable for any groups. One teen noted that the feelings of even those "Aryans" who expressed sympathy could be summarized in the statement "They can't help it, that their parents . . . "—a sentiment of pity but not equality.[50]

Denied social integration, Jewish teens could also expect a dismal future in the German economy. The limits set on Jews at trade and vocational schools, as well as their exclusion from universities and institutions of higher learning, restricted employment possibilities. The Nazis even blocked those few who managed to pass the Ph.D. exam, as did Lotte Dixon in 1937. The Gestapo seized her thesis and notes (and she received the actual degree only after the war).[51] In addition, Jewish job training programs were limited, and Jewish businesses, where a teen might have apprenticed, were closing down. Despite the Jewish community's training centers, the number of applicants continually outnumbered the slots available. Also, decrees time and again eliminated career choices. For example, by 1935 some provinces had declared that women teachers of agricultural home economics could only be "Aryans" and that only "Aryan" women could take exams to qualify as midwives, social workers, or physical therapists. While before 1933 Jewish girls would have looked forward to business or professional careers, by mid-1935 the apprenticeship office for Jewish girls reported that half were applying to become seamstresses. By 1937, when young women had shifted their focus to jobs useful in countries of

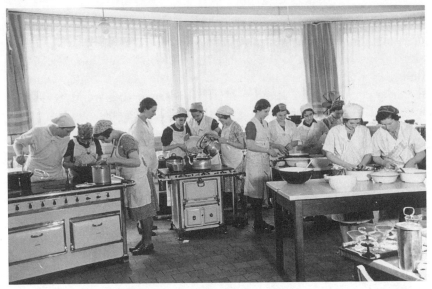

Home economics school in Essen. (Courtesy of the Leo Baeck Institute, New York)

emigration, 24 percent of graduates from Jewish schools planned to learn a craft. They largely preferred tailoring (20 percent), because, as one woman maintained, "sewing knows no language." Sixteen percent trained for domestic service, 13 percent for commerce, and 12 percent for social work. By the end of 1937, about thirty institutions offered some training in home economics. And, lest girls harbor unrealistic notions about continuing at a university abroad, they were warned "that Jewish girls in and out of Germany have almost no chance to study [at the university]. The few scholarships available are only for young men."[52]

What a narrowing of career prospects meant in practice can be seen through the experience of Annemarie Scherman, aged sixteen in 1933. Originally she had wanted to become a goldsmith, but because she was a *"Mischling"* she could no longer apprentice in Germany. So she learned about pediatric nursing, passing the course exam with commendations, but was prohibited from taking the state exam. When she tried to enroll to study medicine at the university, she had to sit on a bench for Jewish students and carry student identification with a yellow stripe across it. Unhappily, she tried to become a medical assistant but found that this pursuit was barred to Jews and *"Mischlinge."* Finally, she took a business course, learning stenography, typing, and other secretarial skills. She passed her exam in 1938 but could not find a job because every application form asked her "racial" history. She finally found a job at a newspaper for a brief interlude and then worked as an assistant to a doctor who opposed the regime.[53] She was lucky compared with those even younger. By 1942, "first-degree *Mischlinge*" could no longer attend any German schools.

Parents and children frequently clashed regarding the vision each had of the child's future. Such clashes were particularly frequent between girls and their parents. One school survey in 1935 indicated that girls preferred jobs in offices or working with children (such as kindergarten teaching), whereas parents thought they should become seamstresses or work in a household setting. Parents were more likely to go along with boys' choices of crafts or agricultural training. Moreover, except for housework, the opportunities for girls were more limited than for boys. Welfare organizations suggested sewing-related jobs, such as knitting, tailoring, or making clothing decorations, whereas options recommended for boys included becoming painters, billboard designers, upholsterers, shoemakers, dyers, tailors, or skilled industrial workers.[54]

To make matters worse, parents seem to have preferred keeping girls home, either to shelter them from unpleasant work or so they could help out. In early 1937, one report on vocational training for youth suggested that 70 percent of girls leaving school refused any sort of training. Parents kept them at home to assist with the household. In his memoirs, for example, Ezra BenGershom described how his father decided that he and his two brothers should receive vocational training but that his one unmarried sister should help out in the house.[55]

In addition to family strategies, the blame for the relatively small number of girls in training programs also lay with Jewish community welfare organizations. They often gave boys preferential treatment in career training and offered them greater varieties of training and subsidies. In 1937, a self-critical report of the Central Bureau for Economic Relief noted that girls made up only 25 percent of its trainees. In 1938, the League of Jewish Women announced that one provincial welfare office had given subsidies to seventy-two boys but only ten girls.[56]

Jewish papers urged families to provide some household training to their daughters, encouraging parents to accept the loss of bourgeois class status implicit in this move. An article entitled "My Daughter Does Not Need That!" chastised mothers who rejected having their daughters trained as servants. Still, the old-fashioned idea that girls did not need a career because they would ultimately marry lingered on in some families, even as that fantasy became more and more inconsistent with reality. Some girls may have felt protected by their parents' decisions. Others were no doubt frustrated, their anxiety stirred by their lack of any training suitable for emigration. Only those who had joined a youth group might have the political perspective and psychological strength to insist on such training against their parents' wishes. In July 1936, the emigration preparatory training school at Gross-Breesen could not fill its girls' section but had to turn down four hundred boys.[57]

CHILDREN LEAVE HOME

Between 1934 and 1939, thousands of parents made the agonizing decision to send their children out of Germany and into the unknown, either on what were called "children's transports" (*Kindertransporte*) or by themselves. At least 18,000 "unaccompanied children" left Germany. Many teenagers departed, often for Switzerland or England, as parents with means found study opportunities for them. Other teens headed abroad on their own after preparing at agricultural training centers. Some of these centers were founded outside Germany, such as the agricultural training center for Jewish apprentices, Werkdorp Nieuwesluis, established in Holland in 1934. By 1936, there were centers in ten other European lands, where 843 young men and 288 young women trained for agricultural careers, the women mostly in home economics.[58]

Still others managed to get out as menial laborers, for girls and young women generally as household servants or apprentices. Typically, they saw their departures as permanent, with few expecting to return. Theirs was an assessment of the long-range political prospects. Many, like Ruth Eisner, had pressed for their whole families to emigrate. When her father refused, the sixteen-year-old finally begged: "At least let me go!" Some children expected to return to Germany to visit their parents. To their dismay, the government soon forbade their reentry. When one fifteen-year-old visited her parents in the mid-1930s, she was threatened with arrest unless she left the country immediately. In 1938, sixteen-year-old Miriam Carlebach understood her Palestine certificate to be a "life guarantee." As she waited to embark, bureaucrats stamped her passport three times: first with the red *J* for Jew; next with permission to take 30 marks out of the country; and finally with a declaration that she would never be allowed to enter Germany again.[59]

Parents searched for family or friends abroad to take in their children. One mother, appealing to her sister in New York in late 1938, declared:

> Lately, I have often been sick of my life, but . . . one has duties to one's children. On June 15, Rolly turned thirteen! . . . I am very concerned about his future. He wants to go to America, not Palestine. Wouldn't it be possible

for you to find a family there who would take the boy in . . . ? Naturally, I
can't think of a separation, but . . . that is how it is for all parents today, all
must send their children abroad![60]

Even before the November Pogrom, British rescue groups, including the
Quakers, brought German-Jewish refugee children to England, but the
numbers were small. Spurred into more intense action by the pogrom,
these groups formed the first major transports of children, leaving Berlin,
Hamburg, and Vienna in December 1938. Zionists also increased their
efforts after the pogrom, bringing more agricultural apprentices into Palestine than ever.[61] The *Kindertransporte* took between 8,000 and 10,000 children to England (after November 1938), 3,400 to Palestine, and some to
other European countries and the United States.[62] There they received foster care or, in the case of Palestine, lived on kibbutzim or in children's
homes until their parents could join them. Many parents never made it.

The children who went to Palestine did so under the auspices of Youth
Aliyah. Pioneered by Recha Freier in Berlin and supported financially by
Hadassah, the Zionist women's organization in the United States, it rescued
over 3,200 children from Germany. It required 60 percent boys and 40 percent girls because of what its leaders considered the division of labor on the
collective farms where the children would work.[63]

For children, the *Kindertransporte* could be a terribly wrenching experience, a considerable adventure, or both. Feelings of adventure crop up in
men's memoirs of their teen years. Charles Marks wrote: "To me it was an
adventure; to [my parents] it must have been agony." Some children went
abroad in one direction while their parents fled in another. In a letter to relatives abroad, one woman worried that her friends were heading toward
Shanghai while their children traveled to England on a *Kindertransport* but
conceded: "None of this devastates us anymore, we are used to much
worse."[64]

For parents, the decision to send off a child was the most excruciating
moment of their lives. The expression "children turned into letters" (*aus
Kindern wurden Briefe*) revealed their despair. One woman recalled that
when she received her papers at eighteen to emigrate to England as a governess, her mother fainted. Many mothers on their own, with husbands
either abroad or in concentration camps, made the agonizing decision to
send their children out of Germany, and they suffered intensely from the
loss of daily intimacy. Herta Beuthner, whose husband was in Argentina,
sent their son to Palestine to avoid his induction at fifteen into forced labor:
"The separation from my only child was heartbreaking. For many days and

nights I lay in my bed, crying, and didn't want to live any more."[65]

Some mothers could not bear the thought of parting from their children. Almost fifty years later, Miriam Gillis-Carlebach recalled that when she told her mother that she wanted to leave for Palestine, Lotte Carlebach covered her face and cried, "My only Miriam." The teenager tried to console her: "But Mommy! Eight children will remain at home with you!" Her mother would not be comforted: "Each child is my only child. I yearn for you already." Whereas Lotte Carlebach sympathized with her daughter's desires and approved of her emigration, Ruth Klüger's mother showed no such understanding. As a result, both mother and daughter wound up in Auschwitz. Both survived, but even late in life, Ruth Klüger recalled her frustration when her mother refused to let her join a children's transport. A young man from the Jewish community had told her mother there was one last chance to send her child to Palestine:

> My heart pounded, for I would have loved to leave, even if it had been a betrayal of her. But she didn't ask me or even look at me once, rather she said, "No. One does not separate a child from her mother." On the way home I struggled with my disappointment, which I could not express to her without hurting her. I believe I never forgave her for this.[66]

These children were willing to cut all ties with their homeland. Parents feared an unknown future abroad. Children, however, reacted almost viscerally to present dangers at home.

By 1939, 82 percent of children aged fifteen and under and 83 percent of youth aged sixteen to twenty-four had managed to escape Germany. The remaining Jewish children and teens had fewer and fewer friends, especially outside the big cities. By 1937, in Hessen-Nassau, for example, seventy-eight communities counted fewer than ten Jewish children and teens, and only thirteen communities counted between twenty and thirty-five children and teens.[67] Opportunities for those increasingly nervous and frightened children who remained—the *Kindertransporte,* like other exits, were never sufficient—continued to dwindle. By July 1941, about 25,000 Jewish children and youth under age twenty-five still lived within the borders of pre-1938 Germany.

5

The November Pogrom and Its Aftermath

The store was boarded up.... Our home no longer offered us ...
security. Our family was now scattered in three different locations.

—SHLOMO WAHRMAN

The November Pogrom struck like lightning, suddenly shattering everything it touched, shocking those who suffered it. Although it represented
the intensification of the political disenfranchisement, economic strangulation, and social segregation that had begun in 1933, no one expected the
widespread violence—a pogrom of the sort connected only with czarist
Russia. The public manifestations of Jewish life in Germany stood covered
with broken glass. Businesses and synagogues were ransacked, Jewish livelihoods destroyed. The Nazis also destroyed private, interior spaces. Homes,
which had previously felt safe, were transformed into nightmares of
smashed furniture and torn feather beds. Jewish men, often humiliated and
beaten, were now forced into concentration camps. Jewish women remained behind, trying frantically to free their men, repair their homes, and
help their families flee for their lives.

THE BACKGROUND TO NOVEMBER 1938

The Nazis stepped up their persecution of Jews in 1938. In March the
German annexation of Austria sparked the public abuse of Jews and the
looting and pillaging of their shops and homes in Austria. In annexing
Austria, the Reich had added 200,000 Austrian Jews, canceling out the
reduction of German Jews by recent emigration. In Germany that same
month, the Nazis enacted the "Law Regarding the Legal Status of Jewish
Communities," the first major piece of anti-Jewish legislation since the

Nuremberg Laws. This law deprived Jewish congregations of legal protection and subjected them to the administrative control of the regime. In addition, they could no longer tax members, a restriction intended to reduce them to penury. The law proclaimed a renewed attack upon Jews.

The noose tightened in the spring, when Jews and "Aryan" spouses of Jews had to assess and report the value of their domestic and foreign property worth over 5,000 marks: "From here it was only a short step to the outright seizure of Jewish property." Jews would have to inform the government of whatever they planned to take abroad and were forbidden from taking valuables out of the country. As if preparing its inventory of sites to be ransacked, the government required the registration and identification of all Jewish commercial establishments in June. A Jewish teenager recalled his fury upon first noticing a sign labeling a "Jewish" store. He tried to erase it. The Jewish owner chased him away, since he had to identify himself as specified by the new regulation.[1] By June, fresh boycotts intensified.

Most ominously, the government rounded up Jewish men and sent them to concentration camps. First it singled out "foreign" Jews. As a result of Germany's intentionally difficult and exclusionary naturalization laws, many of these so-called foreign Jews had actually resided in Germany for generations; about 40 percent were born there[2] but had not achieved citizenship. In February the government ordered the expulsion of "Soviet Jews"—often people whose grandparents had come to Germany at the beginning of the century. Those who had not emigrated by May were sent to concentration camps, from which they would be released only when they had emigration papers in hand.

In its "June Action" the Gestapo arrested about 1,500 so-called antisocial Jewish men, sending them to concentration camps. Most of these men had previously been convicted of minor legal infractions—some 500, for example, of traffic violations. The pettiness of these "crimes" notwithstanding, 146 died at Buchenwald alone while wives, families, and friends exerted major efforts to have the others freed. They, too, would be set free only when they could prove readiness to emigrate. That same summer, the Nazis destroyed three synagogues—in Munich, Nuremberg, and Dortmund. In addition, all Jews were required to have the letter *J* stamped on their passports as of the fall. In January 1939 they would receive a new identity card, also stamped with a *J*. The *J* marked them as easy prey and made looking for housing or jobs impossible, since no one would rent to or hire a Jew.[3]

It was the deportation of Polish Jews—many of them also resident in Germany for generations—that sparked the incident that led to the

November Pogrom. Germany expelled 17,000 Polish Jews on October 27 and 28, 1938, sending them to the Polish border. Poland denied them entry. They languished in a no-man's-land between two borders, in the cold and without food or shelter, while their families and communities became more and more desperate. The deportation of the Polish Jews, usually mentioned only as a prelude to and then overshadowed by the November Pogrom, sent shock waves through the entire Jewish community in Germany.

The manner in which the Polish Jews were deported foreshadowed the brutality to come: officials picked them up without warning, gave them a few moments to pack necessities, allowed them to take only ten marks, and then herded them away. For the first time, the Nazis swept up Jews without regard for age or sex. Various states and cities such as Hamburg, Frankfurt, and Munich rounded up whole families. In Württemberg and Saxony, women and children made up the majority of deportees. One deportee wrote:

> Everyone . . . was loaded onto the wagons. . . . Crying women and children, heartrending scenes. . . . [A]rriving at the border at 5 P.M., we were shoved across it. . . . For three days we were on the platform and in the train station, 8,000 people. Women and children fainting, unconscious, incidents of death, faces yellow as wax. . . . Women and children half-dead. On the fourth day help finally came . . . from the Warsaw Jewish Committee.[4]

Whatever food, clothing, or succor the deportees received came from other Jews. Jewish communities in Germany, too, helped the Polish Jews. In Munich, a leader of the League of Jewish Women quickly organized members to race to the homes of the deportees in order to pack some clothing and food for them. One volunteer discovered five terrified children whose parents had hidden them from the roundup. The oldest was ten. The volunteer slipped them out of the apartment and brought them to an orphanage, preventing their immediate deportation. Those involved in relief activities all felt the imminent threat to themselves. In Hamburg, the women who brought food to the trainloads of Polish deportees returned saying, "And who will bring *us* bread and butter at the train?"[5]

THE POGROM

As the pitiable deportees languished in the cold, wet, no-man's-land between Poland and Germany, young Herschel Grynszpan, whose parents and sister were among them, was driven to despair. He shot Ernst vom

Rath, a diplomat at the German embassy in Paris. The Nazis used the death of vom Rath as a convenient excuse to launch their largest pogrom to date. Organized by the government and Nazi organizations and supported by mobs, the attacks began around 3 A.M. on November 9/10.[6]

Destruction and Persecution

Assailants wielding hatchets and axes ravaged Jewish homes and businesses, while others used incendiary bombs and dynamite to demolish synagogues. Mobs destroyed holy items and books and plundered Jewish homes while forcing Jews to watch. Rowdies rounded up Jews—women and men—half dressed or in their pajamas and herded them into the marketplace or main squares to taunt them. Firemen and police looked on or prevented aid as synagogues and other Jewish property burned, attempting only to save neighboring "Aryan" buildings from destruction.

In the frenzy of this "public degradation ritual," the Nazis went beyond plundering and terrorizing Jewish women and men. They also invaded Jewish hospitals, old-age homes, and orphanages. In Königsberg, a band forced the children of the Jewish orphanage out onto the street in their nightclothes. The freezing children huddled close to the burning synagogue to warm themselves. When Nazis stormed an orphanage in Dinslaken, in the Rhineland, the director ordered the children, aged six to sixteen, outside, assuming that the troopers would not dare harm the children out in the open. Despite the cold, the children scrambled into the street, without coats, running after the director to the town hall to obtain police protection. They encountered about ten police and a crowd of eager onlookers. "We do not give protection to Jews," the police chief announced, "Get out with those children or I'll shoot."[7]

The next morning the SS forced Jews to sweep up the broken furniture, destroyed household items, feathers, and glass that littered the streets. The SS stood around, laughing and taunting. Moreover, the job was left to a community deprived of most of its able-bodied men. The Nazis had systematically rounded up Jewish men and imprisoned them in concentration camps: 11,000 to Dachau; 9,845 to Buchenwald; 9,000 to Sachsenhausen. There, brutality and humiliation reigned. Guards prevented Jewish men from washing and drinking water while subjecting them to long days of torturous exercise, standing at attention, or sitting in the sun without permission to move. The Jewish men suffered sickness, madness, and death. The lucky ones were released if they could prove they were about to emigrate and agreed to sell their businesses for minute sums. The first group left after six days; others stayed for months. The men who were lucky enough to return from internment, with shaved heads and frozen limbs, were often physically and psychologically ravaged. Gerdy Stoppleman's husband left Sachsenhausen in March 1939: "More than his body, my husband's mind was deeply affected. Almost every night he experienced Sachsenhausen concentration camp anew in nightmares so alarming that I feared for his sanity." Still, others faced even worse: "On a daily basis one heard that the ashes of a dead person had been delivered to this or that family. These urns were sent cash on delivery (for which the post office took the sum of 3.75 marks)."[8]

Threatened with worse punishment if they told anyone of their suffering in the camps, many Jewish men were too terrified to tell their families. Others wanted to repress their experiences. Ingeborg Hecht's father, however, described his ordeal in Sachsenhausen: "In a low voice, punctuated by the hollow cough that lingered with him for a long time to come, he recounted his terrible experiences. If he hadn't been our own father, a qualified lawyer, and in his right mind, we would never have believed him."[9]

The November Pogrom claimed the lives of at least one hundred Jews, not counting the camp deaths or suicides occurring shortly thereafter. The pogrom also destroyed hundreds of synagogues and countless homes and shops. Damage was estimated at several hundred million marks: the broken glass alone was valued at 24 million marks. Jews were made to pay a fine of 1 billion marks as punishment for the vom Rath assassination. The government, not the Jews, would collect on insurance payments for damages incurred. The Nazis used the pogrom not only as the occasion to accelerate their plunder of the Jewish community but also to dismantle the Central Organization of Jews in Germany. In 1939, the government forced the Central Association of Jews in Germany (*Reichsvereinigung der Juden in Deutschland*) upon the Jewish community. It would oversee emigration, education, and social welfare programs and would represent all individual Jews in Germany. The Gestapo, not the Jewish community, would appoint its leadership.

German Reactions

The November Pogrom provides examples of the contradictory behavior of Germans toward Jews—a mixture of rampant viciousness, studied ignorance, and occasional kindness. Many Germans joined mobs to attack and burn Jewish homes, businesses, and synagogues. Others chose to take advantage of their Jewish neighbors. In Bavaria, for example, an "Aryan" neighbor offered a Jewish woman and her mother a "deal" after the arrests of their husbands. The Jewish woman should sign over the deed of her house to him and leave Germany. Should they decide to return, he would give it back to them! She declined. Ingeborg Hecht's neighbor chose to make excuses: she gave Ingeborg a big bag of groceries for her father upon his return from Sachsenhausen, assuring her that "the Führer knows nothing of this."[10]

One Jewish woman recalled the events as a mixture of mobs and helpers:

> While I was sweeping up some of the debris, I noticed another mob of hoodlums, among them women. They were armed with axes as they approached [and] proceeded to ransack the entire house. . . . I thought of Anna K., the former parlor maid. . . . Soon we were on our way in hope that there would be some straw bed in her barn. . . . She had two such beds, but we would have to leave early the next day . . . because her brother had become a member of the SA.

Mally Dienemann of Offenbach am Main was deeply touched when her non-Jewish landlady helped clean up her apartment: "Her devotion and guilt . . . knew no bounds. These simple people . . . brought me flowers when I was alone . . . and other Jews must have also known such people in one form or another. For officially we were all supposed to starve during these November days."[11]

What were the reactions of Germans not immediately involved either in the destruction or in helping Jews? While most approved of, or went along with, "moderate" antisemitism, many disapproved of the open barbarism of the November Pogrom: "Shame at the act, shock at its extent, and regret for the property destroyed converged to create a negative reaction." Even if Nazi Party members approved, the large majority of the population condemned the violence—even those who had previously endorsed "moderate" antisemitic measures. Still, there are almost no cases of public opposition to it. In the wake of Hitler's triumphs (incorporating Austria and dismembering Czechoslovakia) and in the shadow of an increasingly terrorist state (in which there were also no protests against the arrest or murder of political opponents), the pogrom was met with silence. In addition, when Germans watched what was happening to Jews they became still more mute, fearing for their *own* lives and property. Some thought the pogrom would only start with Jews and soon spread to other opponents of the system. When neighbors in the small town of "Sonderburg" saw the furniture and possessions of a Jewish family being tossed from a second-floor window—watching in horror as the feathers from the down quilts floated in the air—they tightened their shutters, secured their doors, drew their curtains, and trembled for themselves.[12]

As it was happening, the Nazis referred to the pogrom as the "Jew Action," a typically bureaucratic euphemism. Afterward it became known as "Crystal Night" (*Kristallnacht* or *Reichskristallnacht*)—a term commonly used through the late 1980s. Although the origin of the term is unclear, many Germans used this euphemism to describe the tons of shattered glass spread over public areas, streets, and squares, from the ruined homes and shops of Jews.[13]

A powerful image, mentioned often in Jewish women's memoirs, is that of flying feathers—feathers covering the internal space of the home, hallway, and front yard or courtyard. As in Russian pogroms at the turn of the century, the mobs tore up feather blankets and pillows, shaking them into the rooms, out the windows, and down the stairways. Jews were deprived of their bedding and the physical and psychological sense of well-being it represented.[14] Broken glass in public and strewn feathers in private spelled the end of Jewish security in Germany.

WOMEN'S ROLES AND REACTIONS DURING THE POGROM

The image of feathers flying is one of a domestic scene gravely disturbed. This was women's primary experience of the November Pogrom. The marauders beat and arrested men. Although some women were publicly humiliated, bloodied, beaten, and murdered,[15] most were forced to stand by and watch their homes torn apart and their men abused. Later, women anguished as their men disappeared into concentration camps and many strove, heroically, to free them.

Personal testimonies show the massive terror. In the small town of "Sonderburg," for example, with 4,000 inhabitants and only 150 Jews, one Jewish woman recalled:

> It was around 6 o'clock in the morning when five young fellows came in ... one from Sonderburg who had worked with me at ... the department store for at least ten years. He didn't do anything, he only sent the others in and they destroyed everything. ... They ... told me to go to the window, then they came with an axe but instead of hitting me, they hit the windows. A couple of hours later ... children came by and threw stones in. ... The man who worked with me said nothing: I looked at him ... but he lowered his face. Among the four was the veterinarian and he came to my

father's bedroom and said, "Mein Herr, following orders, we must destroy your house. You and your wife, go out."

The veterinarian had known her father from community sports events. Another woman recalled her experiences as an eleven-year-old in "Sonderburg": "Men . . . ran around axing all our furniture and throwing things out the window. They smashed the closet door and broke all my toys. Afterward, we hid in a closet in a neighbor's apartment." In Berlin, where the pogrom spread unevenly at first, Toni Lessler described the children arriving at her school from various neighborhoods exclaiming that the synagogues were burning. Fearing that they might be attacked at school, she sent them home with their teachers. Many arrived home to find only their distraught mothers: ninety-two of their fathers had been sent to concentration camps. After the pogrom, Jewish schools limped on, taught and directed, for the most part, by women and a few elderly male teachers.[16]

Although the ravage was thorough, in large cities a few escaped the worst because of oversights by the Nazis, because some buildings were protected by "Aryan" owners, because the vandals did not have enough time to get to them, or because, having been forewarned, some families split up and hid. In Leipzig, for example, as arrests of men continued after the pogrom, the Wahrman family split three ways: the father stayed with friends; the mother, aunt, and daughter went to (non-Jewish) neighbors; and the two young sons hid with other neighbors. Eleven years old at the time, one son later recalled: "How sad it was. . . . The store was boarded up. . . . Our home no longer offered us safety and security. Our family was now scattered."[17]

Those fortunate few who managed to escape still experienced days of terror, often trying to distract themselves or calm their families with the kind of avoidance behavior they had used in previous situations. One woman wrote: "We were at the piano and played a Mozart concerto. Often our eyes went to the window, but we did not stop. . . . We did not want to admit disturbing reality. We wanted to spare our nerves."[18]

Immediately after the cataclysm, with men imprisoned, many women continued to hide from further persecution; others had no way of remaining in their ransacked homes. Deprived of their men, women gathered together for consolation, encouragement, and advice. One young woman joined her fiancé's mother in Mannheim, "who had found refuge with about twenty other women and girls in one relative's apartment. All the men were already in Dachau." In another small town, where all the Jews had been herded together and then separated by sex, an observer noted: "We met nothing but young wives and mourning mothers" lingering in the area where the men had been imprisoned. Visiting a local hospital, she saw many women lying in the reception area, "all of them had escaped from small towns [where they would have been recognized] just in time, but did not know any longer where to go."[19] Eventually, most women returned home to clean up the wreckage and salvage a few objects or pieces of clothing. Since most of the dishes, pottery, or porcelain had been smashed, clothing slashed, and furniture axed, cleanup involved throwing away most items or saving shards of family treasures.

The most crucial task confronting Jewish women was to have their men freed. Since 1933, women had frequently represented their husbands to the authorities; now they would have to rescue them. Wives of prisoners were told that their husbands would be freed only if they could present emigration papers. Although no statistics are available to indicate their success, these women displayed extraordinary nerve and tenacity in saving a large number of men and in facilitating a mass exodus of married couples in 1939. Many women summoned the courage to overcome gender stereotypes of passivity in order to find any means to have husbands and fathers released from camps. Charlotte Stein-Pick wrote of the November Pogrom: "I tried ... day in and day out, to find a connection that could lead to my husband's release. I ran to Christian acquaintances, friends, or colleagues, but ... people shrugged their shoulders, shook their heads and said 'no.' And everyone was glad when I left. I was treated like a leper, even by people who were well-disposed toward us." Undaunted, Stein-Pick entered Nazi headquarters in Munich, the notorious Brown House, to request her husband's freedom based on his status as a war veteran. There she was shown her husband, twenty pounds thinner, and begged repeatedly for his release. The Nazis demanded that she explain the finances of her husband's student fraternity, of which he was still treasurer. She did. Upon his release, she had to return to the Brown House monthly to do the fraternity's bookkeeping until she emigrated.[20]

Ruth Abraham impressed not only her family but also the SS with her determination and bravery. During the November Pogrom, she pulled her fiancé out of hiding and led him through the teeming crowds: "His store was in ruins and I found him hiding behind a pillar." She then traveled to Dachau to ask for the release of her future father-in-law. She arrived at the concentration camp in a bus filled with SS men. She assumed that because of her "Aryan" looks she was taken for a member of the League of German Girls. She requested an interview with the commandant and begged for the elderly man's freedom. After three days and the intercession of a Nazi Party member, she succeeded. Again she attributed her success to her looks, since the men she met refused to believe that she was a "full Jew" and seemed to take pity on her. Abraham's unconventional behavior found a conventional reward: the couple married immediately. The rabbi who performed the ceremony had bandaged hands, an indication of the treatment he had received in a concentration camp.[21]

Some women saw not only to their husbands' release and the necessary papers but also to the sale of their joint property. Accompanying her husband home after his imprisonment, one wife explained that she had just sold their house and bought tickets to Shanghai for the family. Her husband recalled that anything was fine with him, as long as they could escape from a place in which everyone had declared "open season" on them.[22] Expressions of thankfulness tinged, perhaps, with a bit of surprise at women's heroism can be found in many men's memoirs. They were indebted to women even after their ordeal, when many men were too beaten in body and spirit to be of much use in the scramble to emigrate.

The testimonies of both men and women emphasize women's calm, dry-eyed, self-control in the midst of turmoil. For example, a Jewish community leader wrote: "The highest praise . . . goes to our wives who, without shedding one tear, inspired the hordes, some of whom had beaten their men bloody, to respect them. Unbroken, these women . . . did everything to have their men freed." Charlotte Stein-Pick recalled her husband's counsel on the day of the pogrom: "'Just no tears and no scene.' . . . But even without this warning I would have controlled myself." Hanna Bernheim, remembering the pain of giving up prized family heirlooms to the Nazis some months after the pogrom, reflected on the dignity and self-control of Jews around her and on her own form of defiance: "I was glad that the Jews I saw behaved well, they didn't show any excitement noticeable to strangers. And I told an acquaintance I met loud enough for the employees to understand it, that I had never cared for these things." When the Nazis confiscated all her valuable ritual objects and jewelry, a Hamburg woman wrote in a poem that expressed her grief and her quiet defiance, "I will separate myself without tears."[23] This stoic calm in the face of danger was not merely a proclamation of female stalwartness to counter the stereotype of female "frailty." German-Jewish bourgeois upbringing had always valued decorum, and so women maintained their dignity as part of their Jewishness in the face of general dishonor. Jewish women's heroism reproached "Aryan" savagery and suggested a new task for women. Traditionally men had publicly guarded the safety and honor of the family and community; suddenly women found that they stood as the defenders of Jewish honor and pride —and of Jewish life itself.

On their own, many women faced the dizzying procedure of obtaining proof of immediate plans to emigrate in order to free a relative from a concentration camp. They had to decide whether to send children abroad while they organized their papers, settled on a destination (if they had not already discussed this previously), sold property, and arranged the departure. In spite of their apparent calm, the inner stress for women was massive.

EMIGRATION

The November Pogrom decisively tipped the balance toward emigration. For those in camps, the only way out was proof of readiness to emigrate, and for those not in camps, the violence influenced their decisions. Psychologists who studied refugee memoirs determined that almost 40 percent of memoir writers did not give up psychologically until 1938 or 1939. It was only after the pogrom that Jews were finally convinced that they faced physical danger. After November 1938, "essentially everyone tried to find a possibility of emigrating."[24]

Obstacles to Emigration

In the period following the pogrom, emigration became the highest priority within the Jewish community. Still, immigration restrictions in foreign countries and Nazi bureaucratic and financial roadblocks stymied Jews. Countries of potential refuge thwarted Jewish entry. Elisabeth Freund described her and her husband's many attempts to leave Germany:

> It is really enough to drive one to despair.... We have filed applications for entry permits to Switzerland, Denmark, and Sweden ... in vain, though in all these countries we had good connections. In the spring of 1939 ... we obtained an entry permit for Mexico for 3,000 marks. But we never received the visa, because the Mexican consulate asked us to present passports that would entitle us to return to Germany, and the German authorities did not issue such passports to Jews. Then, in August 1939 we did actually get the permit for England. But it came ... only ten days before the outbreak of war, and in this short time we were not able to take care of all the formalities.... In the spring of 1940 we received the entry permit for Portugal. We immediately got everything ready and applied for our passports. Then came the invasion of Holland, Belgium and France.... A stream of refugees poured into Portugal, and the Portuguese government recalled ... all of the issued permits.... It was

also good that in December 1940 we had not ... paid for our
Panamanian visas, for we noticed that the visas offered us did not ...
entitle us to land in Panama.

Freund was frustrated with friends who urged them to leave Germany: "As
if that were not our most fervent wish." She agonized: "There are no more
visas for the U.S.A. My husband has made one last attempt and asked our
relatives in America by wire for the entry visas for Cuba. . . . No other country gives an entry permit to German Jews any longer, or is still reachable in
any way."[25]

Once they received permission to *enter* a foreign country, Jews still had
to acquire the papers to *exit* Germany. "Getting out . . . is at least as difficult
as getting into another country and you have absolutely no notion of the
desperation here," wrote sixty-six-year-old Gertrud Grossmann to her un-
comprehending son abroad. Getting the required papers took months of
running a bureaucratic gauntlet, which many women faced alone, meeting
officials who could arbitrarily add to the red tape at whim: "There was no
rule and every official felt like a god."[26]

Bella Fromm summarized the plight of all German Jews: "So far I have
gathered a collection of twenty-three of the necessary documents. I have
made a thorough study of the employees and furniture in fifteen official
bureaus . . . during the hours I have waited." Bewildered, she reported that
she did not yet have all the papers she needed—and this was a few months
before the November Pogrom. Afterward, Mally Dienemann, whose sixty-
three-year-old husband languished in Buchenwald, raced to the Gestapo to
prove they were ready to emigrate. Next she rushed to the passport office to
retrieve their passports.

> After I had been sent from one office to another ... I had to go to ... the
> Emigration Office in Frankfurt, the Gestapo, the police, the Finance
> Office, [send] a petition to Buchenwald, a petition to the Gestapo in
> Darmstadt, and still it took until Tuesday of the third week, before my
> husband returned.... Next came running around for the many papers
> that one needed for emigration. And while the Gestapo was in a rush, the
> Finance Office had so much time and so many requests, and without cer-
> tification from the Finance and Tax offices ... one did not get a passport,
> and without a passport a tariff official could not inspect the baggage.[27]

Finally arriving in Palestine in March 1939, Rabbi Dienemann died from
his ordeal.

By 1939, new arbitrary laws slowed emigration even more. Even with a U.S. affidavit in hand, Else Gerstel could not simply leave "immediately," as her brother abroad urged. "It was impossible even to buy the ship tickets before we had the official permits. And that meant to pay taxes which were much higher than everything we owned. There were several months of red tape, desperate struggle." The elderly were physically ill equipped to endure the strains of this paper chase. Gertrud Grossmann confided by letter: "I dread going to the consulate and possibly standing around there for hours, which is physically impossible for me." The situation deteriorated so much that by 1940 she wrote her son: "Your emigration [in 1938] was child's play compared to today's practically insurmountable difficulties."[28]

As the government harassed the desperate Jews, individual Germans sought to enrich themselves at Jewish expense and Jews, often women, since the men were in camps, regularly encountered corruption. Charlotte Stein-Pick, anxious to get her husband out of a camp and expecting to receive visas from the American consulate imminently, was shocked to learn that there were Germans at the embassy who expected bribes in order to forward her papers. She went to a lawyer, who informed her that it would take 3,000 marks to pay off the swindlers: "I ran around bewildered.... In spite of everything, we German Jews still continued to resist believing the terrible corruption which National Socialism brought with it." In a respectable shipping company's elegant office on Berlin's exclusive boule-vard, Unter den Linden, another desperate woman had to hand over a 100-mark payoff for a place on a ship's waiting list. Moreover, she had to participate in the expensive farce of paying for round-trip tickets because, even though the Germans would have blocked their reentry, her family's visas to Cuba had to be tourist visas. Since this family had hidden money before the government blocked it, she was able to pay for the trip.[29] A situation like this was frustrating and nerve-racking before the war; it could cost Jewish lives thereafter.

Even before the pogrom, the government had no intention of letting Jews escape with their money or property. Afterward it blocked bank accounts more stringently and robbed potential emigrants more thor-oughly. In Berlin, the Gestapo set up a special "one-stop" emigration bureau where: "the emigrating Jew was fleeced, totally and completely, in the manner of an assembly line." When they entered they were "still . . . the owner[s] of an apartment, perhaps a business, a bank account and some savings." As they were pushed from section to section "one possession after the next was taken." By the time they left, they had been "reduced to . . . stateless beggar[s]," grasping one precious possession, an exit visa.[30]

Nazi avarice is illustrated by the experience of the Bernheim family. They left in July 1939, falling prey to the Nazi decree of February 1939 that expropriated all valuable stones and metals from Jews. Thus, before emigrating, Hanna Bernheim packed a suitcase and headed for a Nazi "purchasing post" to give up her valuables:

> There were many people who had three, five suitcases, full of marvelous things: old [bridal] jewelry, Sabbath candles and goblets . . . beautiful old and modern plates. . . . The young officials were in high spirits. . . . These treasures, often collected by generations, were thrown together. . . . They were small-minded enough to take jewelry not at all precious as to the . . . value, but precious to us as souvenirs of beloved persons.

Shortly thereafter, at the airport, agents examined Bernheim's hat box and confiscated a brass clock, toiletries, and underwear. The guard even insisted on a body search. She recalled: "The propellers started. . . and I could only beg the woman to do the examination immediately. She was nice and correct, helped me with dressing, and the French pilot waited. And so I flew out of . . . hell."[31] Nazi insatiability was so great that a dentist warned one woman to see him before departing "and have him cover a gold crown and filling I had with a white coating. A patient of his had missed her ship while the gold in her mouth was removed by a Nazi dentist."[32]

Despite chaos and barriers, the largest number of Jews to leave in one year emigrated directly after the November Pogrom, reaching 78,000 in 1939. The United States, Palestine, and Great Britain took the most German Jews, but Jews left no escape route untried, as the 8,000 who fled to Japanese-occupied Shanghai show. By September 1939, about 185,000 (racially defined) Jews still remained in Germany; their numbers sank to 164,000 by October 1941, when Jewish emigration was banned. Another 8,500 managed to escape between 1942 and 1945. Exact figures of those who left Germany as a result of racial persecution cannot be established, but a good estimate is between 270,000 and 300,000 Jews. That is, close to three-fifths of German Jews managed to flee Germany. Yet approximately 30,000 of those who got out were later caught by the Nazis in other European countries. Ultimately, about half of those Jews who had lived in Germany in 1933 could save themselves through emigration to safe countries. Their friends and relatives who remained behind were murdered.[33]

Packing for Good

When Jews finally reached the stage of packing, they believed their departure would be permanent. Women took charge. As Berta Kamm put it: "Only a woman knows how much there is to deliberate and resolve in such a rushed departure." Packing was so clearly considered "women's work" that some women stayed behind to do it, sending men and children ahead. Packing quickly became an art as Nazi rulings and red tape skyrocketed. To emigrate with one's belongings, one had to receive a permit from the Finance Department. This permit was obtainable only after preparing lists of all the items one wished to take. Lisa Brauer spent an entire week writing "endless lists, in five copies each ... every item entered, every list neatly typed, and in the end I could only speak and breathe and think in shoes, towels, scissors, soap and scarves." Another woman recalled how "a science of emigration advisement came into being [and these advisers] prepared the lists. For example, one was not allowed to say 'one bag of sewing supplies,' but had to detail every thimble, every skein of wool, every snap." Also one could not take just anything: "Only those things were allowed which had been purchased before 1933." Other items could be taken only in limited amounts and only "if the complete purchase price was paid to the Gold-Discount-Bank once again."[34]

After completing the lists, and often with ship or plane tickets in hand, Jews had to await the authorization of the Finance Department. Despite official policy encouraging emigration, the Nazi bureaucracy dawdled and delayed Jewish emigration. Again, connections and bribes seemed to speed up the process and, again, women had to master the world of officialdom and the art of bribery. To obtain the necessary papers before her boat departed, Lisa Brauer begged for assistance from a former student whom she knew was married to someone in the Finance Department. She arrived at the student's door early one morning, when it was still dark, "to avoid being seen and recognized by curious neighbors." Shortly thereafter, a clerk from the Finance Department appeared at her home. Brauer offered him any books in her library. "Three days later I got my appointment at the Finance Department."[35]

With the arduous packing accomplished and papers in hand, some families sent the freight containers, known as "lifts," to interim stations, frequently ports in Holland. They remained there until the family knew its final destination. Some families lost their possessions when access to their containers was cut off by the German invasion of Holland. But others could not even consider packing most of their possessions, since the giant containers and the surcharge demanded by the Nazis for every item cost too much. One man recalled "that these giant containers . . . stood in front of many houses in my neighborhood, with the designation . . . New York or Buenos Aires or Haifa. However, most emigrants could not afford such costly things and traveled to foreign lands with only a few suitcases."

Many emigrants, mourning their loss, sold their homes and furnishings for a pittance. Lisa Brauer, trying to create what she viewed as a dignified moment amid her misfortune, set the table with coffee and cake and invited neighbors to purchase items: "Only a few . . . took advantage and tried to grab as much as they could carry." Dismantling her home after the November Pogrom, Alice Baerwald wrote: "It was so terribly difficult to destroy . . . what one had created with so much love." She had cultivated every plant around the house: "Flowers, nothing but flowers, that was my joy. . . . My children had played and laughed here and romped in the grass with the dogs. And now suddenly to sell to total strangers." The city of Danzig decided the price of her house and chose the buyer. She then sold the contents of her home to "Aryan" purchasers, many of whom complained of *their* plight. Since Nazi ideology asserted that Germans suffered because of Jews, many Germans could simultaneously ignore Jewish suffering, exploit Jews, and lament their own lot. A pastor's wife proclaimed, "We're suffering just as much as you," but Baerwald retorted, "only with the difference that you're buying and I'm selling."[36]

It was clear to the emigrants that their German neighbors were benefiting greatly from their misery and doubtlessly clear to these Germans as well. Placing an ad in the paper, Lotte Popper tried to sell her "bedroom, living room, kitchen furniture." The ad was simply one among many other ads by Jews. She commented: "Yes, the Aryans had it good. They could now beautify their homes cheaply with the well-cared-for furniture of emigrating Jews." Only "the stupid among the populace were persuaded not to buy anything which had been used by Jews. The others, however, crowded the auction rooms, for the belongings [of Jews] were to be had for a song."[37]

Packing gave some women the chance to smuggle valuables out of the country. What their ingenuity managed to salvage was paltry compared with what the Nazis stole from them. Still, it helped some families subsist for a short time when they arrived penniless at their destination and saved precious mementos. While most women packed feverishly under the scrutiny of one or two officials,[38] some women managed to bribe these officials. One woman, who smuggled gold, silver, and jewelry into her bags, commented on the officials who demanded huge payoffs to make this possible: "This corruption of the Germans, which grew into the monstrous, rescued the lives and a modest existence for many people, particularly Jews." A few women bribed officials without consulting their husbands. They knew full well that their plans would have been vetoed, but they hoped to save some valuables for their immediate needs abroad. Else Gerstel, the wife of a judge, hid silverware with "Aryan" friends until the night before she packed. She then paid off packers to hide the silver while "seven Gestapo men were watching." She also smuggled other valuables in a secret compartment of her desk, built especially for this purpose: "I had risked of course the concentration camp and my life, probably all our lives. Alfred had no idea of what I had done. The night before we arrived in Cuba I whispered the whole story in his ear."[39]

Other women smuggled jewelry or money abroad for their relatives. Visiting her grandchild in Switzerland, one grandmother smuggled jewelry on each trip. Alice Baerwald, a resident of Danzig, agreed to smuggle her sister-in-law's jewelry from Berlin to Danzig in order to mail it to her when she emigrated. It was not yet forbidden to send one's own jewelry from Danzig, a "free city" according to the Treaty of Versailles, and she could claim it belonged to her. Then other elderly family members begged her to take their jewelry to Danzig too. None of them wanted to become dependent upon their adult children once they arrived abroad. Even more fearfully, she agreed, noting that "if someone caught me, I'd be finished." A few years later, she reflected: "One lived . . . in such danger that one . . . forgot completely that there could still be a normal life elsewhere. . . . Naturally one did many forbidden things, but because, in fact, everything was forbidden to us Jews, one had absolutely no choice."[40]

Women committed "illegal" acts not only to support their families but also to help the community at large. Beate Berger, for example, smuggled money from Berlin to Palestine in order to buy land for a children's home. Faithful friends, too, helped Jews take valuables abroad. The patient of one Jewish doctor, who was driven to commit suicide because of Nazi persecution, helped the doctor's widow smuggle jewelry and fur coats to Switzerland. She even accompanied the family to the border to assure their safety.[41]

While for many, "packing reduced a lifetime of possessions into three suitcases," for others, the clothing, shoes, and linens they packed had been donated by the Jewish Winter Relief Agency. Having sold the little they had to pay for their voyage, they had nothing left to take with them. The Jewish organization proclaimed: "They should not be uprooted and arrive in a foreign country with the mark of poverty stamped upon them."[42]

Final Farewells

In fear for their lives, some people fled immediately after the pogrom. Alice Oppenheimer, with exit papers in hand and a husband in Buchenwald, packed bags for her five children and looked up the next train to Switzerland. It would leave on a Saturday. Because she was religiously observant, she phoned a rabbi for his advice regarding travel on the Sabbath. He told her to disregard the prohibition against travel since her life was in danger. She left with only some jewelry to sell in Italy in order to tide the family over until its departure for Palestine: "I could sell only a few articles, and those I practically gave away. I had to have some money in hand. How else could I proceed with five children? [In Italy] I bought a loaf of bread for them and said: 'I cannot give you any more to eat, or I won't have enough money.'" Several days later they embarked for Palestine, where they met up with the sixth child. Her husband also joined them, freed after sixteen days in a concentration camp because of his Palestine certificate. Oppenheimer remarked that the camp had "transformed a still youthful man into an old man whom I failed to recognize when he finally landed by boat at Tel Aviv."[43]

For those lucky enough to leave Germany, most faced painful farewells with friends and relatives. "More and more, one learned to say farewell," wrote one woman, as she listed friends who had scattered over the entire world. Moreover, all worried that those left behind would face increasing torment, and neither side knew whether they would ever see each other again. Fleeing shortly after the pogrom, Toni Lessler said her farewells in the only public place left for Jews, the railroad station café. There, no one noticed a few Jewish people visiting with each other. Referring to the Zoo station in Berlin, Lessler wrote:

> As we looked around . . . we saw similar groups to ours . . . friends and relatives who were taking leave from one another, none of whom could find any other meeting place than this dismal train station . . . in the midst of renovation and which offered the most inhospitable sojourn imaginable. I am unable to say how many tears were shed that evening.

When Elisabeth Freund finally escaped, shortly after Germany invaded the Soviet Union, her good-byes were excruciating. In the midst of real terror, having experienced bombings, forced labor, and the removal of Jews to tighter quarters, she tried not to break down: "Just no tears. One must not start that, otherwise one cannot stop. Who knows what will become of these people. In a situation like this, one can no longer say farewell in a conventional way."[44]

Individuals took leave in their own personal ways of what had been their *Heimat*—an almost untranslatable, nostalgic word for a romanticized homeland. In 1962, Ann Lewis and her parents described their feelings as they embarked for England. Ann, ten years old at the time, recalled the farewell at the train station:

> Relatives and friends—perhaps twelve or fifteen people—had gathered to see us off. . . . Everyone had brought presents . . . flowers, chocolate, sweets, magazines, books. . . . I have never forgotten this picture of the little knot of our friends and relations, standing close together as if to give each other mutual comfort, waving to us as the train carried us away. Sometimes I am surprised how often it comes into my thoughts. Although this leave-taking occurred when I was still so young, it marked the most important turning-point of my life . . . the fundamental break with my roots.

Her mother wrote:

> We are waiting at Bahnhof Zoo. . . . Many relatives and friends are there with flowers and presents. The train comes into the station, we get in, the children are excited and are looking forward to opening their presents—the train begins to move, we wave. Everything vanishes, we sit down—try not to think—dull apathy—mind a complete blank, vacant, oppressed, not a single tear. Courage—we *must* win through.

Her father wrote:

> It is comfortable in the compartment . . . the luggage-racks are crammed with suitcases. . . . The four . . . are silent . . . the two adults, their faces looking serious and tired, are gazing with unseeing eyes through the windows, deep in thought. . . . Barely a quarter of an hour from now . . . Germany will lie behind them—Germany, the country which had been their home, where they had experienced happiness and suffering, the land whose language they had spoken—Germany, the country whose landscape was so dear to them . . . the Germany of poets, of thinkers and of the great composers.[45]

Strikingly, even as both parents experienced relief, their farewell thoughts echoed the general orientation of women and men when contemplating emigration: most women covered their pain and maintained a courageous front, while many men looked back, mourning for the country and culture they had once loved and had now lost. Adding to these differences, as we have seen (in chapter 2), were more immediate concerns: women looked forward to a safer environment for their families, while men agonized about how to support them.

It was terribly distressing for Jews to leave their homeland, family, and friends, especially when they saw the present suffering and feared for the future of those left behind. They also worried about how they would fare abroad. Their anguish notwithstanding, these émigrés were the lucky ones, and not only in hindsight. When Toni Lessler confided to a friend that "emigrating is terribly hard," he responded tearfully, "Remaining here is much harder!"[46]

Who Stayed Behind?

A gender analysis of the desire to emigrate (see chapter 2) highlights women's and men's unique expectations, priorities, and perceptions. Women wanted to leave well before their men. Paradoxically, it does not follow that more women than men *actually* left. To the contrary, fewer women than men left Germany. Why?

Although life was becoming increasingly difficult in the 1930s, there were still compelling reasons to stay. First, women could still find employment in Jewish businesses and homes. They could also work as teachers in Jewish schools, as social workers, nurses, and administrators in Jewish social service institutions, and as clerical workers for the Jewish community. And older, educated women found jobs in cultural and social service fields within the Jewish community. Hedwig Burgheim, for example, found challenging and important work. In 1933, she was forced to resign as director of a teacher training institute in Giessen. Thereafter she directed the Leipzig Jewish Community's School for Kindergarten Teachers and Domestic Services, which trained young people for vocations useful in lands of emigration. After the November Pogrom, her own attempts at emigration having failed, she taught at the Jewish school and, by 1942, headed the old-age home in Leipzig. Along with its residents, she was deported in early 1943 and died in Auschwitz. Martha Wertheimer, a journalist before 1933, also found her skills in demand thereafter. She plunged into Jewish welfare work, while also writing books and plays, contributing to the Jewish press, and tutoring English to earn extra money. She escorted many children's transports to England; worked twelve-hour days without pausing for meals in order to advise Jews on emigration and welfare procedures; took great

Office staff of the Jewish Winter Relief Agency, Berlin. The poster with a hand around a collection cup reads "Do Your Duty." (Courtesy of the Leo Baeck Institute, New York)

joy in leading High Holiday services at the League of Jewish Women's Home for Wayward Girls; and organized education courses for Jewish youth who had been drafted into forced labor. Ultimately, she wrote a friend in New York that, despite efforts to emigrate, she was no longer waiting to escape: "A great dark calm has entered me, as the saying of our fathers goes *'Gam zu le'tovah'* ('this, too, is for the best')." She continued: "It is also worthwhile to be an officer on the sinking ship of Jewish life in Germany, to hold out courageously and to fill the life boats, to the extent that we have some."[47]

While the employment situation of Jewish women helped keep them in Germany, that of men helped get them out. Some men had business connections abroad, facilitating their immediate flight, and others emigrated alone in order to establish themselves before sending for their families. Among Eastern European Jews who returned east between 1934 and 1937, for example, the majority were male, even though almost half of them were married. A handful of men, some with wives, received visas to leave Europe from groups hoping to save eminent intellectuals and artists. Women's organizations agreed that, if there was no choice, wives should not "hinder" husbands from emigrating alone, but they argued that it was often no cheaper for men to emigrate without their wives.[48]

Before the war, moreover, men faced immediate physical danger. Men who had been detained by the Nazis and then freed, as well as boys who had been beaten up by neighborhood ruffians, fled Germany early. After the November Pogrom, in a strange twist of fortune, the men interred in concentration camps were released only upon showing proof of their ability to leave Germany immediately. Families—mostly wives and mothers— strained every resource to provide the documentation to free these men and send them on their way while some of the women remained behind. Alice Nauen recalled how difficult these emigration decisions were for Jewish leaders:

> Should we send the men out first? This had been the dilemma all along. . . .
> If you have two tickets, do you take one man out of the concentration
> camp and his wife who is at this moment safe? Or do you take your two
> men out of the concentration camp? They took two men out . . . because
> they said we cannot play God, but these are in immediate danger.

Even as women feared for their men, they believed that they themselves would be spared serious harm by the Nazis. In retrospect, Ruth Klüger reflected on this kind of thinking and the resulting preponderance of women caught in the trap: "One seemed to ignore what was most obvious, namely how imperiled precisely the weaker and the socially disadvantaged are. That the Nazis should stop at women contradicted their racist ideology. Had we, as the result of an absurd, patriarchal short circuit, perhaps counted on their chivalry?"[49]

Despite trepidations, parents sent sons into the unknown more readily than daughters. Bourgeois parents worried about a daughter traveling alone, believing boys would be safer. Families also assumed that sons needed to establish economic futures for themselves, whereas daughters would marry. In 1935, one family sent its son to Palestine because "it was proper for a young man to try to leave and find a job elsewhere." His parents were reluctant to send their daughter abroad. Like other young women, socialized to accept their parents' judgment, she consented to remain behind and even made it "possible for him to go abroad by supporting him financially." As more and more sons left, daughters remained as the sole caretakers of elderly parents. One female commentator noted the presence of many women "who can't think of emigration because they don't know who might care for their elderly mothers . . . before they could start sending them money. In the same families, the sons went their way." Leaving one's aging parent—as statistics indicate, usually the mother— was the most painful act imaginable. Ruth Glaser described her own mother's agony at leaving her mother to join her husband, who had been forbidden reentry into Germany: she "could not sleep at night thinking of leaving her [mother] behind." Men, too, felt such grief, but more left nonetheless. Charlotte Stein-Pick wrote of her husband's anguish: "This abandonment of his old parents depressed him deeply. . . . He never got over this farewell. . . . To be sure, he saw that we could never have helped them, only shared their fate. I almost believe he would have preferred it."[50]

As early as 1936, the League of Jewish Women noted that far fewer women than men were leaving and feared that Jewish men of marriageable age would intermarry abroad, leaving Jewish women behind in Germany with no chance of marrying. Still, the League was not enthusiastic about emigration to certain areas because of anxiety about the possibility of forced prostitution. The League of Jewish Women also turned toward parents, reminding them of their "responsibility to free their daughters" even though daughters felt "stronger psychological ties to their families than sons do, [which] probably lies in the female psyche." As late as January 1938, one of the main emigration organizations, the Aid Society, announced that "up to now, Jewish emigration . . . indicates a severe surplus of men." It blamed this on the "nature" of women to feel closer to family and home and on that of men toward greater adventurousness. It also suggested that couples marry before emigrating, encouraged women to prepare themselves as household helpers, and promised that women's emigration would become a priority. Yet only two months later the Society announced it would expedite the emigration of only those young women who could prove their household skills and were willing to work as domestics abroad.[51] Jewish organizations also provided less support to emigrating women than to men.[52]

That some women and men took the advice to marry before going abroad, or came upon the idea on their own, can be seen from marriage ads in Jewish newspapers. These ads frequently included the requirement that the future spouse be amenable to emigration. For example, in 1936, one woman sought a "marriage partner . . . with the possibility of emigration," while another woman gave the value of her dowry in Swiss francs. A businessman offered a "pretty, healthy, and young woman" the opportunity of emigrating to Palestine together. By 1938, almost every ad announced the desire or ability to emigrate, occasionally boasting "affidavit in hand." Some may have entered into phony marriages before emigrating to Palestine. Since a couple, that is, two people, could enter on one certificate, a quick marriage of convenience, to be continued or broken upon arrival, saved an extra life.[53]

Families were often reluctant to consider Palestine, and the kibbutz, as an alternative for daughters. One survey of graduating classes from several Jewish schools in late 1935 showed that 47 percent of the boys but only 30 percent of the girls aimed for Palestine. Statistics for the first half of 1937 indicate that of those taking advantage of Zionist retraining programs, only 32 percent were female. Overall, fewer single females than males emigrated to Palestine: between 1933 and 1942, 8,209 "bachelors," compared with 5,080 "single" females, entered from German-speaking lands.[54]

Those young women who actually wound up in Palestine preferred the cities. The majority of German-Jewish girls and young women did not take available positions on kibbutzim or in agricultural training centers but rather took jobs as cooks or milliners. Better jobs, such as social workers, kindergarten teachers, and nurses, were much harder to find. While emigration consultants encouraged young women to take up the adventures of kibbutz life, articles appearing on Palestine, often written by committed Zionists, must have given pause. In one such article, the male author described a situation in which eight young women cared for fifty-five young men. They cooked, washed "mountains" of laundry, darned hundreds of socks, and sewed ripped clothing, working long days and into the night. But even more was expected of them. They were to do the emotional housework as well:

> A friendly word at the right time will bring a young man to his senses who once had a dozen shirts ... and now noticed that his last carefully maintained shirt was taken by another. ... Whether the kibbutz thrives is up to the girls! They have to mother one, be a comrade to the other ... and have the endlessly difficult task of always remaining in a good mood [and] smiling.

Such reports, plus the numerous news items regarding Arab-Jewish discord, left most young women looking elsewhere for refuge.[55]

The growing disproportion of Jewish women in the German-Jewish population also came about because, to begin with, there were more Jewish women than men in Germany. In 1933, 52.3 percent of Jews were women, owing to male casualties during World War I, greater marrying out and conversion among Jewish men, and greater longevity among women. In order to stay even, a greater absolute number of women would have had to emigrate. The slower rate of female than male emigration, however, meant that the female proportion of the Jewish population rose from 52.3 percent in 1933 to 57.5 percent by 1939. After the war, one woman wrote:

> Mostly we were women who had been left to ourselves. In part, our husbands had died from shock, partly they had been processed from life to death in a concentration camp and partly some wives who, aware of the greater danger to their husbands, had prevailed upon them to leave at once and alone. They were ready to take care of everything and to follow their husbands later on, but because of the war it became impossible for many to realize this intention and quite a few of my friends and acquaintances thus became martyrs of Hitler.[56]

A large proportion of these remaining women were elderly. Age, even more than being female, worked against timely flight; together they were lethal. Between June 1933 and September 1939, the number of young Jews in Germany under age thirty-nine decreased by about 80 percent. In contrast, the number of Jews over sixty decreased by only 27 percent. As early as 1936, a Jewish woman released from prison for her work in the communist resistance recuperated in a sanatorium. She remarked upon its "dismal milieu": "The guests [were] nearly all old people who had remained behind by themselves. Their children were either in prison camps or in Palestine, the U.S.A., and still farther away. . . . [They] longed for death." By 1939, the proportion of people over sixty had increased to 32 percent of the Jewish population; by 1941, two-thirds of the Jewish population was past middle age. In Berlin alone, the number of old-age homes grew from three in 1933 to thirteen in 1939 and to twenty-one in 1942. Already in 1933, the elderly had consisted of a large number of widows, the ratio being 140 Jewish women over the age of sixty-five to 100 men. By 1937–38, 59 percent of the recipients of Jewish Winter Relief aged forty-five and over were female. In 1939, 6,674 widowed men and 28,347 widowed women remained in the expanded Reich.[57]

In short, in slightly less than eight years and drastically increasing after the November Pogrom, two-thirds of German Jews emigrated (many to European countries where they were later caught up in the Nazi net), leaving a disproportionate number of old people and women. Jewish newspapers featured articles about old women whose children had emigrated, whose living quarters were small, whose help had disappeared, whose finances were meager. Thrown together, sometimes in old-age homes, sometimes as paying guests in the homes of other Jews, these women passed their days reliving memories of better times. Financial worries plagued them, but they were even more tormented by not knowing their children's exact whereabouts or circumstances. They constituted a "community of old people, who supported . . . and consoled each other." When Elisabeth Freund, one of the last Jews to leave Germany legally in October 1941, went to the Gestapo for her final papers, she observed: "All old people, old women" waiting in line.[58]

6

War and the Worsening Situation of Jews

[We're] not afraid of the bombings.... That is a danger we ... share
with ... millions.... We are only afraid of the Gestapo.

— ELISABETH FREUND

Well before the outbreak of World War II, Jews endured warlike conditions.
But after Germany went to war, the Nazis accelerated their economic and
social persecution. The government confiscated Jewish business and personal property and limited food and clothing purchases. It herded Jews
together, tagging them and compelling them to do forced labor, and it
banned Jewish emigration. Jewish women and men shared increasing
deprivations. They also faced frightful bombings and even more dreadful
news of concentration camps. On a daily level, women remained responsible for shopping, making meals stretch, repairing clothing worn to shreds,
organizing their children's schooling and free time, and, even in ghetto
housing, providing a home life and community for their families.

THE IMMEDIATE PREWAR PERSECUTIONS

Restrictions and Responses

While the viciousness of the November Pogrom alerted Jews to the acute
physical dangers of remaining in Germany, the decrees following it put an
end to the hopes of any who might have believed that Jews could continue
to eke out an existence. Economic ordinances after November 9/10, 1938,
prohibited almost all employment and business activity to Jews, forced
"Aryanization" of all remaining Jewish firms and property, demanded a
punitive tax on Jewish assets, and ordered the deposit of cash and other

valuables into blocked accounts controlled by the government. For access to their money, Jews had to apply to the government and bring proof of why they needed it. Thus, Jews had to write for special permission to take their own savings out of these blocked accounts. They had to submit formal requests for funds to buy a new winter coat, pay doctor bills, or pay off old debts. A "control agency" decided whether Jews could withdraw their own money on a regular basis and what amount they might remove. By 1939, when Jews had been excluded from the general welfare system and more than two-thirds of all German Jews had no source of gainful employment, these accounts kept many from sinking into abject poverty.[1] Others managed on Jewish community welfare. Still others subsisted on the starvation wages they received as conscripted labor since the government had decreed, on December 20, 1938, that unemployed Jews who would become burdens on public welfare could be compelled to work (see chapter 7).

"But there were always things that hurt worse than the loss of possessions," wrote one woman, referring to the social isolation she had experienced. Within days of the pogrom, Jews were further segregated: their access to public places, including certain streets, denied; their visits to theaters, movies, concerts, and exhibits prohibited; their public school attendance banned. In January 1939, the government forced Jews to add the name "Israel" or "Sarah" if their first names did not appear on a list of identifiable Jewish names. These names were also inserted in telephone books, announcing a person's racial status to anyone who cared to look. Moreover, the government dissolved all remaining Jewish political organizations. The remaining 213,000 "full" Jews could read the texts of the latest anti-Jewish laws in the heavily censored *Jüdischer Nachrichtenblatt*, the only Jewish paper allowed after the November Pogrom, or could hear the decrees announced in synagogue.[2]

Observant Jews found Nazi contempt for their religion painful to bear. For example, in 1939, the government chose the most sacred day of the Jewish year, Yom Kippur, to confiscate radios owned by Jews. As a result, observant Jews had to miss prayer services and disregard Jewish strictures against working on the holidays as they hauled their bulky, heavy radios to government offices and waited on line to deposit them.

Memoirs describe how the besieged Jews met new restrictions. Ready to emigrate, one couple rented a room at the railroad station hotel but were banned from its restaurant. They "had . . . to take their meals in their bedroom." Fancier hotels, like the Reichshof in Hamburg, pasted small stickers into their room assignment cards asking "guests of the Jewish race" to have their meals in their rooms rather than in the hotel restaurant. The only other restaurants still accepting Jews were at the railroad station. Else and Alfred Gerstel, intent on celebrating their twenty-fifth wedding anniversary in December 1938, finally ate a meal in the waiting room of a Berlin railway station. When they returned home, friends and relatives surprised them with a small party: "Everybody had to bring their own cutlery, as we all had already given up our silverware with the exception of one spoon, one knife, one fork for each person."[3]

Some rules could be circumvented more easily than others. When Jews could no longer buy clothing, many women mended and repaired old garments. For those with money, the black market provided forbidden products. Bribes helped, too. One woman paid a "sympathetic, needy Aryan soul" for clothing stamps (but was stymied when she could not go to a store and purchase the necessary items herself). Jewish communities also helped needy Jews with food and clothing, utilizing the volunteer work of many Jewish women. When, by mid-1940, Jews could no longer own private telephones, they made use of public ones, braving the wrath of some Germans. Elisabeth Freund recalled trying to use a public phone before they, too, were prohibited to Jews in December 1941. She met with the fury of an "Aryan" woman who ripped open the door of the booth and dragged her out, screaming: "We Aryans have to wait. The Jews are always in the booths! Out with the Jews! Out! Out with all Jews from Germany!"[4]

As the Nazis relentlessly restricted the realm in which Jews negotiated their lives, Jews also faced the general pre-war scarcity that began to touch most middle- and working-class Germans. Observers for the Social Democratic Party reported a paucity of raw materials and certain foods as early as 1934. By 1935, they noted shortages of pork, butter, fat, rice, cheese, and eggs, adding that the Nazi Women's Organization was organizing lectures on baking without fat and using ersatz products, and that newspapers were urging husbands to greet the loss of meat and fat "with a friendly face."[5]

Jewish witnesses commented on these general scarcities, often attributing them to the war production rumored to be in progress. Recounting prewar conditions in Frankfurt, Erna Albersheim wrote: "Milk was of poor quality.... The bread was hardly edible.... Rolls were gray.... Onions [were] sold by the piece when the grocer had any. Butter was rationed.... All woolen material had to contain 30 percent wool. We were not allowed to tell our customers that they were not getting pure wool." She drew the conclusion that resources were being diverted from consumer goods to preparations for war. She recounted the joke about a worker in a baby carriage factory who stole parts for his own baby and tried to screw them together at home: "It's awful," he said to his wife, "every time I think I have everything just right, it turns out to be a machine gun."[6]

In late autumn 1938, the chief European correspondent of the *New York Times* visited Berlin, "a city of short rations and straitened friendships." Conditions continued to deteriorate in the spring and summer of 1939 as prices began to rise and the government rationed some foods. In a south German city, it became increasingly difficult to run a household in the months before the war: "I had ... to bring my ration card to the dairy.... Once a week they had ... eggs for 2 hours.... Though not admitted by the authorities there was some inflation already, the food prices had risen a good deal."[7]

Jews encountered not only general prewar scarcity but also an extremely difficult housing situation. During the November Pogrom, many Jews had to leave their homes immediately. Even the tenants of Jewish homes for the aged, bequested by Jews, had to leave within forty-eight hours. They hardly knew where to go, as often their children had already left the country. In April 1939, a "law" permitted "Aryan" landlords to give Jewish tenants immediate notice of eviction, after which Jews could find rooms only with the permission of local authorities. In May the government began to remove Jews who were living among the "Aryan" population by pushing them into *Judenhäuser* ("Jew houses") or forcing them to cram into designated apartments. They had to share overcrowded apartments and even rooms. Some families were able to take in relatives. In Düsseldorf, as the younger members of the family emigrated, Ruth Glaser's grandmother took in her husband's brother and his two sisters.[8] The old people lived together, subject to further deprivation.

Mixed Marriages

Both the November Pogrom and the establishment of *Judenhäuser* prompted the Nazis to further refine their notions of mixed marriages.[9] The excesses of the November Pogrom had caused grumbling among the populace, especially among those who had relatives married to Jews. Also, the establishment of *Judenhäuser* raised the question of whether the "Aryan" partners were to live in houses designated for Jews, and, if so, which "Aryans"? The Nazis decided that as of the end of April 1939, there would be two kinds of mixed marriages. A "privileged" mixed marriage consisted of a mixed couple whose child had been baptized or an "Aryan" man and a Jewish woman, regardless of whether they had offspring. The "nonprivileged" marriage involved an "Aryan" woman and a Jewish man who were childless or an intermarried couple whose child had been enrolled in the

Jewish community as of September 1935. There were far more "privileged" than "nonprivileged" mixed marriages, since children of intermarriages tended to be baptized. "Nonprivileged" couples and families were forced to live in *Judenhäuser,* and the Jewish partner and their children, known as *Geltungsjuden* since the Nuremberg Laws, that is, recognized and treated as Jews, were later forced to wear the Star of David. In contrast, "privileged" couples could remain in their own apartments and the Jewish partner did not wear the star. Although these categories were clearly defined by the state, they were sometimes flexible, adjustable, and corruptible as people tried to have themselves reassigned to the "privileged" category.[10] Also, Nazi officials in small towns did not always understand or acknowledge the requirements involved in each of the categories.

Even before these legal refinements, an August 1938 diary entry of an "Aryan" woman married to a Protestant of Jewish descent described their agony: "We see others living in peace . . . know they do not have to fear the newspaper, decrees, or party conventions and I tremble at everything." She continued: "Every day brings hundreds of pinpricks, humiliations, anxieties." Moreover, many non-Jewish wives tried to maintain their composure to protect their Jewish husbands from the guilt and fear they felt for thrusting their wives into these crises. When the Gestapo came to her home to confiscate her radio, a Christian woman was "distressed but I didn't want to let my husband know because he would always say, 'You have to suffer so much because of me.'" Jochen Klepper, a Protestant clergyman and popular hymn writer married to a Jewish woman, and thus in a "privileged" situation, wrote in February 1939 that "Aryan" women married to Jewish men were "so much more disadvantaged than Jewish women with Aryan husbands. . . . Every misfortune landed on [the "Aryan" women] which we others were spared given the current state of affairs." Once he was forced to wear the Star of David, the philologist Victor Klemperer refused to appear in public with his "Aryan" wife, fearing that she would be insulted by strangers who saw them together.[11]

The Nazi decision to privilege male over female "Aryans" reflected Nazi misogynism and the higher status of males in German society. The "household" was defined by its male head. In addition, "Aryan" men married to Jewish women still served in the military (until they and "first-degree *Mischlinge*" were banned in April 1940, the month Germany invaded Denmark and Norway), and the Nazis feared that the morale of these men would suffer if their families were treated like Jews. In addition, Nazi leaders may have assumed that women were passive but that men would protest their own forced transfer—or that of their wives and children—into a

Judenhaus. Finally, the Nazis probably transformed into racial law the sexist German legal practice regarding marriages with foreigners: when German women married foreigners, they lost their German citizenship, but when German men married foreigners, their wives became German citizens. In other words, German women lost their blood ties to the *Volk* when they married "out," and Jewish women gained some protection from being "incorporated" when they married "in."[12]

OUTBREAK OF WAR

Curfews, Rations, and Judenhäuser

Even before the war, Jews had experienced social death in German society. The Nazis had expropriated them, forced them to do hard labor, and almost completely segregated them. The war itself provided the occasion for massive isolation, expulsion, and ultimate annihilation. The government continually expanded its persecution, from subjecting Jews to a profusion of bans, to marking them with the Star of David, to deportation and death. Although various government organs passed 229 anti-Jewish decrees from the November Pogrom until the outbreak of war, another 525 decrees tormented Jews between the outbreak of war and the "Final Solution."[13]

On January 30, 1939, Hitler made a speech predicting the destruction of the Jewish "race" in the event of a world war. On September 1, 1939, Germany unleashed the war. The government placed a curfew on all Jews: 8 P.M. in winter and 9 P.M. in summer. Although by this time few Jews ventured out after dark anyway, these legal restrictions magnified their social isolation. They prevented Jews even from visiting friends after a long day's work. Some people disobeyed the curfews, but they ran grave risks doing so. Rolf Kralovitz defied the curfew often, attending his beloved, and also forbidden, opera. His anxious mother spent evenings worrying about how she would cover for him if the Gestapo suddenly inspected their *Judenhaus* to check that all residents had obeyed the curfew: "Although my mother was happy that I was interested in opera ... she was very worried when I returned home late from the performance."[14]

The issue of food plagued Jews far more than that of curfews. The government imposed food rationing on all Germans on August 28, 1939, three days before Germany started the war. Although rationing was neither strict nor comprehensive during the early war years, as the war dragged on the government cut fat, sugar, potato, and (ersatz) coffee allotments. From a prewar average of 3,000 calories per person per day, "normal consumer" intake gradually dropped to about 2,000 calories by 1944. Thus, official food rations to "Aryan" consumers did not fall below subsistence until late in the war. Even then, "the looting of a continent (and the government's concern about the hunger in World War I being repeated) made sure that German rations were by far the highest in Europe." For Jews, but not for "first-degree *Mischlinge*," caloric intake plummeted immediately.[15]

Starting in 1939, the government limited when and where Jews could shop. In some cities, the stores accessible to Jews charged them more than other consumers. Jews (mostly women) had to go to special offices for their ration cards stamped with the word *Jew*, while "Aryans" received their ration cards at home from their block warden. The government also cut food rations, leading to malnutrition and disease. Jews received less meat and butter than "Aryans" and no cocoa or rice. The government continually reduced the list of foods available to Jews. By January 1940, rationing for Jews became more stringent, as they were denied legumes, most fruit, and meat. Only Jews who did heavy labor were still allotted 200 grams of meat per week, compared with "Aryans" doing heavy labor who received 1,000 grams per week. The only recourse, for those with means, was the growing black market in foodstuffs. Others occasionally bartered with friends or, more rarely, received a handout from a compassionate "Aryan."[16]

Many Jews feared starvation almost as much as they feared the Gestapo. The dire food situation of the Klemperers, a "nonprivileged" mixed couple, illustrates the plight of many Jews, although, with relatively more "Aryan" contacts, the Klemperers were probably better off than most "full" Jews. In his diary, Klemperer noted how gaunt his friends looked, how much weight they had lost, and how he and his wife Eva never satisfied their own hunger at mealtime. When they visited friends to exchange food, his wife, the "Aryan," carried the "pure Aryan vegetables"—such as asparagus—for which Victor Klemperer would have been imprisoned. By the second year of the war, the search for food sometimes caused Eva Klemperer to hunt from early morning until late at night. They bartered with other Jews, and did favors and extra chores in return for food from those who had a bit more. By August 1942, as deportations were progressing, Klemperer noted his own "typical hunger stomach," swollen like a "drum." He regularly stole potatoes and bread from one of his *Judenhaus* neighbors. He rationalized his behavior by recording that non-Jewish relatives were providing her with so much extra food that it was spoiling. By the war's end, he and his wife were surviving on food they had begged from non-Jewish friends and he had "hallucinated" a decent meal.[17]

Jews were usually restricted to only one hour of shopping per day. Such restrictions were much more cruel than apparent at first glance, and they affected Jewish women, who did most of the shopping, disproportionately. First, most able adults worked the entire day. In Breslau, where Jews could shop only between 11 A.M. and 1 P.M., these rules made shopping nearly impossible. In Berlin, where shopping took place between 4 and 5 P.M., Jews raced to the nearest store after work. Second, supermarkets, as we know them today, were nonexistent: "shopping" involved running to the baker, the butcher, and the greengrocer. There were usually long lines and short stock, and Jews had to wait behind all "Aryan" customers or shop in stores designated for Jews. Stores ran out of food well before everyone had bought their share. Thus, Jews often had to run to yet another store or return the following day. With luck, a decent grocer might set some food aside for a Jewish customer who had left off a shopping list earlier in the day.[18]

The list of forbidden foods regularly grew longer. In 1941, in addition to the already prohibited foods, it included canned foods, fish, poultry, smoking goods, coffee, and milk, even skim milk. Jews could no longer buy apples or tomatoes and were limited to particular vegetables. When a shortage of potatoes developed, stores displayed signs stating: "Foods in Short Supply Are Not Sold to Jews." Jewish parents could purchase milk only as long as their children were small. Jewish children could not purchase candy or even artificial honey. Food prohibitions were enforced not only by merchants. Even if one managed to acquire some forbidden goods on the black market, it was dangerous to store them. The Gestapo conducted sporadic house searches to make sure that Jews were not hiding forbidden foods.[19]

To exacerbate matters, "Aryan" women often appointed themselves guardians of the food pantry. For example, an enthusiastic Berlin Nazi regularly terrified a neighboring Jewish child. The little girl, on her way to the grocer, "came out of our entrance with a shopping bag. This woman stood right in front of it. Diagonally across from us hung the pharmacist's large round clock. It was shortly before 4 and she said, 'You're not allowed to go shopping yet, I won't let you out of here.'" Erna Becker-Kohen, in a "privileged" mixed marriage, tried sending her small son for milk in her Berlin neighborhood: "The women railed mercilessly that the Jew-woman had sent her child shopping when she is forbidden to do so; therefore they don't want to wait on the little fellow anymore.... Even mothers have no empathy." Like other Jews, she attempted to shop in another part of town where she was not as easily recognized and confronted less often, except for occasional comments about her dark hair and dark eyes.[20]

Once Jews were forced to wear the Star of David, trying to shop at off-hours or in stores not designated for Jews meant removing the star and, hence, gambling with one's life. In Leipzig, one Jewish woman who had taken off her star in order to shop noticed the Gestapo entering. Dreading a search, she quickly grabbed the star and tried to swallow it, choking to death. Similar incidents occurred in Berlin:

> In Oranienburger Street, I saw a Jewish woman who had been denounced by a Nazi woman because she allegedly bought some groceries with a "non-Jewish" card. Terrified, this poor woman put the card in her mouth and swallowed it in the presence of the police who took her to the station house. Our friend, Lotti Fischer, from Berlin Pankow, was denounced because she bought milk with "Aryan" cards for her sick mother. She, her mother, and brother were deported [and] her property was confiscated by the state.[21]

By 1940, the government prevented Jews from buying shoes, lingerie, and clothing. Nor could they buy the material with which to make or darn clothing or repair their shoes. Moreover, public laundries were off-limits to Jews, and only designated Jewish shoemakers were permitted to repair the shoes of Jews. Even teenagers could not buy clothing and had to wear threadbare and noticeably outgrown garments. In Hamburg, in June 1939, one destitute mother managed to acquire a new winter coat for her growing son from the Jewish community. Thereafter, the community provided one pair of shoes for him in May 1940, exchanged his coat for a used one, and allowed him to have his shoes repaired for the last time in January 1941. By 1942, needy Jews sometimes received the hand-me-downs of neighbors who had committed suicide or had been summoned for deportation. Receiving such clothing was patently illegal, since the government confiscated all Jewish property.[22]

In addition to making food and clothing scarce for Jews, the Nazis turned Jews into refugees within Germany. Government agencies forced Jews out of their homes and into new ones on short notice and kept them moving from one place to another. Jews had to sell more furniture with each successive move into tighter and tighter quarters. Often an entire family was squeezed into a small room; sometimes complete strangers were jammed together. The poet Gertrud Kolmar, sharing an apartment with her father and several strangers, wrote her sister: "Since my bed is in the dining area, I actually have no refuge anymore, no space to myself, and the feeling of homelessness . . . has grown ever more powerful." Also, the new lodgings left to Jews were underheated and delapidated. In the winter, frost formed inside the rooms, since fuel deliveries were never adequate. Usually in old buildings, the rooms were often infested. Ruth Klüger wrote of the dark, insect-ridden room she shared with her mother: "You turn off the light and imagine the bugs crawling out of the mattresses. Then you get bitten, turn on the light and wail loudly, because the disgusting vermin are actually walking around in the bed."[23]

In Berlin, Jews received five days' notice to evacuate their apartments and were allowed to rent rooms only in houses still owned by Jews. They had to search frantically for new apartments while still showing up for their long shifts at forced labor. In Leipzig, the Nazis forced a widow, whose four children had emigrated but whose own attempts had met with failure, to leave her apartment in April 1940 for a one-room sublet. In February 1941, they compelled her to leave that room for an unheated sublet, and in September they made her move into a room in a *Judenhaus,* which she shared with a stranger. These moves preceded the final one, to Riga, from which she never returned.[24]

By 1943, most of the few remaining Jews lived in *Judenhäuser,* the last stop before their deportation. In some cities these houses were located in a single neighborhood, concentrating Jews in a ghetto-like area. Indeed, Jews who lived there often referred to it as a "ghetto." Most of these houses accommodated only Jewish families. Some, however, separately housed "nonprivileged" mixed marriages and Jewish members of mixed marriages (particularly those in which the "Aryan" spouse had died or had divorced the Jewish spouse), while others lumped them together with all-Jewish families.[25]

An integral part of daily life in many *Judenhäuser* was the dreaded "spot checks" by the Gestapo to search for forbidden food and to make sure that the Star of David was tightly sewn on clothing. In Dresden, these "spot checks" were in reality mini-pogroms. The Gestapo, spitting at residents and hitting them, regularly burst into Jewish apartments, destroyed whatever furniture or bedding was left, and stole money and food. Rejecting the taboo against hurting old people, especially women, Gestapo agents kicked, slapped, or punched elderly women or smeared their faces and clothing with food. In 1942, Gestapo members attacked women between the ages of seventy and eighty-five in Dresden's Jewish old-age home. Jews lived in terror on the streets and at home. "Fear and hunger fill the day," wrote Victor Klemperer in June 1942: "Will I be beaten up and spat at today?"[26] For the people in his *Judenhaus,* daily life had degenerated into a state of perpetual fear.

The inability of many Jews to find adequate living quarters did not concern the government, which considered barracks acceptable. In Cologne, for example, the Nazis forced 2,000 Jews to relinquish residences owned by non-Jews. Given three days' notice, the Jews moved into barracks erected for Russian prisoners of war during World War I. Klara Caro wrote:

> They reminded me of the Roman catacombs, except that here it was a matter of sheltering living human beings, not dead ones. Due to the dripping water, the damp odor of mold spread. Everything needed to serve the most primitive needs was missing. . . . 20 persons . . . crammed together in one room. Everyone could bring along a bed, table and chair, that meant separating from the last things to which one was attached. All other remaining possessions were expropriated by the Gestapo. How touching it was, that those affected understood, even in this miserable little spot, that it was within their power to smuggle in something tasteful, whether a vase with a flower, a colorful cloth, a small picture.

In Dresden, those crammed together considered themselves lucky, especially after deportations started: "It was not Poland, it was not a concentration camp!"[27]

Despite the dire situation of Jews in *Judenhäuser* and barracks, the cacophony of voices and the impossibility of privacy, Jews living there created a community of connection and concern, some even finding a new "extended family." Holding on to their bourgeois values and way of life was a matter of integrity and identity, of resistance against "Aryan" dehumanization. Jews shared and bartered food with each other, consoled each other after the arrests of friends and family members, gave gifts and services. No longer integrated into German neighborhoods and no longer allowed to frequent German shops, ride on public transportation,[28] or work with German workers, most "full" Jews were spared much of the public enmity they had previously faced and could aid and comfort each other. In Dresden, an elderly woman left a suicide note to the members of her *Judenhaus* thanking them deeply for their "heartfelt courtesy" toward her while she lived there. Her careful words exemplify most of these relationships: not chosen friendships but bonds forged out of necessity and commiseration. Else Behrend-Rosenfeld, in charge of the 320 Munich Jews crammed into the barracks at Berg am Laim, commended the internees:

> Orthodox and Liberals, those baptized as Catholic and Protestant, the for-
> merly rich and poor, the highly educated and those from very simple
> social circles had to live and get along with each other. And, naturally, not
> everyone demonstrated good will. . . . we did our best to mediate, and then
> it became clear . . . that we had been successful . . . : In Berg am Laim we
> had become a true community.

Parents continued, even with limited means, to provide some of the remnants of bourgeois education for their children. Anneliese Winterberg
fondly recalled the six months of piano lessons she received as a child in
Bonn, where 474 Jews were squeezed into a former cloister during their last
months before deportation. Only 9 ultimately survived. In some *Judenhäuser,* younger residents created a small theater and staged performances.
In Leipzig, teenagers gathered to listen to a forbidden gramophone that
belonged to an "Aryan" woman married to a Jewish man. They danced to
old records on Sundays: "We were more carefree than the adults, who suffered greatly from the persecution."[29]

While most turned to their community for social support, many also
turned to religion for moral sustenance. In these years, Rabbi Joseph
Carlebach received hundreds of questions regarding Jewish ritual and
Jewish law, with the queries to him increasing dramatically as other rabbis
fled. Thus, even as the situation deteriorated around him, his wife, and
children, he felt compelled to stay on to serve the religious needs of the
remaining Jews in Germany. As late as the winter of 1943, regular prayer
services continued in Hamburg, and the community had built a new *mikvah* (ritual bath). In Bonn, regular religious services took place in the
Judenhaus, including a wedding right before a deportation, and outside
Munich, Orthodox Jews prayed in the cloister of a nunnery where they had
been herded.

Memoirs and letters do not dwell on religious life in the *Judenhäuser,*
perhaps because religious Jews took their observance so much for granted
that remarking on it would have seemed superfluous. Even Salomon
Samuel, a rabbi, rarely mentions more than a passing "Sabbath" in his
letters. Yet documentation exists that the Sabbath and holidays were
commemorated even in the Jewish Hospital in Berlin—which may be
characterized as the last official residence of Jews in Germany. Furthermore, a description of Jews from Cologne conducting a Passover Seder in
the Theresienstadt concentration camp suggests that such observances
surely took place in the less horrifying atmosphere of the *Judenhaus.* In
Theresienstadt in 1943, Rabbi Caro gathered between twenty and thirty

people in a room intended for five. There were no chairs, so the women and men sat on the floor.

> The Seder plate consisted [of] a carrot, a little bit of [inedible] green, a bone and salt water.... The Rabbi ... celebrated the Seder, reading the *Haggadah* and a *Chasen* [cantor] from Prague ... chanted the well-known songs. It belonged to the satanic tricks of the Nazis, that on Jewish holidays they invented special cruel punishments. So all of a sudden the lights went out.... But the Rabbi went on saying the *Haggadah* by heart.... Never [had] "Leschana Habaa Bejerushalayim" [Hebr. for "next year in Jerusalem"] been said with more fervor."[30]

The Star of David

From September 19, 1941, on, Jews over the age of six had to identify themselves by wearing a large yellow Star of David with the word *Jew* (*Jude*) written in black, Hebrew-like letters on it. The *Judenstern*, as it was dubbed by the Nazis (Jews more often referred to it with the more respectful *Davidstern*, while some ironically dubbed it "der Orden pour le sémite," the Semite's medal), had to be securely sewn onto garments and worn on the left side of the chest. Jews had to pay ten pfennigs for each star—"a lot of money" to many—and needed several stars to assure that all their outerwear was marked. Even bridal couples had to wear the star, the bride on her wedding dress.[31]

The introduction of the star signaled a new stage in persecution. "This was the most difficult day in the twelve years of hell," according to Victor Klemperer. Every person wearing a star "carried his ghetto with him, like a snail its house." With the yellow star blazing from their coats, Jews could be identified, vilified, and attacked with impunity. Those who had earlier dared to circumvent shopping rules, limitations on public transport, or restrictions on entertainment could no longer do so unless they removed their star. This was a severe crime; even a loose star could be cause for sending its wearer to a concentration camp.

The Star of David affected Germans as well, blatantly confronting them with Jewish misery. Until its introduction, and with the exception of the November Pogrom, the Nazis had discriminated against Jews with measures that other Germans could claim not to see or could quickly forget. For example, after the decrees that forbade Jews from attending public entertainment, Jews simply "disappeared" from audiences. When the government blocked the wealth of Jews, few Germans, besides the bureaucrats and bankers responsible, took notice. Of course, shopkeepers knew the rules limiting purchases by Jews; neighbors watched Jews emigrate or saw them evicted; and children joined in the harassment of Jewish peers at school and saw their eventual expulsion. The yellow star, however, did not just brand Jews but revealed who was left. Many, having promoted and become accustomed to the social death of the Jews, were surprised that "so many" Jews were still around. Some Germans responded with shock or sympathy, others with embarrassment. Although there were occasional out-bursts of hostility against the "star bearers" (*Sternträger*), most Germans remained indifferent. Some strangers stuck cigarettes, fruit, or other tokens of sympathy into the pockets of Jews, while others moved away from them, shouted at them, or looked through them. That Jews were easily identifiable was now woven into the daily lives of Jewish and non-Jewish Germans.[32]

Jews themselves, according to Ruth Klüger, often date the moment they had to begin wearing the star further back than the actual event: "That is because the isolation of Jews was already in full swing before September 1941." Unlike most other Jews, she continued, "I can't say that I did not want to wear the Jewish star. Under the circumstances it seemed appropri-ate." Most Jews, however, felt the full torment intended. A sixteen-year-old boy "felt naked. . . . The star seemed as big as a plate and to weigh a ton."[33] Some tried to hide the star by holding a briefcase or shopping bag in front of it—also a punishable offense.

The most courageous or rash—depending on whether or not they were caught—were those who ventured out without their star. Inge Deutsch-kron was such a quick-change artist. She would

> duck into a doorway, take off my coat, and put on the jacket without a star that I carried with me. It was not an entirely risk-free procedure. If an informer were to see me, I would suffer the same fate as those whom the Gestapo stopped on the street to check whether their star was sewn on tightly enough. . . . I went through my coat-changing routine often, not only because Jews were barred from using public transportation except when going to and from work, but also because our grocer would not have been able to wait on us if I had come in wearing the star. . . . And of course I continued to go to concerts and the movies and theater. . . . not wearing the star made life much more bearable.

To spare loved ones pain or worry, some Jews even hid the star from each other. One Jewish grandmother, whose daughter in a "privileged" mixed marriage and grandson did not have to wear the star, removed her coat with the star on it before she entered the child's room.[34]

The Nazis marked not only people. After March 1942 Jewish homes also had to display a Star of David—probably to facilitate the roundups of Jews. In Hamburg, for example, Jews had to place a Star of David near their names at the entrance to their building foyer. If a non-Jew lived in the apartment, too, then each tenant had to hang a separate nameplate and put a star by the Jewish name.[35]

Even before the imposition of stars, many Jews had already been recognized as such by their non-Jewish neighbors. Even Jews in "privileged" mixed marriages, who did not have to place a star on their clothing or residences, were shunned by "Aryan" neighbors, who sometimes reported them to the Gestapo. In Krefeld, for example, neighbors complained that Jews were gathering in the home of an "Aryan" man married to a Jewish woman. The husband explained that his wife had many relatives in town and that these were visits by relatives, not meetings. Still, he had to promise that the visits would cease. Neighbors then proclaimed that the couple had acquired illegal furniture. Luckily, the couple could prove that the old clothing and chest of drawers which they had recently received were legally inherited from the wife's sister. Other neighbors informed the Gestapo that the couple had ten baptized, Catholic children. Four had been born after the Nuremberg Laws, thus giving the local party leader pause: "We have no interest in having even more half-Jews result from this marriage."[36]

Erna Becker-Kohen found similarly hateful neighbors in Berlin. When the Germans invaded Poland, her "Aryan" husband worried that in their war frenzy, the neighbors might beat his wife and child to death. As a result, he brought them to a convent. Sadly, they remained there for only a few weeks because another guest refused to live near a Jew, and a nun, who "felt very German," did not want to encounter the mother and child either. Becker-Kohen noted that no one even sympathized with her baby son. Upon their return home, a loyal priest visited her and "the old lady who lives under our apartment opened [her door] in order to look him over from head to toe. He just stood there cheerfully and asked her for permission to look at her just as closely." When she left her small son outside a store for a moment that following summer, neighborhood boys threw stones at him. By early 1942, another priest walked her home from church because he worried that her neighbors would hurt her. She commented:

> To be sure, we live in a completely "respectable" neighborhood, where many upstanding civil servant families live, yet as good National Socialists they do not believe they should leave the Jewish women in peace. Their hatred is boundless. When these people think they can cast their good upbringing aside, they are surely even more dangerous than the gangsters around the Alexanderplatz.

Becker-Kohen's neighbors, unfortunately, did not have a monopoly on odious behavior. In October 1941, the members of her Catholic church choir refused any longer to sing with a "Jew." This was not an isolated incident. Some churches asked converts to sit on separate benches, others asked them not to attend services so that other Christians would not be deterred from coming to church, and still others discussed separate services.[37]

THE BOMBINGS: POPULAR AND JEWISH ATTITUDES

During the war, popular attitudes increasingly hardened toward the Jews. The Allied bombings began in late 1940 and intensified the following years, with the heaviest raids on Berlin escalating after August 1943. As bombings took their toll, the government repeatedly pinned blame for the war on the Jews, dubbing the bombings "Jewish sky terror." The war became the "Jewish war." Primed by antisemitic propaganda since 1933, the population was quick to pick up this theme. Even many who disliked or opposed the Nazis were confused or infected by the atmosphere. "The Jews are responsible for this," proclaimed Lilly Wust in March 1943, surveying the rubble around her home in Berlin. This same Lily Wust helped to hide her Jewish lover and aided other Jews in hiding. Victor Klemperer reported that after enduring air-raid attacks with workers who opposed the war, one declared, "They are getting rich as a result of this war, these few swinish Jews [*Saujuden*]. It really is the 'Jewish war.'" Disheartened, Klemperer concluded, "None were Nazis, but all were poisoned."[38]

Germans as well as Jews were required to hide in bomb shelters. Of course, Jews were segregated from "Aryans"—isolated in dark, cramped spaces. Elisabeth Freund recorded: "There are ... punishments if one does not come.... In our building, as everywhere, there are separate air-raid shelters for Aryans and Jews. The Aryan shelter is large and roomy, so that a number of beds and couches can be placed there. The Jewish shelter is so small and crowded that we can only sit." It was in these shelters that some Germans chose to vent their antisemitism on nearby Jews. Even though she remained in a secluded section of the shelter, Erna Becker-Kohen and her child were taunted by their German neighbors. She wrote: "I fear the people more than the bombs."[39]

Uncomfortable shelters and hateful neighbors were relatively minor issues for Jews during the bombings. Already exhausted from forced labor, long nights in bomb shelters drained them terribly. Elisabeth Freund wrote: "It is totally impossible to sleep there. . . . Heavy labor, and then to sit in the shelter for five, six hours." Assuming that if she continued to endure sleepless nights she would fall ill, she asked a doctor to certify that she was too sickly to go to the shelter. Also, the fright of nearby hits and the danger to their own lives did not leave them unconcerned.[40] Jews observed the blackout rules set up for air raids, letting down heavy shutters, draping their lamps with black paper. Many Jews lost their homes and remaining few possessions. The crippled Jewish communities tried to alleviate immediate needs. In Hamburg, where Jews suffered greatly from the bombings, the Jewish community set up special offices to help those in desperate straits, collected furniture and clothing donated by Jews fleeing the country, and distributed the goods to bombing victims.[41]

Exhaustion and fear notwithstanding, the anonymity of the bombings came as a relief to Jews who dreaded more personal attacks. Ruth Fleischer recalled: "The war's outbreak was something else altogether from Crystal Night because Crystal Night touched our personal life as Jews. . . . I took the war indifferently because it was a general circumstance." Although Jews suffered and died in the bombings, these attacks threatened Jewish lives in an arbitrary manner; the deportations threatened them in a far more direct and systematic one. Thus, when postwar Germans recalled the Nazi era, they emphasized the horrors of the bombings. Jews, on the other hand, did not stress the bombings either during or after the war. They dreaded the Gestapo far more. Freund remarked: "I'm not afraid of the bombings, even if it isn't exactly pleasant, and one never knows whether one will survive until the next morning. That is a danger we . . . share with many millions. . . . We are only afraid of the Gestapo."

Most important for Jews, the bombings held out hope. They were signs of a possible German defeat and the end of the Nazi nightmare. Fleischer continued: "I thought that perhaps this war would bring us luck and be our rescue."[42]

JEWISH SOCIAL LIFE IN WARTIME

By the beginning of the war, most families were already split apart and scattered in many directions. Jews who got out with their children left behind elderly parents or widowed mothers, while others could not escape but managed, at least, to send their children to safety. Elisabeth Freund commented on the fate of Jewish families:

> There is hardly a Jewish family left that hasn't been violently torn apart, whose members have not been scattered over the entire world, parents without their children, wives without their husbands. . . . And all without news of one another, without knowing whether their relatives are still alive in the concentration camps.

Trapped in Germany, the elderly were intensely lonely. In 1940, a mother wrote her grown son of a dream:

> Last night I had a wonderful dream. Walter, you appeared in person, took both of my hands in yours and said: "Why are your fingers so rough?" "That's from all the housework," I said and then you stroked my two little fingers. It was the first time that I dreamed of one of my children and saw them so alive before me. I was very happy.[43]

Children left behind found little respite from the harshness of daily life. In Breslau, a rare trip to a candy machine on the Goethestrasse brought cheer. Even before the war, children had wondered how they were "supposed to concentrate in school when things were so bad at home." Now school itself was full of distractions as new students appeared, old students disappeared, and teachers vanished without a word. Even Lotte Kaliski, who had founded and directed the school that bore her name, had to sneak out of the country without saying good-bye to the children and to most of the teachers.[44] The beginning of deportations in October 1941 made the situation more dreadfully unstable. In Vienna, Ruth Klüger noted that what mattered in school was who had been "picked up" (i.e., deported) and who had gone into hiding or could still flee the country: "You came into the class and looked around. Perhaps those who were absent were ill, more likely one would never see their faces again." As the number of students and teachers dwindled, schools closed down and the remaining children were crammed into another school—and yet another. The new classrooms became increasingly more dilapidated, just as the children's clothing got thinner and more shabby.[45]

Most parents worked as forced laborers in factories and had no one to care for their children after school or during school vacations. "Where was one to put these poor, overly nervous children, who after these last years with their terrible experiences needed a holiday rest especially badly?" wondered Elisabeth Freund. In past years, Jewish school administrators had organized excursions into the forests, but it was no longer possible to use public transportation. Even if they could have, parents worried that the children might be attacked by rowdies. In addition, in 1941 the Gestapo forbade Jews from taking excursions in the forests. Parks had been forbidden even longer. Even at the Jewish day care centers, neighbors objected to noise if the children played outdoors. The Jewish community finally came up with a solution: "transforming every free spot in the Jewish cemeteries into playgrounds with sand boxes for the smaller children." The bigger children could weed the graves. In this way the children got some fresh air and stayed busy. In addition, the graves remained in good repair, something for which no extra Jewish workers were available and which, inexplicably, had been demanded by the Gestapo. Freund wrote: "That is what things have come to now: In Germany the cemeteries are not only the final resting place for the old people, but also the only spot where Jewish children can play."[46]

As if school and leisure time were not frustrating enough, teens who completed their education found life at forced labor even more disheartening. Unlike the "Aryan" apprentices, Jewish teens learned nothing. They were supposed to remain unskilled laborers. Even the few teens who attended Jewish vocational schools faced restricted instruction because of limits set on Jews. One woman reported on her experiences between October 1940 and September 1941, learning to be a cook: "You can imagine that at this time, when Jews had limited access to food, we received no regular cooking instruction.... When I look at my ... report card, [and see] that we learned to cook for special *diets,* I have to laugh, we were *always* on a diet back then!"[47]

High-strung children or teens could not retreat to peaceful homes since parents, too, suffered enormous stress. Ruth Klüger recalls that "death, not sex was the secret about which grown-ups whispered, about which one would have liked to have heard more." She would feign sleep, listening with rapt attention to the horror stories the adults shared. She wondered why parents kept stories about deaths from children, "since there was nothing else worth talking about." Moreover, she realized that most children understood on some level what threatened them: "On the street below, Nazi rascals ran around with their small pointed daggers and sang the song about Jewish blood spurting from the knife. One didn't have to be very clever to understand, rather it took more than minor mental acrobatics to misunderstand."[48]

Families could neither prevent nor remedy the mental illness that

A rare photo of a bridal couple wearing the Star of David. The government required Jews to wear the star on September 19, 1941, and confiscated their cameras on November 13, 1941. This photo and other documents were hidden by Heinz Zaspel, a non-Jewish plumber, given him by Gabriel Nathensen, possibly a friend or relative of the couple. No one ever returned to claim the mementos from Mr. Zaspel. In Lange, Davidstern und Weihnachtsbaum *courtesy of the Forum Verlag, Leipzig.*

resulted from this kind of terror. Hapless souls might turn to non-Jewish psychiatric professionals, since Jews could no longer practice. These "Aryan" doctors showed little sympathy or understanding. In fact, some of them were involved in the Nazis' euthanasia program. When a Hamburg Jewish woman complained to a doctor that people treated her "like the worst swine" and wanted to kill her, he treated her for paranoia and depression. The doctor commented in her files: "Full of hypochondriacal fears." She was deported a year later.[49]

Despite the failure of families to stave off disaster, many Jews still clung to traditional notions of marriage and family. Jews continued to marry until their own deportations—perhaps as a form of silent protest or defiance, perhaps determined to survive, or die, with a committed partner. In November 1941, Hermann Samter, an official in the Berlin Jewish Community, wrote: "Characteristic for the present time is not only the high number of suicides (among us), but even more the flood of marriages. Shortly before our end, almost every relationship leads to marriage." His last letter, of February 7, 1943, announced that he had just married his fiancée in order to prevent her imminent deportation. In a stroke of luck, he got permission both to marry her and then to free her from the assembly point at the Grosse Hamburgerstrasse. Shortly thereafter, they were both deported and murdered.[50]

Although rare, pregnancies have also been documented. Elisabeth Freund noticed that several of her forced labor coworkers were pregnant. She wondered about this:

> First, there are hardly any contraceptives available anymore, and they are very expensive. But then, having children is probably contagious, the result of the endless propaganda for large families. After all, there's nothing more beautiful than a healthy, laughing baby. All the Aryan women have some, and are always having more, and talk incessantly about their children. In this hopelessness, the Jewish women, who no longer have anything else, at least want to have a child . . . so that their life has some meaning. Even if they have to leave the child in an institution to be cared for during the week, at least there is some joy in their dreary existence.

When one Jewish woman miscarried after lifting heavy crates, her coworkers expressed differing opinions:

> Some find the situation dreadful, the others say it is better this way, what's to become of a Jewish child in Germany, the mother would just have to

put it in an institution immediately. The Aryan supervisor expressed her opinion as follows: " ... it is surely better this way for you and the child." ... I could not ... get it out of my head. ... It's about [the fact] that in this country, where so many children are born ... even *one* Jewish child more is a misfortune. With this, judgment is passed on all of us.[51]

Ruth Abraham, who delivered her baby in December 1942, desired to have a child despite the frightful conditions she endured: "As improbable as it sounds, in spite of everything I wanted to have a child at this time, and I as well as my parents were overjoyed when this happened and I became pregnant." Her husband, on the other hand, "was very depressed during the entire pregnancy. I tried to encourage him."[52] When her sister's family was deported, she and her husband abandoned their own apartment in the same neighborhood in terror that they would be next. They tore off their stars and sought refuge with their one remaining relative. Suddenly Abraham's labor pains began. To avoid endangering the relative, the couple returned to their own apartment, telephoning a midwife and Jewish doctor from a booth on the street. Her husband attended her throughout the night of labor. The doctor arrived as the baby's head appeared. He delivered the baby but not the afterbirth, fleeing as an air-raid alarm blared. The Abrahams immediately brought the infant girl to an "Aryan" woman who had offered to care for her, and they began their life in hiding.[53]

Some Jews and "Aryans" also continued to court each other, as the cases of "race defilement" in Gestapo files show. They became secretly "engaged," considered themselves "married," and sometimes even covertly lived together. One couple displayed real ingenuity. In 1942, a Catholic priest secretly married Chorazy, an "Aryan" man, and Leonie Werner, a *"Misch-ling"* who was in hiding. In 1943, Chorazy legally married Leonie's widowed "Aryan" mother. Then the two young people could live together (with the mother) without neighbors suspecting them of "race defilement." They had two children whom they had to hide. Others also had babies. For example, one "first-degree *Mischling*" lived with his "Aryan" girlfriend illegally because their marriage had been prohibited. They feared being denounced by neighbors for "race defilement" and so led circumspect lives. When his "wife" was about to deliver their baby, he brought her to the hospital but could not claim to be the father. He paced the streets unable to acknowledge his wife or child: "Then I was struck by the thought that I was about to become a father and I began to cry bitterly."[54]

Most Jews turned exclusively to each other, with family and friends providing sources of sustenance, information, and evaluation. Even after

March 1942, when Jews could no longer ride public transportation, thus limiting visits to each other, Ilse Rewald and her husband walked over an hour to visit her brother-in-law, who had invited them to a house concert. Young singles also sought each other's company. As late as 1942, some young Berliners met to dance to recordings, mostly of the fox-trot, at the home of a friend. There were few refreshments because of meager rations, and the group had to disband before the 8 P.M. curfew for Jews. The elderly were the most isolated. In January 1939, sixty-six-year-old Gertrud Grossmann reported to her son abroad: "We live entirely cut off from the world around us." Two years later, she wrote that she no longer saw friends because she and they hardly left their homes.[55]

Of course, Jews shared bad news with each other, an increasingly depressing pastime: "One was never free from the terrible discussions about the war and our own fate. . . . Each one told terrible new stories; they were unbearable, and unfortunately most were not exaggerated." Still, a sense of solidarity in misery prevailed: "Each one trembled with the others' news . . . which added to our own misfortune. Self-sacrificing friendships and a readiness to help each other arose which only perilous times and a merging of fates can create."[56]

The few who retained non-Jewish friends found them a source of solace and aid. Ilse Rewald stressed the solidarity of "our Christian friends." They still visited her and her husband at night, even after the Rewalds had to mark their residence with a star. Some brought food. Ultimately, they helped the Rewalds survive in hiding. Elisabeth Freund recalled (around May 1941) that such friendships were encouraging but also mutually burdensome:

> When we are together with Aryans . . . we are supposed to explain things because after all they know nothing of our difficulties. That upsets us and is just as hard on the listener. . . . We know enough who feel the treatment of Jews in Germany is a terrible disgrace. It is like a curse that sticks to us; being together with us must be torture for our Aryan friends.[57]

What often struck Jews about the Germans they encountered was how little they seemed to know or admitted to knowing about the extremes of official antisemitism. Freund recalled an exchange in which a saleswoman asked why she was buying steel cutlery. Freund explained that Jews could no longer own silverware. The reaction was anger: "How can you tell me this? I'll never, ever believe it! . . . I will always love and admire my Führer! Even if all the Jews want to tear him down. He is my Führer, he is the greatest person of our age!" More often, Germans reacted with surprise, whether feigned or real. In April 1942, Victor Klemperer noted that a German had commented to a Jewish friend: "I see many more Jews on the streets of late." He had no idea that Jews could no longer take trams and were being forced to walk long distances. Klemperer's own close friend, an "Aryan" woman who stored his diaries at great risk, offered to buy furniture from him well after Jews were forbidden to sell their own property. As late as June 1944, an "Aryan" factory worker wished Klemperer an enjoyable summer. When he responded that he avoided long walks because of the yellow star, she rejoined, "Then I wouldn't wear it outdoors!" She was surprised when he informed her that such an infraction could cost him his life.[58]

"Aryan" obliviousness impressed Jews, but not as much as "Aryan" complaints about their *own* suffering. In October 1939, an embarrassed "Aryan" couple, trying to shoo their Jewish friend of thirty-one years out of their apartment, lamented that the Germans were now paying for the misdeeds of the Nazis against the Jews. Shortly after Germany attacked the Soviet Union, Elisabeth Freund found herself on a boat next to an "Aryan" woman. Not aware that Freund was Jewish, the woman grumbled to her about the untrustworthy Russians and worried about her seventeen-year-old-son. Of course, she added, "the Führer surely knows better!" Aware that she was breaking a new rule denying Jews the right to take even short excursions and terribly nervous that the Gestapo would do a spot check and catch her, Freund thought:

> If it weren't all so bitterly serious, one could actually laugh about it: there we are, sitting on the . . . steamboat. The bells from the Potsdam Garrison Church ring out "Forever loyalty and upright honesty!" And this poor little woman pours her heart out to me, the non-Aryan. One can almost feel pity when she explains how the German *Volk* has been so treacherously betrayed by the evil, evil Russians. She believes it and doesn't see that they've all been betrayed by their own government.[59]

Even when acknowledging the plight of Jews, many Germans relativized it or told Jews how lucky they were to leave their homeland. When Freund's clothes began to look shabby, a German coworker asked about them. She explained that Jews had not received clothing ration cards since the beginning of the war. Surprised, he considered this predicament and concluded: "Actually, the difference is not really so great. You have no clothing ration cards and get no socks,—we have some [cards] but there are no socks to be bought. It comes to the same thing." Upon finally receiving permission to emigrate in October 1941, Freund walked to the factory gate with an "Aryan" who had to accompany her, presumably to make sure Jews would not steal anything. The man said: "I wish you good luck, you will be better off than all of us here." Similarly, a salesman, curious that she wanted to purchase sunglasses, exclaimed: "What, you're going to America, a land without war! I wish I could switch places with you!" Neither exchange revealed any recognition of the terrible persecution of the Jews—not even from the "Aryan" who witnessed their forced labor—and in both cases the Germans perceived the Jews as luckier than they.[60]

ANNA AND SALOMON SAMUEL:
THE ODYSSEY OF ONE ELDERLY JEWISH COUPLE

The plight of Anna and Salomon Samuel illustrates how two individuals faced the increasing indignities, isolation, and privations of the war years. Their lives offer a firsthand account of how the many elderly Jews trapped in Germany endured the last years of Nazi evil.[61]

In 1932, Anna and Salomon Samuel, then aged fifty-eight and sixty-five, respectively, retired to Berlin. He had served as a rabbi in Essen since 1894, and they had raised four children, all of whom emigrated to Palestine before the war. Although the children tried desperately to rescue their parents, all efforts failed. While agonizing about being so far away from their children, the couple experienced emotional support in their correspondence with a young German woman, Else Schubert-Christaller, a Christian scholar of Judaism, whom they grew to love like a daughter. The only details remaining of their lives are those which Schubert-Christaller collected: their 500 letters and the boxes of memorabilia and scholarship they sent her for safekeeping.

These letters depict not only daily life but also the gendered way in which wife and husband dealt with their circumstances. Anna Samuel was the housekeeper, her husband the scholar. Typically, as Anna Samuel faced the increasing challenges of furnishing meals, clean clothing, and a comfortable abode, Salomon Samuel reread Goethe's *Wilhelm Meister*, studied Jewish history, and provided intellectual comfort, and hence moral support, to his immediate Jewish community. Salomon Samuel's letters discussed philosophical issues, with only hints of the dire situation until close to the end, when deportations began.[62] His erudition and kindness brought his wife pride and pleasure. Moreover, just as scholarship kept him engaged and remote from the increasingly dismal situation, household tasks kept Anna Samuel busy and distracted as well: "*One* good thing: one is kept occupied, so that the harried, freezing time passes more quickly."[63]

In May 1939, with the curtailment of shopping hours and rations for Jews, Anna Samuel wrote that shopping had become "horrible—such long trips, no more Jewish shops anymore—everything so alien." Shopping for everything in the one hour allotted to Jews unnerved her daily. Their meals, even the Sabbath meal, contained no meat. Milk, too, became impossible to purchase by February 1941. Thanks to the potato flour and meat stamps sent by Else before Passover, the Samuels could observe the religious regulations and enjoy the rare taste of meat for the holiday. Both wrested some happiness from the Seder.[64]

Nazi regulations were only part of the problem. Anna Samuel also endured jeers from neighbors whenever she went shopping. In December 1941, with the yellow star on her coat, she was taunted by teenage girls: "So close to the festival of love . . . hatred was not stilled. . . . And *such* big girls, who could reflect on what they are doing!" One year later, she remarked that trips into town felt like running the gauntlet. In May 1942, she wrote: "The bad children! Maybe they are supposed to clear us off the streets. Everything is so premeditated today." With sad amusement she commented on the "Aryan" porter's baby, whom she enjoyed from afar because "it always smiles at me."[65]

Besides suffering pervasive hunger, the Samuels endured brutal winters with little coal. At first, Jews received half the regular coal rations, but later even that apportionment was revoked. Often, in fact, the government simply confiscated their heating supplies. Sympathetic observers reported that "elderly people in particular suffer terribly in the bitter cold." The Samuels were always cold. In January 1940, Anna Samuel wrote: "From 8 in the morning until about 3 we fend off cold and hunger." She, her husband, and her sister-in-law sat in front of the tiny tiled stove wearing their coats. By the winter of 1941, the Samuels rarely had heat. When the Nazis confiscated their water heater and sun lamp the following summer, the couple mourned the loss of these items, "which saved us . . . from freezing *to death,* not from *freezing. . .!*"[66]

The bombings took their toll on the aging couple, sixty-six and seventy-three-years-old in 1940. Taking shelter, night after night, through three-hour raids exhausted them. Poverty also plagued them. Living as frugally as possible, they remained in debt to their Christian friend, which embarrassed and pained them. Most debilitating was their dwindling hope of ever seeing their children again. Without the money or connections to escape from Germany, they approached their only remaining hope, the Palestine Office, to ask about illegal emigration. There they learned that they were too old for that route: "In plain language, *we* would *not* be considered for illegal emigration. . . . We were *too* old! They left us not even a sliver of hope, the mean ones!"[67]

Moving into *Judenhäuser* frightened and exhausted them. At first they lived in modest quarters, sharing them with Salomon Samuel's sister. But these became too expensive once the Nazis placed an additional tax of 15 percent, known as the "social compensation tax," on Jews only. Their intention to find a cheaper place notwithstanding, they soon heard rumors that they would be ordered to move—"Everything is so uncertain!"—and, in fact, soon were so ordered. They had to divest themselves of furniture and books: "It is so hard for my husband to hand over so many books! A Jew should have wings. Should not become so comfortably earthbound!"[68]

They settled into their new abode, one room in a Jewish old-age home, in June 1941, the month Germany invaded Russia. Anna Samuel wrote: "It's a bit difficult all right, for example, no running water in the room, only in the hallway, [where] there is always a hubbub." She tried to organize their room, "and *one* room has to hold everything, without seeming totally uncomfortable! The desk stands by the window, my husband is already writing at it." Always the good homemaker, she worried:

> How will I create order, even the most modest level of comfort out of all this chaos, when . . . every kitchen amenity is missing. . . . Where will I wash something? There is an electric hot plate in the hallway—but it is always in use. . . . To get to the shower, I have moved my *first* rising to between 5 and 6. Then I go back to bed.[69]

To their shock and dismay, no sooner were the Samuels settled than they were ordered to move again, this time to Berlin-Köpenick. In August 1941, their suitcases and baskets surrounding them, Salomon felt "banished from the city." Anna understood this move as a narrowing in, a closing down of options. She nevertheless tried desperately to keep their newest home—a tiny room—as pleasant as possible: "Our little room is interchangeably a sleeping, eating, and living room, but it is *too* small to make it *cozy*. . . . And my husband worries me, he has become so thin . . . and looks so forlorn!"

In Köpenick, they no longer had access to water in the hallway.

> It is embarrassing . . . to be dependent on one water pipe located near others. . . . Here, in the *entire* little house, there is only *one* in the kitchen. . . .

So I often fetch the indispensable liquid in the late evening hours when everyone has fallen asleep, or in the early morning when everyone is *still* sleeping! . . . A little inconvenient, unfamiliar! One notices *how* spoiled one was.[70]

In October 1941, when Anna Samuel began to hear of deportations, she reflected: "And our poor, tiny room has prepared us gently for more hardship!"[71] In hindsight, we know that nothing could have equipped the Samuels to fathom the genocide the Nazis were perpetrating against Jews in Eastern Europe at the very moment Anna Samuel wrote these words. Nor could the Samuels have ever been prepared for the suffering they endured and the death they met in Theresienstadt.

7

Forced Labor and Deportations

Berlin is judenfrei.   — JOSEPH GOEBBELS

In the last years of the German-Jewish community, Jews suffered exhaustion from forced labor, hunger, and deprivation and, perhaps even worse, overwhelming sadness and fear. They missed their friends, their lively communities, the lives they had once known. Parents longed for children who had emigrated even as they were deeply grateful that the children were safe. Most horrifying were the trains that awaited them for their "evacuation" or "departure."

FORCED LABOR

By the end of 1938, Jews older than fifty made up half of all Jews remaining in Germany, and one-fourth of Jews were in need of financial support. An "army of impoverished and jobless Jews . . . threatened to become a burden on the German *Reich*." In December 1938, the government ordered that unemployed Jews be assigned to jobs. In 1939, all public welfare for Jews ceased. Only 16 percent of Jews were still employed after 1939 (and over half of these were workers). The American Jewish Congress reported sadly that German Jews, "stripped of their property, declassed and pauperized . . . were . . . worth little more than their . . . slave labor value."[1]

With the outbreak of war and a severe labor shortage, industry as well as public and private businesses demanded Jewish workers. Local and central authorities drafted even self-supporting Jews to report for work, although, officially, forced labor affected only the unemployed on welfare. Other Jews, subject to intimidation and pressure, were forced to "volunteer."

Steps for mobilizing Jewish labor commenced. By May 1940 in Berlin, all

Jewish men between eighteen and fifty-five and all Jewish women between eighteen and fifty had to register with the Jewish community's division in charge of forced labor. By the summer of 1940, there were still 72,327 Jewish residents in Berlin, of whom 25,000 women and 16,000 men between the ages of eighteen and sixty were "fit" for forced labor. In early 1941, about 20 percent of the remaining Jewish community of Germany worked in forced labor, many in armaments. That March, the Reich formally drafted all Jews between fifteen and sixty-five into forced labor. From 1941 on, Germany exploited Jewish forced labor to the maximum, even importing Eastern European Jews after Germany had been declared "free of Jews."[2] In the winter of 1944–45, most people defined by the Nuremberg Laws as "first-degree *Mischlinge*," Jews married to "Aryans," and even "Aryan" men married to Jewish women were inducted into forced labor.

The daily life of most Jews consisted of at the very least ten hours of forced labor. Government bureaucrats, unrestrained by formal age limits, forced much older Jews to work, including women as old as seventy. In Dresden at the Zeiss-Ikon factory, Jewish forced laborers sympathetically named the section of fifteen and sixteen year old Jewish girls the "kindergarten."[3] Generally, Jewish workers were segregated from "Aryans," except "Aryan" supervisors. The government decreed in October 1941 that Jews would be denied all "Aryan" workers' rights. Jews were paid only for "work done" and could not claim sickness, maternity, or death benefits; family or child allowances; holiday pay; or pensions. They generally received the lowest wages and were taxed at the highest rate. Also, Jews were fair game for impatient supervisors. They could be bullied relentlessly and dismissed without notice. Jews were relegated to particularly hard and dirty work, such as construction; road work; rubbish disposal; cleaning public toilets and sewage plants; or sorting coal, rags, and bones. When working the night shift, which occurred frequently, Jews could not take shelter during bombings, and those at home worried about their loved ones.

Middle-class, middle-aged Jews found factory work particularly difficult, since they were not only untrained but also slower compared with younger "Aryans." Victor Klemperer, formerly a professor, recorded his chagrin when his supervisor disparaged his work: "You're getting stupider all the time.... I'd be ashamed to produce such shit!" Klemperer tried "time and again to appreciate the comedy of the situation, but the humiliation torments me a great deal." He knew that a few "Aryan" women produced far more than his group of retired Jewish men and worried that this could hasten deportation for the Jews. He was right to worry: dismissal could lead to deportation. One woman, compelled to do forced labor with 900 other women at Siemens-Schuckert-Werke AG, recalled her fear of not meeting the production target: "You had to meet your target or else you were in danger of being picked up." She helped the older people, "since they could not do the set amount." Mistakes could result in arrest for sabotage.[4]

Jewish women labored in a variety of industries. The Nazis noted that "Jewish women proved to be highly skilled winders" in armaments factories. They were forced to work for Siemens electrical works and for I. G. Farben industries, where some toiled in knee-deep water while SS men drove them on with whips. Jewish women also worked in factories producing dyes, batteries, or rat poison, or cleaned trains and streetcars. One fifteen-year-old, for example, worked first in an ammunition factory and then cleaned army troop transport trains. Sometimes she crawled under the cars to oil them.[5]

Working conditions were dismal. For Jews, there were no safety protections normally provided to "Aryan" workers. At Siemens-Schuckert, for example, Jewish women had to dip tin into chemicals using two hands whereas "Aryan" women could use only one hand. Also, eating and sanitary facilities were minimal or lacking. Ilse Rewald worked in a munitions factory where Jews were barred from using the canteen and there was only one toilet for all the Jewish forced laborers. Forced labor was usually dirty—so dirty that other Jews could identify Jewish female forced laborers by their grimy appearance. Manfred Fackenheim-Field, an accountant for the Berlin Jewish Community until he was deported in 1943, wrote: "Because all these jobs were particularly dirty, the one piece of 'soap' (ersatz clay soap) that one could get with a ration card wasn't enough. One recognized these Jewish women immediately because of their involuntary uncleanliness."[6] The labor was heavy, backbreaking, and mind-numbing, the environment often excruciatingly hot, and the hours long. One Jewish woman described forced labor on an estate, where she worked from 6 A.M. until late evening, bent over harvesting carrots and potatoes. She slept with the other forced laborers in a barn, with "my little suitcase for a pillow." Yet heavy labor did not earn Jews more rations. This woman ate nothing but a "thin soup."[7] The lack of protein left most Jews in forced labor greatly weakened.

For those remaining in their hometowns, forced labor exacerbated the other problems of daily life: the search for food and fuel, the compulsory changes of apartments with short notice, the ongoing deportations (after October 1941), and the bombings. For housewives doing forced labor, there were the extra responsibilities of shopping, cooking, laundering, and housekeeping in cramped quarters. While spouses and friends could provide some solace, shift work often prevented them from seeing each other.

Camilla Neumann reported that she regularly missed seeing her husband for six days on end: "But every evening there were a few dear lines from Ludwig on my night table, and naturally I, too, put a little note for him on the dinner table every day. . . . Before I went to bed I . . . prepared breakfast for Ludwig." Many women also cared for elderly parents and children. When the Nazis closed most remaining Jewish day care centers in the late fall of 1942, some forced laborers had to leave their babies at home unattended except for a brief daily feeding by a visiting nurse. Doing forced labor in Berlin, Elisabeth Freund, reflected:

> When I see how these women work and how they have to earn a few extra marks by moonlighting; how they have to wake their children before 5 A.M. . . . to bring them to daycare; how in the evenings and on Sundays they wash and sew and keep everything orderly in the one room that most often serves the entire family; how they manage to acquire a few groceries by waiting endlessly in shops; how they magically create a new child's dress out of an old curtain; how they work themselves to death and how each woman bears her individual fortune — it is admirable! What right do I have to consider my own fate so intolerable?[8]

The activities at the Ahawah day care center in Berlin offer a glimpse into these lives. Mothers doing forced labor brought their children to the center around 5 A.M. The children played in the courtyard, took baths, and ate their meals at the center. "They were serious children. . . . They laughed less than others, they also cried less. It was as though they wanted to make as little trouble as possible for us," reported a caretaker. They were probably also lethargic from malnourishment. Late in the evening, dead tired, the mothers picked up the tots and went home. This routine continued until February 1943. Then the Nazis deported the children and their caretakers without warning. When the mothers arrived, they found empty strollers and cribs. Neighbors watched the mothers' mounting horror as they realized that their children had been taken from them: "The mothers stood there for hours crying."[9]

While anxiously awaiting her visa to the United States, Elisabeth Freund was forced to work in a laundry on the outskirts of Berlin. She was grateful not to be in a munitions factory, since her children were in England and she did not want to produce the munitions that might harm them, or in a battery factory, which she had heard was dangerous and dirty. For backbreaking work at the laundry, unmarried Jewish women earned about 14 marks, while married women earned 12.50 marks weekly. Married women whose husbands also worked were docked some pay for being "double earners." Unskilled "Aryan" women netted twice as much; even an "Aryan" cleaning woman in Berlin earned about 20 marks a week plus her meals. Jewish girls received even less: a fifteen-year-old in a Berlin uniform factory earned 30 pfennigs an hour; another teenager earned 50 pfennigs an hour at Siemens. Freund calculated that with car fare at 1.80 marks a week and the "social compensation tax" on Jews of 15 percent deducted immediately, she earned about 1.50 marks a day, which was supposed to cover all her expenses. Because the cost of living was high and their salaries so low, most women on the night shift at Freund's laundry moonlighted in the mornings. Freund, too, worked in a photo lab for a few extra marks between sleeping, shopping, housekeeping, and working. Within a short time, however, most women had to give up their extra jobs because the forced labor was too exhausting. In June, the heat from the steam presses and hot water reached 116 degrees Fahrenheit in the steam press room and 104 degrees in the rest of the hall.[10]

Occasionally, the Jewish women got sick from the heat or burned themselves on the machines. The managers at the laundry, however, dispensed medications and salves only to "Aryans." Later, at another factory, when Freund needed medicine she was allowed to go to the nurse, a woman she referred to as a "brown nurse" (i.e., Nazi nurse): "She did not speak a word to me, just shoved a measuring glass with medicine toward the corner of the table . . . so that I didn't even know . . . whether it was for me. Probably this servant of brotherly love feared that even one word to a Jewish woman was too much." Forced labor conditions did not allow either lengthy sicknesses or time to recuperate. When Freund's doctors recommended some time off because she had lost twenty-five pounds and could no longer stand the hot steam presses, the laundry fired her.[11]

Her next job was in a "radio factory"—which turned out to be an armaments plant. There she received 18 marks a week doing work that her supervisor warned was "indescribably monotonous." But Freund was grateful to be back at work, fearful of worse jobs, and thankful that she had been spared such work in her previous life: "Now I am happy to be here again and do this boring work. Working men and women do this their whole lives. How good it was to be able to learn something, that earlier everything beautiful and interesting in the world was available if only one wanted it." Many Jewish women and men expended extra mental energy to endure the monotony of jobs—in which "every hour had 600 minutes." Ilse Rewald tried to raise her spirits during her dull, tedious work by jotting down ideas for stories or poems on a small piece of paper. She feared being caught doing this, but "I can stand the monotony of the work, the noise of the machines, and the long stretch of the day better this way."[12]

In general, a strong will to survive—with health and luck—helped the forced laborer. Freund, for example, despite weakness and ringing in her ears, continued to work: "This is a matter of will power, and I must manage. If one has to, everything is possible." When she was forced to do even heavier work, she slaved on: "I continue to work. I have to continue, I have to carry on, I have to see my children alive once again, I cannot allow myself to be destroyed here." By late 1941, when deportations had begun, those who remained at forced labor, like Rewald, considered themselves lucky. No matter how difficult their job, they thought that at least they were still needed and hoped their labor would prevent their deportation.[13]

Jewish friends played a crucial role in making forced labor at all tolerable to Jewish workers. There may have been some tensions between bourgeois Jews, who had never before worked in a factory, and their proletarian coreligionists. But most reports, like that of Elisabeth Freund, stressed the extreme importance of new on-the-job friendships: "I travel home with a neighbor.... We make plans to meet the next day. Perhaps we can stay together. All the women who already know one another or who are just getting to know one another have this one wish: to stay together. It reminds me of children, who are less afraid in the dark when in twos." Freund later worked with a young woman who "knows a lot of poems by Goethe and Schiller by heart, just like me." Although talking was forbidden, "if we are not observed while tying up cartons, we can really enjoy ourselves." Freund observed other women banding together to make life more bearable as well: a group of young kindergarten teachers "continued to maintain a study group, and read Pestalozzi and Montessori two mornings a week. They think they can carry it off." These teachers knew many folk songs, and Freund and others sang with them when the strict "Aryan" supervisor was not around. They were either unaware of the irony of Jewish forced laborers singing German folk songs, or perhaps intended to spite those Nazis who believed "Jews must not desecrate German music," by asserting it was their music too. More practically, they believed that "work went more smoothly with singing."[14]

Companionship while singing, as well as while walking home through the outskirts of Berlin on lovely spring nights, gave Freund and her friends a bit of pleasure in their otherwise harrowing lives:

> These wonderful starry May nights. The smell of lilac wafts from every garden.... We have found a path through the gardens and over a

meadow.... The way the moon ... and the stars glitter and glow, that is an
experience that can't be taken from us even by this slave labor, and that
always helps us find a little consolation in the face of our terrible fate.

Rewald, too, affirmed the importance of her new friends, all of whom had
lost someone dear to them during the ongoing deportations. Shortly after
Rewald's mother was deported, a coworker baked her a birthday cake "on
the first birthday that I ever spent without my mother. She had to save a
long time for the ingredients to give me a little pleasure."[15]

DESPAIR AND SUICIDE

From the beginning of forced labor, Jews understood that their situation
was radically deteriorating. In 1941, probably in late spring, the Nazis
decided upon the "Final Solution," the annihilation of European Jewry.
When Germany invaded Russia, death squads followed close behind, murdering hundreds of thousands of Jews. By the fall, the Nazis set into motion
the extermination of Jews in all of German-occupied Europe.

The systematic deportation of German Jews, what the Nazis called
"waves" of deportations, purportedly for hard labor, began in October
1941. Before that date, the Nazis had undertaken isolated expulsions of
Jews from Germany, such as the deportation of Polish Jews in October
1938, the Jews of Stettin in February 1940, or the Jews of Baden and the
Rhine Palatinate in October 1940. Between October 15 and November 4,
1941, the first twenty "transports" (a Nazi euphemism), with about 1,000
people each, originated in various German cities and headed for Lodz. The
first transports from Berlin left on October 18, 1941. By December, the
killing was in high gear, and some of the extermination camps were already
operating at full force.

The deportations created a new level of despair among Jews. Toward the
end of 1941, Elisabeth Freund wrote: "Everything is getting worse, and the
worst is, that the hopelessness of our circumstances gets clearer all the time.
It's happening to me too, I am so disheartened, I don't know how I can bear
it." She soon heard of the deportations of Jews from Breslau and the murder of Otto Hirsch, one of the leaders of German Jewry, in the Mauthausen
concentration camp: "It is so terribly upsetting. This helplessness! It's as
though we are all sitting in a trap!" Another forced laborer, whose mother
had just been deported, whose "Aryan" husband had been jailed for an anti-
Nazi remark, and whose child had nearly died and lay recuperating in a
hospital crib, despaired of life. She saw her mother, her husband, her child

behind bars. Eventually her husband returned, weighing ninety pounds and looking "as if he were one hundred years old." She no longer entered bomb shelters, convinced that if a bomb did not kill her a concentration camp would—and she preferred the bomb.[16]

Desperation was hardly new in the daily life of Jews. But from late 1941 nervous breakdowns, depression, and suicides became more and more common. Almost every memoir mentions one or more suicides. The rate of suicide—higher among Jews than non-Jews even before Nazism—had risen steeply with early Nazi brutality. It mounted during the anti-Jewish boycott in 1933. Between 1932 and 1934, the Jewish suicide rate was 50 percent higher than that of the rest of the population. In that period, 334 Jews committed suicide, including 122 women. Suicides increased further with the annexation of Austria in 1938 and surged sharply during and directly after the November Pogrom. An American living in Hamburg wrote that after November 9: "Families we had known, prosperous, content and happy, were now in a state of nervous collapse. . . . Suicides were a daily occurrence." One woman declared: "I felt I had my face slapped so often that it took all my self-command not to succumb to a nervous breakdown, as did many of my friends. Suicides occurred frequently. I dreaded the telephone bell. It so often announced a new tragedy."[17] The torrent of suicides in the 1930s notwithstanding, the most acute epidemic of suicides occurred during the deportations of 1942 and 1943. These suicides angered the Nazis, who waited for the unsuccessful suicides to recover in order to send them to their state-controlled deaths.

In a study of suicides within the German-Jewish community, Konrad Kwiet labels them "a mass phenomenon." In normal times, the suicides of 0.03 percent of a population (30 suicides per 100,000) would be high. Although suicide statistics are difficult to determine, Kwiet estimates that under Nazi rule roughly 10,000 Jews committed suicide or attempted suicide, 3,000 to 4,000 of these during the deportation years. Even a conservative estimate of 5,000 suicides would mean that almost 1 percent of the 525,000 Jews in Germany in 1933 took their own lives (i.e., about 100 suicides per 100,000). The suicides during the deportation years from 1941 to 1943—at least 3,000 in a Jewish population of about 134,000—meant that the rate jumped to over 2 percent of the Jewish population. In Berlin, the estimates were about 4 percent as the suicide curve ran parallel with the deportations. Among those who received their notification to be deported, the estimated suicide rate soared to 10 percent. Some Jewish sources suggested that one-quarter of Jewish deaths in Berlin were suicides.[18]

Few Jews who committed suicide left suicide notes, but memoirs tell of the suicides of relatives, friends, and acquaintances. Since most memoirs were written after the genocide, the suicides are almost always seen in the context of a potentially far more horrible death. The memoirs respectfully consider the person's motivations. Thus, they omit the kind of lamentation, frustration, or dejection that under normal circumstances would probably accompany a description of another's self-inflicted death.

Although the suicides of Jews in Germany superficially fit typical sociological patterns of suicides because of advancing age, loneliness, and grief, they do not fit the typical psychological profiles of suicides—anger and aggression against the unloved self. Kwiet notes that sources "speak of careful preparations, of conversations and memories of a happy German childhood, of people remembering their children who have left Germany, and of those who in the final hours turn for solace to the German classics ... Goethe and Schiller ... Bach and Beethoven." These Jews died by their own hand in order to preserve a sense of their own dignity and agency—even "Germanness." Many died surrounded by German cultural artifacts: Jewish men sometimes wore their army medals. And, like one eighty-year-old woman, they believed that their children would understand their decision. They succeeded in their despair-driven desire for a "death of their own,"[19] in some ways stealing it from the Nazis.

Those who mourned the suicides did not criticize or pity them. They rarely condemned them for flouting religious proscriptions against suicide. Nor did the mourners blame those who died for leaving the living more desolate than ever. For example, Nora Rosenthal understood her husband's suicide during the November Pogrom in terms of his "[inability] to stand the strain of Nazi persecutions," even though he left her the entire "agony, ... responsibility, [and] ghastliness" of getting herself and two children out of the country.[20] Those reflecting on the suicides of relatives or friends often admired the courage it took to end one's own life. Lily Krug, whose brother returned from a concentration camp after the November Pogrom, nursed him through the first stage of a nervous breakdown, hiding from him the poison that he, a doctor, kept in his home: "I hid the veronal and thought I had outwitted him. What was my horror one morning to find him dead in bed! His features suffused with peace, his suffering forgotten. I did not cry, I envied him." Occasionally friends and family members either knew about the potential suicide, were present during it, or aided it. Even the doctors at the Jewish Hospital in Berlin "were of a divided opinion as to whether it was better to save the sick of this category or to allow them to pass away peacefully."[21]

Fragmentary suicide statistics, memoirs, and the work of Kwiet suggest that more men than women committed suicide—at least in the early Nazi years. The first wave consisted of men who felt the shock and despair of losing their jobs in the civil service and in the professions. Next came those in business and commerce whose livelihoods were threatened or destroyed. Early suicides also included men who were staggered by the lawlessness of the regime. They preferred death to the "degradation and humiliation" they were experiencing, sometimes leaving statements about their suicide, possibly in the hope of influencing public opinion. One man wrote: "I have chosen a voluntary death in order to shock my Christian friends into awareness. . . . How much I would have preferred to lay down my life for my fatherland. Do not mourn me, but endeavor to enlighten people." In the final years, more men than women held responsible positions in the Jewish community and committed suicide when the Nazis ordered them to help organize deportations.[22]

In general, before Nazism fewer Jewish women than men had committed suicide in Germany. In the Nazi era there were more and more women who, driven to despair, saw no alternative but death. A Jewish tennis champion killed herself shortly before 1935 in order to spare her "Aryan" husband difficulties; the Jewish wife of an "Aryan" lawyer killed herself before 1936 to enable her husband to support their family. In the wake of the November Pogrom, one woman—hopeless about her plight and fearful of becoming a burden on strangers—appealed to her husband to consider a joint suicide. Forlorn that both her children had emigrated, depressed that she had lost her home, and terrified of being arrested, she proposed: "We should . . . separate ourselves forever from this world by throwing ourselves . . . into the Neckar [river]." The husband argued against suicide for the time being, and each promised that if either committed suicide it would only be with the other. The husband's arrest, for a technical detail related to their packed furniture, drove the wife to despair, and she killed herself. Before taking the pills, she wrote a letter to her husband and children, asking their forgiveness. "Please try to understand me. I am desperate, crushed without hope. I can't continue to breathe. I am afraid of the prison walls which await me. . . . Forgive me that I leave you like this. I am powerless. . . . My heart is tearing apart. I am perspiring with fright day and night."[23]

In the later years, during the deportations, the number of female suicides may have caught up to, or even surpassed the number of male suicides. Suddenly Nazi reports indicate that "three Jewesses committed suicide" or that "five elderly Jewesses" attempted suicide, usually before deportations. The first and obvious reason for the increase in female suicides is that, as has been seen, more Jewish women than men remained in

Germany. The gradual realization that the deportations meant death, especially for the elderly, may have impelled many aged women, often widowed,
to commit suicide. Kwiet suggests that the average age of suicides during
the deportations was between sixty and seventy.[24]

Whereas in the early 1930s many suicides were impulsive, by the time of
deportations, as reports and rumors raced through the *Judenhäuser*, the
vast majority of them seem to have been deliberate. Women and men
planned these later suicides carefully, paying an exorbitant price for the
drugs or chemicals with which to kill themselves, and carefully choosing
the time to do the deed. In one case, a *"Mischling"* grandson did his eighty-
three-year-old grandmother's bidding by helping her into a gentle suicide:
she talked about her youth, happier days, and read from Schiller. Then she
took a large number of sleeping pills and "in the end she fell asleep."[25]

Sometimes Jews planned joint suicides, sometimes entire households
committed suicide together. Ilse Rewald reported on the joint suicide of an
elderly couple when they learned of their imminent deportation. They took
sleeping pills after the man had pinned every medal he had ever won as a
soldier on his suit, perhaps in hopes of shaming the Nazis who would find
his body. In one of several examples of elderly sisters committing suicide
together, family members tried to dissuade the sisters, but eventually gave
in to the "composure of the aunts and the arguments of their long-time
friend that the two elderly women would not even be able to survive the
transport to the camp. Someone provided the two women with cyanide
and during the night before their deportation they died in their own beds
—between fresh sheets and with flowers on the table." Elisabeth Freund
described the joint suicide decision of two women and their ninety-year-
old mother. The younger women thought they could probably survive the
deportations, but not their old mother. They decided to die together:
"When we get our notice to vacate the apartment, then we will sit down in
the kitchen with mother and turn on the gas. That is the only act of love
that we can still perform for our mother."[26]

Raul Hilberg has written that German Jews had the means to kill themselves with far less pain than Eastern European Jews, who would later have
to resort to more violent methods, such as jumping out of windows or
prompting shootings by ghetto guards. While some German Jews, too,
committed suicide violently, probably more tried to end their lives peacefully and in a refined manner, and many had the means to do so. They had
been bourgeois and, where possible, they chose quiet and private deaths.
Many took the barbiturate veronal, the suicide drug of choice, "the last
protest of people who faced the prospect that even their own deaths would

be taken from them." By mid-1942, Victor Klemperer had dubbed veronal "Jewish drops" and wondered: "Where do all these people get veronal?" Some procured it from their doctors, asking how many pills constituted a lethal dose. Others had to pay high prices on the black market. Doing forced labor, one woman sold her genuine Persian rug for 1,000 marks— the going rate for the thirty or so tablets of veronal she needed to kill her-self. She took them upon receiving her deportation notice. The American reporter Howard K. Smith, remarking on suicides in the early 1940s, reflected: "It was death one way or another, and the sensible ones chose it the sooner and easier, rather than the later and harder."[27]

"Suicide hardly shocks us anymore, we envy those who muster the courage"; these words reflected the attitude many Jews had developed. Hermann Samter's letters, commenting on the suicides of two of his older female relatives, summarized the situation: "It is shocking, how matter-of-factly this subject is discussed today. . . . Two female cousins of Aunt Nelly took their lives . . . before their deportation. . . . The people have just totally had it. And then, the fear of what still awaits them in the East. One can't say anything if someone so deliberately makes an end of it."[28]

DEPORTATIONS:

THE TRANSITION FROM SOCIAL DEATH

TO PHYSICAL ANNIHILATION

Officially, the Nazis used euphemisms to describe murder. They spoke of "evacuation to work in the East," "resettlement," or "departing"—as though the Jews had chosen their fate themselves. Moreover, Nazi decrees, such as what Jews should pack for Auschwitz (including one suitcase or backpack, one pair of work boots, two pairs of socks, two shirts, two under-pants, two wool blankets, bed linens, and one sweater) deceived Jews into hoping they would actually be put to work. Notwithstanding the Nazis' cynical euphemisms and duplicitous directives, Jews spoke of being "taken" (*geholt werden*) and worried for their safety. Ultimately, "almost all deported German Jews were murdered. . . . Their specific fate differed from place to place, but the final result was always the same."[29]

The first deportations came as a shock, but word quickly spread among Jews. People anxiously anticipated the dreaded notice sent by the Gestapo via the local Jewish community. It ordered them to prepare for "evacua-tion," explaining when and where to report and how much luggage and money to take. The agony of waiting began. The elderly Samuel couple, for example, began to expect deportations in October 1941, even wondering whether it would not be better to be deported sooner, rather than later, because there might be "no room" later on. On November 12, 1941, Anna Samuel wrote her non-Jewish friend Else Schubert-Christaller that a sign had been posted on their old-age home in Berlin-Köpenick that read "Confiscated by the Commandant's Office" —a signal to her of imminent deportation. The sign disappeared a few days later. By April 1942, Anna and her seventy-five-year-old-husband, Salomon, paid regular farewell visits to friends whose deportation notices had arrived. In July they expected a government official to assess their "wealth," and they had already acquired backpacks for their "trip." A letter of August 3 warned Else that they were preparing for "departure" (*Abwanderung*). For months they had been sending her mementos in the hope that these would one day reach their children in Palestine. Now they packed a last shipment of Salomon Samuel's scholarly writings, and he asked for a toothbrush and hat (which Jews could no longer purchase). He dreaded the process of deportation and wished that it were already behind him.

Salomon Samuel wrote that they would be going to Theresienstadt, about which he had heard "favorable things"—although he maintained his skepticism. Established in late 1941, Theresienstadt was considered by most Jews as the "preferred" camp, for the elderly, war veterans, and functionaries of the Jewish communities. Although the German-Jewish survival rate was higher there than in other camps, Jews still died en masse from disease and malnutrition, and most of the others were sent on to Auschwitz to be gassed. Finally, on August 17, the couple learned that they would be picked up within three days. The torture of anticipation ended on the third day, when they were moved to the assembly point at the Grosse Hamburgerstrasse. Within weeks of their arrival in Theresienstadt, they had both died —four days apart.[30]

As with Anna and Salomon Samuel, the notice of imminent "evacuation" usually arrived with a list for Jews to fill out, describing the property they were leaving behind. Many of these lists remain today in German archives, often recorded in the shaky handwriting of the elderly, specifying every item not packed in the fifty kilograms permitted on their journey. The government confiscated the property left behind for its own use or to auction it under a cynical Nazi decree of November 1941, the "Eleventh Decree to the Reich Citizenship Law." This decree mandated the automatic seizure of property of German Jews who had left or would leave the country. At the pubic auctions, "good Aryans fought like jackals over a carcass" to acquire Jewish property. Some auctions took place in the former homes of Jews, where small crowds gathered after reading announcements in the newspapers. Howard K. Smith reported on one auction in the apartment of his former neighbors, two elderly women:

> When the auctioneer opened the Bernsteins' door . . . one could see on the table inside two tea-cups still half-filled. . . . The auctions were ugly spectacles, with ill-tempered citizens crying curses at one another . . . threatening with all the standard threats to have one another arrested and to call friends "high up in the party" into their squabbles.

Since the "Eleventh Decree" did not pertain to Jews sent to Theresienstadt, which was located in "greater" Germany, the Nazis forced these Jews to give up their property by perpetrating a cruel hoax: they promised "perpetual care" in exchange for all property left behind. After this plunder of Jewish property, the Nazis charged Jews a third-class train fare for their "trip to the East" and stole the contents of their suitcases when they arrived.[31]

The property of Jews often wound up in neighbors' homes and government offices. When Harry Kahn returned to his hometown in Württemberg in 1945, he personally retrieved his property. A Nazi teacher's widow lived in his parents' house; the leader of the Nazi women's organization had acquired their bedroom set; their rug embellished the town's revenue office. Often bureaucrats kept some of the finer pieces for their own use. When a mother and daughter returned to Leipzig from a concentration camp, they went to a local official to ask for their property back. The official explained that it would be difficult to find the pieces. The mother pointed to the chair he was sitting on and said, "That, for example, belongs to me!" She had photos to prove it.[32]

While some of the deportees left home by themselves, members of the Jewish community administration, the police, or the Gestapo accompanied others. In the area around Marburg, Jews had to mail their keys to the finance ministry, marked with the name and address of the "previous" tenants. Ruth Alton-Tauber, "evacuated" from Berlin in October 1941 with her six-year-old son, recalled how he grabbed two teddy bears on their way out the door. As they left their apartment, the Gestapo unscrewed their nameplate from their door: "This small act touched me deeply. All at once I became conscious of the fact that we no longer had a home or a homeland." In Berlin, many Jews walked to their destination, five or six abreast, escorted by police. Often trucks stood waiting in front of buildings from which Jews were being deported. Ruth Abraham watched her sister's family seated in such a truck for hours while the Gestapo and its dogs led other Jews to it.[33]

Amazingly, given the sheer terror they felt, Jews left quietly, "confronting this new calamity with dignity." Fourteen-year-old Cordelia Edvardson, considered a "Jew" by the Nazis, said good-bye to her Catholic parents, who made the sign of the cross on her forehead and gave her a tiny silver cross to safeguard her. Earlier she had cried alone but now, full of dread as she was escorted to her doom, she held firm: "I didn't want it to be said: 'She was torn, crying, from the arms of her mother and taken to Theresienstadt.' No, instead one day people should say: 'This was the fate of Cordelia Maria Sara, and she had the strength to bear it. Alone.'"[34]

Usually, the deportees were taken to an "assembly point" (*Sammelstelle*), where they waited until the trains to the East became available. While some assembly points were in synagogues and other Jewish communal buildings, the Nazis cruelly located others in slaughterhouses. In Dortmund, a *"Mischling"* daughter who made her way into a large hall to say a last good-bye to her mother wrote: "They were in the 'Exchange,' which was at the cattle market by the slaughterhouse, they were brought to the slaughter-house(!) . . . There lay the Schacher family. . . . He was half dead." In Leipzig, Rolf Kralovitz and his family, given one day's notice, hurriedly packed and left home—only to wait in a school for three days. There they had to turn in their identification cards and wedding rings. At the assembly point in the Berlin Levetzowstrasse synagogue in the fall of 1941, more than 1,000 men, women, and children awaited their final deportation sleeping on straw on the icy marble floor. Government bureaucrats collected their work papers, bread coupons, tax documents, and money. Ruth Abraham's father, who was at that assembly point, handed her a properly executed receipt for the 6,000 marks he had been forced to sign over to the government from his blocked bank account "for his stay in the concentration camp." Guards did a body search, "and after that the luggage was ransacked and shamelessly robbed." Both the Gestapo and, under its direction, girls from the Nazi youth organization rummaged through the luggage, stealing the last remainders of money, jewelry, food, and soap. Then all Jews under age sixty had to walk to the railway station.[35]

Officials at some assembly points split families, while others allowed them to stay together. In Dortmund, for example, families remained to-gether, lying on straw, with little but their own provisions to eat. In con-trast, in Berlin, as early as the end of 1941, parents could not request deportation when their children were taken or vice versa. Even when called to the assembly point as one unit, a family was often torn apart upon arrival. Elisabeth Freund heard news of families forcibly split up at the Levetzowstrasse synagogue assembly point in Berlin:

> The scenes that took place there are supposed to have been indescribable.
> Families were separated, married couples were torn apart, children
> dragged away, parents left behind. Already during the arrests, in the apart-
> ments, people took their lives. There in the synagogue it goes on. Body
> searches take place, suitcases are ransacked. . . . Everything is taken from
> them that has monetary value, as well as soap, combs, . . . scissors, brushes,
> everything that a civilized person needs.

In breaking up families, the Nazis dealt the most painful blow besides death itself. Many people hoped to be deported *with* their families. A seventeen-year-old *"Mischling,"* for example, braved the Gestapo's wrath by stealing into the building where her mother was imprisoned. When an officer asked her if she wasn't afraid to be inside this particular building, she responded: "At least I'm with my mother." Ilse Rewald, too, ran to the Gestapo to beg that either her mother's deportation be postponed or she and her husband be allowed to accompany her mother: "We still believed that nothing could happen to us as long as we weren't torn apart."[36]

While most Jews hoped to keep their families together, a few saw separation as the only viable strategy. In Berlin, Jewish mothers, ordered to assemble for deportation, left their infants at a Catholic hospital in the hope that the babies, at least, would be spared.[37] Many people who went into hiding were the sole remaining members of their families. They decided to hide after their families had been deported or had refused to go along when their deportation notices came, opting for separation from their families as their only chance to survive.

The final stop in Germany was the railroad station. The hapless victims arrived by foot or squeezed in vans, and then were herded, accompanied by kicks and insults from the Gestapo, onto trains. Some were carried on stretchers, some babies in cardboard suitcases because the Gestapo had confiscated their carriages as a "luxury." In the Berlin Putlitzstrasse station, a group of Jewish women led by Bertha Falkenberg, the former chair of Berlin's League of Jewish Women, distributed the maximum provisions tolerated by the Gestapo—for a one-day train trip, although the trips took longer. The women spent days preparing sandwiches for the thousand-person transports and then provided water, some form of coffee, and soup at the station. They helped people search for lost baggage, although most property had been kept, purposely, by the Gestapo at the assembly point. Between 1941 and 1943, Falkenberg's group dwindled from forty to eight as they, too, were deported.[38]

Old people receiving a meal at the Pestalozzi Street kitchen of the Jewish Winter Relief, late 1930s. (Courtesy of the Leo Baeck Institute, New York)

Population statistics make clear that the deportees were mostly elderly and women. Two-thirds of the deportees were forty-five years of age or older. Moreover, 32,000 more Jewish women than men remained in Germany in 1941 and were deported from there. The preponderance of the elderly and women appears in one example after another. In June 1941, the remaining Jews of Bonn were interned in a cloister: 300 women and 174 men. Of the German-speaking Jews deported to the Lodz Ghetto in 1941, 81 percent were older than fifty and 60 percent were women. When the last Jews of the village of Poembsen (in Westphalia) were deported, it was "almost only elderly women." In the 1980s, the writer Regina Scheer looked over about 50,000 files in the "confiscation" archives of the financial ministry of Berlin and Brandenburg and was able to glean information about the fates of those who had passed through Auguststrasse 14/16, Berlin, a building that functioned as a *Judenhaus*, a day care center, and an old-age home. She found that thousands of people had passed through this address en route to their deportations: "More women than men were deported. In these years, Auguststrasse 14/16 must have been a house of old women." By late 1942 and early 1943, the deportees from this house included not only older women but also women in their early twenties. They were the nurses and caregivers whose jobs had become superfluous after the aged, sick, and very young had been deported.[39]

"*Mischlinge*" and Jews in mixed marriages were better off than "full" Jews because they were not automatically destined to be murdered, but they were not automatically spared from deportations either. The Nazis exempted "*Mischlinge*" and Jews in mixed marriages from the early deportations, but later there were major regional variations, and local offices acted arbitrarily. In Frankfurt, for example, even Jews in "privileged" mixed marriages were deported to Theresienstadt as early as 1942. Later, "*Mischlinge*" brought up as Jews, Jews in mixed marriages who had remained enrolled in the Jewish community, and Jews in mixed marriages that had been dissolved by death or divorce were subject to deportation, generally to Theresienstadt. In most cases, the Nazis kept them there rather than shipping them to a death camp. The widowed or divorced Jewish parent from a previous mixed marriage was frequently spared if there was a minor "non-Jewish" (that is, baptized) child. In Hamburg, the Gestapo continually taunted a Jewish mother, "Wait 'til the boy turns ten and you'll be on the next transport." His tenth birthday came just as the war ended.[40]

By 1942 the Gestapo forced or tricked some "Aryans" into divorcing their Jewish spouses and vice versa. The files of the fourteenth transport from Hamburg document several such cases. In April 1943, the Gestapo summoned a Jewish woman who had lived separated from her "Aryan" husband for years and informed her that she "had to dissolve the marriage and depart [*abwandern*] to Theresienstadt." In two incidents, the "Aryan" wives of Jewish men suddenly divorced them in October and December 1942, respectively. Both divorces appear highly suspicious, occurring in long-standing partnerships. In one, the couple had been together for thirty years and the social workers described "the touching manner" in which the sixty-six-year-old wife cared for her seventy-six-year-old husband. In September 1942, she told the Jewish community that her husband was "unable to travel" (*transportunfähig*), and two months later she divorced him. The Gestapo probably tricked the women, perhaps promising that a divorce would help their mates, or threatened immediate deportation if a divorce was not forthcoming. In both instances the men were deported on the fourteenth transport and murdered. In a similar divorce case, after the husband was deported, the wife killed herself.[41]

In some places, the Gestapo harassed Jews in mixed marriages into signing false confessions or accused them of false crimes. The result was deportation and death. One woman reported that the Gestapo would regularly summon her "Aryan" father to headquarters, deride him for remaining married to a Jewish woman, and shout and spit at her mother. Besides humiliating them, the officers terrorized them by threatening their incarceration. The agonies of intermarried Jews notwithstanding, they were the Jews with the best chance of surviving. Of the German Jews who survived Nazism without emigrating, only 1 percent were *not* partners in mixed marriages.[42]

By late 1944, Jews in mixed marriages, too, faced deportation to the East, although only sporadically and arbitrarily. Many went into hiding. In January 1945, the government planned to deport Berlin Jews in mixed marriages to Theresienstadt, but these plans were only partially carried out because of transportation difficulties. Still, a transport of 1,000 Berlin Jews from mixed marriages went to Theresienstadt in February 1945. That month the Nazis also ordered the deportation from Dresden of the seventy remaining Jewish spouses in mixed marriages; only the famous saturation bombings saved their lives. While the fate of Jewish spouses in "mixed marriages" and of "first-degree *Mischlinge*" was uncertain throughout most of the war, the Nazis' intentions became clearer toward the end. Historian Ursula Büttner argues that in 1945 Jews in mixed marriages were about to be murdered and only the war's end saved their lives.[43]

Hamburg statistics illustrate the increasing proportion of mixed marriages that remained as Jews in wholly Jewish marriages were deported. Historically, Hamburg had high rates of intermarriage. In 1925, for example, 13.7 percent of marriages in which there was one Jew were mixed. By 1940 (after many Jewish couples had fled and others had moved from smaller towns into Hamburg), 42.7 percent of marriages in which there was one Jew consisted of mixed couples. By November 1941, there were 879 marriages between Jews, 1,036 mixed marriages, and an additional 198 Jews who had been in a mixed marriage and had small children. Thus, the deportations (and some last-minute emigration) raised the proportion and the number of mixed marriages relative to marriages in which both partners were Jewish. The same pattern existed throughout Germany: by the end of the deportations the majority of Jews left in Germany (including those with false papers or in hiding) were those in "privileged" mixed marriages. As irony would have it, one Jewish forced laborer was protected by her "privileged" status, while her "Aryan" husband, a communist, remained imprisoned the entire time.[44]

Gertrud Hammerstein's letters show just how terrifying the deportations were. Since Jews working in certain professions or war industries could ask for extensions or plead with superiors to get them, Hammerstein, the fifty-eight-year-old mother of a nurse who worked at the Jewish Hospital in Berlin, was safe until her daughter Hilde's name showed up on a deportation list. In October 1942, she wrote to another daughter and her son-in-law in England that she was giving her letters to someone who would forward them after the war, since she had little hope of surviving. If sent to Poland, she was certain she would perish. She noted that no one had received correspondence from deported relatives or friends in six months. Still, she hoped that Hilde and her new son-in-law, Willy, because they were young, would survive. She wrote that the next transport for Poland was leaving in the morning and she could still be called at the last minute: "If the 1,000 [person objective was] not filled, someone else was fetched. . . . This time 200 little children."[45] Moreover, it looked like Jews who had not yet been deported were going to starve: she reported that Jews could purchase only cabbage, turnips, and beets. For lunch Willy ate only 420 grams of bread and a half pound of lettuce.

In November 1942, Hammerstein related that 560 employees of the Jewish community received only eight days' notice to leave for Poland. Later, while shopping during the one hour permitted to Jews, she saw her deported friends' furniture loaded onto a truck: "It is too sad; [to see] that which one has loved one's whole life long, strewn to the winds." Only one other person was left of her earlier, large circle of friends. She also provided the transport number of their Uncle Paul, "because [with this number], it will be possible later on to find out if one is still alive and where."[46]

Gertrud Hammerstein wrote her last letter on December 10, 1942, recognizing that "daily, hourly" she could "reckon on giving up everything that was beloved and dear" to her. Resigned to an approaching doom, she reflected on her life, which, despite the "last year of horrors," had been a good one. Then she wrote her final farewell:

> So, my dear child, if I do not survive the end of the war, be certain that . . . my wishes for you are with you each day. Throughout your life you were a beam of sunlight for those around you, stay as you were and you will be a joy to yourself and others. You, dear Fritz, I press your hand again in spirit, you are beloved and dear to me, also remain as you were. . . . So farewell, my beloved little Katie, stay happy. . . . You have brought me only happiness. . . . I embrace you with all my heart. Your Mother.[47]

None of the three survived.

As the Nazi war against the Jews progressed, the official "evacuation" letters ceased and Nazi dragnets scoured the streets and factories, finding Jews and shoving them into closed trucks. In Berlin these surprise roundups, or razzias, began toward the end of 1942 with the arrival of Alois Brunner and his Viennese "deportation specialists." As the deportations sped up, deportees were either routed eastward to ghettos in Poland, Latvia, and Lithuania —staging grounds for further deportations to concentration and extermination camps—or sent directly to their deaths. By war's end, from Berlin alone there had been 65 transports to the East and over 120 to Theresienstadt. Among the latter were the so-called aged transports (*Alterstransporte*) of Jews older than sixty-five—whom the Nazis could not pretend were fit for hard labor. Even as Soviet troops began to liberate concentration camps in the East, the Germans relentlessly rounded up the remnants of German Jewry, sending them to camps closer by. Of the 164,000 Jews in Germany in October 1941, one estimate has only 14,500 left in July 1944, and deportations continued into the spring of 1945.[48]

The Berlin roundups were the occasion, on February 27, 1943, for the Rosenstrasse protest against the deportation of Jews. During its "factory action" that day, the Nazis seized Jews at their forced labor sites and took them directly to the assembly points. There, the Gestapo segregated intermarried men, some intermarried wives, and some *"Mischlinge"* in a separate building on Berlin's Rosenstrasse. "Aryan" wives, much like Jewish women after the November Pogrom, took the initiative to rescue their husbands. Hundreds, maybe a few thousand, demonstrated openly for the release of their men. They were joined by relatives, friends, and some strangers, standing fast despite savage threats by the Gestapo and the SS. On March 6, the first of approximately 1,500 prisoners were released.

The Nazis may have had their own reasons for releasing these Jews. The regime worried about the morale of "Aryan" relatives and, in light of the defeat one month earlier at Stalingrad, may have been unwilling to antagonize broad sections of the population. Also, the Nazis may have intended that some of the released prisoners would fill the administrative positions of recently deported Jewish communal workers. They not only released the prisoners but also, to the amazement of the victims, even returned some who had been "mistakenly" sent to Auschwitz. The Rosenstrasse protest was the only demonstration in Nazi Germany against the deportation of the Jews—in this case, mostly Jewish relatives. It should not detract from this demonstration to recognize that kinship played a crucial role among the demonstrators, but it is a telling reminder that there was no such protest on the basis of moral opposition alone.[49]

In June 1943, the Nazis closed down the Central Association of Jews in Germany (*Reichsvereinigung der Juden in Deutschland*), deporting its last administrators and appropriating its remaining resources. Of the top thirteen leaders, only Rabbi Leo Baeck and Moritz Henschel survived in Theresienstadt. A rump Central Association remained in the Jewish

Hospital in Berlin, sharing it with an infirmary for Jews who were to be "cured" before they were deported and some doctors and nurses. Also interned there were *"Mischlinge"* and Jews from mixed marriages, Jewish prisoners of the Gestapo, and Jews who worked for the Gestapo (see next chapter). The 800 residents of the Jewish Hospital were the only Jews officially remaining in Germany when the war ended.[50]

What Jews Believed

Nazi authorities left the phrase "deportation" purposely vague to hide its nature from both the victims and the rest of the German population. Moreover, Jews were segregated, scattered, and had unequal access to information compared to non-Jews. They were generally isolated from other Germans and, with the exception of the few other Jews with whom they worked or lived, from each other. They were not allowed radios and seldom had close relatives serving in the military or in officialdom. But a far more effective barrier to their comprehension was the sheer inconceivability of the genocide. Even those who received information frequently reacted with disbelief or repressed it. Some despaired upon learning of their fate, while others denied its possibility.

As early as March 3, 1940, with the deportations from Stettin, some Jews had an inkling of what to expect. Else Behrend-Rosenfeld asked her diary: "And what will these people do in Poland? Is the idea to give them work? So why have they taken the aged with them?" Moreover, rumors of the murder of "useless eaters" and the mentally ill—"also 'Aryans'"—circulated within the Jewish community. During the early, systematic deportations—although Jews were told that they were being "resettled in the East," and some believed they would be doing forced labor—there were already whispers about "gas wagons": "When my parents spoke about this at home in the kitchen, I was sent out." In the summer of 1941, Willy Cohn entered into his diary the "gruesome, barely conceivable [news] that 12,000 Jews had been shot in Lemberg." Victor Klemperer, whose contacts in his Dresden *Judenhaus* included Jews in mixed marriages with ties to non-Jews, wrote in January 1942, "rumor, but ... believable.... Evacuated Jews near Riga ... were *shot.*" In March he noted, "Concentration camp is apparently identical with a death sentence," and "I heard the most horrible concentration camp ... was Auschwitz (or something like that)." April 1942 brought news of mass murders of Jews in Kiev, including small children. According to Ruth Abraham, when she helped her elderly parents climb into the truck to the assembly point in July 1942, both knew what awaited them. They were resigned to a "horrible end, rather than remaining in a horror without end."

About that same time, Howard K. Smith wrote that "transportation" to Russia meant "death by slavery" and that the "fondest hope" of the elderly Jews he knew "was to die quietly and from natural causes; not torture."[51]

Those who listened to forbidden radios could hear BBC reports of mass murders in June. By mid-1942, rumors of mass murder circulated via the Jewish rumor mill known as the "mouth radio" or *Mundfunk* (a wordplay on *Rundfunk,* or radio). Soldiers, home on leave from the eastern front and sworn to secrecy, confirmed the rumors, telling trusted relatives or friends, who informed Jewish friends. In addition, relatives of deported Jews were already wondering why they no longer received word from them. By late 1942, there were widespread rumors in Germany of the gassing of Jews.

In November 1942, Rabbi Stephen Wise of New York publicly announced and the U.S. State Department confirmed the mass murder of 2 million Jews and the Nazi intention to murder all the Jews of Europe. The BBC reported on this. In December 1942, Britain, the United States, the USSR, and nine allies condemned the Nazis' "extermination of the Jewish People in Europe." That month, Ruth Abraham's husband, terrified of the approaching birth of his baby, was assured by another Jewish forced laborer that "if millions of Jews go through gas and your wife brings a new Jewish life to the world, [the baby] will bring luck [*Massel*] for all of you." By that time the Nazis had already killed nearly 4 million European Jews, at least two-thirds of them in 1942 alone, a year Raul Hilberg has called the "most lethal . . . in Jewish history." Whereas in late 1941, Ilse Rewald had assumed that deportations meant a ghetto and forced labor, by late 1942 she had heard of mass murders: "It is clear that every 'evacuated' person is going toward his death."[52]

Thus, by the time of the Rosenstrasse protest, most remaining Jews harbored a suspicion about what awaited them at the end of deportation. The ultimate terror may have remained hidden, but the deportations represented a clear threat to their liberty and, in a less systematic way, to their health and safety: "At the same time that many truly believed they were being sent to camps merely to perform hard labor, they looked upon arrest and deportation as spelling their end."[53]

Still, not all Jews were privy to information or rumors, and, even then, hearing is not necessarily believing. There were always those Jews, like those Germans, who did not, or could not, grasp what the rumors meant. They expected the worst—they did not expect the unthinkable. Inge Deutsch-kron recalled that she had heard about gassings and executions over the BBC in November 1942. Yet she and her mother absolutely refused to believe the "literally unbelievable" until an "Aryan" friend confirmed the reports. A *"Mischling"* son, whose father was deported, also refused to believe what he had heard, although he harbored dire misgivings. Years later he recalled that when his aunts and uncles were sent to Lublin, they

> were told they were being sent to work camps and we pretended it was so. "Well," we said, "by now they're bringing them new shoes." And later we said, "Well, they don't write, but let's hope they are well." But everybody knew they weren't being sent to a work camp. Everybody was lying to each other and nobody admitted the truth. But everybody knew. We didn't dare admit the truth. It was impossible.

Hence, even as rumors abounded, some Jews continued to "believe" that they would be doing hard labor. Nurse Frieda Cohn, who during the height of deportations had discovered double and triple suicides, wrote after the war that she was so depressed by these experiences that she had wished to be deported too: "What that really meant wasn't known yet." As late as mid-1943, the Jewish resistance group Chug Chaluzi (Pioneer Circle; see chapter 8) prayed for deported parents and friends but recited the special Jewish prayer for the dead only for those whom the Nazis had murdered before the deportations.[54]

"Mischlinge" and Jews in mixed marriages doing forced labor personally came across proof of the horrors taking place in the East. In 1943, one Jewish man, married to an "Aryan," worked at a rag and scrap shop, sorting clothing taken from army trucks returning from Poland. He opened leather handbags to sort the contents, finding Jewish passes and letters in German and Yiddish begging for food. One day he found children's shoes with blood on them. He went home and wept with his wife. Then they went into hiding. But another Jewish woman failed to draw the correct inferences from a similar experience. Edith Wolff, a *"Mischling"* who later helped organize the Chug Chaluzi, was arrested for giving another woman a false food ration card and sent to the penitentiary at Cottbus. There, some women told her of a strange incident. They had been asked to sort clothing with yellow stars on it and had found necklaces, rings, and watches in the hems and linings; the clothing itself was soiled with dirt, blood, and human excrement. Wolff did not understand what this meant, although she inferred from the stars that the clothing had belonged to Jews and assumed that they had hoped to save a few things to help them survive their deportation. Only much later did she realize the full import of this evidence—the Jews had "literally sweated blood" as they were about to be killed.[55]

As late as 1944, there was confusion among the few remaining Jews in mixed marriages and among *"Mischlinge."* Whereas Helmut Krüger, a *"Mischling"* whose mother was deported to Theresienstadt, wrote that all knew of concentration camps, but "we knew nothing about extermination camps," Victor Klemperer reported a conversation in which his friend estimated that over 6 million Jews had been murdered by shooting or gas. Moreover, he knew of a soldier who had reported on the horrific murders of Jews in the East, confiding: "When we received whiskey, we already knew what would happen."[56]

What Germans Saw, Heard, or "Knew"

Between 1941 and 1943, the Nazi regime deported most of the Jews in Germany. Of the 164,000 "full" Jews counted in the census of October 1941, only 51,000 remained in Germany in 1943. Terrorizing the daily lives of all Jews, deportations also touched the daily lives of many Germans in both small towns and big cities. In the small town of "Sonderburg" in the Rhineland, for example, only 12 of the original 150 Jews remained in 1942. Of these, one man was ninety-four years old, three people were in their seventies, seven were in their sixties, and one was in her fifties. During the night of July 25, 1942, an SS officer told each Jewish person to assemble the following morning. A neighbor saw one couple leave their home around 7 A.M. When she told her parents, her mother cried and refused to look and her father pulled down the shades. In a rare instance of a German revealing what she saw happen to Jews, a woman reported in the 1970s on the "Sonderburg" deportations. She told a former Jewish neighbor that she had seen a furniture van, "filled with Jews. I saw Mr. Miller and all the others sitting there quietly. One of the workers from my store ran forward with a blanket, which he placed over old Mr. Miller's knees." The Nazis then forced the elderly Jews to stand in the square in front of the synagogue, in open view of anyone passing by.

Of the almost 73,000 Jews in Berlin at the beginning of the deportations, only 6,000 remained there by mid-1944. During the winter of 1942–43, Berlin workers en route to the morning shift could see vans with Jews inside, but it was a Jewish forced laborer, Marcella Herrmann, who recorded what she saw. The back of the van was covered by a curtain, which did not reach the floor. She noticed: "the feet of people who were obviously sitting on benches. . . . There were feet in women's shoes, pretty shoes next to worn shoes, feet wrapped in rags, others in dilapidated slippers. . . . Whose feet are those? What kind of people are those? What is in store for them? I was seized by horror."[57] How many German laborers saw similar scenes or asked similar questions? Or helped sort soiled clothing from the East?

Other Jewish witnesses made clear how much the Berlin populace saw. In July 1942, Ruth Abraham, desperate to say a last farewell to her parents, walked three hours (since Jews could not take public transportation) to the assembly point at Schulstrasse, Berlin: "I arrived at about 6 in the morning; curious people had gathered in front of the building and were gloating over the misery that had befallen their fellow citizens, the Jews. . . . I wound my way through the hateful crowd of people into the building where the unlucky ones were." Near the Berlin Levetzowstrasse synagogue assembly area, Herta Pineas noted "how the house owners and storekeepers stepped in front of their doors and observed at great length the loading of the Jews into the furniture vans." Later, she assisted at a train station: "The people living around the Putlitzstrasse station observed in masses from the bridge across the rails how these transports . . . departed from an open platform . . . and supposedly they knew nothing of these things?" Indeed, those Berliners anxious to be informed did hear rumors about the destiny of the Jews. As early as mid-September 1941, Ruth Andreas-Friedrich—a German who wanted to know because she helped to hide Jews—feared that deportation would mean death. That December she wrote: "The Jews are disappearing in throngs. Ghastly rumors are current about the fate of the evacuees."[58]

Nor did the government—despite rigorous attempts to murder Jews secretly, under the cover of "night and fog"—remain entirely silent about the fate of the Jews during the implementation of the "Final Solution." Hitler's famous speech to the Reichstag of January 1939—filmed, broadcasted, reprinted in newspapers, and repeated with slight variations in September 1942—blamed Jews for fomenting war. It ended with the ominous prophecy that this war would not see the "Bolshevization of the earth and thus the victory of Jewry, but the annihilation of the Jewish race in Europe." In November 1941, Minister of Propaganda Joseph Goebbels referred to Hitler's threat. Goebbels wrote an editorial in *Das Reich*, a widely read newspaper, entitled "The Jews Are at Fault!" He announced: "We are now experiencing the fulfillment of this prophecy, thus a fate is carried out against the Jews that is, to be sure, hard, but more than deserved." Moreover, he warned that if Germany lost the war, Jews would turn into wolves "hurling themselves upon our *Volk*, our women and children, in order to realize a vengeance unlike anything that has occurred in history." He apparently realized the preponderance of elderly women in the Jewish population at that time, for he warned that if Berlin Jewry seemed made up of "fragile old women" it was only because Jews were looking for sympathy. He cautioned that no matter how "fragile and pitiable" they were, they belonged to the same world Jewry attempting to bring the United States into the war.[59]

Information about the mass executions and gassings was available to Germans from the same sources available to Jews, as well as from administrators and settlers in the eastern territories and from businessmen and others in contact with German industries at the camps. Most significantly, over 3 million soldiers set upon "Jewish Bolshevism" in the East. As the war progressed, more and more soldiers either saw or participated in anti-Jewish atrocities. Some of them wrote letters home describing the brutal murders they had committed or witnessed, including those against women and children. Many of these letters exhibited pride in a job well done or an ideological determination to annihilate the Jewish people: "There is only one solution for Jewry: Extermination." On leave or recovering from wounds, soldiers shared their experiences. If Jews *indirectly* found out about the exterminations from soldiers home from the front, surely many more Germans heard of or read letters about the slaughter directly.[60]

In interviews with Germans after the war, many acknowledged that Jews "disappeared" or "vanished," although few admitted to having known the destination. During the war, few had openly questioned why Jews "disappeared" or how. Some wanted them to "disappear"; others were afraid to ask; still others hoped to exonerate themselves later by not "knowing" now. That most Germans knew or suspected the truth about the camps is hardly at issue any longer; as David Bankier put it, "They knew enough to know that it was better not to know." Moreover, those Germans who chose ignorance had an easy time of it, since Jews had been so thoroughly ostracized and segregated before their deportation.[61]

Germans might have understood the fate of the Jews in the context of a war of extermination against the Soviets, and they might have merged the specific annihilation of the Jews with the atrocities against Poles and Russians. The pivotal question here is not *what Germans knew* about the genocide but rather who *chose to believe the facts* that were emerging.[62] A conscientious and concerned German could figure out that the Jews were being exterminated. The knowledge of Germans, however, should be distinguished from that of those Jews who did not or could not draw the correct inferences. The disbelief of the victims, suffering from lack of information and isolation, is different from the disbelief of the perpetrators and bystanders, whose callous disregard about the fate of the Jews is striking.

Ultimately, many Germans denied knowing or negated information about the genocide because they had erased Jews from their consciousness and their consciences. The "social liquidation [of the Jews] preceded [their] physical annihilation by many years." Many Germans participated in perse-cuting Jews, either in their official positions (such as in the Gestapo, the Party, or the civil service) or in the course of their daily lives; most other Germans either applauded, ignored, or denied the persecution. Except dur-ing the November Pogrom, few Germans ever objected to the plight of the Jews. Aside from the Rosenstrasse demonstration, made up mostly of wives and relatives, there was never a mass demonstration against the deportation of Jews. Thus, by the time of their deportation, Jews had already been condemned to "social death."[63] Physical death lay several hundred miles away.

8

Life Underground

I had terrible hunger pangs, but worry about where I was to spend the night made all the pain seem insignificant.

— CAMILLA NEUMANN

Most Jews waited until the last moment to "dive," once they were certain the Nazis intended to kill them. Hiding may have been somewhat easier for women than men, but it was extremely dangerous and nearly impossible for all Jews. They lived in dread, fearful for their own safety and that of the people who hid them. Since "the prospect that Europe's Jews saw before them was not one of simply holding out until a preordained liberation date set for May 1945 at the latest,"[1] they showed enormous courage in defying the fate the Nazis had prepared for them. The Germans who hid them showed compassion and daring, revealing the possibility of resistance to genocide.

GOING INTO HIDING

By August 1942, Erna Becker-Kohen, living in a "privileged" mixed marriage, noticed fewer and fewer yellow stars in Berlin: "One doesn't see many Jews on the streets anymore, most have been taken, one knows nothing about them." Those German Jews who remained in Germany had either gone into hiding or were in mixed marriages—although they, too, were in danger and in many cases hid. About one-third of the Jews in hiding had refused to comply with their deportation orders, others had hidden just before the orders arrived. "Hiding" could mean ducking out of sight for the duration of the war or removing the yellow star and assuming an "Aryan" identity, with or without papers. Jews became fugitives, "submerging" or "diving" into the underground, to avoid detection by the Nazis. Known as

"U-boats," another term for submarines, they referred to their condition as *"untergetaucht"* (submerged) and to themselves as *"getauchte Juden"* (submerged Jews).[2]

To decide on an illegal, underground existence was profoundly difficult, since an Allied victory was not at all certain. Indeed, until the Battle of Stalingrad—more than a year after the deportations had begun—the Axis seemed to be winning. The decision to defy deportation appeared to many to be open-ended and, hence, impossible. How long could they find refuge with strangers? How long could their money or false identities last? Only once the war had turned against the Nazis could some Jews hope for an end to their suffering.

Most Jews who hid did so after the official notices of deportations ceased and the arbitrary roundups of Jews began in late 1942. By then, their attitudes and perceptions had changed: they had already seen friends and relatives deported, and rumors were spreading. It was especially after parents and elderly relatives had been taken that many decided it was time to hide. Ilse Rewald and her husband resolved to defy their fate only at the last minute, when the arbitrary roundups began, and only after the last remaining members of their families were deported to what they knew was a certain death. In January 1943, each took off the Star of David, left their apartment, and no longer reported to work. Gabriel Ritter's mother waited until the last possible moment, the end of February 1943: "We were looking out of the window . . . and we saw how the Jews were being taken from the rear house. My mother . . . tore off our stars. We got dressed quickly and really catch-as-catch-can: I remember that my mother put on the wrong skirt with the wrong jacket." The Ritters did not have a destination. With only the clothes on their backs and some money the mother had stashed away, they called various non-Jewish acquaintances. One agreed to hide them for three days and then found another family who hid them for over a year.[3]

For those who had not hidden earlier, the roundup of Jewish forced laborers at the end of February 1943 was the final push. During this "factory action," about 10,000 Jews, over 7,000 in Berlin, were hauled out of the factories where they worked and were deported. Some Jewish workers had been warned by German coworkers or foremen of the impending action and chose that day to start hiding. The factory action shocked those remaining Jews who had counted on the priority of war production and their own importance as useful laborers to stay their own deportations. It made clear that the Nazis' obsessive hatred would engulf even Jews doing valuable labor.[4]

THE DILEMMAS OF AN ILLEGAL LIFE

Though estimates vary widely, some suggest that between 10,000 and 12,000 German Jews went underground. Only about 25 percent actually survived; the rest were denounced, caught by the Gestapo, or died from malnutrition, exposure, or the bombings. Those who defied deportation embarked upon an illegal life. For the middle-aged, this was an existence for which nothing in their bourgeois backgrounds had prepared them, either emotionally or practically. The younger generation, which had grown up under Nazism, may have been more adept at the necessary machinations for living illegally, especially in groups. Nevertheless, memoirs often stress how agonizing illegality was, not simply because of its dangers but because these law-abiding people had been left no choice but to become outlaws.

Men in hiding were in greater danger of being caught than women. Since most German men of military age had been drafted, men walking the streets were looked upon with distrust and were subject to frequent identity checks. Toward the end of the war, there were manhunts for possible deserters or escaped forced laborers. As a result, unless men in hiding had foolproof false papers, they left their refuge only infrequently. Jewish women could blend in among German women more easily as servants or nannies. Indeed, one Jewish woman, introduced as the hider's aunt, had an ersatz coffee now and then with the Nazi block warden, while another, introduced as the hider's fiancée, had to accept the suspicious and dangerous friendship of a leader of the Nazi women's organization.[5]

In a study of sixty-five testimonies culled from memoir collections and autobiographies, Avraham Seligmann offered some insights about hiding. In his work, the ages of those who hid ranged from twelve to fifty-nine; about half were between thirty-one and forty-nine. On occasion, babies and small children faced the hardships of hiding, usually with their mothers. About 40 percent were married (72 percent to Jews and 28 percent to non-Jews). Seligmann estimates that an equal number of men and women went underground. Yet there is reason to believe that fewer women than men went into hiding, although this is an area in need of further research. First, it was harder to hide with children. Second, some families thought that men, especially sons, could withstand the harshness of hiding better than daughters. Third, while in the 1930s women were eager to flee from danger by emigrating, in the early 1940s some women may have feared hiding as even more dangerous than forced "relocation" or "evacuation" to the East.

Seligmann's data suggest that 47 percent of those in hiding hid with family members. This figure seems high, since even couples who went into hiding together had to split up on occasion to avoid suspicion. For example, the Collm family—Steffi, Ludwig, and their small daughter, Susi—went into hiding together but changed quarters about every three weeks, sometimes the mother and child finding shelter together, sometimes the husband and wife. Only toward the end did all three manage to reside together. Such family separations were excruciating, especially during the bombings. The Collms reported losing contact with Susi for eight days after a particularly severe bombing in an area where she was hidden. They agonized until they got word of her safety.[6]

As the war and the Gestapo threatened the fugitives, the daily struggle for their lives became even more exhausting and debilitating, but it was also radically simplified: daily life became a search for shelter and food. Carrying a backpack or small suitcase with the barest essentials, many Jewish fugitives left their old neighborhoods, where they could have been easily recognized, and approached non-Jewish coworkers, friends, and relatives for their first shelter. They stayed with acquaintances, with acquaintances of acquaintances, with couples in "privileged" mixed marriages, or with these couples' relatives and friends. Others, relying on sheer nerve rather than calculation, approached total strangers, since they knew not one soul they could trust. Only about half the Jews in Seligmann's study actually knew the people who first hid them.

Although some Jews prepared a first shelter and a network of helpers before they "dove," many sought refuge spontaneously, just as their hiders made impetuous decisions rather than following carefully thought-out strategies. In 1942, twenty-three-year-old Erna Puterman knocked on her friend's door, declaring: "Today they took my mother." Her friend responded: "Then you'll stay here." The hider and her three children shared their two rooms with the Jewish woman until the war's end. Fearing imminent deportation, Irma Simon packed one suitcase and started walking down her street to find a place to store it. Because it was heavy, she paused for a moment. Looking around, she noticed her shoemaker's shop. She asked him if he might store her suitcase. He did more: he and his brother helped to hide her, her husband, and their son. Both Berliners, Puterman and Simon wound up sharing their helpers' apartments with them. This was common in Berlin, where most rescuers lived in three-room, rented apartments, sharing them with the Jews they hid.[7]

In their new surroundings, Jews with light hair and eyes had an easier time avoiding suspicious stares than Jews with darker hair and complexions. Referring to the dark-haired, dark-skinned caricatures of Jews that many Germans believed, one Jewish fugitive stressed that these stereotypes saved many Jewish lives, since most Germans "never suspected . . . German-looking people of being Jewish." The same Nazi stereotypes may have prevented some dark-haired Jews from finding shelter. In her study of people who hid Jews throughout Europe, Eva Fogelman noted that potential rescuers feared the greater risk of hiding a Jewish person fitting the Nazi stereotype: "A Jewish woman who could pass as an Aryan, with blond hair and blue eyes, was more likely to be offered shelter than a Jewish man with identifying traits . . . dark curly hair, a hooked nose, dark eyes . . . a circumcised penis." For those passing as "Aryans," looks mattered, but bearing, appearing confident, was also essential.[8]

Although grateful for any shelter, many Jews who hid made do with few amenities, even fewer than in the *Judenhäuser*. In some places they had buckets rather than toilets, in others a communal dish rather than individual place settings. Frequently there was no way of bathing; sometimes they became infested with lice. Jews found temporary refuge in unused rooms, attics, cellars, workshops, storerooms, or showrooms; behind staircases or false walls; or in storehouses or barns. Thus shelters were often cramped, dingy, and damp. In Berlin, small garden sheds on the outskirts of town provided frequent, if dangerous, refuge; the Gestapo, aware of the potential for hiding there, made regular sweeps through these areas. Shelters were often dark and lacked sanitary facilities, other than buckets. Moreover, many Jewish fugitives had to remain motionless for days on end. The sheer boredom drove some into the streets, where they were caught, while a "stubborn acceptance of monotony" saved the lives of the more patient.[9] Others had to leave their shelters early and return late each day in order to avoid arousing the suspicion of their protectors' neighbors or friends.

The classic tale of Jews in hiding is that of Anne Frank and her family, who remained in one Amsterdam refuge from 1942, when they "dove," until 1944, when they were denounced and arrested. Unlike the Franks, however, many Jews in hiding changed lodgings frequently, sometimes to minimize questions that neighbors might ask their hosts, sometimes because they had not told their unsuspecting hosts the truth for fear of being turned away. Seligmann's data indicate that about 300 Germans were needed to hide sixty-five Jews. Inge Deutschkron and her mother hid with at least twelve people in as many places in the course of twenty-seven months. A resistance group moved Jewish "guests around from one to another. You take them one night, we'll take them the next. Permanent guests are suspicious looking." One Jewish wife in a "privileged" mixed marriage and her daughters left Berlin to spend two and a half years walking from village to village:

> Every single day, no matter what the . . . weather, we walked on. . . . Often we were cold and . . . hungry, and we slept in farmers' shacks. . . . I used to break into those shacks. . . . I brought a map along . . . and made sure that we never went to a village more than once. I asked farmers . . . for food. I told them that we had been bombed out of our home and were trying to make our way to relatives. . . . Sometimes farmers gave us . . . food [and] a place to sleep. The farmers wouldn't have helped us at all if they had known that we were Jewish. . . . I dyed my hair blond. . . . One of my daughters . . . had blond hair.

Seligmann found that about one-quarter of the Jews he studied had one main hiding place, that the great majority had at least two main places to hide, and that virtually all had extra sites lined up in case of emergencies.

Emergencies included not only distrustful neighbors or alert block wardens but also bombings. The latter caused large sections of the German population to lose their shelters, including many Jews in hiding. However, the bombings also had a positive side for Jews, giving some the occasion to blend in with other "bombing victims" and to pretend that they were "Aryans" whose legal identification papers had been "destroyed" and who required new ones. Importantly, even though Jews in hiding suffered from the bombings, they gave all Jews hope that the Allies would win the war.[10]

In desperation, some Jews sought shelter in public places. The young people in the Jewish resistance group Chug Chaluzi (Pioneer Circle), for example, endured many "street nights" when they slept in coffeehouses, bars, waiting rooms, and streetcars, probably blending in with others who had lost their homes as well. In Berlin, telephone booths could serve as emergency shelters. Camilla Neumann reported:

> I had terrible hunger pangs, but worry about where I was to spend the night made all the pain seem insignificant. . . . Suddenly I discovered several telephone booths. . . . I had found my lodging for the night. . . . I spread . . . newspapers out in the booth and squatted down. There could be no thought of sleep, of course, but at least I would not be seized by the police patrol.

In the small town of Weiden, one woman hid in twenty-three different places in two years, including a mill and a railroad inspector's booth.[11]

Besides shelter, other significant problems concerned identity papers, food, sickness, and money. Living illegally, Jews could no longer use their identity cards, stamped with a large *J*, or their ration cards. A foolproof fake document could play a critical role in survival, as could an even more difficult to acquire legal document (such as a postal identity card). Either could satisfy possible questioners. Some Jews tried to obtain illegal identification cards from underground groups. The Rewalds managed to get false papers from a man who had supervised the husband during his forced labor. By 1944, this forgery was essential, since Rewald had to support her husband, who could no longer risk being seen in public.

Jews without false identification cards or their protectors had to resort to the black market for food. But even those in relatively secure hiding places, like Irma Simon, lost a great deal of weight and nearly starved. Others, like Blanca Rosenberg, an Eastern European Jewish woman who took on the false identity of a Polish forced laborer in Heidelberg, survived only by stealing food from the Nazi family she served: "My food ration was that of a forced-labor slave—a small loaf of bread. Stupefied by the ration, I turned to Cesia [the maid whom she was to replace]. 'How do you manage on this ration?' . . . She smiled. 'Look, you're the cook, so fill up a bit on the soup you're making.'" She began to lose weight and sneak food from the pantry. Since the housewife counted the ripe fruit on the trees, Rosenberg could not steal from the garden. She stole an egg now and then from under a hen and ate it raw: "Unlike the fruit trees, the chickens never gave me away." Those with neither false identities nor access to helpers often went without food for days or ate wild berries and roots.[12]

Jews in hiding suffered injuries from the bombings and dreaded serious illnesses such as pneumonia and tuberculosis because of their undernourishment and exposure to the elements. Pregnancy must have also been of concern. Seeking medical aid created serious risks, since doctors might demand identification and hospitals required it. Even with papers, men would be endangered by their circumcision. Jews, even women in childbirth, steadfastly avoided medical personnel or hospitalization.[13]

As hard as it was to survive in hiding, it was even more dangerous—to one's helpers—to die. Irma Neumann, married to an "Aryan," and hence "privileged" (although she, too, went into hiding at times), tried to save her sister Erna by finding her a tiny room in Berlin, which she shared with a working-class woman. Exceedingly malnourished, Erna developed a high fever and a bronchial infection in February 1943. A doctor, whom Irma entreated to help her sister, recommended hospitalization; but hospitalization was impossible. Her sister had only Jewish identification. Erna soon died of heart failure. Irma and the roommate had to dispose of the body:

> The most horrible hours of my life began. We two women waited until 12:30 at night until all was still in the building, where 44 (!!!) occupants lived. Then we took the ... body, which we had hidden in a sack, and dragged it four flights down.... The desperation and the fear of getting caught gave us superhuman strength. It was just enough to uncover the corpse and set it into the impenetrable night. That was my farewell to my beloved sister.[14]

In addition to papers, food, and health, money was critically important, although not always absolutely essential. About one-quarter of the hiders in Seligmann's sample demanded money, valuables, or some form of work from the Jews they hid. Some demanded money as a prerequisite for providing shelter; some needed money to buy food to feed the people they were hiding. Also, most Jews in hiding wanted to pay for their expenses if they could. But money was not always available. Some, like one seamstress, sewed in return for food and shelter. Some young women even resorted to exchanging sex for shelter, including working in brothels in Berlin. Although memoirs rarely mention the issue of money, it is occasionally clear that a person in hiding had some money. Ruth Abraham stashed money away before going into hiding; Erna Becker-Kohen received money from her "Aryan" husband. She even made donations to the parishes in which she found refuge, so as not to feel like a beggar.[15]

Jews often concealed their real identities from their hiders, both to avoid being refused shelter and to protect their hosts from implication in their ruse, which could cost them prison sentences and, possibly, their lives. Indeed, in Seligmann's study, although 85 percent of Jewish fugitives revealed their Jewishness to their first rescuer, close to half concealed it from their second hider, with many (31 percent) pretending to be Christians. Correspondingly, many people preferred to remain ignorant of the identity of the person they protected. In addition to Jews, army deserters and forced foreign laborers who had escaped were on the loose. Between hiders and hidden, much was assumed and left unsaid—and hiders who knew often feigned ignorance.[16]

Some Jews even hid in Nazi families. Blanca Rosenberg worked for Nazis during the last year of the war, pretending to be an Eastern European forced laborer. The household consisted of seven children. She did backbreaking work from 5:00 A.M. until 10:00 or 11:00 at night. She also had to fake sympathy for the antisemitic complaints of the housewife, who, like many of her class, benefited from the persecution of Jewish women or the forced labor of Eastern European women, although never acknowledging it: "Oh ... the miseries this war has produced. And all this misfortune brought down on us by the damn Jews." Still, Rosenberg was grateful. A false identity in one household provided a relatively safe haven: "I passed.... An invisible little maid, to whom no attention need be paid, I began to lose my perennial wariness, and my shattered nerves settled."[17]

Although at times some Jews had the urge to reveal their identities, as a result of a "need to belong to the Jews," most realized the jeopardy of doing so. Erna Becker-Kohen was an exception; a convert to Catholicism, she felt compelled, even while hiding, to identify as a Jew: "Worried that people will think I have used my Christian beliefs as a cover for my Jewish origins, I tell all people ... of my Jewish ancestry. This honesty is due Christianity and my Jewish racial compatriots.... I will never give up this candor, even if I know I am putting myself into great danger."[18]

False identities became somewhat easier to acquire once the Allies began heavy bombing—as, for example, in the massive attacks on Berlin in August 1943—destroying neighborhoods and registry and documentation offices. Then Jews could claim to be refugees whose homes and records had been destroyed. In Münster, a Jewish woman used the pretext that all her documents had been destroyed to request papers from the authorities. She then applied for and received an Evacuated Family Support Certificate. A Jew could also pick up a perfectly good identity card from a corpse on the street. One woman, describing how fervently she longed for an identity card, recalled seeing dead bodies on the street after a bombing: "Then I got the idea, check if they have an identity card on them.... And in that moment I took off and was lucky!" In early 1945, as the Soviets moved westward, some Jews could acquire proper papers by claiming that they were refugees from the East. Still, more than half of Seligmann's sample continued to use their own names, some without any false papers, others with false papers proclaiming their "Aryan" status in their own names.[19]

Most Jews in hiding lived in constant terror of detection, fleeing when the police or Gestapo approached the premises. Alice Goldstein, for example, was in bed when the Gestapo raided her friend's apartment where she was hiding: "Thank God I had the presence of mind to make my bed with the speed of light and to hide in the closet in my nightgown, with my clothing in my hands. A miracle occurred, the officers did not open the closet, even though they carefully searched the apartment. I feared they would hear my heartbeat." Ilse Rewald worked illegally in a laundry run by a distant non-Jewish relative. When officials entered to spot-check the papers of the workers, she quickly ran away. In 1943, she wrote: "We live . . . only from day to day, worrying about our sheer survival doesn't give a moment's respite."[20]

Jews in hiding feared not only almost all "Aryans"—for any neighbor, block warden, mail carrier, or grocer could denounce them—but also Jewish "catchers," Jews hired by the Gestapo under the pretext that their lives would be saved, to track and denounce other Jews. In Berlin there were about fifteen to twenty Jewish catchers. The most famous was Stella Goldschlag, the "blond Lorelei," as she was known to the submerged Jews. On one weekend alone, she led the Gestapo to sixty-two hiding Jews, finding them in cafés and apartments and on the streets. A resistance group known as the Society for Peace and Reconstruction, which consisted of Jews in hiding and Germans and worked to save Jews and to distribute antiwar propaganda, tried to intimidate Stella by sending her a "death sentence" in the mail, with little success. Ursula Finke was caught on a train station platform by another Jewish catcher in 1943.

> In total desperation I took account of my life and knew that first they would beat me half dead and then they would transport me to Auschwitz. . . . The approaching train appeared . . . as my salvation and with one leap I threw myself in front of the train. I came to consciousness as someone called: "Turn off the electricity." Lying under the train, I heard an excited group of people on the platform who probably thought I had done this because of a love crisis and were now also scolding. . . . It was as if I had lost my mind, I felt no pain, only despair, and screamed: "You should be a persecuted Jew some time!"

Two railroad workers pulled her from under the train. Because her foot was smashed, her German captors postponed deporting her and instead sent her to the Jewish Hospital. She remained there until the war's end.[21]

Edith Bruck, uncovered by two Jewish catchers in November 1944, experienced her own capture with a sense of peace at last, like those Jews who after long foreboding faced deportation with relief. Surviving her ordeal in Ravensbrück, but weighing only eighty-eight pounds and suffering from tuberculosis, she wrote of the thoughts that accompanied her to the camp: "The whole pack so disgusted me that I was glad to depart to Ravensbrück adorned with my Jewish Star. . . . Above all, I was certain that no one would pursue me anymore."[22]

Besides the ongoing dread and danger of detection, bombings, particularly for Jews in major cities (where most hid), were an ever-present threat to refuge, life, and limb. Many Jews could not seek safety in bomb shelters, since these were available only to people with proper identity papers. Other Jews avoided the bomb shelters because they feared endangering not only themselves but also their hiders. Still others so feared the bombs that they dared to enter public shelters, although often avoiding those directly attached to the house in which they actually lived. Thus, part of the daily life of those in hiding included the "constant ... alarms, the burning houses and burned-out apartments, blocked-off streets blanketed in black smoke, bombed-out people and disturbed children ... and blocks of ruins." The bombings forced many Jews to flee major cities. As the war progressed, Jews increasingly found spots in small towns and villages.[23]

In sum, hiding meant keeping out of harm's way—whether from informers or bombs—and finding means of sustenance. But it was also, as Eva Fogelman has shown, a "tedious, enervating job, more like an assembly-line worker's duties" for Jews and their hiders. Ruth Andreas-Friedrich portrayed the rescuers as "risking their necks every hour and every day for a couple of miserable bread coupons, a temporary emergency shelter. ... No one who did not go through it themselves can imagine how difficult it can be to provide even the simplest assistance under such circumstances." Both Jews in hiding and their rescuers became weary of "endless days of deception and anxiety."[24] Thus, hiding took a heavy psychological toll, requiring enormous courage and patience from hiders and hidden. Of Jews, hiding also demanded a will to survive that could withstand the most severe challenges. One young woman, exhausted by running from the Gestapo, sleeping *under* a bed during the day, and frequenting pay toilets in train stations at night, found a brief respite with a soldier "who liked her." When he was summoned to the front, she found another shelter, only to be bombed out of it. On her last visit to a Jewish woman friend, she said: "I can't go on; I'm too tired. They'll catch me and kill me." Then she disappeared forever.

Rather than face discovery and deportation, some Jews in hiding may have committed suicide, while others were driven close to suicide. Alice Goldstein, whose two grown children had been deported, twice decided upon suicide. In March 1944, she found herself in Oberkassel, standing in deep snow, with nowhere to go. She resolved to jump off the Rhein Bridge but, noticing soldiers nearby "who would have gotten me out right away," changed her mind. A year later, with "not a slice of bread to eat," she decided to take the veronal she had been saving "as a last refuge." Luck intervened. Goldstein met a stranger who took her in, and she survived.[25]

The psychological toll of hiding was compounded by the terrible grief and guilt Jews felt about surviving after their families had been deported. Could they have done more for their loved ones? Could they have warned them? Could they have helped hide them? Lotte Paepcke, for example, safely hidden in a monastery, later wrote: "It was generous, this . . . life. [But my] soul withdrew from that alien, borrowed peace and wandered [eastward] to the place of [its] allotted fate: toward calamity and ruin." Such moments of guilt notwithstanding, most Jews in hiding were determined to defy those who would have exterminated them and, sometimes, to help others escape as well.[26]

JEWISH RESISTANCE

Although hiding was usually an isolated struggle by Jewish individuals or sometimes parts of a family, there were attempts at mutual support. In Berlin, Jewish fugitives tried to counter their isolation by meeting in cafés and by developing a "Jewish grapevine." They warned each other of the whereabouts of catchers. They traded information about the acquisition of false identity cards and the possibility of border runners who might smuggle Jews out of Germany. Some formed small groups of Jews already in hiding, like Felice Schragenheim's ten friends, who found shelters and false documents for other Jews.[27] Berlin provided a unique opportunity in this regard, since Jews trudging from village to village or hiding in small towns had few other Jews with whom to speak.

The Chug Chaluzi was one Jewish resistance group. In the summer of 1942, Edith Wolff, who would organize the group, persuaded a reluctant Jizchak Schwersenz, a teacher and Zionist youth leader, to go underground: "Only in this way can you save the children!" They began to prepare to save children and young people from deportations and organized the Chug Chaluzi after the "factory action" in February 1943. The group viewed saving Jewish lives as a form of political resistance: "We're combating Hitler with every life we save!"[28]

Its members tried to develop Jewish consciousness, to strengthen Jewish solidarity, and to prepare for a Jewish life in Palestine after the war. Consisting of about twenty young women and men (although at times it grew to forty), the group divided its illegal work between physical survival and cultural survival. Members met regularly, often daily, to exchange information and to organize meals and lodging for each other, and they routinely frequented public theaters, concerts, operas, and movies. In the summer, they met in the Grunewald and other parks; in the winter, in a variety of hiding places. Bombings did not stop them; they would gather one hour after the all-clear signal. Their cultural activities, with a socialist and Zionist bent, included study groups, religious practice, and visits to cultural events in Berlin. They rarely went anywhere in groups of more than two, and if they traveled as a group they pretended not to know each other. When the entire group met, only two people would arrive at the destination every fifteen minutes.

Their weekly schedule included hiking and sports on Sundays, attending Berlin cultural events on Mondays, studying Hebrew or English on Tuesdays, discussing Palestine and Zionist history on Wednesdays, analyzing the Hebrew Bible on Thursdays, and meeting on Fridays. They planned their most important meetings for Saturdays, the Jewish Sabbath, when they prepared for the cultural event they would attend the following week. They would read the opera or play they planned to see. They were particularly moved by Goethe's *Egmont*, whose "struggle for the liberation of his people seemed so close to our own lives at that time." They also read Jewish history and Jewish literature on the Sabbath. Then they engaged in political discussion or talked about themes of general interest. They ended the Sabbath with the traditional *Havdalah* ceremony, using ersatz items: a flashlight, leaves, and a taste of cognac in place of the customary candle, spices, and wine.[29]

Members of the Chug Chaluzi had to guess the dates of Jewish holidays, since the last Jewish calendar in their possession was for the year 5700 (1939–40). When holidays "occurred," they decorated whatever meeting place they had chosen with flowers and two candles. Then, in place of the *challah*, a traditional bread, they shared some gray war rolls. Sometimes they prayed together, although they could not hold actual services. On Yom Kippur, the Day of Atonement, they prayed in the cellar apartment of a worker's family near Alexanderplatz. Remarkably, most members of the group's inner circle survived, probably because of the help of non-Jews (particularly those connected to the communist resistance and living in "privileged" mixed marriages), their own group solidarity, and financial aid from Zionist organizations abroad, not to mention the pluckiness of youth, sheer nerve, and good luck.[30] Other resistance groups were not as fortunate.

While the Chug Chaluzi was organized for some Jews to provide mutual support in hiding, other Jews joined German political groups to resist the Nazis. If the number of Jews in hiding was small, then the number engaged in organized political resistance was smaller still, since Jews were not only terribly isolated but also on the run. Their meager numbers should come as no surprise, since non-Jewish Germans who opposed the Nazis did not form political resistance groups of major significance either. The historian Arnold Paucker has written astutely: "[The belief] that Jews as a group . . . could have waged something like direct political resistance in a Nazified country whose own democratic organs had failed miserably or had been brutally destroyed, belongs quite simply to the realm of fantasy."[31]

Yet there were Jewish women and men who attempted to hurt the regime in connection with underground groups or even as lone individuals. They engaged in a broad range of oppositional activities, showing remarkable courage and taking considerable risk, often paying with their lives. Edith Wolff, on her own, pasted anti-Nazi slogans wherever she could, mailed them to bureaucrats, or slipped them into books. Peter Edel, with connections to a communist worker, stuck news of the war or the simple message "End It!" in factories, in streetcars, and on buildings in the center of Berlin. Some Jews maintained contact with German political resistance groups; some joined communist groups that attempted to undermine German morale and the war effort. In communist groups, Jews were clustered into Jewish cells, apparently for security reasons. Historians of Jewish resistance estimate that more than 2,000 Jews were active in antifascist underground activities at various points between 1933 and 1943, the majority in the earlier years before mass emigration. Paucker reminds us: "If this is measured proportionately against the size of the German population, the Jewish figure would be the equivalent of a mass movement of 600,000 to 700,000 active German antifascists. And [the Germans] certainly can't claim anything like that!" Quite young for the most part, these Jewish men and women "were primarily motivated by antifascism and they were often only loosely connected with the established Jewish community." This is not, however, to deny any Jewish motivation: even the resistance group around Herbert Baum, consisting of German Jews who shifted between discussions of Marxist literature, Judaism, and Zionism, tried to create some kind of Friday evening "atmosphere"—without much success, according to one member. Hunted as Jews and as leftists, their identities and the impetus for their actions were extremely complex.[32]

The Herbert Baum Group was the largest German-Jewish resistance group. Formed in Berlin between 1938 and 1939, this procommunist group first met to study and hike together. By wartime, the group consisted of young forced laborers, many of whom had made contact on the job. In 1941, the average age was twenty-two. The group's core consisted of about

30 members, and its outer circle another 40 to 50, although as many as 150 may have been connected at one point or another. Women made up nearly half the core, a proportion that far surpassed the share of women in the general antifascist resistance. Its members studied Marxism, printed antifascist leaflets, and helped people who lived illegally. Attempting more visible sabotage, the group organized an arson attack against the Nazi propaganda exhibit *The Soviet Paradise* in May 1942. In reprisal, the Nazis arrested and executed Baum and twenty-seven members and sympathizers and also shot over 250 other Berlin Jews. Only four members of the Baum Group's inner circle survived.[33]

Jewish women were involved in organized political resistance. Some had been politically committed to socialist or communist parties before 1933, while others, like Marianne Prager-Joachim from the Baum Group, were young adolescents in 1933. Judaism formed the cultural identity of some of the women, while having barely touched others. Whatever their identification with leftist politics or Jewishness, Jewish women participated in either mixed resistance groups or exclusively Jewish ones. Although women were crucial to the infrastructure of the resistance groups—as in the broader organized resistance throughout Europe, most groups would have collapsed without them—few women actually functioned as leaders. The only known Jewish group consisting entirely of women was active in and around Berlin. Led by Eva Mamlok, its members had belonged to the Jewish youth movement. During the period when the Nazi-Soviet pact was observed, it was this group, not those associated with the communists, that continued its antiwar propaganda. Only one member of the Mamlok group survived.[34]

Two Jewish women offer a glimpse into two different paths of Jewish resistance. Edith Wolff was born to a Jewish father (who later would be deported and murdered) and an "Aryan" mother. She and her two sisters had been baptized. As a student in the late Weimar Republic, she had belonged to the international, pacifist youth movement and was familiar with Marxist and Zionist writings. In 1933, at the age of nineteen, she converted to Judaism in solidarity with the Jewish people. That year she also began a personal campaign against the Nazis, leaving her own anti-Nazi tracts in library books, phone booths, and other public places and sending threatening postcards to Nazi bureaucrats. Because her aunt had removed Edith's name from the registry of the Jewish community, she was regarded as a *"Mischling."* This classification entitled her to "Aryan" rations of food, textiles, and cigarettes, and made it easier for her to help other Jews. When the deportations began, she found ways to hide young Jews or plan their escape from Germany altogether. Her work brought her into contact with individual resisters within the Confessing Church and the Catholic Action. When the final roundup of Jews began in February 1943, she helped organize the Chug Chaluzi, intent on saving "the leftovers" from the Nazis.[35] After the war she emigrated to Palestine.

Recha Rothschild chose a different course. Before the Nazi seizure of power, she had lived the life of a "new woman" and joined the Communist Party. After her arrest by the Nazis in 1933, her communist worldview, she wrote, sustained her during her three-year imprisonment. Upon her release, she emigrated to France, where she joined the communist resistance, helping German refugees, publicizing events in Germany, and providing aid to the Spanish Republic. Imprisoned in Gurs, a French internment camp in the Pyrenees, Rothschild managed to escape and continue her underground activities in France. During the German occupation, she worked for *Our Fatherland* (*Unser Vaterland*), a resistance newspaper that her group Free Germany (*Freies Deutschland*) slipped to the occupation troops. She survived, she believed, because the communists supported her physical and psychological existence, providing funds as well as "friends and sympathizers." After the war she chose to live in East Germany.[36]

THREE ACCOUNTS OF HIDING

The accounts of Irma Simon, Ruth Abraham, and Erna Becker-Kohen, three Jewish women who hid in Germany during the last years of the war, evoke the texture of feelings and the range of ordeals experienced by Jews in hiding. Their stories lend immediacy to the harrowing dilemmas such fugitives faced. They illustrate both the unremitting terror confronted by all "U-boats" and the singularity of each experience.

On the surface, these three women had little in common other than having grown up in secure, middle-class Jewish homes. They had different feelings toward their religion; they had varied contacts with the non-Jewish world; and one had married a Catholic, conferring on her "privileged" status. During the 1940s each woman hid differently: one ran back and forth between Berlin and the eastern provinces; another stayed primarily in one Berlin apartment; and the third trudged from village to village in the Bavarian and Austrian countryside. Their differences notwithstanding, all three watched their world turn sinister and faced the insecurities, hunger, and sheer terror of going underground.

These three stories also show a wide spectrum of actions by Germans: from those who refused to have anything to do with Jews (or, worse, who could have looked the other way but actively chose to persecute them), to those who unknowingly provided Jews with shelter, to a tiny minority of brave and generous people who welcomed the victims of persecution. If caught, the hiders risked brutal interrogation, imprisonment, and concentration camps. Men were also sent to the eastern front as punishment. Yet, however perilous their gamble, the consequences for hiders were not inevitable. After getting caught hiding a Jewish woman, one mother of four children merely received a reprimand.[37] The risks taken by the hiders never matched the risks of the "U-boats": the hider had a choice, the Jewish fugitive had none; if caught, the hider had a chance to survive, the Jewish person faced immediate death.

Irma Simon

Irma Simon, born in 1900, studied foreign languages and, at the age of twenty, married a man twenty-eight years her senior. During the 1930s, two of her sisters fled to the United States and two brothers escaped to New Zealand. She remained behind because her mother could not emigrate. Another brother also stayed and was killed in Auschwitz.

As a forced laborer at Siemens in Berlin, Irma Simon was warned one day in advance by a non-Jewish foreman of the imminent "factory action" —the roundup of Jewish workers on February 27, 1943.[38] She kept her husband and nineteen-year-old son, Fritz, home from work that day. The three of them agonized about what to do. Her husband, a veterinarian, volunteered that he had planned ahead, acquiring the means for the family to commit suicide rather than be murdered: "He held his arms high with his fists clenched. Then he opened his hands, and three glass capsules lay on the palms. 'What's that?' I asked. 'Prussic acid,' he said. 'Or do you want to wait until they come and ask, May we escort the ladies and gentlemen to their execution?'"

Seeing her son's pained expression, Irma withstood her husband's entreaties. After a day of unbearable tension, Irma Simon exploded: "We have to do something! 'And what should we do?' my husband asked. 'There must be someone in all of Berlin who will help us!' 'I don't know of anyone,' he said. 'Maybe you can find someone to keep a suitcase for you. But someone who will take the risk of hiding three Jews, that you won't find.'" The three had no reason to believe that any of the Germans they knew, whether neighbors, clients, or former friends, would help them. Insisting on some action, Irma Simon packed a suitcase of important belongings. She walked about one hundred yards down Lehrter Strasse and, miraculously, found her protector—a shoemaker. Years later, she said: "To think that this casual acquaintance would offer us even the smallest amount of help actually defied all reason. But in my despair I tried to do the unthinkable."

The shoemaker's brother August Kossmann, a smith, offered her family shelter. She stared at him: "A person whom I had never seen in my life calmly promised something that anyone in this city of millions, Berlin, would have considered insane." This worker—a communist, but not associated with any underground group—strove entirely on his own to save this previously well-off bourgeois family. August Kossmann took Irma and Fritz to his tiny three-room apartment in Lichterfelde. There, she pretended to be a widow, now engaged to Kossmann. She wore a black hat and veil for the duration of her ruse. Fritz, who was of army age, pretended to be her invalid son. The shoemaker hid her husband, although within a short time bombs destroyed the shoemaker's home. Then Dr. Simon, too, wound up with August Kossmann.

Irma Simon left her home with only one dress, which she dyed black to conform to her new identity as a "widow." She would wear this dress, covered only by two aprons that Kossmann found her, for the duration of the war. Her husband had packed some silverware and some morphine from his practice. They sold these items to buy bread. Their meager resources, however, did not last long. Irma Simon began life in hiding weighing 130 pounds and ended it at 84 pounds.

In constant dread of discovery by the neighbors, Irma Simon frequently pretended not to be in the apartment. Hence, she could not heat the apartment and froze during Kossmann's working hours, from 5 A.M. until 5 P.M. Because the toilet for Kossmann's apartment was off the stairway in the hall and she could not be seen using it, a pail served as her toilet. One neighbor, Mrs. Grüneck, was not only a member of the Nazi women's organization but also the most intrusive of block wardens. She incessantly demanded to see Irma's identity card and made pointed inquiries into Fritz's "leave" from military service. As a result of her prying, Fritz had to "return to the front" within weeks of being hidden. Kossmann gave him shelter in his garden shed on the edge of town and regularly delivered food to him by bicycle. At one point, Grüneck confronted Irma Simon: "I hear you are a Jew." In such cases, nerve was the only recourse left to Jews in hiding. Irma pretended to be so insulted that she threatened to go right to the police, ostensibly to embarrass the block warden: "You know I want to marry Kossmann, how can you say such a thing!" Grüneck retreated, but Kossmann decided it was time for Irma to disappear until the situation calmed down. Irma would visit her "father," supposedly a Pomeranian peasant. When Grüneck heard this, she attempted to garner food from the hapless couple. To provide the

"Pomeranian" food for the block warden and some basics for himself and his dependents, Kossmann worked overtime for local farmers. Always hungry, Irma Simon recalled: "Sometimes I almost cried in fury when we brought these delicacies down to Mrs. Grüneck. We lived—Kossmann, my boy and me—on one ration card." When her husband moved in, Kossmann also provided for him.

When Irma Simon had to "visit her father," she spent those weeks in the garden shed with Fritz. The shed was an unheated, windowless shack less than six feet high and four by five feet in area. For light, Kossmann carved a small hole into the roof and put a glass plate on it. When it rained, Irma and Fritz removed the plate and caught some water for washing themselves. A table served as a bed. Every day Kossmann delivered food to Fritz and Irma, emptied their latrine bucket, and covered up the waste so as not to alert the Gestapo. He then backed away from the small shed, covering his tracks, which could have given them away. Fritz and Irma spoke with each other in whispers, for the owners of nearby sheds could walk past at any time and the Gestapo regularly checked the shed area. She described her first night there: "I almost died of fear when strange sounds startled me awake the first night. 'Rats' said my son. 'For God's sake don't scream, they won't bite.'" Of the two, Irma had the better situation: Fritz remained in the shack for two years, surviving the cold and loneliness with leg muscles so atrophied that he could not walk when he was first liberated. Irma found relative safety in Kossmann's apartment. Finding shelter for a man of military age proved far more difficult than finding shelter and a cover story for a woman.

A cover story notwithstanding, Irma was severely limited by her lack of a false identity card. She was particularly vulnerable to bombings, since without an identity card she could not enter bomb shelters. During bombings, Irma and her husband sat upstairs watching the windows burst and parts of the walls crumble. Although frightened, she always felt "better a bomb than the Gestapo." She also sorely missed an identity card when she came down with pneumonia. Luckily, the doctor who examined her did not require identification, but he insisted that she would die if she did not go to the hospital immediately. Knowing that the hospital would require a legitimate identity card, Irma and her protector refused, and she remained at home.

The Simons were totally isolated from other Jews and assumed, like many other Jews in hiding, that they were the last Jews left. They knew of no other Jews in hiding until close to the end of the war, when a non-Jewish man and a Jewish woman sought shelter in Kossmann's daughter-in-law's apartment. There the young woman gave birth with only her lover to assist her. Irma rarely left the apartment in order to keep a low profile. Luckily, with the exception of the block warden, most neighbors seemed not to take much notice of her—"they were all so busy with their own problems"—but she was always afraid.

At some point in 1943, Kossmann and Irma Simon became lovers. She was forty-three and he fifty. "He was not the type to have insisted that I sleep with him," she declared years later. The relationship was mutual. She admired his strength, his calm, and his certainty that they would all make it. She described him as big—he was over six feet—strong, and handsome, perhaps in contrast to her husband, who was much older than she and terribly frightened and beaten. After the war, she emigrated to the United States with her husband and son. Her son joined the army, and Irma worked until she could establish her husband in his own apartment. Then she returned to Berlin to live with August Kossmann until he died in 1973. She remained in Berlin, where she had many friends, and died there in 1995.

Ruth Abraham

Born in 1913, Ruth Abraham was convinced that her looks helped her during the Nazi years—"I look absolutely Aryan, blond hair and blue eyes, a straight nose and well developed."[39] Despite many attempts, all her efforts to emigrate failed.

In December 1942, Abraham was almost nine months pregnant. As she walked to work wearing her yellow star, a woman, Maria Nickel, approached her and offered to help her once her baby was born. She suggested that Abraham place the newborn in front of Nickel's door so that she could say it was a foundling. She would care for the infant, along with her own two children, and would allow the Abrahams to reimburse her only for actual expenses. Fearing a trap, but desperate, Ruth Abraham had to overcome her own distrust of Nickel and then convince her husband to do the same.

By January 1943, Abraham realized: "According to everything I had seen and had heard on illegal radio broadcasts from abroad, deportation meant certain death." She decided to collect the money she had hidden at her workplace. On January 18, 1943, Abraham and her husband tore the yellow stars from their coats and left their apartment to face the bombed and burning streets of Berlin. Just then, her labor pains began, and the couple returned to their building basement, where she gave birth. She brought her newborn daughter to Maria Nickel. For the duration of the war, they shifted the baby back and forth between them: "Whenever an acceptable, safe hiding place turned up for me, I took the child. Whenever I had to hide the child from people, I always either stuffed pillows in her mouth [or] put her to sleep with red wine." Maria gave Ruth a postal identification card, which she had tricked a postal clerk into providing, with Maria's name and Ruth's photo. Not wishing to "burden her husband with the truth," Maria simply took his driver's license and gave it to Ruth's husband. Now the Abrahams had false identity papers, although ones that were not the most definitive and could implicate the Nickels.

The Abrahams headed to their first shelter in Küstrin, due east of Berlin, an address they had bought "for a lot of money." They lived with a poor peasant woman. They were less hungry there than in Berlin: "The peasants were happy to give their products for black market prices; in general, you could get anything for money." Their peace lasted only until June 1943. Then SS officers roared up to the hut on their motorcycles and confiscated their papers, insisting that Ruth's husband and five-month-old infant looked Jewish. When the SS drove away to check their papers, Ruth, a devout Jew, asked her husband to say a prayer of blessing over their child, fearing this was the end.

The Abrahams quickly agreed to split. Her husband jumped on his bike and fled, while Ruth, pushing the baby carriage, headed for the only train to leave that day for Berlin. Suddenly the carriage broke. She raced toward a peasant, who had previously sold her black market goods, and begged him to take her to the train, which he did: "In this tension and mortal danger it was clear to me that they must have seen on my face that I was a hunted Jew." Fearing an SS inspection in the train, she asked the conductor if she could sit in the cattle car because her baby was agitated. He agreed. In Berlin, she immediately phoned the Nickels to warn them of the danger. They had already been through a harrowing interrogation by the Gestapo but were able to plead ignorance and were released with a warning.

Homeless with her baby in Berlin, Ruth tried to find a contact. Her father's accountant, a Dutchman, had once told her that if she were ever at her wits' end, she should contact his friend, the Dutch consul. With nowhere else to turn, she approached the consul, who no longer held an official position since the German army had overrun his country. He offered his apartment keys, which, to her horror, she could not accept. The apartment was in her old neighborhood, where she would have been recognized. She begged for further assistance, but the consul refused. "[I was] at the end of my strength, homeless, hunted by the Gestapo and without papers, completely broken physically and psychologically. When I looked at my baby I was seized by the nerve to say . . . to the consul: 'If you can't help me, then I'll stay here and end my life here. That would not be what the Queen wants.'" He left the room and returned with his secretary, who provided shelter for the mother and child in her own apartment. There Ruth and her baby faced nightly bombings in a sixth-floor apartment in the center of Berlin, and she had no idea of her husband's whereabouts. Terrified of the bombings, she fled to another hideout near Küstrin but was forced to return to Berlin before long. She gave the baby to Maria, but the bombings became so severe that mothers with small children were evacuated. Since Maria was listed as having only two children, Ruth took her baby back.

Without identity papers and relying on her "Aryan" looks, she left Berlin and wandered from village to village, asking for shelter and trying to blend in with the many "Aryan" women and children whose homes had been bombed. Finally, she found an attic room with peasants who subscribed to the rabidly antisemitic *Stürmer*. She paid handsomely for the privilege of living in their freezing space and cooking where they prepared the feed for their animals. She washed her laundry—including diapers—in ice-cold water.

Two incidents at the time (probably 1944) gave her hope and countered her extreme sense of isolation. One day a Polish prisoner of war asked her if she were a Jew: "I did not answer and he comforted me—be strong, the end of the war is near. He . . . listened to the English station every night. . . . If I wanted, I could listen. . . . Hearing that was like opium, and that thought, that liberation and deliverance were near, gave me new courage to go on living." When a dog bit her baby, she found a doctor to attend to the wound: "The doctor asked for my identity papers and I told him I didn't have any. When I started to cry he comforted me with the words, 'I'm a half Jew,' and with that we understood each other."

She remained in the countryside, separated from her husband, until January 1945. Underground in Berlin,

> he spent time in movie theaters, streetcars, and wherever he could find quarters for a few nights. People whose help we had never expected risked their lives for him, poor people from simple backgrounds who did it out of feelings of humanity. [There was] a vegetable store where my whole family had shopped. My husband lived there for months.

By late in the war, the plight of Jewish men hiding in Berlin was at its most perilous, since all able-bodied men were drafted into the *Volkssturm*. Somehow, her husband found Ruth in her hiding place: "It was like a miracle that he was able to come to me. My husband arrived at 2 in the morning and got my attention by throwing a stone at the attic pane. I went to the window and recognized him." Their landlords prepared to escape from the advancing Soviets and "couldn't understand why we weren't preparing for flight, like they all were doing. Of course I said we would follow them, but I wasn't in a hurry." With the appearance of the Russians, the Abrahams could admit their true identities: "Now we no longer needed to keep it a secret that we were Jews and we told everyone present. This confession was like a bombshell. Now it was so easy for these people to say, 'we suspected it all along and that's why we kept you.'"

Attempting to flee the area because it was too close to the war front, the Abrahams joined a group of foreign forced laborers: "I shudder to describe the trip that we and hundreds of forced laborers set out on.... Every step [was] over corpses and dead animals, on foot and on broken-down vehicles we moved slowly forward.... Among all these wretched people, I was the only woman with a child." They paused in Landsberg an der Warte, where the Soviets arrested her husband, despite his insistence that he was Jewish. She remained in Landsberg until spring:

> Without my husband I just vegetated; everything was so hopeless. I was losing my strength and could hardly get out of bed. Suddenly I heard a knock.... A gardener asked me for a piece of bread for a beggar.... I went to the door ... and recognized my husband as the beggar. Dressed entirely in rags ... how can you describe such a reunion. The child was afraid of her father, whom she no longer recognized ... and I realized right away that he was a very sick man.

He had diphtheria. Summoning her last reserves of energy, she nursed him to recovery. Then Russian soldiers brought the family back to Berlin. By this time Ruth suffered from tuberculosis. She managed to recover and, in 1948, emigrated to the United States with her family: "What an irony of fate. Now we no longer needed any affidavits at all, and were considered displaced persons, and ... when our lives were at stake, our papers weren't adequate and America was closed to us." In 1965, seventeen years after they had last seen her, the Abrahams were delighted to pay for Maria Nickel to attend the wedding of their daughter, the child she had helped save.

Erna Becker-Kohen

Erna Becker-Kohen had lived in a "privileged" mixed marriage as a devout convert to Catholicism. She changed shelters most often, because her dark hair, dark eyes, and "rather foreign appearance"[40] called unwelcome attention to her. Her memoirs were written in diary form with exact entry dates.

Are they an actual contemporaneous record? On the one hand, the possibility seems unlikely, since she was often forced to carry whatever essentials she needed on her back, even through deep snow. Yet the entries exhibit an emotional immediacy and, often, a tone of complaint, uncertainty, and desperation unlike memoirs written after the fact. This suggests that perhaps this testimony—whether written fully on that day or jotted down hastily and completed shortly after the war—was as urgent to her as her most basic necessities.[41]

Becker-Kohen gave birth to her son during Christmas 1937. Despite fears for her child, the pregnancy and anticipation had been "the most solemn, most beautiful of my life" (March 1938). Tiny Silvan was baptized by a Jesuit priest. Shortly thereafter, she and her husband, Gustav, brought the infant to see their parents in Frankfurt. There she found that her brother had left for Brussels, her sister was packing for Chile, and her mother was searching for a place to live, having been evicted from her apartment.

By 1940, as her neighbors' hostility grew, she sought refuge in Upper Bavaria. Until February 1941, she and Silvan found respite among priests in Grünau. Back to Berlin, they spent nights in a bomb shelter, segregated from the others, and days hiding in their own apartment, afraid to be recognized in the neighborhood (February 1941).

Her double identity as a Jew and a convert plagued her: "Could I leave Judaism in such difficult times? Because, on the surface, it is a turning away."[42] Once she found herself in a church, crying over the ruins of the synagogues in Frankfurt: "When I passed the destroyed synagogue, I could not keep tears from flowing down my cheeks. . . . I entered the Capuchin monastery in the old city, hoping to find some comfort there" (April 1941).

Becker-Kohen often commented on her husband's devotion. Employed in a lab as an engineer, he withstood incessant pressure to divorce her. Moreover, the Gestapo harassed the couple, showing up at their apartment to search it for "suspicious" materials and to confiscate the radio.[43] In the summer of 1942, Gustav realized that all civilians were to acquire gas masks. When he asked for a mask for his wife, the official responded: "Gas masks are surely pointless for Jews"(August 1942). Gustav, like Erna, was often deeply depressed. Their only form of diversion was to play the piano for each other. When Gustav played, she sat near him: "I imagine myself in another, peaceful world, in which I, too, am a person of full worth" (January 1943).

Intensely religious, Becker-Kohen had befriended several priests. Through their good offices, the family spent some months at safe addresses in

Austria during the summers of 1941 and 1942. A Father Erwin, in particular, remained loyal, continuing to visit the family and to engage in theological discussions with her. A number of churchgoers, however, caused her and other converts grief, objecting to "Jews" taking communion or sharing pews with them.

On March 6, 1943, the Gestapo came for Erna Becker-Kohen. They told her to pack her necessities because they were unsure whether she would return: "My little boy, who was standing next to me, began to scream loudly at those words. . . . They brought him to a neighbor . . . while they loaded me on to a truck. . . . My child's cries . . . still ring in my ears." Nearly crazed, she ran through the hallways of the assembly point at the Grosse Hamburgerstrasse, found an office, and pleaded for release. Because of her status in a "privileged" mixed marriage, she was freed. But she realized she had been lucky. From that time on, she dreaded deportation: "I live in permanent fear of disaster" (May 1943). Silvan, too, worried, asking out loud in the streetcar one day: "Mama, when is the Gestapo coming for you again?"

On June 15, 1943, Father Erwin came to her apartment to urge her to leave Berlin immediately. She packed quickly: "Several suitcases of clothes, a large basket of laundry. Wait! The photos as souvenirs of more peaceful times. . . . Take the valuable jewelry! I might need it on the way. . . . We are traveling into the unknown." Her first shelter, through the intercession of another priest, was in Tannheim in the Austrian Tyrol (August 1943). Fearful of the mayor, a vicious Nazi, she left town in December 1943 for Salzburg. There, the woman who had promised to take her in reneged. Hungry and exhausted, with nowhere else to go, Erna and Silvan visited a priest who had helped them in the past. The priest, however, had become frightened, wanted to disassociate himself, and managed to find them a room for only one night—unheated, unlighted, without even a candle. They returned to Tannheim, finding refuge with an elderly peasant couple, Michl and Sefa. But just as Erna Becker-Kohen found shelter by pretending to be from a bombed-out city, she also had to make way for others actually suffering that plight. Even without knowing her Jewish identity, the mayor insisted that the town was only for evacuees from Essen and Innsbruck and that she should return to Berlin (February 1944).

Just then (and a half year since their last meeting), her husband arrived in Tannheim. He looked "like a skeleton" and was seriously ill. He had been overworked, underfed, and also terribly lonely. Erna was doubly alarmed: she worried about her partner, whom she loved, and she realized that his existence provided her only shield. The peasants with whom they had stayed found another place for them four hours away by foot. Despite

Gustav's frailty, the family fled there, pulling a sled with their belongings. The house was "completely neglected and covered with dirt from top to bottom.... I can not shake the feeling of being lost" (March 1944). When Gustav returned to Berlin, mother and child stayed on with the peasants, their seven children, and the four children of an evacuated family from Bremen (end of March 1944). After an outbreak of scabies among all the children, Erna decided to leave. Trudging through meter-high snow, her six-year-old "behaved very bravely on the road and told me again and again, as he clambered in my footsteps, 'You don't have to worry about me, I'm very good at this'" (April 1944).

To avoid calling attention to themselves, she found five different lodgings within two weeks, paying dearly or working for her keep. Ordered out of one town, they headed east and, in one village, went from house to house asking for a place to sleep: "however, nothing but suspicious questions, rejecting faces everywhere." During May and June, still searching for hiding places, Erna Becker-Kohen began to despair. Believing that her son would be able to survive with peasants she had befriended, she decided on suicide with an overdose of digitalis (June 1944). She was rescued, noting in her diary the bottomless dread she felt as she regained consciousness.

They continued to wander. By the end of August, they found quarters in Pfronten, run by a Catholic mayor. There they lived with peasants who refused to feed them, forcing them to walk two hours to the nearest inn: "Then catastrophe hit. I got sick.... They were even reluctant to feed my little boy, and [he] often suffered from hunger. Once he came from watching the cows ... and told me he was so hungry ... that he lay under a cow and milked it into his mouth" (September 1944). Her pleas to the mayor for a different abode met with success, and he found them a bed in a local orphanage run by the Sisters of Mercy. Feeling recovered after two weeks there, she and Silvan found brief refuge in a home recommended by the nuns.

This peaceful period was interrupted in mid-October by news that the Nazis had required Gustav, like many "Aryan" men married to Jewish women, to do forced labor. Driven by a sense of duty and assured that Silvan could remain in the orphanage, Erna decided to travel to Berlin: "Because I was aware of how dangerous my trip could be (bombings, arrest because I had no papers, betrayal by my dear neighbors), I spoke beforehand with the ... director of the orphanage, who promised ... to keep an eye on Silvan in case anything should happen to me" (October 1944). Luckily, the trains were too packed for identification checks. Erna insisted on sneaking into her old apartment to pack Gustav's bags. His destination was the forced labor camp at Nikolassee, on the outskirts of Berlin—"I went along until the barbed wire, then we had to separate."

When she returned to her son, she learned that the Nazi Party in Pfronten had discovered their whereabouts. They headed out once more (October 1944) with Erna lifting Silvan over many difficult passages covered by avalanches. By the time she arrived in the village of Häselgehr, she suffered severe heart problems and a high fever and had to stay in bed for three weeks. Luckily, a kindly priest cared for her. Nevertheless, her heart had been damaged by the overdose of digitalis and her harried existence. A doctor told her that she would not last another six months in this kind of life.Yet as soon as she was well enough to move on, she found several new shelters that lasted until February 1945, when she was ordered to leave the area entirely.

Despite her wanderings, she began to feel hopeful. She knew from illegal radio broadcasts that the war was winding down. By the end of April, a month in which she had to find five shelters, Erna wondered whether the Americans would arrive before she was exiled from her latest refuge: "My nerves are stretched to bursting, having to wait is almost impossible to bear."

Erna Becker-Kohen and Silvan were finally liberated in May 1945. She looked on in amazement as the hostility around her vanished and people who had been cruel suddenly tried to befriend her. At the end of that month, through a chance meeting with a German-Jewish refugee from Bonn, now an American military doctor, she learned of the genocide that had taken place: "So those were the 'resettlement camps.'" All of her relatives had been murdered.

Her new despair and health problems notwithstanding, she searched for her husband. By October 1945 there was no word from her husband, and she began to consider killing herself and her child:

> I cannot bear being the only survivor of my big family. . . . If I find out for certain that Gustl is dead, I will no longer want to live, along with my child, either. What are we doing here? We are all alone, even today still despised by most people. I will only be doing my little boy a favor by sparing him the hard fate of a person with no home anywhere on Earth.

Not until January 1946 did Erna find out that Gustav was alive. When they reunited, he could hardly walk and suffered from tuberculosis. Almost six feet tall, he weighed only one hundred pounds. He would never fully recover and died in 1952. Erna and Silvan settled in Freiburg in 1954 after a failed attempt to make a new life in Chile.

After the war, between 3,000 and 5,000 Jews came out of hiding in Germany. In Berlin, a city that once encompassed 160,000 Jewish Berliners, about 5,000 to 7,000 Jews hid, of whom only 1,400 survived.[44] Fewer than 1 percent of the original Jewish population of Germany in 1933 were rescued by their countrymen or women; most had been persecuted by them.

Irma Simon, Ruth Abraham, and Erna Becker-Kohen are the "success" stories of hiding: a middle-aged woman and her family, whose rescuer also became her lover; a young, blond woman and her baby, whose husband hid elsewhere; and a young, dark-haired convert to Catholicism and her "*Mischling*" son, whose "Aryan" husband was punished for her continued existence. "Success" is only in comparison with those whom the Nazis found and murdered. Although their physical lives were saved, they experienced irretrievable loss and immeasurable grief. Their previous lives and health had been ravaged. Moreover, they faced the agonizing disclosures of the genocide; each lost parents and siblings, as well as nearly her entire extended family and many friends. The Nazis had destroyed their homes, desecrated their synagogues, and robbed them of their *Heimat* while most Germans had stood by, complicit or applauding. Two of the three saw their marriages blown apart by the "Third Reich." Whatever property they had once owned was withheld from them after the war, only to be returned—grudgingly—decades later and, in many cases, never at all. One started a new life in America, and two spent their final years in Germany after their attempts abroad faltered. There were no "happy endings."

Conclusion

"Suppose that an earthquake destroys not only lives, buildings, and objects but also the instruments used to measure earthquakes," wrote French philosopher Jean François Lyotard referring to the enormity of the Holocaust and the inadequacy of our attempts to fully understand it. But even if the massive violence and inhumanity of Germany's war against the Jews remain ultimately incomprehensible, we can begin to understand the smaller steps taken on a daily level. In the 1930s, Nazi Germany succeeded in enforcing social death on its Jews—excommunicating them, subjecting them to inferior status, and relegating them to a perpetual state of dishonor. On a daily, grass-roots level, Nazi persecution provoked a sharp break in previous relationships. Gradually but relentlessly, friends, neighbors, clients, and employers turned away from Jews, placing them beyond the pale of German social life and empathy. Although the road to Auschwitz was, indeed, "twisted"—conceived and implemented piecemeal —the social death of Jews was unswerving.[1] Imposed by the government, it was sustained, with some notable exceptions, by the German population. The German "racial community," through its complicity in, approval of, or indifference to the persecution of these newly marked "enemies," helped pave the way toward the physical extermination of the Jews. The social death of Jews and German indifference to their increasingly horrific plight were absolute prerequisites for the "Final Solution."

JEWISH RESPONSES

For Jews, society and politics lurched wildly and ominously in the years after Hitler's triumph. Their responses to the Nazi threat varied, corresponding to the stages of persecution. In memoirs and interviews, almost all German Jews described their immediate pain and shock, their uncertainty and apprehension when the Nazis came to power. The early terror created, as we have read, "fear, fear, fear." And yet, the occasional lulls in Nazi persecution—"only a small dose to begin with ... then a brief pause. Only a single pill at a time and then a moment of waiting"[2]—caused perplexity and allowed hope. Dealing with the confusion of daily life in Nazi Germany and seeking to survive from day to day—that is, simply living one's life—distracted some Jews from making the painful decision to flee or deceived them into thinking they could hold out until they were trapped. In the pursuit of pragmatic solutions, even in extraordinary times, contemporaries may have missed or misread the danger signals in their daily lives.

The desire of Jews to find some workable arrangement also provided occasions to accommodate and to go on with their lives amid Nazi villainy. Most attempted to "normalize" their lives at first, hoping the regime would come to an end. There was some reason for hope: experiences were uneven. They differed according to where Jews lived—insults and isolation were not always immediate and not total, especially in big cities. They differed according to whether Jewish businesses were under attack—some persisted, doing well, even if many others declined or shut down. Gender and age, too, created distinctive experiences. Clinging to the familiar during the "catastrophic gradualism" of the early Nazi years was a tool for survival rather than an illusory response to the menace of Nazism.[3]

Despite policies that succeeded in expelling Jews from their surrounding society socially, morally, and even physically, Jews made every effort to maintain a semblance of their previous daily lives. On a communal level, Jewish organizations persevered, offering religious, cultural, and social initiatives for a community under siege. Confiding to a colleague in June 1941, Rabbi Leo Baeck showed satisfaction that German Jews had struggled successfully to maintain "schools, religious observance, and charity."[4] Jews could attend their own educational and vocational institutions, enjoy Jewish Cultural Association concerts, plays, and lectures, and rely on an extensive social service network. Outside the safety of the Jewish community, individuals continued to work (although frequently not at jobs of their choice), meet friends (although far fewer non-Jews than before 1933), and take excursions (aware of where Jews were "not wanted"). Families continued to celebrate special events, both secular and Jewish, with parties and cheer. Teens, as we have seen, also broke the rules, attending forbidden theaters, showing up in areas where Jews were "not wanted," or enjoying the silliness (and danger) of mockingly imitating Nazi leaders. In other words, a vital and intense Jewish life continued, even in Nazi Germany.

Jews' attempts to go on with their lives notwithstanding, Nazism intruded relentlessly into the innermost sanctums of private life. Jewish couples had to contend with unprecedented and complicated eventualities when deciding whether to court, marry, have children, or divorce. Antimixing laws and Germans' hardening attitudes toward "racial defilement" invaded the most intimate of relationships. Unmarried Jews had to face the sudden politicization of their sexuality, avoid or hide love ties with "Aryans," or suffer the brutal consequences of their "crimes." The regime threatened the bonds of marriage and the very fabric of family life for "mixed" couples. Marriages between "Aryans" and Jews had to withstand enormous pressure from government, employers, friends, and families to split. Those that remained intact—the majority—faced ostracism and deprivation, although most Jewish spouses' lives were spared.

Nazism also affected the lives of Jews in public. As the overwhelming majority of Germans began to treat Jews like the second-class human beings they were decreed to be, Jews kept as low a profile as they could. Many withdrew from social circles, often before they were expelled, and others fled abroad. Many learned new languages and new skills, preparing for future emigration if it became necessary. Most adjusted to daily deprivation and insult, trying to remain calm and maintain their honor in the face of the dishonor they suffered. It took enormous energy to preserve self-esteem when confronted by lawlessness, economic decline, and social ostracism. Adjusting to circumstances beyond one's control and protecting one's self-respect were necessary human responses, defense mechanisms that helped them to endure daily life and remain true to their own image of themselves.

Remaining faithful to their way of life and to their human integrity rarely detracted from efforts to emigrate. Between 270,000 and 300,000 Jews managed to flee Germany—about three-fifths of German Jewry. These facts notwithstanding, it has been common, with hindsight, to criticize German Jews for not having emigrated quickly enough, for hoping they could remain in Germany, for loving Germany too much, for not seeing the writing on the wall. This is a profound and cruel distortion. Although many German Jews did love Germany and did not want to leave, many more could not leave. In the early years, the Nazis had deceived and confused German Jews, allowing them to maintain some hope. After the November Pogrom almost all German Jews tried desperately to flee, realizing that there was no future for any Jew in Germany. Those who could not were trapped by their obligations or their economic and social circumstances. Some were elderly or cared for elderly parents. Others could not obtain visas or jump the hurdles set up by the Nazis to inhibit escape. In any case, perceptions by Jews of their predicament—either before or after 1938—were *never* the crucial factors affecting emigration. Punitive emigration taxes, "blocked accounts," and Nazi plunder, creating the specter of abject poverty abroad, discouraged many, especially family breadwinners and the elderly. Most important, lands of refuge heartlessly shut their doors.

By the outbreak of war, only a remnant of the Jewish community remained. Life was reduced to daily survival. Unlike "Aryans" who worried about bombings and their relatives fighting as soldiers, Jews mourned those who had already died at the hands of the Nazis. Most avoided public exposure—so effectively, in fact, that many non-Jews were surprised that "so many" Jews remained once the Star of David forced them into glaring visibility. During the bombings, Jews were less anxious about death from the sky than at the hands of the Gestapo. The bombings were "so everyday one did not see [them] as that dramatic anymore." The cruelties were harder to endure. Jews suffered "the fairy-tale horror of our existence: fear at every knock on the door, persecution, humiliation, life-threatening danger, hunger (real hunger), constant new prohibitions, ever more gruesome enslavement, ... absolute helplessness."[5]

On June 19, 1943, Goebbels declared Berlin "free of Jews" (*judenfrei*). The Central Association of Jews in Germany had been dismantled earlier that month. The deportations had terrorized Jews relentlessly since late 1941. The deportees had known they were being "taken," not "evacuated." Although the "ultimate terror remained hidden," they had viewed deportation "as spelling their end."[6] The only German Jews left in Germany were those in mixed marriages, those in hiding, and those in some *Judenhäuser* or the Jewish Hospital in Berlin. They all hoped to hold out until the Allies had conquered Germany. Of the over 500,000 Jews who had lived in Germany at the beginning of the Nazi era, only approximately 15,000 German Jews survived within the pre-1938 borders.

GERMAN PERPETRATORS AND BYSTANDERS

Within prewar Germany society, Germans—the government and the many who eagerly anticipated, supported, or went along with Nazi racial laws—transformed Jews into outcasts. During the war, they increased anti-Jewish restrictions, burdens, and penalties until Jewish daily life in Germany became more and more like confinement in a concentration camp without walls. Thus Germans organized and enforced the social death of

Jews. Their presence in this book is conspicuous not just for what they witnessed but for what they did. In the 1930s there were moving exceptions based on loyalty, honor, and plain decency, and in the 1940s there were Germans who risked everything to hide Jews. But most Germans suspended the exercise of decency and the normal civilities that make a society function and, significantly, suspended them before laws or decrees required them to do so.

The disenfranchisement of Jews was carried out in an increasingly ruthless context as political "enemies" were beaten, incarcerated, and murdered. Germans saw, heard, and read about these events. Many participated in them. When we explore the question of how much Germans knew about the later genocide, we should keep this earlier era in mind: from 1933 to 1939 the savagery of political repression and violence against "others" increased and was not hidden from the public. This brutality provided the setting in which the "master race" turned Jews into permanent outcasts, making it difficult for Jews to work or run a business, to shop, to cook traditional meals, to find rental apartments, to maintain friendships with non-Jews, and to educate their children. Fearful of their own regime *and* seduced by its seeming successes, many Germans stood by or celebrated as Jews lost their professional practices and businesses and had to sell—to them!—for a pittance. The even more rapid escalation of anti-Jewish violence after November 1938 took place in the context of a triumphant terrorist regime, basking in its victories over Austria and Czechoslovakia. The Nazis confiscated all remaining Jewish businesses, drafted Jews into forced labor, and sequestered them in *Judenhäuser*. They blatantly robbed Jews of their personal jewelry and precious heirlooms and their few remaining assets. During the war, they slashed Jewish food rations and prohibited Jews from buying medications, clothing, or soap, denied them public transportation, and segregated them in bomb shelters.

Historians have noticed that when Germans are asked about the uncomfortable issue of the Holocaust, many quickly bring up the war.[7] The "Jewish war," as some Germans described it, is remembered as a disaster for the German people as victims. The bombings stood out as the German civilian war experience. This is not the place to analyze how their self-image as victims might have alleviated German responsibility, embarrassment, or guilt regarding the genocide, nor how much serious damage was actually wrought. Instead, it is worth noting that our information regarding the deprivations that Jews endured within Nazi Germany rarely comes from Germans, who were, or claim to have been, too preoccupied with everyday concerns to pay much attention to the regime's practices or rhetoric. Our information comes almost entirely from the victims—not from "Aryan" workers who observed the increasing shabbiness of Jewish workers' clothing, not from "Aryan" children who taunted Jewish children, and certainly not from neighbors who saw Jews evicted from their homes or banished them into separate areas of bomb shelters.

Jewish victims' accounts belie the conclusions of German historians who have failed to find antisemitism in their sources. Moreover, these stories contradict the claims of many Germans that they "did not know" what was happening to the Jews.[8] The Jewish victims regularly point to public, gratuitous, and unnecessary cruelty—cruelty not coerced by any external threat. They encountered "Aryans" who went out of their way to be malicious: the woman who told the baker that he should not deliver rolls to Jews; Germans who ferreted out "Jewish features" on trams; the housewives who hindered a *"Mischling"* child from buying milk; the bureaucrats who prohibited Jewish children from playing outdoors. Moreover, they met Germans who took advantage of their misery, extorting money and goods from them before furnishing them with emigration papers. Further, Jews met thousands of Germans who bought goods cheaply from emigrating Jews, all the while complaining of their own problems. Other Germans fought like "jackals over a carcass"[9] at the auctions of Jewish property, benefiting from the deportation and murder of the owners. This everyday view from the victims' perspective has been badly missing from histories of German daily life during the Nazi era.

Some historians have explained the behavior of the German population in the face of the persecution and genocide of the Jews as the result of a combination of authoritarian mentality and moral apathy, "not so much an antisemitic bias." They have blamed the growing distance between Jews and non-Jews after 1933, both physical and social, for German "ignorance and indifference" toward Jews. On the other extreme is the recent argument that, generations before the Nazis, Germany—uniquely—adopted an "eliminationist antisemitism" that craved the annihilation of Jews. The Nazis mobilized this violent hatred, permitting "ordinary Germans" to take pleasure in tormenting and, ultimately, exterminating Jews.[10]

This study challenges both sides. It shows that, with poignant exceptions, particularly those people who hid Jews, many Germans took an active—not passive—role in persecuting Jews and that throughout the Nazi era German racism was widespread, deep, and invidious. Still, "ordinary Germans" balked at rampant violence against Jews. They were *not* bent on killing Jews as much as ostracizing them from society. Their racism led them to hope that the Jews would simply "disappear"[11]—first, economically and politically, then socially—and, later, to avert their eyes when this process escalated hideously.

This wish among Germans that Jews "disappear" was not the same as wishing for or condoning genocide. Nevertheless, it is valuable to examine the meaning of these "disappearance" wishes for people on both sides of the "racial" or ethnic divide.[12] It is also crucial to analyze how endemic prejudice becomes epidemic, how bigotry turns into massacre. Simply because so many Germans wished for the Jews to disappear does not mean that we can leap to the conclusion that genocide was inevitable in the 1930s. Unless one reads history backward, the 1930s were highly ambiguous. They were frightening, even ominous, but gave no clear indication of the genocide to come. What the 1930s do show us is how intensely menacing racism is, how it demeaned the perpetrators as it devastated the victims, how social death can lead to physical death.

Racism showed no mercy toward either the young or the old. Official government policy, but also teachers, peers, neighbors, and strangers, targeted children, destroying the childhood and youth of tens of thousands of young Jews. One can only wonder how previously sheltered, hopeful, and lively children could cope with increasing ostracism and the cruel narrowing of options in their lives. Jewish schools provided brief solace but soon shrank as more children emigrated. The Nazis closed them forever in June 1942. Beyond the school yard, Jewish children had to negotiate public spaces where strangers as well as former friends treated them heartlessly. This everyday evil is the story that is, not surprisingly, omitted by German witnesses—how they participated in the persecution even of children. Ultimately, the majority of children escaped with their families or "turned into letters" as they fled. A few survived in hiding, and about 20,000 under the age of eighteen were murdered as the Nazis strove to eradicate the Jewish "race" in its entirety.[13] The aged fared even worse. Unwilling to become burdens on their children abroad or unable to maneuver through the Nazi bureaucracy, they sent their young out first and were then trapped by events. In 1941, two-thirds of the Jewish population was past middle age. About 61,000 elderly people—the majority female—remained in Nazi hands.

Racism was not gender-neutral either. In imagery and practice, the Nazi government and most Germans treated Jewish women differently from Jewish men. Nazi propaganda castigated Jewish men as cheats and traitors, depicting them as greedy bankers and pimps. The Nazis persecuted Jewish men early on, culminating with their arrests during the November Pogrom. With rare exceptions, Nazi policy before the deportations bowed to taboos against physically abusing women in public. Thereafter, however, the Nazis treated men and women similarly, with shocking savagery, whether in forced labor or by tearing them away from their families and loading them onto trains bound for the East.

Gender influenced how the victims of immeasurable cruelty strove to save themselves. At various stages of persecution, Jewish women responded differently from men. Women's roles in the family and society in prewar Germany affected both their approach to events in the 1930s and their options during the war. They reacted to the Nazi threat earlier than men, pushing for emigration. When the Nazis blocked Jewish men's economic survival, Jewish women took on employment or trained for new jobs. Jewish women also strained to rescue loved ones from the clutches of the Gestapo. As the family became more central to the practical and emotional needs of Jews, women took on the increased burdens of daily survival, from living in tighter quarters, to preparing ersatz foods, to providing sociability and diversion. Housewives and mothers strove to preserve a sense of "normalcy" in the midst of desperation—while learning to cope with less and to expect even worse.

Women maintained their dignity amid their despair by remembering who they really were, not who their enemies said they were. They preserved shrinking family and friendship circles, which drew sustenance from each other. They also volunteered to aid the Jewish community. During and after the November Pogrom, Jewish women displayed extraordinary determination. As they toiled to clean up the debris, they doggedly sought the freedom of their male relatives. They now knew with certainty that their lives in Germany faced qualitatively new hardships and cruelties. Most embarked on the dizzying chase from bureaucracy to bureaucracy to free their men, paying bribes where necessary, and doing everything in their limited power to find a haven abroad. As the regime plundered their belongings, Jewish women tried to overcome the myriad obstacles to escape, facilitating the exodus of thousands. Yet, when emigration turned into a rout, more Jewish women were trapped. Some were widows, too aged to leave; others had sent husbands ahead; still others hesitated to leave their parents or did not have the wealth or vocations required by countries of refuge.

Examining women's experiences raises the following question: Why, until recently, have historians looked primarily at men in studying the Holocaust? It seems clear that "the end—namely, annihilation or death—does not describe or explain the process," that "along the stations toward extinction . . . each gender lived its own journey." To raise the issue of gender can never place blame on other survivors for the disproportionate deaths of Jewish women. Blame rests with the murderers. To raise the issue of gender also does not place it above racism. We know that the Nazis did not want "to share the earth with the Jewish people."[14] I have emphasized the importance of gender not only because it helps us to tell a fuller, more intimate, and more nuanced story but also to give Jewish women a voice long denied them and to offer a perspective long denied us. Studying the ways in which women and men were treated differently and the frequently distinctive manner in which they reacted demonstrates how gender influenced decisions and destinies. Gender mattered, especially in extreme situations. As the Nazis closed in on Jewish life, Jewish women's stories were at the heart of Jewish history.

Notes

INTRODUCTION

Epigraph: Tolstoy, *War and Peace*, trans. Rosemary Edmonds (New York, 1978), 887.

1. Antisemitism is spelled without a hyphen except where it appears in quotations. See Shmuel Almog, "What's in a Hyphen?" in *SICSA Report*, No. 2 (Summer 1989). "Willing" in Goldhagen, *Executioners*; ten-year-old in Deutschkron, *Outcast*, 7, 14.

2. Orlando Patterson introduced the term "social death" to describe the slave condition. Three features add up to the social death of slavery: personal domination, excommunication from the "legitimate social or moral community," and a perpetual condition of dishonor. A history of Jews in Nazi Germany illustrates many similarities (with important differences). See: *Slavery* and *Freedom*.

3. With some exceptions, this book does not tell the story of the significant minority of working-class, Eastern European Jews residing in Germany. See: Yfaat Weiss, "The Encounter Between German Jewry and Polish Jewry During the Nazi Era" (Ph.D. diss., University of Tel Aviv, 1996).

4. Christabel Bielenburg, interview in film *World at War: A New Germany.* (Thames Television: London, 1977).

5. Nauen, Research Foundation, 10.

6. "[M]en without" in Hilberg, *Perpetrators*, 127; "being" in Ringelheim, "Reconsideration," 400.

7. Memoirs are so compelling because they express writers' feelings and allow the multiple voices of Jews to be heard. But memoirs raise questions about the failures of memory and the writers' assumptions. How do a writer's motives affect the substance of the memoir? Also, since repressing danger played a large part in maintaining one's sanity in the early Nazi years, how can we see the secrets people kept from themselves? Further, does "memory" of the 1930s change with knowledge of the later genocide? With these concerns in mind, I have sifted through diaries and letters written during the 1930s and early 1940s, a collection of memoirs at Harvard University written by German émigrés (both Jewish and non-Jewish) in 1940 when the genocide was still inconceivable to most, and memoirs written after 1945, many in the 1960s and even some in the 1980s.

8. See, for example, the Bavaria and Ruhr projects. Broszat et al., eds., *Bayern* (especially *Herrschaft und Gesellschaft*, vols. 2–4); and Niethammer, ed., *"Jahre."* These studies have also been the model for innumerable local studies by history workshops. See also: Nolan, "Historikerstreit" (1988, 1990). Jews do appear in Herbert's work, *Foreign Labor* and *"Reichseinsatz,"* but for the most part they are not German Jews.

9. Baldwin, *"Historikerstreit,"* 16; Fritzsche, "Where did all the Nazis Go?" 191–214. See also: Friedländer's and Diner's articles in *Nationalsozialismus,* ed. Diner; Nolan, "Historikerstreit" (1988); Kocka, *Sozialgeschichte,* 162–74.

10. Ulrich Herbert (see note 8) and Alf Lüdtke are among the historians who draw these connections. Lüdtke examines how the "privatization of politics and the politicization of the private" became routine, that is, normal. Lüdtke, "'Formierung,'" 19. See also: Gerstenberger, *Normalität,* introduction; Peukert, "Alltag," 57.

11. Nolan, "Historikerstreit" (1990), 239; Trommler, "Normality," 119–38; von Saldern, "Hillgrubers," 166–67; "permeated" in Geyer, "The State," 218.

12. Frank Stern, "Antagonistic Memories: The Post-War Survival and Alienation of Jews and Germans," in *Memory and Totalitarianism,* ed. Luisa Passerini (Oxford, 1992); Friedländer, "Controversy," 108.

13. Strauss, "Emigration," I, 316–17. Between 1933 and Sept. 1944, the number of Jews in Germany declined from 525,000 Jews by religion to less than 15,000 "Jews" by "race." In 1933, 15 percent of German Jews lived in towns of under 10,000 and 3.4 percent in towns of 10,000 to 20,000. There were 1,700 Jewish communities. Cahnmann, "Village," 107.

14. Baumann showed that in 1933 in some small south Baden towns a far greater percentage of Jewish women worked. "Beziehungen," 34. See also: *IF,* Feb. 23, 1933, 9; Silbergleit, *Bevölkerung,* 108.

15. Silbergleit, *Bevölkerung,* 108.

16. In 1933, the female Jewish population consisted of 45 percent housewives, 41 percent single women, and 14 percent widows. Rosenthal, "Population," 250. In 1929, about one-quarter of all German-Jewish students were women. In 1932, 1,408 Jewish women, or 7 percent of all women, studied at German universities.

17. Schleunes, *Twisted Road,* 7. See also: Rosenthal, "Population," 233–73. In 1930, twenty out of one hundred Jewish marriages were mixed, but conversions were down in comparison with the Imperial era. Schmelz, "Entwicklung," 42, 52–53.

18. Huerkamp, "Akademikerinnen," 319. For the SPD, see: Wickert, "Sozialistin."

19. "Goethe" in Mosse, *German Jews,* 14; German-Jewish culture in Brenner, *Renaissance*; Schorsch, "German Judaism," 67–74.

20. In *The Making of the Jewish Middle Class,* I used memoirs to show how families maintained or changed Jewish life, how Jews forged friendship and family networks to create a Jewish cultural, religious, and social context, and how fundamental *Bildung* (education and cultivation) was to German-Jewish identity.

21. Goldhagen, *Executioners.*

22. "Moderate" in Niewyk, *Weimar,* 80; Straus in Niewyk, *Weimar,* 93–94.

23. "First state," in Burleigh, *Racial State,* 22.

24. The term "race" is discussed by Henry Louis Gates, Jr., ed., *"Race," Writing, and Difference* (Chicago: 1985). "Mixed marriage" is another problematic term: before the Nazis came to power it denoted a marriage between individuals of different religions, but afterwards it marked a couple of mixed "races." I have chosen to write it without quotation marks to remain close to the way these couples were described before 1933.

25. Hildesheimer, *Existenzkampf.*

CHAPTER I

Epigraph: Arendt in Günter Gaus, *Zur Person: Porträts in Frage und Antwort* (Munich, 1964), 22.

1. Gruner, "Reichshauptstadt," 230. Mob violence also occurred in some small towns and cities.
2. Limberg, *Durften*, 37–38.
3. Lang, Harvard, 34, 108. On burning papers, see also: Lewinsohn, Harvard, 1. Her husband was a socialist and half-Jewish.
4. Deutschkron, *Outcast*, 8. See also: Braun-Melchior, LBI, 31C; Lisa Frank, Yad Vashem, 8; Popper, Harvard, 58.
5. Bamberger, LBI, 15.
6. Milton, "Holocaust," 298–300. The five women in Wickert, "Sozialistin."
7. *Reichsgericht* and *Kammergericht*, Rothschild, LBI, 117.
8. She was never deported from prison and survived. Baronowitz, Yad Vashem, 3.
9. Hostages and Hohenstein in Milton, "Holocaust," 298–300. Milton also notes that before 1939, about 25 percent of the women held in "preventive detention" were Jewish. For an exception, a woman arrested on financial grounds, who spent eighteen months in prisons before 1939, see: Lohr, Harvard; Plaut in Händler-Lachmann, *Purim*, 198; Leipzig in Lange, *Davidstern*, 205–6.
10. "Naked" in Klemperer, *Zeugnis*, I, 11; Nuremberg in Kahn, LBI, 13; police refusal and "defenseless life" in Limberg, *Durften*, 133, 143.
11. Sichel, Harvard, 77; Krug, Harvard, 17.
12. Strauss, "Emigration," I, 342–45. On the fur trade, see: Fred Grubel and Frank Mecklenburg, "Leipzig: Profile of a German-Jewish Community," *LBIYB*, (1977).
13. "Best business days" in Lohr, Harvard, 26. Civil servants could lose their jobs for shopping in stores owned by Jews. Barkai, "Existenzkampf," 159. See also: Schleunes, *Twisted Road*, chap. 3. For excesses, see Richarz, *Leben*, III, 293.
14. Hanau and Dortmund in Richarz, *Leben*, III, 161, 231–32.
15. Nathorff, *Tagebuch*, 38; Albersheim, Harvard, 33; Eisenstädt, Yad Vashem, 1–2.
16. Richarz, *Leben*, III, 222; Kershaw, *Opinion*, 240–46. For Hessen, see Richarz, *Leben*, III, 96–98. On firing help (in Nördlingen): Hamburger interview.
17. Breslau in Plum, "Wirtschaft," 284; small businesses in Baerwald in Limberg, *Durften*, 102–3; cattle dealer (near Fulda) and tenants in Limberg, *Durften*, 119, 143; "free of Jews" (literally, "clean of Jews") from Schleunes, *Twisted Road*, 145. After the war, many families tried to reclaim their losses. These claims were denied by officials of the Federal Republic who argued that Jews had not been forced to sell during the early years.
18. Cleaning woman in Kliner-Lintzen, "vergessen," 336–43; small businesses from Barkai, "Existenzkampf," 155 and "Volksgemeinschaft," 41.
19. There were 3,030 Jewish attorney/notaries and 79 patent attorneys still working in Germany in June 1933, when some people had already fled. They represented 16 percent of all lawyers practicing in Germany. Plum, "Wirtschaft," 282. Number affected by laws in Strauss, "Emigration," I, 326. Until July 1938 about 3,000 (out of about 8,000) Jewish doctors still practiced. Thereafter, only 709 Jewish "caretakers of the sick" (*Krankenbehandler*) could treat Jews. Of 4,500 Jewish jurists, only 1,753 still practiced in July 1938. Thereafter, only 172 could be "consultants" to other Jews. Barkai, *Boycott*, 29, 121–22.
20. Fromm, *Blood*, 170.
21. Bergas, LBI, 2. Jobless Jewish teachers vied for teaching jobs within the Jewish community or set up their own tutoring lessons. Staatsarchiv Hamburg, 522–1 Jüd. Gemeinden, #297B Band 4, Vorstandsprotokollen 1933–34, and Bundesarchiv, Coswig: Jüd. Frauenbund Verband Berlin, folder 21. "Half Jews" were eventually also fired from school service, some becoming tutors as well. Becker-Kohen, LBI, 22. For the sad experience of a teacher who retained her job until early 1935, but whose students became increasingly hostile, see: Röcher, *Schule*, 73, 118–19.
22. Stephenson, *Women*, 155–56; Bankier, *Germans*, 69.

23. Thomas Mann, *Tagebücher 1933–34*, ed. Peter de Mendelssohn (Frankfurt am Main, 1977), 46 (he used the word *Vermauschelung*, an antisemitic term, to denigrate the way Jews ostensibly talked or thought, in describing Kerr); Popper, Harvard, 28.

24. Berlin was the home of 45 percent of all Jewish doctors; another 30 percent practiced in other big Prussian cities. There were about 9,000 "non-Aryan" medical doctors on April 1, 1933. Plum, "Wirtschaft," 282, 291; Kater, "Physicians," 49–77; Grenville, "'Ärzte,'" 191–206; Necheles-Magnus in Limberg, *Durften*, 52–53.

25. In Prussia and Berlin the proportion (in 1925) of women doctors was 21 percent and 40 percent, respectively. In June 1933, there were 587 Jews among 4,367 women doctors in Germany. Huerkamp, "Akademikerinnen," 319; Nathorff, *Tagebuch*, 40.

26. "Traitors" in Limberg, *Durften*, 56.

27. Huerkamp, "Akademikerinnen," 325; Scholem in Gay, *Jews*, 256.

28. On businesses, see Kliner-Lintzen, *"vergessen,"* 336–43; on licensing, see Behnsch-Brower, LBI, l.

29. Rosenthal, "Population," 262; Gruner, "Reichshauptstadt," 232; Vollnhals, "Selbsthilfe," 377. It is estimated that about 40,000 Jews, or one-fifth of the working population, were unemployed in late 1936.

30. Women's jobs in *BJFB*, Jan. 1934, 7; March 1935, 2; *IF*, Feb. 23, 1933, 9; *JWS*, 1931, 77–78. In 1934 in Berlin, for example, the number of unemployed Jews rose to 27,203, of whom 42 percent of the females and 30 percent of the males seeking jobs found them. Vollnhals, "Selbsthilfe," 372, 375.

31. "Expedient" in *IF*, July 14, 1938, 12; "relatively few" in *IF*, Jan. 13, 1938, 13–14; midlife in *CV*, June 25, 1936. See also: *IF*, July 14, 1938, 12; *CV*, Aug. 25, 1938.

32. Abraham, LBI, 2; sewing furs in *Community*, ed. Foster, 28–30; mother and daughter in Brauer, LBI, 53.

33. Lewis, LBI, 264.

34. Hamburg in Meyer-Gerstein, LBI, I, 36; courses described in Bundesarchiv, Coswig: 75C Jüd. Frauenbund, Verband Berlin, folder 37; home economics in Bundesarchiv, Potsdam. Jüdische Haushaltungsschule, Frankfurt am Main, 1925–39 (49.01 10250); Zentralstelle für jüdische Wirtschaftshilfe (Economic Relief) in Heuberger, *Zedaka*, 324; *Hachsharah* in Rosenstrauch, *Nachbarn*, 6l.

35. In 1933–34 in Berlin, of those seeking retraining, 51 percent of women and only 26 percent of men were over the age of thirty (of these, 15 percent of the women and 8 percent of the men were over forty). In 1936, of 106 new "home caretakers" (*Hauspflegerinnen*), about one-fourth had been commercial employees and another one-fourth had previously been housewives. *JWS*, 1937, 80.

36. *JWS*, 1933–34, 118–21; 1937, 8–9; *IF*, May 21, 1936; *BJFB*, Oct. 1938, 14.

37. Blau, "Last Days," 199; Kramer, "Welfare," 183; soup kitchens in Bauer, *Brother's*, 125; clothing in *JWS*, 1938, 82.

38. A total of 75,000 Jews received Winter Relief in January 1936. These included mixed marriages in which the head of household was Jewish and foreign Jews. *IF*, Jan. 16, 1936, 1. By 1939, in Germany as a whole, Jewish Winter Relief subsidized 26 percent of a greatly diminished and aging population. See also: Barkai, *Boycott*, 92–99 and "Existenzkampf," 164; Kramer, "Welfare," 183.

39. Kramer, "Welfare," 179. The most needy were Jews forty-five years or older and single people. "Remedy," in Schwarz, "Tschaikowsky," 118, 120.

40. Bauer shows the Joint Distribution Committee providing major portions of the Central Organization's budget. *Brother's*, 127. See also: Kramer, "Welfare," 180; Vollnhals, "Selbsthilfe," 407. The Central Organization of German Jews (*Reichsvertretung der deutschen Juden*) was forced to change its name in 1935 to the Central Organization of Jews in Germany (*Reichsvertretung der Juden in Deutschland*).

41. "No sympathy" in Alexis de Tocqueville, quoted by Geyer in "Reconsidered," 59–60. See also: Struve, "Economy," 471. Prinz quoted by Schwarz, *Lager*, 34.

42. Berlin in Gruner, "Reichshauptstadt," 234; Bab, LBI, 191. In Hamburg, a landlord called the police when his tenants erected a *sukkah* in his garden. He asked that the police stop this "Jewish shamelessness." Before 1935, the police refused. Popper, Harvard, 47. Officially, Jews lost their protection as tenants in 1939.

43. Wahrman, *Forget*, 53–55, 115. Even in the aftermath of the November Pogrom, his father slaughtered chickens. See also: Händler-Lachmann, *Purim*, 95, 111.

44. *Kochbuch für den Jüdischen Haushalt* (Berlin, 1935). For recipes, see: IF, May 21, 1936, 13; *FIG*, May 1933, 215–16; *BJFB*, Nov. 1937, 13. See also: Schoenewald coll., LBI, III, 10.

45. Lewis, LBI, 252.

46. Garlic in Baerwald, Harvard, 33, and Limberg, *Durften*, 120–21, 130–31; restaurant in Limberg, *Durften*, 141–42.

47. "Aryan" couple in Limberg, *Durften*, 130–31; "passing" in Angress, *Fear*, 6–7.

48. Train incident in Limberg, *Durften*, 130–31. School incidents in Richarz, *Leben*, III, 236; Rosenstrauch, *Nachbarn*, 32; and Vogel, *Forget!*, 226. Unless otherwise noted, quotations from Richarz are translated by me and are not from the English version of her book.

49. Fromm, *Blood*, 119–20. Klemperer notes this conflation as well. *Zeugnis*, I, 554, 564.

50. Danzig cases in Baerwald, Harvard, 42–43; Fromm, *Blood*, 104.

51. In 1949, a public opinion survey in the Allied occupation zones determined these figures. They are very high, given that Jews were a tiny percentage of the population. Stern, *Whitewashing*, 255.

52. Popper, Harvard, 27–28, 32. See also Neumann, Harvard, 63, on silent shoppers.

53. Villagers in Limberg, *Durften*, 152, 174; Sabbath in Helfand, "*Halakhah*," 95.

54. Villages and Ihringen in Baumann, "Beziehungen," 123; Fulda in Limberg, *Durften*, 118, 120.

55. Windows and tar in *Sopade*, 1935, 1037 (Westphalia); Gladenbach in Moritz, *Verbrechen*, 77–80.

56. Small towns in Baumann, "Beziehungen," 126; "kicked off" and 1937 funeral in Limberg, *Durften*, 130, 152; Leipzig in Lange, *Davidstern*, 27. Struve documented divisions that arose around funerals *before* the Nazi takeover. "Entstehung," 83–84.

57. Leipzig (around 1935) in Lange, *Davidstern*, 19–23; sign and spying in Limberg, *Durften*, 133, 148.

58. Brauer, LBI, 42–43. The incident occurred in 1938. See also: Mommsen, "Reaktion," 374, 378; Kater, "Everyday," 129–59.

59. Thanks to Peter Pulzer for this insight.

60. Kahle, Harvard, 6; Popper, Harvard, 34; new positions in Segal, LBI, 45–47. See also Lessler, LBI, 21–22.

61. Stein-Pick, LBI, 40; Freund, LBI, 104–5.

62. Nuremberg in Kahn, LBI, 16; Appel in Richarz, *Life*, 352–53.

63. Dortmund in Richarz, *Life*, 352; Rhineland in Henry, *Victims*, 92.

64. Bernheim, Harvard, 35–36.

65. Albersheim, Harvard, 36; Becker-Kohen, LBI, 21.

66. For example, it was brave of a non-Jewish woman to bring food to a Jewish friend in his apartment. Monjau, LBI, 13.

67. Bielenberg, *The Past Is Myself* (1968; reprinted London, 1986), 30, cited by Martin in "Autobiography," 192.

68. Bad Dürkheim in Steckelmacher, Yad Vashem, 3; Arendt interview in Gaus, *Zur Person*, 22.

69. Kahn, LBI, 16.

70. Kahle, Harvard, 12.

71. *Volksgemeinschaft* in Geisel, "Erinnerung," 14. On voluntary informers, see also: Gellately, "Gestapo," 673–74; Mallmann, *Herrschaft*, 241. Prejudices in Bankier, *Germans*, 81. For more

on denunciations, the "key link between the police and the people in Nazi Germany, [which made] the terror system work," see Gellately, "Gestapo," 664, 669, 673‒74, 677, and his *Gestapo*. Later, with men at the front, the proportion of women denouncers increased. Johnson, "Women," 33‒69. Local laws frequently forced Germans to break all relations with Jews much earlier than 1941. Mommsen, "Reaktion," 428‒29.

72. Quaker was Hilde Koch, Harvard, 67, 82, 113‒14; "traitors" in Krug, Harvard, 17.

73. Bergas, LBI, 1; Appel in Richarz, *Life*, 352.

74. Nazi Party members kept commercial ties to Jews, some until as late as 1938. Mommsen, "Reaktion," 387, 430‒31. "Disgusting" in Broszat, *Bayern*, I, 450.

75. "Spared ourselves," in Hayum, LBI, 86; cafés in Glaser, LBI, 16‒17; Lewis, LBI, 251‒52.

76. "Insensibility" in Bankier, *Germans*, 81; "discipline" in Gellately, "Gestapo," 677; "race" in *Sopade*, 1936, 27.

77. See: Herbert Freeden, "Kultur," in *Nazi Germany*, ed. Paucker.

78. Düsseldorf in Glaser, LBI, 14; synagogues in Helfand, "*Halakhah*," 95. On the early disbanding of synagogues, see: Händler-Lachmann, *Purim*, 113‒14.

79. Bab, LBI, 185; "window" in Rovit, "Collaboration," 151; "stubborn refusal" from Freeden, "Kulturbund," 65‒66; "laugh together" from Mariam Niroumand, quoted by Rovit, "Collaboration," 144. See also: Strauss, "Autonomy," 138; Freeden, *Theater*; Geisel, *Premiere*; and Akademie der Künste, *Vorstellung*.

80. University town in Bernheim, Harvard, 43. Meyer-Gerstein was one such speaker, LBI coll., I, 38‒39.

81. The male-led Reichsvertretung never recognized the importance of the League. Thalmann, "Frauen," 296. *BJFB*, Jan. 1935, 10; quote from *BJFB*, Dec. 1935, 13. See also: Kaplan, *Feminist*.

82. "Emotional" in *BJFB*, June 1935, 9‒10; professions in *BJFB*, Dec. 1935, 13; "disintegration" in *BJFB*, Dec. 1935, 13; Buber in Sichel, *Challenge*, 76. See also: *BJFB*, Sept. 1936, 3‒6. League activities in: (Bochum) *BJFB*, May 1935, 10; (Gelsenkirchen) *BJFB*, Feb. 1935, 5; (Munich) *BJFB*, Feb. 1935, 12 and *Rundschau*, March 14, 1935, 18; (Königsberg) *BJFB*, Jan. 1935, 10. For concerts, exhibits: *BJFB*, Jan. 1935, 10; Feb. 1935, 5; May 1935, 10; Sept. 1936, 3‒6.

83. *Rundschau*, Feb. 14, 1935, 18. See also: Bundesarchiv, Coswig: 75C Frl, Jüd. Frauenbund Verband Berlin, Medizinische Fachgruppe, folder #20.

84. *BJFB*, June 1936; Dec. 1936. Affiliates provided a variety of training, e.g.: crafts (Breslau, Frankfurt am Main, and Hamburg); tailoring (Hamburg and Cologne); infant nursing (Neu Isenburg and Frankfurt am Main); teacher's aide training (Frankfurt am Main); courses for governesses (Cologne); and technical teachers' training (Frankfurt am Main). The Home Economics School of the League of Jewish Women at Wolfratshausen expanded all classes. *BJFB*, March 1938, 3.

CHAPTER 2

Epigraph: Reiner in *Durften*, ed. Limberg, 156.

1. Harvard in Allport, "Personality," 14‒15.

2. Allport, "Personality," 14; "Life" in "Laura Pelz" in Morris, "Lives"; "special element" in Rudolf Lennert, quoted by Stern, *Whitewashing*, 37.

3. Dienemann, Harvard, 25.

4. "Ill tidings," in Richarz, *Life*, 402; "doorbell" in Limberg, *Durften*, 156; "idle men" in *Durften*, 174.

5. Party in Richarz, *Life*, 405.

6. Limberg, *Durften*, 141‒42.

7. Glaser, LBI, 15‒16; Grubel (vacation in 1937), memoirs, LBI, 15; Elly Busse, Berne, Switzerland, told Atina Grossmann that she ordered by phone to avoid trouble. April 1993.

8. *Sukkah* (1936) in Händler-Lachmann, *Purim*, 125. About one-third of the respondents to the Harvard study turned to religion for comfort. Sixty-eight percent of the respondents consid-

ered themselves Jewish, although some of the Christians were converts from Judaism. Allport, "Personality," 16. Glaser, LBI, 16–17; Prinz, "Rabbi," 232–38. See also: Nussbaum, "Ministry."

9. "Mass" in Cohn, "Bemerkungen," 45, 48; Haluz in Bentwich, *Youth*, 25.

10. "Prevailing conditions" in Lixl-Purcell, *Women*, 92; Klemperer, *Zeugnis*, I, 24, 26, 66, II, 104, 191, 654; Dienemann, Harvard, 23a.

11. Fromm, *Blood*, 197; "parents" in Marks, LBI, 8.

12. Heroines in *BJFB*, Feb. 1935, 12; "duty" in *BJFB*, July 1938, 13.

13. *IF*, Feb. 27, 1936; March 19, 1936; June 25, 1936; *CV*, Feb. 27, 1936; Feb. 24, 1938, 17.

14. E.g., "Junge Mädels lernen der Mutter helfen," in *CV* April 9, 1936; "Häusliche Erziehung," in *IF* March 19, 1936 and May 21, 1936; "head" in *IF*, May 21, 1936; exchanges in Glaser, LBI, 16. See also: *FIG*, Jan. 1936, 137.

15. Becker-Kohen, LBI, 31; men and housework in *BJFB*, October 1938, 14; "North American" in *BJFB*, Oct. 1938, 4; "Aryan husbands" in *BJFB*, Dec. 1935, 8; "consideration" in *IF* May 19, 1938, 19. See also: "Der Ehemann im Haushalt," in *IF*, May 19, 1938, 19.

16. *BJFB*, June 1935, 9–10. Scientific management is discussed by Nolan in *Modernity*, 42 and chap. 10.

17. *CV*, April 23, 1936; "merriment" in *CV* May 27, 1936; women also took gymnastics courses entitled: "Must housework exhaust us?" Bundesarchiv, Coswig: 75C Frl Jüd. Frauenbund: Verband Berlin, folder 37. See also: *CV*, March 17, 1938, 11 on energy-saving utensils.

18. Daily help in *IF*, March 19, 1936; *FIG*, Nov. 1935, 73–74; male help suggested in *IF* March 26, 1936; male help hired in *Sopade*, Jan. 3, 1936, 21; adding to stress: Illo Heppner, conversation, Washington, D.C., Dec. 1991; Bab, LBI, 179; composer in Geiger-Kullmann, LBI, 62–64; Nazi help in Brauer, LBI, 31.

19. "Mutti, hast du Zeit für mich?" in *CV*, Feb. 27, 1936; "Mutti ist so nervös!" in *CV*, Sept. 16, 1936.

20. *CV*, Aug. 25, 1938, 8.

21. League in Edinger letter in the Schoenewald coll., LBI, IV, 1 and *BJFB*, Oct. 1935, 2; candles in *IF*, Feb. 17, 1938, 16; Becker-Kohen, LBI, 4. See also: Segal, LBI, 93–94.

22. The Harvard team called denial "dynamic psychological mechanisms of a protective nature." Allport, "Personality," 14.

23. Housework in Allport, "Personality," 14; "drown worries" in Dienemann, Harvard, 25; "dismantle" in Baerwald, Harvard, 65; "spirit" in Brauer, LBI, 38.

24. "Wrong one" in Dienemann, Harvard, 25; "Wir werden jetzt alle Vegetarier,—dann sind wir doch von hinten—'Arier.'" Wolff, Yad Vashem, 01/247, 22.

25. Wolff, Yad Vashem, 01/247, 14, 21–22.

26. Kahn, LBI, 21.

27. Greece in Kahn, LBI, 23; Lewis, LBI, 264. See also: Kurt Ball-Kaduri, LBI, 30; Brauer, LBI, 43, 57.

28. Lore Steinitz about her mother, Irma Baum. Note to the author entitled "The first 'sit in,'" Jan. 7, 1995, also deposited at the Leo Baeck Institute, New York.

29. Abraham, LBI, 2.

30. "Daylight" in Limberg, *Durften*, 141; SS and SA in Geiger-Kullmann, LBI, 72. See also: Bundesarchiv, Coswig: 75C Jüd. Frauenbund Verband Berlin, folder 37 — "Protokoll der Arbeitskreistagung vom 2 Nov. 1936 re. Gefährdung der Jugendlichen."

31. Behnsch-Brower, LBI, 4–5.

32. Bick, Research Foundation, 18; husband's depression in Honnet-Sichel, Harvard, 72–73; Cohn, Yad Vashem, 5.

33. Teenager (from Lippehne near the Eichwald) in Limberg, *Durften*, 213–15; Lewis, LBI, 251–52; destitution in Kramer, "Welfare," 183. In the first three months of 1937, for example, over 55 percent of migrants were women. Quack, *Zuflucht*, 60–61.

34. *IF*, June 25, 1936; *CV*, March 10, 1938, 3.

35. Rural Jews in Baumann, "Land" (Baden-Württemberg), 40; Appel in Richarz, *Leben*, III, 237.

This gender-specific reaction in dangerous situations has been noted by sociologists and psychologists: men tend to "stand their ground," whereas women avoid conflict, preferring flight as a strategy. See also: Kliner-Fruck, "*Überleben*," 79. Although there were also women who were afraid to leave, they were in the minuscule minority. Gay, "Epilogue," 364.

36. Gompertz, LBI, 7.

37. Leonard Baker, *Days of Sorrow and Pain: Leo Baeck and the Berlin Jews* (New York, 1978), 238.

38. "His status" in Berel, LBI, 16; Shanghai couple described by their daughter, Evelyn Rubin, at Queens College, December 1988, and in the *Long Island Jewish Week*, Nov. 19, 1978.

39. Lore Segal, *Other People's Houses* (New York, 1958). See also: Quack, *Sorrow* and *Zuflucht*, chaps. 4 and 6.

40. Women in the economy in Claudia Koonz, "Courage," 285 and *Mothers*, chap. 10; Jewish sector in Barkai, *Boycott*, 2–3, 6–7, quotes on 80–83.

41. Axelrath, Harvard, 37. She and her husband spent twelve years (1927–39) in Hamburg. They were the only Jews in the American colony.

42. "Impending danger" in Koonz, "Courage," 287; "judges" in Gerstel, LBI, 71.

43. Segal, LBI, 45–46, 61. See also: Drexler, Harvard; Hamburger, LBI, 40–41; Spiegel, *Retter*, 15; Hilda Branch in Rothchild, *Voices*; Eisner, *Allein*, 8; Morris, "Lives," 93.

44. "He laughed" in Segal, LBI, 45–47, 61; "so seriously" in Allport, "Personality," 3.

45. Wyden, *Stella*, 47; Salomon in Felstiner, *Paint*, 74. Carol Gilligan's theories may apply here: men tend to view and express their situation in terms of abstract rights, women in terms of actual affiliations and relationships. *In a Different Voice: Psychological Theory and Women's Development* (Cambridge, Mass., 1982).

46. Nauen, Research Foundation, 8; Bernheim, Harvard, 53; "decent German" in Hamburger, LBI, 41, 46.

47. Stein-Pick, LBI, 2, 38; Swiss bank in Bamberger, LBI, 5; pregnancy in Deutsch, Harvard.

48. Gerstel, LBI, 71; "sixth feeling" in Foster, *Community*, 28–30.

49. Bloch, Research Foundation, 6, 8; the lawyer was Braun-Melchior, LBI, 32.

50. "Quota" in Strauss, LBI, chap. 8, 44; "hell" in Bernheim, Harvard, 45; Gerstel, LBI, 76.

51. Hellwig, Harvard, 25–26. See also: Edel, *Leben*, 149–50; Bab, LBI, 180.

52. The agencies were the Hilfsverein, the Hauptstelle für Jüdische Wanderfürsorge, and the Palästina Amt. Wyden, *Stella*, 48, 88. For the Nazi plans, see: Schleunes, *Twisted Road*, 183–84, 197–98.

53. In 1933, over 35 percent of the Jewish population was older than fifty, by 1938, more than half were older than fifty.

54. "Expensive" in Wyden, *Stella*, 48; taxes in Barkai, *Boycott*, 99–100, and Marrus, *Unwanted*, 131; Stoppleman, LBI, 6.

55. Accounts in Barkai, *Boycott*, 99–100; Marrus, *Unwanted*, 131; and Walk, *Sonderrecht*; hesitating in Grubel, LBI, 12.

56. Lewis, LBI, 269–70; Fromm, *Blood*, Aug. 10, 1938, 238.

57. On foreign consulates, see: Staatsarchiv Hamburg, Oberfinanzpräsident, 314–15, 9UA2: "Auswanderung jüdische Emigranten, 1936–1941."

58. Blonder in Vogel, *Forget!*, 12; "We know" in Lixl-Purcell, *Women*, 84; sex for papers took place after the November Pogrom, private interview.

59. Walk, *Sonderrecht* (Nov. 16, 1937); Bundesarchiv, Coswig: 75C Hil HICEM Prague 5 Coordinating Committee for Refugees: Domestic Bureau (Fragebogen 1939).

60. Strauss, "Emigration," I, 357. It is estimated that about 60,000 to 65,000 refugees in total left Germany in 1933 and that about 40 percent of these (not all of whom were Jewish) went to France. Shortly after 1933, Paris began to restrict the flow. Rita Thalmann, "L'Immigration Allemande et l'opinion publiques en France de 1933 à 1936," in *La France et l' Allemagne 1932–1936*, ed. Comité d'histoire de la 2e Guerre mondiale (Paris, 1980), 149–50; Bauer, *Brother's*, 138–39; Marrus, *Unwanted*, 146–47; Vicki Caron, *Uneasy Asylum: France and the Jewish Refugee Crisis, 1933–1942*, forthcoming.

61. Leipzig in Wahrman, *Forget,* 77–78. See also: Evelyn Pike, *The Long Island Jewish Week,* Nov. 19, 1978.

CHAPTER 3

Epigraph: Becker-Kohen, LBI, 1.

1. Burleigh, *Racial State.*
2. Despite Jewish law whereby the mother's faith is determinative, more children of Jewish fathers and Christian mothers remained Jewish. *ZDSJ,* July 1906, 107–8. Eleven percent from: Blau, "Mischehe," 46.
3. The estimates for *"Mischlinge"* (officially called *Judenmischlinge*) in 1933 are 292,000. See Strauss, "Emigration," I, 317, and his "Autonomy," 127. In 1935, the Nazis estimated 475,000 "full Jews" and 750,000 "first- and second-degree *Mischlinge."* Grenville, "'Endlösung,'" 102. Noakes argues the 750,000 figure is exaggerated. Using figures from the census of 1939 (when many Jews had already emigrated), he finds 52,005 "first degree" and 32,669 "second-degree" *Mischlinge.* "Development," 292–94. See also: Beate Meyer, *Die Verfolgung jüdische "Mischlinge" in Hamburg* (Hamburg, forthcoming). Thank you to Beate Meyer for sharing some findings with me.
4. Mason, "Women," 95; Bajohr, *Fabrik,* 220.
5. For marriages between Jewish men and Jewish women, see note 9. The increase in Jewish marriages between 1933 and 1935 was proportionally greater than it first appears, since this was a period of emigration. *Statistisches Jahrbuch,* 52–59 (1933–1941/42). "Sumptuous" in Grubel, LBI, 11.
6. In Breslau, Behnsch-Brower, LBI, 2; Ruth (Sass) Glaser, LBI, 37. Blackmail is mentioned quite frequently in the early Nazi years. For examples: *IF,* March 12, 1936, 2; May 21, 1936, 4.
7. (Sass) Glaser, LBI, 46, 48; "please" in Lixl-Purcell, *Women,* 26.
8. Statistics in Schmelz, "Entwicklung," 53; Strauss, "Emigration," I, 317; and Büttner, "Persecution," 271.
9. Intermarriage statistics from 1931 until 1939:

Religion of People Marrying in 1931:

	Prot	Cath	otherChrst	Jew	Other	total
Jewish men	600	180	10	2,484	110	3,384
Jewish women	291	95	9	2,484	110	2,989

Religion of People Marrying in 1933:

Jewish men	764	297	17	2,174	116	3,368
Jewish women	275	89	8	2,174	127	2,673

Religion of People Marrying in 1935:

Jewish men	217	82	1	2,751	53	3,104
Jewish women	84	31	1	2,751	34	2,901

Religion of People Marrying in 1936:

Jewish men	25	15	2	2,665	16	2,723
Jewish women	11	9	—	2,665	12	2,697

Religious Affiliation of People Marrying in 1938 in the *Altreich*:

	Prot	Cath	other	Jewish
Jewish men	18	5	1	2,851
Jewish women	19	5	1	2,851

Religious Affiliation of People Marrying in 1939 in the *Altreich,*
Austria, Sudeten, and Memel:

Jewish men	10	13	1	2,152
Jewish women	40	21	2	2,152

In 1932, 27 percent of Jewish men and 18 percent of Jewish women married non-Jews. In 1933, 35 percent of Jewish men and 20 percent of Jewish women married non-Jews. By 1936, only 3 percent of Jewish men and 1 percent of Jewish women married non-Jews. The *Altreich* was within Germany's pre-1938 borders. *Statistisches Jahrbuch*, 52–59 (1933–1941/42).

10. Abrams, *Special*, 22.
11. For the definitions of various "non-Aryans," see: Raul Hilberg, *Destruction*, I, 72–80, and Blau, *Ausnahmerecht*, 64, for the exact wording.
12. Advertising in Hilberg, *Perpetrators*, 152. A chart with marriage possibilities was published in the *Zeitschrift für Standesamtswesen*, Berlin, March 10, 1936, and reprinted in Rosenstrauch, *Nachbarn*, 36. A similar chart is in Kleiber, *Fremdgängerinnen*, 82.
13. Proving they were not Jews in Büttner, "Persecution," 274; Bundesarchiv, Koblenz, R18 Reichsministerium des Innern files: R18/5246, fiche 6 (letters asking to prove that writer or writer's relative is "Aryan") and R58/161 (for Jewish claims of unwed "Aryan" parentage. These come from *Meldungen aus dem Reich*, June 26, 1941, Berlin, SD Lagebericht, 21–23); names in Bundesarchiv, Koblenz R18/5246 (fiche 6); dispensation in file R18/5065. See also: Cohn, "Bearers," 327–66.
14. Shaven heads in Czarnowski, *Paar*, 102; the Paris list was not complete in Author unknown, *Gelbe Fleck*, 213. See also: Eisner, *Allein*, 70–71.
15. Halting intermarriages in: Pätzold, *Verfolgung*, 93, 97; Noakes, *Documents*, 533. In Berlin, the number of mixed marriages dropped dramatically from 663 (1933) to 367 (1934). Gruner, "Reichshauptstadt," 257. Courts in Müller, *Juristen*, 99; Noam, *Gericht*, 62; priest in *Sopade*, 1937, 938; Berlin in Gruner, "Reichshauptstadt," 233; local SA in Bankier, *Germans*, 44; *Stürmer*, Nr. 40, Oct. 1935, in Author unknown, *Gelbe Fleck*, 211.
16. "Aryan" lover in Ehre, *Gott*, 124; Gellately, *Gestapo*, 147. See also: *Sopade*, 1937, 1568; Müller, *Juristen*, 105–9; Noam, *Gericht*, 112–13.
17. "Determining" in Noam, *Gericht*, 118; custody in Gellately, *Gestapo*, 172. Later, both sexes faced punishment — also when Germans had sexual relations with other "inferior" races — but German women were also humiliated in public. Kleiber, *Fremdgängerinnen*, 114–16; 1938 case in *Sopade*, 1938, 747.
18. Treason in Müller, *Juristen*, 112; harsher in Noam, *Gericht*, 111, 115. After 1939, Jewish "career offenders" could face the death penalty. Müller, 119–121. "Protective custody" in Noam, *Gericht*, 118; execution in Broszat, *Bayern*, I, 485.
19. "Sex-craved" in Müller, *Juristen*, 112; 1938 incidents in *Sopade*, 1938, 765; false accusations in Leyens, LBI, 18. See also: Müller, *Juristen*, 121–23; *Sopade*, 1935, 1033, 1036, 1038.
20. Appeals in Bundesarchiv, Koblenz: R18 Reichsministerium des Innern files: R18/5065, R18/5244. Out of thousands of requests to the Ministry of the Interior, about a dozen

received permission to marry. Büttner, *Not*, 30. Fromm wrote about Paul von Schwabach, *Blood* (July 28, 1938), 238 (see also Fritz Stern, *Gold and Iron* [New York, 1977], 547 re. the same man).

21. Leningrad in Bundesarchiv, Koblenz: R18 Reichsministerium des Innern files: R 22/4426 Rassenschande 1939; Heydrich in Büttner, *Not*, 30.

22. Abortion had been illegal even before the Nazi seizure of power. Atina Grossmann, "Abortion and Economic Crisis," in *Biology*, ed. Bridenthal, 66–86. Germans faced forced sterilization as of July 14, 1933. Bock, *Zwangssterilisation*, esp. 347–48, 355, 357–60. See also: Aly, *Cleansing*. Rumors in Büttner, *Not*, 36. Two months after the Wannsee Conference of January 1942, Jews were exempted from forced sterilization. Bock, *Zwangssterilisation*, 347–48, 355, 357–60.

23. On "Aryans": Mason, "Women," I, 102; Frevert, *Women*, 232.

Children born to Jews 1933–39

Year	Jews by "race"	Jews by religion
1933	1,246	1,146
1935	1,139	1,046
1939 (to May 31)	325	284

Table from *Statistik des Deutschen Reiches*, vol. 552, as cited by Strauss, "Emigration," I, 319.

24. Delay in Freyhan, LBI, p. 7; Becker-Kohen, LBI, l.

25. In 1940, Nazi leaders discussed allowing German-Jewish women to have abortions, but the decision was postponed. Bock, *Zwangssterilisation*, 163; see also, Quack, *Zuflucht*, 58–59. Klüger, *leben* 28; Wysbar in Limberg, *Durften*, 195–97.

26. "Relatives" in Büttner, *Not*, 13; baptism in Owings, *Frauen*, 457; adultery in Abrams, *Special*, passim; Brandenburgisches Landeshauptarchiv: PrBr Rep 12 B St Potsdam 80 and Bundesarchiv, Koblenz, R18 Reichsministerium des Innern files: R18/5246 (fiche 7). By May 1941, only 263 of 9,636 petitions asking for "Aryan" status or to be "upgraded" in *"Mischling"* status succeeded. Noakes, "Development," 319.

27. Phases in Büttner, *Not*, 13–14, 23, 32–33. See also: John Grenville, "'Endlösung,'" 91–122. "Confessions" in Moritz, *Verbrechen*, 7–8, 248–53, 258.

28. Krüger, LBI, 20.

29. Krüger, LBI, 5, 16, 24, 41.

30. Mother-in-law in Jauffron-Frank, LBI, 31–32. See also: Owings, *Frauen*, 456; Runge, *Onkel*, 58–59, 95.

31. Grandmother in Lange, *Davidstern*, 242; Becker-Kohen, LBI, 3.

32. Klemperer, *LTI*, 179–80; Blau in Richarz, *Life*, 466.

33. Hitler Youth in Jacobson, *Selves*, 236, 243. See also: Limberg, *Durften*, 137.

34. In Hamburg, for example, the divorced Jewish mother of a baptized child could not be deported until the child was ten. Ruth von Bialy, interview. Although *"Mischlinge"* were banned from the army in April 1940, this was not strictly enforced until October 1942. Krüger received the Iron Cross in Oct. 1940 (LBI, 41/1, 48). "Second-degree *Mischlinge*" were not discharged.

35. *IF*, April 23, 1936; Walk, *Sonderrecht*, 198, 221, 241, 345. The law forbidding "interracial" adoptions was proclaimed on April 12, 1938. Removal of children in *Sopade*, 1939, 210; children dissociating in Lange, *Davidstern*, 185–99, and in Limberg, *Durften*, 137–38.

36. Custody in *AJYB 5698 (1937/38)* (Philadelphia, 1937), 332, and Büttner, *Not*, 31–32. Taking child from "Aryan" mother in *Sopade*, 1936, 974; eighteen-year-old in Lange, *Davidstern*, 159–60; soldier in Lange, *Davidstern*, 213–14.

37. *"Mischling"* son in Limberg, *Durften,* 232; Edvardson, *Kind,* 55–56; rejected child in Lange, *Davidstern,* 185–99; Jewish Hospital in Elkin, "Kinder," 262–65.
38. Schmelz, "Entwicklung," 43; Klüger, *leben,* 54–55.
39. Hamburg couple in Meyer-Gerstein, LBI, II, 14; Wyden, *Stella,* 50. See also Hilda Branch in Rothchild, *Voices.*
40. Resignation (Jan. 26, 1937) in Blau, *Ausnahmerecht,* 37; relief in Kramer, "Welfare," 186.
41. At first, confusion prevailed as courts denied or granted divorces and then reversed themselves on appeal. Courts in Müller, *Juristen,* pp. 100–103; Pätzold, *Verfolgung,* 76; *GemBer,* July 21, 1934, 4; *IF* Feb. 27, 1936. "Downfall" in Owings, *Frauen,* 105. See also: Jacobson, *Selves,* 238. For threats and bribes to "Aryans" to divorce Jews, see: Morris, "Lives," 99, 108, and Ostow, *Jews,* 25–26.
42. Göring in Sauer, *Dokumente,* II, 84. See Para. no. 1333. Since 1940, "experts" had discussed the murder of both members of the mixed marriages in Poland if the "Aryan" partner did not accept divorce. In the occupied Baltic countries the Germans tested forced divorces as of 1941. Götz Aly, "Nachwort," in Krüger, *Der halbe Stern,* 134. See also chapter 7 on forced labor of "Aryan" spouses.
43. Donath, Harvard, 18.
44. Büttner, *Not,* 57, 298 n. 253. Büttner notes only 7 percent of mixed marriages in Baden-Württemberg ended in divorce and 10 percent of those in Hamburg (through October 1942). The Hamburg figure is over 20 percent in Meyer, *Verfolgung* (forthcoming). See also: Deutsch, Harvard; Donath, Harvard; Frevert, *Women,* 237.
45. SA uniform in Runge, *Onkel,* 94–95. According to Eva Wysbar, most mixed marriages in the film industry broke up, although a minority emigrated. Limberg, *Durften,* 195–97, 200.
46. "Insurmountable" in Stern, *Whitewashing,* 8–9; doctor in Ehre, *Gott,* 116–24, 128, 154–57.
47. Journal was *Deutsches Recht* quoted in Noam, *Gericht,* 60. Case from October 1939, Frankfurt am Main in: Noam, *Gericht,* 70.
48. Divorce in Lange, *Davidstern,* 186–88. Lundholm believes her father denounced her to the Gestapo. She survived Ravensbrück. *Die Zeit,* June 10, 1994, 24.
49. Woman in Hellwig, Harvard, 30; man in Limberg, *Durften,* 138–39.
50. On divorces, Limberg, *Durften,* 137; on gender, Koonz, *Mothers,* 192; "gentile wife" in Bernheim, Harvard, 49. For wives divorcing Jewish husbands, see: Kamm, Harvard, 38–39; Edel, *Leben,* I, 151, 217, 222, 284; Koehn, *Mischling,* 13, 19. Bertolt Brecht, *The Jewish Wife and Other Short Plays,* trans. Eric Bentley (New York, 1965), 15, 17. The play was written in the mid-1930s, copyright 1942. In Hamburg, court records show that more "Aryan" women divorced their Jewish spouses. Meyer, *Verfolgung* (forthcoming). More research is needed on other cities before we can draw definitive conclusions.
51. Dresden in Albersheim, Harvard, 69; theater director in Krüger, LBI, 35, 62, 66.
52. Kästner in Stern, *Whitewashing,* 86; Scholem, *Berlin,* 30; prosecuted in Friedlander, "Judiciary," 32; mixed marriages in Schmelz, "Entwicklung," 43; German divorce rates in *Statistisches Jahrbuch,* 58 (1939/40), 70.

CHAPTER 4

Epigraph: Klüger, *leben,* 7.
1. Since Germans distinguish between *Schüler* (equivalent to our elementary and high school students) and *Student* (someone who attends the university), I have used "pupil" and "student," respectively.
2. Sit apart in Marks, LBI, 4; classes in Littauer, Harvard, 21; grades in Lessler, LBI, 22–24.
3. Mother's Day in Richarz, *Life,* 353–54. By the end of 1933, Nazi youth groups contained 47 percent of boys between ten and fourteen in the *Deutsches Jungvolk* and 38 percent of boys between fourteen and eighteen in the Hitler Youth proper. Fifteen percent of girls between

ten and fourteen joined the *Jungmädelbund* and 8 percent of girls between fifteen and twenty-one joined the *Bund Deutscher Mädel.* The Hitler Youth Law of December 1936 called for the incorporation of all German youth, and a law of 1939 made "youth service" compulsory. Detlev Peukert, "Youth in the Third Reich," in *Life,* ed. Bessel, 27–28.

4. Angress, *Fear,* 10. These are common themes. See also: Eisner, *Allein,* 8.

5. Pails in Lessler, LBI, 22–23; *Gymnasium* in Felstiner, *Paint,* 34.

6. Kallmann, LBI, 29, 39, 42–44.

7. Magdeburg in Drexler, Harvard; (Sass) Glaser, LBI, 14, 17–18.

8. Scherman, Yad Vashem, 1; song in Meynert, "Jugend," 63.

9. School leaving because of hostility in Vollnhals, "Selbsthilfe," 332–33, 337, 339. See also: Colodner, *Education,* 50; Röcher, *Schule,* 58. Universities in Huerkamp, "Akademikerinnen," 327.

10. Kuhn in Owings, *Frauen,* 452; Sheba in Vogel, *Forget!,* 57.

11. Parents lied in Meynert, "Jugend," 58; "scream" in Lange, *Davidstern,* 186. See also: Koch, Harvard, 104. For a "proud to be 'different'" response see: Scherman, Yad Vashem, 1.

12. "Half-Aryan" in Büttner, *Not,* 25; nephew in Krug, Harvard, 14.

13. Hellwig, Harvard, 29–30; Nazi teacher in Richarz, *Leben,* 234. See also: Limberg, *Durften,* 230; Segal, LBI, 78–79.

14. Joseph Benjamin Levy, LBI.

15. Son in Heims, *Berlin,* 73, 76; "lying" in Bernheim, Harvard, 50–51.

16. Limberg, *Durften,* 217–18.

17. *Angst* in Felstiner, *Paint,* 52; swimming in Meynert, "Jugend," 63; "loneliness" in Hellwig, Harvard, 30. See also: Littauer, Harvard, 14–15.

18. Meynert, "Jugend," 62; Limberg, *Durften,* 217–18.

19. Limberg, *Durften,* 208.

20. Lessler, LBI, 22.

21. Class trip in Dienemann, Harvard, 23a; ten-year-old in Limberg, *Durften,* 210–11.

22. Werner Stein in *New York Times,* Nov. 10, 1992, B3 (article on the Kaliski School in Berlin).

23. Colodner, *Education,* 49, 65; Röcher, *Schule,* 71, 92–93, 99; Vollnhals, "Selbsthilfe," 331, 342, 348–54.

24. Pforzheim in Sussmann, LBI, 3; Berlin in Limberg, *Durften,* 221.

25. Lessler, LBI, letter from her sister; Breslau in Littauer, Harvard, 28; "torture" in Limberg, *Durften,* 226; "Aryan neighbors" in Bundesarchiv, Potsdam: 49.01 Reichsministerium für Wissenschaft, Erziehung, und Volksbildung; 5368 Private Waldschule Kaliski.

26. Kaliski school in *New York Times,* Nov. 10, 1992, B3. See also: Michael Daxner, "Die Private Jüdische Waldschule Kaliski in Berlin, 1932–1939," and Joseph Walk, "Jüdische Erziehung als geistiger Widerstand," both in *Nazi Germany,* ed. Paucker.

27. "Separation" in Stein-Pick, LBI, 28; Lessler, LBI, 22–23; "fifteen-year-old" in Angress, *Fear,* 13; Paucker, "Anmerkungen zum Verhalten jüdischer Jugendlicher unter der NS-Diktatur," *Ausstellungszeitung, Juden im Widerstand,* Berlin, March–June 1993 and *Tagesspiegel* (Berlin), November 15–16, 1994. See also: Limberg, *Durften,* 220.

28. Change in Bundesarchiv, Potsdam. 49.01 Reichsministerium für Wissenschaft, Erziehung, und Volksbildung, 5595 Yawne Schule, Köln; emigration in Vollnhals, "Selbsthilfe," 330; school in Limberg, *Durften,* 219.

29. Lewis, LBI, 248; Wahrman, *Forget,* 74; vans in Krüger, LBI, 21; Klüger, *leben,* 13–14.

30. Stein-Pick, LBI, 28.

31. Wahrman, *Forget,* 70.

32. Boys in Lessler, LBI, 27; "tickets" in Dwork, *Children,* 23; six-year-old in Owings, *Frauen,* 450–52; unobtrusive in Limberg, *Durften,* 215–16.

33. Her parents fled later. (Sass) Glaser, LBI, 18.

34. Orthodox in Wahrman, *Forget,* 55; Lewis, LBI, 252–59.

35. Deutschkron, *Outcast*, 3–4; finances in Dwork, *Children*, 11–12; Shabbos in Wahrman, *Forget*, 85. See also: Limberg, *Durften*, 214–15; *BJFB*, Aug. 1938, 8.

36. Homework and Gardner in Kliner-Lintzen, "*vergessen*," 299–300.

37. "Fight" in Meynert, "Jugend," 64; boxer in Vogel, *Forget!*, 199; "rudeness" in Allport, "Personality," 17.

38. Donath, Harvard, 18.

39. Newspapers in Angress, *Fear*, 17; "anxiety" in Meynert, "Jugend," 57; "childhood . . . over" in Owings, *Frauen*, 104; Gillis-Carlebach, *Kind*, 123–98.

40. Strauss, "Emigration," #I, 318; (Sass) Glaser in Lixl-Purcell, *Women*, 13; Danzig in Baerwald, Harvard, 36–37.

41. See: Chaim Schatzker, "The Jewish Youth Movement in Germany in the Holocaust Period" (I) in *LBIYB*, 1987, 157–81, and (II) in *LBIYB*, 1988, 301–25; Walter Oppenheimer, *Jüdische Jugend in Deutschland* (Munich, 1967); Hermann Meier-Cronemeyer, "Judische Jugendbewegung" (I) in *Germania Judaica*, Jg. VIII, Heft 1/2 and (II) in *Germania Judaica*, Jg. VIII, Heft 3/4, Cologne, 1969; Hilde Landenberger, "Die soziale Funktion der jüdischen Jugendbewegung" in *JWS*, 1936; statistics in *JWS*, 1936, 100.

42. Bund in *Gemeinschaftsarbeit*, 72, and Löhken, *Widerstand*, 97. "We loved" in Henry Kellermann, "Recollections," *LBIYB*, 1994, 322–24. He claims a larger number of 9,000 to 15,000 members.

43. Breesen in Angress, *Fear*, 43–154. JPF stood for *Jüdische Pfadfinderbund Deutschlands*. The JPF-MH claimed 6,000 members by 1936. For the Zionists, see: *Gemeinschaftsarbeit*, 55.

44. Angress, "Erfahrungen," 89–104; allegiances in Arnold Paucker, *Israelitisches Wochenblatt*, Nov. 4, 1994, 10.

45. Conversation with Arnold Paucker, Jerusalem, March 1995.

46. Bielefeld in Meynert, "Jugend," 67–68; (Sass) Glaser, LBI, 18.

47. Limberg, *Durften*, 297–98.

48. Gompertz, LBI, 1, 8–9.

49. Nurse in Jacobson, *Selves*, 170–71; Edvardson, *Kind*, 57.

50. "Behaved" in Vogel, *Forget!*, 59; "pity" in Büttner, *Not*, 26.

51. Dixon, Yad Vashem.

52. Home economics training in Colodner, *Education*, 86; seamstress in *BJFB*, May 1935, 5; "sewing" thanks to Renate Bridenthal, who quoted her mother; university in *CV*, March 3, 1938, 6. See also: *BJFB*, Feb. 1937, 2–3; Bodo Becker, "Das 'Jüdische Erholungsheim Lehnitz,' " in *Wegweiser durch das jüdische Brandenburg*, ed. Irene Diekmann and Julius Schoeps (Berlin, 1995), 388.

53. Scherman, Yad Vashem, 2–3.

54. *JWS*, 1935, 185–89, and *JWS*, 1937, 140–43.

55. Vollnhals, "Selbsthilfe," 391; BenGershom, *David*, 56.

56. Subsidies in *Informationsblätter*, Aug./Oct. 1937, 59–60; Bureau in Vollnhals, "Selbsthilfe," 391; League in *BJFB*, March 1938, 3.

57. "My daughter" in *IF*, Feb. 17, 1938, 16; Gross-Breesen in Angress, "Jugend," 219. It may be that Eastern European Jewish women took greater advantage of these career programs. Maurer, "Ausländische," 205. A partial list of career training schools for girls in *CV*, March 3, 1938, 6.

58. Straus, "Emigration," I, 328; Wetzel, "Auswanderung," 460–61; Gertrude van Tijn, "Werkdorp Nieuwesluis," *LBIYB*, 1969, 182–99.

59. Eisner, *Allein*, 8. She left in January 1939; fifteen-year-old in Bernheim, Harvard, 52; Gillis-Carlebach, *Kind*, 209.

60. Lange, *Davidstern*, 28.

61. In England, the Quakers took in 300 children from Vienna by November 1938 and the Children's Inter-Aid Committee brought in 150 up to 1938 and another 300 by the end of 1938. Barry Turner, *And the policeman smiled* (London, 1990), 21–22, 40, 43. By the end of

1939, about 18,000 young people had entered Palestine without their parents.

62. Strauss, "Emigration," 328; Reinharz, "Hashomer," 334. Turner, *policeman,* states that 10,000 children were brought into England.

63. Youth Aliyah was launched officially in 1934, although Freier began it in 1932. Until April 1939, Youth Aliyah sent 3,229 children from Germany to Palestine. Thank you to Sara Kadosh of the Joint Distribution Committee Archives for the figures from Germany. Bentwich claims 7,000 children brought into Palestine (*Youth,* 62, 82), and others claim 10,000 by 1944 (*Ten Years Children and Youth Aliyah 1933–1944* [London: Children and Youth Aliyah, 1945?], 2).

64. "Adventure" in Marks, LBI, 6; "devastates" in letter from Gertrud Grossmann, Jan. 17, 1939. Thank you to Atina Grossmann for sharing these letters. See also: Dienemann, Harvard, 25; Vogel, *Forget!,* 210.

65. "Letters" in Bab, LBI, 184; governess in Kliner-Lintzen, "*vergessen,*" 303; Beuthner in Lixl-Purcell, *Women,* 58. This conscious act of separation of parents and children was so excruciating that many in the resistance who rescued children later realized that they were able to do this work precisely because they had not yet had children. Dwork, *Children,* 51, 65.

66. Gillis-Carlebach, *Kind,* 198; Klüger, *leben,* 62. See also: Nathorff, *Tagebuch,* 149.

67. Strauss, "Emigration," I, 318; *JWS,* 1937, 163.

CHAPTER 5

Epigraph: Wahrman, *Forget,* 116–18.

1. Property decree of April 26, 1938. "Seizure" in Schleunes, *Twisted Road,* 221; teenager in Lange, *Davidstern,* 23.

2. Maurer, "Abschiebung," 62.

3. Buchenwald and synagogues in Thalmann, *Crystal,* 16–20; wives in Behnsch-Brower, LBI, 4–5.

4. Letter of Nov. 19, 1938, from Otto Buchholz, quoted by Maurer, "Abschiebung," 52–53. See also: Sybil Milton, "The Expulsion of Polish Jews from Germany, October 1938 to July 1939," *LBIYB,* 1984; Yfaat Weiss, "'Ostjuden' in Deutschland als Freiwild. Die nationalsozialistische Aussenpolitik zwischen Ideologie und Wirklichkeit," *Tel Aviver Jahrbuch für deutsche Geschichte* 25, (1994), 215–33.

5. Munich in Stein-Pick, LBI, 34; Hamburg in Meyer-Gerstein, LBI, I, 41. See also: Wahrman, *Forget,* 90; Maurer, "Abschiebung," 62–63.

6. Anti-Jewish actions began around November 8, escalating dramatically during the actual pogrom and continuing through November 11. Lauber, *Judenpogrom.*

7. Peter Loewenberg, "The Kristallnacht as a Public Degradation Ritual," *LBIYB,* 1987; Königsberg in *Sopade,* 1939, 219–20; Dinslaken in Thalmann, *Crystal,* 84–85. On another Jewish orphanage, see: Benz, "Rückfall," 34.

8. Jewish women organized emergency aid near the concentration camps as men were released. See *Sopade,* 1939, 924. "Sanity" in Stoppleman, LBI, 5; urns in Littauer, Harvard, 33.

9. Hecht, *Walls,* 59.

10. Neighbor in Stein-Pick, LBI, 40; Hecht, *Walls,* 59.

11. "Sweeping" in *LBI News,* no. 56 (1988), 4–5; Dienemann, Harvard, 34.

12. "Shame" and "moderate" in Bankier, *Germans,* 85, 87; "Sonderburg" in Henry, *Victims,* 116–18.

13. Pehle, "Preface," *November,* vii–viii.

14. Albersheim, Harvard, 28; Axelrath, Harvard, 43; Baerwald, Harvard, 72.

15. Women were not "exempt" from violence. See: Albersheim, Harvard, 63; Baerwald, Harvard, 58; Anonymous, LBI, 5; Henry, *Victims,* 116–17; Baumann, "Land," 38; Günther Haselier, *Geschichte der Stadt Breisach am Rhein* (Breisach, 1985), 450; Moritz, *Verbrechen,* 94–97, 232–33; *Sopade,* 1939, 920; Sauer, *Dokumente,* II, 25–28; Lauber, *Judenpogrom,* 110–14, 221–33; Thalmann, *Crystal,* 70, 81. Also, women were taken hostage for husbands: Lixl-

Purcell, *Women*, 71; *Sopade*, 1939, 922. Finally, the aged, female and male, were not spared physical brutality either: *Sopade*, 1938, 1340. Four Nazis who had assaulted Jewish women were, interestingly, expelled from the Party, whereas twenty-six men who had killed Jewish men received no punishment. Hilberg, *Destruction*, I, 46.

16. "Sonderburg" in Henry, *Victims*, 117–18; Lessler, LBI, 32; Epstein, LBI, 8 (describing the Philanthropin in Frankfurt am Main).

17. Wahrman, *Forget*, 116–18.

18. Allport, "Personality," 6.

19. Mannheim in Abraham, LBI, 3; small town Anonymous, LBI, 4–5.

20. Stein-Pick, LBI, 41–45.

21. Abraham, LBI, 3–5.

22. "Open season" in Limberg, *Durften*, 325.

23. "Praise" in Gompertz, LBI, 10; Stein-Pick, LBI, 39; Bernheim, Harvard, 56, 63; Hamburg (Paula Kleve) in Gillis-Carlebach, *Kind*, 238. See also: Albersheim, Harvard, 33.

24. Psychologists in Allport, "Personality," 4; "everyone" in Lange, *Davidstern*, 27.

25. Freund in Richarz, *Life*, 413–15.

26. Letter from Gertrud Grossmann, Jan. 17, 1939; "god" in Bernheim, Harvard, 51.

27. Fromm, *Blood*, 238 (July 20, 1938); Dienemann, Harvard, 35.

28. Post-1939 laws in Bernheim, Harvard, 63–64; Gerstel, LBI, 76. See also: Nathorff, LBI, 127–33; letters from Gertrud Grossmann, Jan. 3, 1939; Feb. 22, 1940. The government continued to add new impediments to emigration. In 1941, it forbade the emigration of combat-fit Jewish men between the ages of eighteen and forty-five. It also forbade the emigration of women between those same ages. Freund, LBI, 166.

29. Stein-Pick, LBI, 37; also bribes to have husbands released from camps in Moses, Harvard, 44; payoff in Brauer, LBI, 51.

30. Alexander Szanto in Barkai, *Boycott*, 152.

31. Bernheim, Harvard, 55–56, 66; see also Lessler, LBI, 33.

32. Gerstel, LBI, 76, 80, 86.

33. Strauss, "Emigration," I, 317–18, 326–27.

34. Kamm, Harvard, 27, 31; "women's work" in Freyhan, LBI, 7; Brauer, LBI, 56; "before 1933" in Freund, LBI, 144–45. See also: Bab, LBI, 198; Limberg, *Durften,* 203.

35. Brauer, LBI, 57.

36. Containers in Lange, *Davidstern*, 30; Brauer, LBI, 55; Baerwald, Harvard, 65–67.

37. Popper, Harvard, 75; "stupid" in Honnet-Sichel, Harvard, 80.

38. Brauer, LBI, 54, writes of a bailiff (*Gerichtsvollzieher*) and Freund, LBI, 178, of a custom's official (*Zollbeamter*) coming to the home. See also: Glaser, LBI, 71.

39. "Corruption" in Moses, Harvard, 44–45; Gerstel, LBI, 77–79.

40. Grandmother in Glaser, LBI, 38; Baerwald, Harvard, 73, 75. Blocked accounts and prohibitions re. money in Walk, *Sonderrecht* (April and Dec. 1936); Barkai, *Boycott,* 100, 138.

41. Berger in Scheer, *Ahawah*, 265; patient in Lixl-Purcell, *Women*, 53.

42. "Packing" in Vogel, *Forget!*, 202; "uprooted" in Schwarz, "Tschaikowsky," 119.

43. Lixl-Purcell, *Women*, 78.

44. "Farewell" in Bab, LBI, 193; Lessler, LBI, 34; Freund in Richarz, *Life*, 423.

45. Lewis, LBI, 275–77.

46. Lessler, LBI, 33.

47. *JWS*, 1937, 7–13; 27, 78–81; Barkai, "Existenzkampf," 163; Burgheim, archives, LBI; Hanno Loewy, ed., *In mich ist die grosse dunkle Ruhe gekommen, Martha Wertheimer Briefe an Siegfried Guggenheim* (1939–1941), Frankfurter Lern-und Dokumentationszentrum des Holocaust (Frankfurt am Main, 1993), 6, 9, 13, 15, 22, 37.

48. Returning east in Maurer, "Ausländische," 204; "hinder" in *BJFB*, December 1936, 5.

49. Men beaten in Eisner, *Allein*, 8; Nauen (whose father was secretary of the Hilfsverein in Hamburg), Research Foundation, 15; Klüger, *leben*, 83.

50. "Proper" in Morris, "Lives," 43; "the sons" in *BJFB*, April 1937, 5; Glaser, LBI, 26, 71; Stein-Pick, LBI, 46. Another daughter who remained with her parents in Erika Guetermann, LBI.

51. *BJFB*, Dec. 1936, l. Bundesarchiv, Coswig: 75C Jüd. Frauenbund, Verband Berlin, folder 37. Protokoll der Arbeitskreistagung vom 2 Nov. 1936; Aid Society (Hilfsverein) in *CV*, Jan. 20, 1938, 5; March 3, 1938, 6.

52. For example, in 1937, of the 7,313 émigrés supported by the emigration section of the Central Organization of Jews in Germany, there were approximately 4,161 men and 3,041 women. The Hilfsverein supported 3,250 men and 2,512 women. The Palestine Bureau supported 911 men and 529 women. *Informationsblätter*, Jan./Feb. 1938, 6–7. Overall immigration into the U.S. showed a higher proportion of men, evening out only in 1938–39. See: *AJYB 5699 (1938–39)* (1938), 552–554; *5701 (1940–41)* (1940), 608–9; *5702 (1941–42)* (1941), 674–75; Quack, "Gender," 391; Backhaus-Lautenschläger, *standen*, 30 (who claims more women than men entered between 1933 and 1941, although this encompasses Jews and non-Jews).

53. Businessman in *IF*, March 5, 1936; "affidavit" in *IF*, Oct. 13, 1938, 16; see also Klemperer, *Zeugnis*, I, 462 (Feb. 1939). Phony marriages in Wetzel, "Auswanderung," 453; Kliner-Fruck, "*Überleben*," 140; Backhaus-Lautenschläger, *standen*, 62.

54. Surveys in *JWS*, 1935, 188. The programs included: Hechaluz, Habonim, and Makkabi Hazair. *Informationsblätter*, Aug./Oct. 1937, 60. Palestine statistics in "Jewish Immigration from Germany during 1933–1942 (includes Austria … Czechoslovakia and Danzig …)," reprint from "The Jewish Immigration and Population" issued by the Dept. of Statistics of the Jewish Agency.

55. *JWS*, 1933–34; "friendly word" in *IF*, Jan. 16, 1936, 15; June 25, 1936, 9.

56. "Mostly" in Lixl-Purcell, *Women*, 92. Women were also a majority of the Jewish populations of German-dominated Europe: Hilberg, *Perpetrators*, 127; *IF*, Feb. 27, 1936; Blau, "Population," 165.

57. On age, see Strauss, "Emigration," I, 318–19, and Blau, "Population," 165; "dismal" in Rothschild, LBI, 125–26; old age homes in Gruner, "Reichshauptstadt," 242, 251; Winter Relief in Vollnhals, "Selbsthilfe," 405, and *BJFB*, Oct. 1938, 4.

58. Disproportionate number of elderly women in Richarz, *Leben*, 61; *JWS*, 1937, 96–97, 161–63, 200–01; Klemperer, *Zeugnis*, I, 475; *IF*, Jan. 16, 1936; Freund, LBI, 146.

CHAPTER 6

Epigraph: Freund, LBI, 58–59.

1. Barkai, *Boycott*, 136–38. See also: Kwiet, "Stufen," 545–659. Requests in Staatsarchiv Hamburg; Oberfinanzpräsident Hamburg; Sicherungsanordnung—Sperrkonto, Generalakten.

2. "[H]urt worse" in Hellwig, Harvard, 28; statistics for May 1939 in Strauss, "Emigration," I, 326.

3. Bedroom in Bernheim, Harvard, 46; Reichshof guest card at the U.S. Holocaust Memorial Museum, Washington, D.C.; Gerstel, LBI, 77. See also: Drexler, Harvard, on railroad restaurants.

4. "Sympathetic" in Lixl-Purcell, *Women*, 101; volunteer work in Behrend-Rosenfeld, *Allein*, 75, 86, and Henschel "Arbeit," 35–36; Freund in Richarz, *Life*, 421.

5. *Sopade*, 1934, 398–413, and 1935, 1394–95.

6. Albersheim, Harvard, 21, 28, 37 (written around 1940). On wool, see also Lohr, Harvard, 33.

7. *New York Times* correspondent Frederick Birchall in Fromm, *Blood*, 8; diary in Bernheim, Harvard, 61–61a. See: Enssle, "Life," 8.

8. Glaser, LBI, 65–66, 74. See also: Bernheim, Harvard, 49.

9. See also: Büttner, *Not*, 42–43.

10. Thank you to Herbert Strauss, who reminded me of this and mentioned the case of a Jewish man who had his daughter baptized well after the cutoff date of 1935 and was then placed

into the "privileged" category. Edith Wolff tells of a similar attempt to "rise" into the "privileged" category. Yad Vashem, 01/247, 17–21.

11. "Aryan" woman in Büttner, *Not*, 36; Gestapo in Fleischer (a pseudonym) Morris, "Lives," 97; Klepper, *Unter dem Schatten Deiner Flügel. Aus den Tagebüchern der Jahre 1932–1942* (Stuttgart, 1968), quoted in Büttner, *Not*, 42. Klepper's wife received "privileged" status, but her daughter by a previous marriage to a Jewish man was a "full Jew." All three committed suicide when the daughter's deportation seemed imminent. Klemperer, *LTI*, 177.

12. Kleiber, *Fremdgängerinnen*, 39; Czarnowski, *Paar*, 176.

13. Walk, *Sonderrecht*.

14. "Opera" in Lange, *Davidstern*, 31, 33.

15. Ersatz in *Sopade*, 1940, A40–71; calories in Enssle, "Life," 9; "looting" in Gerhard L. Weinberg, "Iconoclasm: German Plans for Victory, 1944–45," *Central European History*, 26, no. 2 (1993), 218. Stoppleman asserts that the rations for Jews were half those for "Aryans." LBI, 3–4.

16. In Kassel, Jews were charged 10 percent more: "Report of March 17, 1942," in Milton, *Joint*, 216; malnutrition in Freund, LBI, 29. The *average* "Aryan" worker received 500 grams of meat per week. *Sopade*, 1940, 49. Handout in Cohn, *Breslau*, 25.

17. Klemperer, *Zeugnis*, I, 679, II, 52, 87, 112, 114, 138, 147, 152, 158, 175, 189, 192–93, 203, 227, 541, 651.

18. Shopping in Fackenheim-Field, LBI, 9, and Runge, *Onkel*, 38.

19. Freund, LBI, 29–30, 49–50, 74.

20. Nazi neighbor in Rosenstrauch, *Nachbarn*, 118; Becker-Kohen, LBI, 31–32.

21. Choking in Lange, *Davidstern*, 35; Berlin in Fackenheim-Field, LBI, 9.

22. Outgrown garments in Freund, LBI, 125; Hamburg in Staatsarchiv Hamburg, Jüd. Gemeinde: 992n Band 4; hand-me-downs in Klemperer, *Zeugnis*, I, 541, 550, 562, 572, 576, 689–90, II, 59, 140, 443, 614.

23. Kolmar, *Briefe an die Schwester (1938–1943)*, ed. Johanna Zeitler (Munich, 1970), quoted by Beatrice Eichmann-Leutenegger, "Die Dichterin Gertrud Kolmar, 1894–1943," *LBI Bulletin* 85 (1990), 30; Klüger, *leben*, 60. See also: Lange, *Davidstern*, 209; Fackenheim-Field, LBI, 14.

24. Berlin in Freund, LBI, 70, 74; Leipzig in "Briefe einer Mutter, 1939–1942," Stern coll., LBI. See also: Lange, *Davidstern*, 31–32.

25. Marlis Buchholz, *Die hannoverschen Judenhäuser*, Hildesheim, 1987. "Ghetto" in von Bialy, interview, 1992.

26. Spot checks in Lange, *Davidstern*, 159. See also Klemperer on spot checks: *Zeugnis*, II, 141, 143, 215. On Dresden house searches, see II, 19–20, 41, 46, 51, 57, 61, 94, 102, 121, 142. On attacks against old women, see II, 72, 79, 82, 95, 111–12, 121, 199, 228; and against old people, II, 111, 151.

27. Klara Caro coll., LBI, "Der Untergang des deutschen Judentums," 2; Dresden in Klemperer, *Zeugnis*, II, 285.

28. "Extended family" in Beck, *gad*, 54. In September 1941, Jews were forbidden from traveling during peak hours and were segregated and made to stand in public transport. In March 1942, municipal transport was forbidden to them unless they worked over 7 kilometers from home.

29. "*Herzenshöflichkeit*" in Klemperer, *Zeugnis*, II, 216 (as supportive community, II, 278, 397, 462); Behrend-Rosenfeld quoted in Kwiet, "Stufen," 650–51. In Bonn, the cloister was the Kloster der Benediktinerinnen "Zur ewigen Anbetung." "Erinnerungen von Anneliese Winterberg" reprinted in Rothe, "Jüdinnen," 294–95. Leipzig in Lange, *Davidstern*, 43. Jews and "nonprivileged" mixed marriages had to give up their record players and records in June 1942. For conflict and envy, see: Deutschkron, *Outcast*, 115.

30. Gillis-Carlebach, *Kind*, 224–25, 252; *mikvah* in Christiane Pritzlaff, "Synagogen im Grindelviertel ... " in *Ehemals in Hamburg zu Hause*, ed. Ursula Wamser and Wilfried Weinke (Hamburg, 1991), 28. Bonn in Rothe, "Jüdinnen," 294–95; Munich in Kwiet, "Stufen," 636;

Samuel in Genger, *Herzen*; Hospital in Elkin, *Krankenhaus*, 64 (who refers to the hospital as a ghetto rather than a *Judenhaus*, 60–65). Klara Caro coll., LBI, "A Seder night to remember," 1–2. For a diary with regular entries regarding worship, see: Cohn, *Breslau*.

31. Bride in Lange, *Davidstern*, 129; "Orden," a wordplay on a Prussian medal of honor, in Cohn, *Breslau*, 58; "a lot" in Scheurenberg, *Leben*, 80.

32. Cohn describes the "exemplary" and embarrassed reactions of non-Jews in *Breslau*, 59–60.

33. Klüger, *leben*, 48; boy in Scheurenberg, *leben*, 79–80.

34. Deutschkron, *Outcast*, 97–98; grandmother in von Bialy, interview, 1992.

35. Staatsarchiv Hamburg: Jüd. Gemeinden 992 1; Klemperer, *LTI*, 179.

36. Hauptstaatsarchiv Düsseldorf: Gestapo files on Judenfreunde, RW58 65442 (around Sept. 1940 and Dec. 1942).

37. This was the Frauenkloster at Schlachtensee. Becker-Kohen, LBI, 5–6, 21, 25; on churches, see Bankier, *Germans*, 122.

38. "Sky terror" in *Völkischer Beobachter*, March 3, 1943; Klemperer entitled one of his chapters "The Jewish War," noting Nazi usage. *LTI*, chap. 26, esp. 102–3; also *Zeugnis*, II, 8, 541, 638–39, 690; Wust in Fischer, *Aimée*, 53.

39. Freund, LBI, 58; Becker-Kohen, LBI, 9. See also Lixl-Purcell, *Women*, 97. Strangely, Jewish observers describe these neighbors in gender-neutral terms, although women outnumbered men on the "home front."

40. Freund, LBI, 58.

41. Staatsarchiv Hamburg. Familie Plaut D38 (Dienstliche Korrespondenz und privater Schriftwechsel).

42. Fleischer in Morris, "Lives," 106; Freund, LBI, 58–59. Klemperer, too, feared the Gestapo more than bombs, II, 474, 606, 656.

43. Freund, LBI, 123–24; letter from Gertrud Grossmann, Feb. 7, 1940, 1.

44. Breslau (Sept. 29, 1941) in Cohn, *Breslau*, 61; "concentrate" in Hecht, *Walls*, 34; Kaliski in *New York Times*, Nov. 10, 1992, B3.

45. Klüger, *leben*, 13–14.

46. Freund in Richarz, *Life*, 416. Most park benches had been forbidden since the outbreak of war, but in some cities, like Berlin, they had been forbidden earlier. Gruner, "Reichshauptstadt," 235. On cemeteries see: Freund (on Berlin) in Richarz, *Life*, 416; Klüger (on Vienna), *leben*, 58; Klemperer (on Dresden), *Zeugnis*, II, 376, 389, 403; Cohn, *Breslau*, 43.

47. Teens in Freund, LBI, 126; diet in Scheer, *Ahawah*, 227.

48. Klüger, *leben*, 7–8, 59.

49. Lilli Segal, *Die Hohenpriester der Vernichtung: Anthropologen, Mediziner und Psychiater als Wegbereiter von Selektion und Mord im Dritten Reich* (Berlin, 1991). See also: "Das Schicksal der jüdischen Patienten im Nationalsozialismus," in *Totgeschwiegen 1933–1945: die Geschichte der Karl-Bonhoeffer-Nervenklinik*, ed., Arbeitsgruppe zur Erforschung der Geschichte der Karl-Bonhoeffer-Nervenklinik (Berlin, 1988), and Aly, *Cleansing*. Hamburg woman in Ernst Klee, "Die Psychiatrie krankt an ihrem Menschenbild," *Die Zeit*, June 10, 1994, 16.

50. Samter, Yad Vashem (letters of Nov. 30, 1941, and Feb. 7, 1943). People also "married" in hiding. Edith Wolff, Yad Vashem, 01/326.

51. Freund, LBI, 82, 159.

52. Abraham, LBI, 6–7.

53. Abraham, LBI, 9.

54. Files in Gellately, *Gestapo* and Gordon, *Hitler*, chap. 7. Leonie (Werner) Hall, Yad Vashem; becoming a father in Krüger, LBI, 61. See also: Kliner-Lintzen, "*vergessen*," 336–39.

55. Rewald, "Berliner," 3; Berliners in Wyden, *Stella*, 154; Grossmann, Jan. 3, 1939, 2, and Dec. 8, 1940.

56. "Never free" in Freund, LBI, 53; "trembled" in Rewald, "Berliner," 6.

57. Rewald, "Berliner," 5; Freund, LBI, 53.

58. Freund, LBI, 139; Klemperer, *Zeugnis*, II, 66–67, 324, 536.

59. Couple in Richarz, *Life*, 405; Freund, LBI, 91–92.

60. Freund, LBI, 141, 176, 178. This denial of Jewish suffering and emphasis on German suffering permeated the postwar era, since, it was hoped, German victims could not be held responsible for the ravages of Nazism. Stern, *Whitewashing*, 92.

61. *Statistik des Deutschen Reiches*, vol. 552.4, from Benz, *Juden*, 734.

62. Genger, *Herzen*, 177, 195 (letters of Jan. and June 1942).

63. Genger, *Herzen*, 178 (Jan. 1942).

64. Genger, *Herzen*, 99, 112, 120, 134, 137.

65. Genger, *Herzen*, 140, 172, 178, 190.

66. Coal in American Jewish Congress, *War*, 26; "bitter cold" in *Sopade*, 1940, 258; Genger, *Herzen*, 111, 113, 116, 172, 197.

67. Genger, *Herzen*, 121–22, 133, 193.

68. Genger, *Herzen*, 132, 141.

69. Genger, *Herzen*, 143–45.

70. Genger, *Herzen*, 151–53, 155, 178.

71. Genger, *Herzen*, 163 (Oct 1941).

CHAPTER 7

Epigraph: Goebbels (Minister of Propaganda) in Ralf Georg Reuth, *Goebbels* (Munich, 1990), 252.

1. "Army" in Kwiet, "Labour," 390; "stripped" in American Jewish Congress, *War*, 23.

2. Statistics in Gruner, "Reichshauptstadt," 243–44, 247; Kwiet, "Labour," 393–94; Barkai, *Boycott*, 159–62; and Stern, *Whitewashing*, 24–27. Female "first-degree *Mischlinge*" did hard labor near home, whereas male *"Mischlinge"* and "Aryan" men married to Jews were sent to hard labor camps. Noakes, "Development," 351. See also: Krüger, LBI; Lange, *Davidstern*, 89–91; Becker-Kohen, LBI, 84–85; Struve, "Economy," 463–82. Struve notes that the labor draft began as early as fall 1943.

3. Freund, LBI, 11, on older women; "kindergarten" in Klemperer, *Zeugnis*, II, 77.

4. Segregated in Josephy, Yad Vashem, 2 (who stayed in Germany to care for her parents and described a fence separating Jews and "Aryans"), and Kwiet, "Labour," 392–93, (sabotage, 399); Klemperer, *Zeugnis*, II, 496; "target" in Erpel, "Struggle," 410.

5. War industry in Kwiet, "Labour," 392, 401; I. G. Farben in Leonie Hall, Yad Vashem, 2; rat poison in von Bialy, interview, 1992; trains in Owings, *Frauen*, 458, 463.

6. Tin in Erpel, "Struggle," 410; Rewald, "Berliner," 2; Fackenheim-Field, LBI, 10.

7. Lixl-Purcell, *Women*, 58.

8. Neumann in Richarz, *Life*, 439; day care in Elkin, "Kinder," 248; nurse in Cohn, Yad Vashem, 6 (Nov. 1942); Freund, LBI, 161.

9. Scheer, *Ahawah*, 122, 231–32, 240. Ahawah is Hebrew for love. Deportations occurred at other daycare centers as well. Kwiet, "Stufen," 583.

10. Freund, LBI, 11, 25, 27, 80–81; girls in Kwiet, "Stufen," 578.

11. Freund, LBI, 20, 100–102, 110–11, 140.

12. Freund, LBI, 111–13, 131; "600" in Klemperer, *Zeugnis*, II, 370; Rewald, "Berliner," 2.

13. Freund, LBI, 95–97; Rewald, "Berliner," 2. See also: Klemperer, *Zeugnis*, II, 11.

14. Tension in Deutschkron, *Outcast*, 84; Freund, LBI, 14, 16–17, 64, 68.

15. Freund, LBI, 68; Rewald, "Berliner," 6.

16. Transports in Friedlander, "Deportation," 212; Freund, LBI, 74, 88–89. Hirsch was murdered in 1941. "Bars" in von Bialy, interview.

17. American was Axelrath, Harvard, 29; "slapped" in Krug, Harvard, 14. Suicide rates in *AJYB 5698 (1937–38)* (Philadelphia, 1938), 336–37; *Sopade*, 1939, 923; Kwiet, "Refuge," 166. See also: Kwiet, *Widerstand*, 196–216.

18. In prewar Germany, about 28 per 100,000 Germans committed suicide, compared with only

12 British citizens in 1936. In 1932–34, suicides were highest in Berlin: 70 Jewish suicides per 100,000 and 49 non-Jewish suicides. Kwiet, "Refuge," 146, 148, 155. Ten percent in Kwiet, *Widerstand*, 205. The one-quarter figure was in the *Jüdisches Nachrichtenblatt* of March 20, 1944, in *AJYB 5701 (1940–41)* (1940), 345, and in Blau: "Last Days," 200, "Population," 172. See also: Klemperer, *Zeugnis*, II, 92, 162.

19. "Preparations" in Kwiet, "Refuge," 166; eighty-year-old in Kwiet, "Stufen," 653. Rainer Maria Rilke, *The Notebooks of Malte Laurids Brigge* (London, 1930) "It is rare to find anyone who wishes to have a death of his own. . . ."

20. Lixl-Purcell, *Women*, 52, 54.

21. Krug, Harvard, 25; friends and family in Kwiet, "Refuge," 167; doctors in Richarz, *Life*, 452; a nurse who tried to save the suicides in Mrs. A, Yad Vashem, 5a.

22. Lawlessness in Limberg, *Durften*, 133; "degradation" in Jauffron-Frank, LBI, 23–24; "shock" and organize deportations in Kwiet, "Refuge," 147, 149, 154.

23. Fewer women than men (of all faiths) committed suicide between 1933 and 1939. See: Kwiet, "Refuge," 141, 147, 154; tennis star in Author unknown, *Gelbe Fleck*, 261–66; letter in Guggenheim, LBI, 4.

24. Kwiet, "Refuge," 150 (n. 38), 151–53, 164–65.

25. Grandson in Kwiet, "Refuge," 167.

26. Rewald, "Berliner," 3; "aunts" in Monjau, LBI, 13; Freund in Richarz, *Life*, 422. More joint suicides in Author unknown, *Gelbe Fleck*, 261–66; sisters in Krüger, LBI, 20.

27. Hilberg, *Perpetrators*, 171–72; "protest" in Geisel, "Erinnerung," 16; Klemperer, *Zeugnis*, II, 122, 173; rug in Rewald, "Berliner," 4; Smith, *Train*, 190.

28. "Shocks" in Rewald, "Berliner," 4; Samter, Yad Vashem (letter of Feb. 13, 1942). Some Jews, like Ruth von Bialy's mother, took veronal with them when they were deported, to use if necessary. Von Bialy, interview.

29. In German, the terms are *zum Arbeitseinsatz nach Osten evakuiert, Umsiedlung, Verschickung,* and *Abwanderung* (which also means "wandering away"). Packing in Fischer, *Aimée*, 35 (directive of Feb. 20, 1943); "murdered" in Friedlander, "Deportation," 217.

30. Genger, *Herzen*, 25, 162, 165, 186, 200, 205–7, 210, 212, 214.

31. See, for example, lists in Hamburg, Oberfinanzpräsident 314–15; F2372, F2074, F1410, and Scheer, *Ahawah*, 201; "Eleventh decree" in Friedlander, "Deportation," 215–16; "jackals" in Smith, *Train*, 190–91. The state's pretext for auctioning was the "treasonous behavior" of Jews. Lange, *Davidstern*, 45–46. See also: Klemperer, *Zeugnis*, II, 288, 290, 316; Kwiet, "Stufen," 569.

32. Kahn in Franziska Becker, "Das beschwichtigte Gedächtnis oder: Wie man sich in einem schwäbischen Dorf an die Verfolgung der Juden im Nationalsozialismus erinnert," in *Landjudentum im Süddeutschen-und Bodenseeraum*, ed. Vorarlberger Landesarchiv (Dornbirn, 1992), 203–4; chair in Lange, *Davidstern*, 197.

33. Keys in Händler-Lachmann, *Purim*, 229; nameplate in Alton-Taubler, LBI, 2; Abraham, LBI, 9.

34. "Dignity," in Beck, *gad*, 79; Edvardson, *Kind*, 77.

35. Dortmund in Kliner-Lintzen, "*vergessen*," 342–33; Kralovitz in Lange, *Davidstern*, 45; see also Düsseldorf slaughterhouse in Morris, "Lives," 106, 110; Abraham, LBI, 6; "ransacked" in Wyden, *Stella*, 100–101; girls in Richarz, *Life*, 450.

36. Dortmund in Kliner-Lintzen, "*vergessen*," 342–33; Berlin in Samter, Yad Vashem (letter of Dec. 28, 1941); Freund in Richarz, *Life*, 421; "*Mischling*," in "The Liberation from Rosenstrasse," film by Michael Muschner (research by Nathan Stoltzfus); Rewald, "Berliner," 4. See also: Samter, Yad Vashem, letter of Dec. 28, 1941, and Morris, "Lives," 153.

37. Scheer, *Ahawah*, 181, 185.

38. Richarz, *Life*, 448–50.

39. Richarz, *Leben*, III, 61; see also Fraenkel, *Jews of Austria*, 526. Bonn in Rothe, "Jüdinnen," 282; Barkai, "Lodz," 282–83, 288; Poembsen in "memoirs of Tante Emma," 31, Simon Gruenewald

coll., LBI; Scheer, *Ahawah*, 208, 213–14. In the town of Witten, 64 percent of the deportees aged fifty to fifty-nine were women. Kliner-Lintzen, *"vergessen,"* xxxii, table 3. Kliner-Fruck estimated that 20 percent more German-Jewish women than men were murdered by examining the Gedenkbuch des Bundesarchivs Koblenz, *"Überleben,"* 96. That more Jewish women than men were murdered throughout Europe has been suggested by Rittner, *Voices*, 3; Ringelheim, "Reconsideration," 394–96; Felstiner, *Paint*, 204–07.

40. Frankfurt in Stern, *Whitewashing*, 32; *"Mischlinge"* in Lange, *Davidstern*, 182–84; Theresienstadt in Hilberg, *Destruction*, II, 438. "In most cases" because I have come across intermarriages where the Jewish partners—falsely accused of a misdemeanor—were sent to death camps, as well as cases where the divorced Jewish partner was sent to her death. See also: Abrams, *Special*, 213. "Minor child" could, at first, be sixteen, then the Gestapo lowered the age to fourteen and, later, to ten. Staatsarchiv Hamburg: Familie Plaut D38, letter of Jan. 19, 1944, and von Bialy interview.

41. "Dissolve" in Staatsarchiv Hamburg, Jüd. Gemeinde 992n, Band 5. Thanks to John Grenville for explaining the element of trickery involved in some of the Hamburg cases and for telling me the last incident.

42. Couple in Brenner, *Weiden*, 104–5; survivors in Blau, "Population," 166.

43. Late 1944 in Seligmann, "Illegal," 346; January 1945 in Gruner, "Reichshauptstadt," 254; transport of 1,000 in Büttner, *Not*, 69; Dresden in Klemperer, *LTI*, 272. While Büttner argues their fate was sealed, Benz contends their fate was unclear. Benz, "Überleben," 684.

44. Staatsarchiv Hamburg, Jüd. Gemeinde 991a: "Ein Beitrag zur Geschichte der . . . Gemeinde in Hamburg . . . Herbst 1935–Mai 1941," 35, 42; communist husband in Lange, *Davidstern*, 242.

45. Hammerstein, Yad Vashem, letters of Oct. 1942.

46. Hammerstein, Yad Vashem, letter of Nov. 2, 1942.

47. Hammerstein, Yad Vashem, letter of Dec. 10, 1942.

48. Brunner in Gruner, "Reichshauptstadt," 251, and Felstiner, *Paint*, 165; transports in Rürup, *Berlin: Bilder*, 316, 317, 319. Population statistics in Strauss, "Emigration," I, 326. These statistics include suicides and a very high death rate from malnutrition and forced labor as well.

49. Gruner, "Reichshauptstadt," 253; Gernot Jochheim, ed., *Frauenprotest in der Rosenstrasse* (Berlin, 1993); Nathan Stoltzfus, *Die Zeit*, July 21, 1989, 9–12, "Widerstand des Herzens," in *Geschichte und Gesellschaft*, 21 (1995), 218–47, and "Dissent in Nazi Germany," *The Atlantic*, Sept. 1992, 86–89; "The Liberation from Rosenstrasse," film by Michael Muschner (research by Nathan Stoltzfus); Siegfried Cohn, Yad Vashem, 3; Gross, Yad Vashem. For more on the "Factory Action" of February 27, see chap. 8 and Stoltzfus, *Resistance*. A similar factory action in Hamburg, also protested, but individually, by wives, ended with the murder of the Jewish husbands in Auschwitz. Meyer, *Verfolgung*.

50. Elkin, *Krankenhaus*; Stern, *Whitewashing*, 41–44. A group of Jews also remained at the Berlin-Weissensee cemetery.

51. Behrend-Rosenfeld, *allein*, 78; "useless eaters" in Cohn, *Breslau*, 35, 39, 60; "gas wagons" in Rosenstrauch, *Nachbarn*, 116; "12,000" in Cohn, *Breslau*, 46; Klemperer, *Zeugnis*, II, 9, 47, 68 (Auschwitz also in II, 259, 312); Abraham, LBI, 6; Smith, *Train*, 185, 187–88.

52. Mid-1942 in Edvardson, *Kind*, 75; what soldiers knew in Walter Manoschek, *Judentum*, and Omer Bartov, *Hitler's Army: Soldiers, Nazis and War in the Third Reich* (New York, 1992); relatives in Klemperer, *Zeugnis*, II, 64, 173; rumors in Bankier, *Germans*, 112; joint statement in Bauer, *Jews*, 83; Abraham, LBI, 8; Hilberg, *Destruction*, III, 1220; Rewald, "Berliner," 3, 6. On late 1942, see also: Klemperer, *Zeugnis*, II, 270, and Deutschkron, *Outcast*, 124.

53. Jacobson, *Selves*, 17.

54. Charlotte Delbo, an Auschwitz survivor, described people arriving at Auschwitz: "They expect the worst — not the unthinkable." *Auschwitz and After* (New Haven, Conn., 1995), 4; Deutschkron, *Outcast*, 128; *"Mischling"* in Abrams, *Special*, 80; Cohn, Yad Vashem, 5; Chug in Wolff, Yad Vashem, 01/326, 17.

55. Rag shop in Sussmann, Yad Vashem, 2; Wolff, Yad Vashem, 01/326, 7–8.

56. Krüger, LBI, 72; Klemperer, *Zeugnis*, II, 606, 616, 640.
57. Statistics in Strauss, "Emigration," I, 326; "Sonderburg" in Henry, *Victims*, 119–20; Berlin in Gruner, "Reichshauptstadt," 254; Herrmann, Yad Vashem, 4.
58. Abraham, LBI, 6; Pineas in Richarz, *Life*, 450; Andreas-Friedrich, *Berlin*, 83.
59. *Das Reich*, Nov. 16, 1941, 1, as cited in *Die Zeit*, June 2, 1995, 16.
60. Freya von Moltke learned of the gassings from her brother, who had been to Auschwitz to recruit laborers. Owings, *Frauen*, 252. "Extermination" in Walter Manoschek, *Judentum*, letter of Dec. 1942. Klaus Harpprecht's father, for example, was a pastor to whom soldiers confessed about the mass executions of Jews, partisans, women, and children. His father told his family, and Klaus told his classmates and, later, his army comrades. *Die Zeit*, May 12, 1995, 16.
61. "Disappeared" in Stern, *Whitewashing*, 220–237, and in Scheer, *Ahawah*, 26–27, 121–22, 178, 184, 207, 232; Bankier, *Germans*, 115.
62. Atrocities in Bankier, *Germans*, 107, and *Die Zeit*, May 12, 1995, 16; question in Mommsen, "Genocide," 220.
63. "Social liquidation" in Stern, *Whitewashing*, 230; "social death" in Patterson, *Slavery*.

CHAPTER 8

Epigraph: Neumann in Richarz, *Life*, 447.
1. Jacobson, *Selves*, 16.
2. Becker-Kohen, LBI, 32. One-third in Seligmann, "Illegal," 344; "untergetaucht" in "Report of 30 Nov. 1943," in Milton, *Joint*, 222.
3. Rewald, "Berliner," 6–7; Ritter in Jacobson, *Selves*, 71.
4. Some historians argue that the Nazis saw Jews as economically retrograde. Götz Aly and Susanne Heim, "Die ökonomie der Endlösung, Menschenvernichtung und wirtschaftliche Neuordnung," *Sozialpolitik und Judenvernichtung: Gibt es eine ökonomie der Endlösung*, ed. Aly, Heim et al. (Berlin, 1983).
5. Seligmann, "Illegal," 345; manhunts in Maren Krüger, "Alltag," 301. For servants, see: Scheer, *Ahawah*, 246, and Rosenberg, *Tell*.
6. Seligmann's sources come from the Kaduri, the Wiener, and the general collections in Yad Vashem, as well as autobiographies. Collm, Yad Vashem, 4, 12.
7. Seligmann, "Illegal," 351. On U-boat's initiative, see Fogelman, *Conscience*, 61; on spontaneity and Puterman, see: Martina Voigt, *Die Zeit*, Apr. 8, 1994, 6; Simon, tapes, LBI; three rooms in Krüger, "Alltag," 298.
8. "German-looking" in Wyden, *Stella*, 157; "traits" in Fogelman, *Conscience*, 61, 139. Still, some Germans also helped Jews, "although we didn't look exactly Germanic." Rudolf Demant, Yad Vashem, 3. On bearing, see: Nechama Tec, *Dry Tears: The Story of a Lost Childhood* (Oxford, 1982), 34–37, 89 and Lenore Weitzman's essay in *Women in the Holocaust*, ed. Weitzman and Dalia Ofer (New Haven, Conn., 1998).
9. "Monotony" in Ruth Gay, "Outwitting the Final Solution," *Horizon*, Jan. 1977.
10. Seligmann, "Illegal," 349–50 (of Jews with two main shelters, 25 percent used between ten and forty other hiding places); Deutschkron, *Outcast*; "guests" in Andreas-Friedrich, *Berlin*, 83–84; "walked on" in Morris, "Lives," 129–30.
11. Chug in Edith Wolff, Yad Vashem, 01/326, 14; Neumann in Richarz, *Life*, 447; Brenner, *Weiden*, 82.
12. One hider claimed everyone used the black market. Krüger, "Alltag," 299; Rosenberg, *Tell*, 141–44; berries in Brenner, *Weiden*, 82.
13. Abraham, LBI, 13; Scheer, *Ahawah*, 180; Simon, LBI.
14. Neumann, Yad Vashem, 2.
15. Seamstress in Ilselotte Themal, "Meine Erlebnisse während der Zeit der Judenverfolgungen in Deutschland, 1933–1945." Thank you to Ruth Gay for sharing these memoirs with me. According to Konrad Kwiet, brothels in Berlin are mentioned in several Wiener Library mem-

oirs. Conversation of Feb. 6, 1996. See also: Kwiet, *Widerstand*, 155. In the Brandenburgisches Landeshauptarchiv: PrBr Rep 12 B St Potsdam 80, a *Rassenschande* case involved exchanges of sex for shelter. The Jewish women were sent to their deaths. Voigt reports that "sex was demanded of a whole slew of Jewish women." *Die Zeit*, Apr. 8, 1994, 7. Money in Seligmann, "Illegal," 339; Collm, Yad Vashem, 2; and Becker-Kohen, LBI, entry for end of June 1944.

16. Seligmann, "Illegal," 352; Krüger, "Alltag," 302.

17. Rosenberg, *Tell*, 140, 142–43, 163; German housewives in Inge Marssolek, "Bürgerlicher Alltag in Bremen," in Gerstenberger, *Normalität*, 118.

18. "Belong" in Jacobson, *Selves*, 88; Becker-Kohen, LBI, 8.

19. Refugees in Josephy, Yad Vashem, 3; certificate in Spiegel, *Retter*, 63; corpse in Kwiet, *Widerstand*, 156; eastern refugees in Deutschkron, *Outcast*, chap. 15; false papers in Seligmann, "Illegal," 349.

20. Goldstein, Yad Vashem, 2; Rewald, "Berliner," 7.

21. Wyden, *Stella*, 156. Stella survived, was imprisoned by the Russians, and remained in Germany after her release. "Death sentence" in Schieb-Samizadeh, "Frieden," 57; Finke, Yad Vashem, 6.

22. Scheer, *Ahawah*, 246–47

23. Avoiding shelters in Abraham, LBI, 11–12 and Lange, *Davidstern*, 91; public shelters in Krüger, "Alltag," 301; "burned-out" in Kwiet, *Widerstand*, 156. In Seligmann's sample, the percentage of Jews in small towns increased from 18 percent at the beginning of hiding to 33 percent after the bombings. "Illegal," 354.

24. "Tedious" in Fogelman, *Conscience*, 83; Andreas-Friedrich, *Schattenmann*, 128–29.

25. Young woman in Herrmann, Yad Vashem, 3; Goldstein, Yad Vashem, 3.

26. Paepcke, *Ich wurde vergessen. Bericht einer Jüdin, die das Dritte Reich überlebte* (Freiburg, 1979), 103–5.

27. Schragenheim in Fischer, *Aimée*, 109, 117, 121–22.

28. "Combatting" was the motto of Nathan Schwalb-Dror of the Geneva branch of the Zionist organization, Hechaluz. Zahn, "Chug," 169, 184.

29. How did they get the tickets for cultural events? Schwersenz stood all night at the box office, which also served as his night's shelter, since it was assumed that he was in line to be the first to get tickets. Wolff, Yad Vashem, 01/326, 11–15.

30. Week and holidays in Wolff, Yad Vashem, 01/326, 15–16. See also: Beck, *gad*, 103–89; Zahn, "Chug," 159–205.

31. Paucker, "Widerstand," 47.

32. Wolff in Zahn, "Chug," 165–69; Edel, *Leben*, I, 266, 281; Jewish cells in Geisel, "Erinnerung," 17; Paucker, "Resistance," 3–21, and *Standhalten*, 28; Baum in Eric Brothers, "Wer war Herbert Baum?" in Löhken, *Widerstand*, 87. See also: Charlotte Holzer, first a member of the Baum Group and later involved in sabotage. Holzer, Yad Vashem, and Stern, *Whitewashing*, 41–44.

33. Baum in Kwiet, *Widerstand*, 114–139; Paucker, *Standhalten*, 57; and Margot Pikarski, *Jugend im Berliner Widerstand. Herbert Baum und Kampfgefährten* (Berlin, 1978). (Pikarski's is an East German publication in which the Baum Group is a purely communist one.) Erpel, "Struggle," 402.

34. Roderick Kedward, "The Maquis and the Culture of the Outlaw," in R. Kedward and Roger Austin, eds., *Vichy France and the Resistance: Culture and Ideology* (London, 1985); Renée Poznanski, "Shield-Bearers of the Resistance? Women in the French Jewish Underground" (paper presented at the Women in the Holocaust Conference, Jerusalem, June 1995). See also: Vera Laska, ed., *Women in the Resistance and in the Holocaust* (Westport, Conn., 1983). Mamlok in Paucker, "Resistance," 13.

35. For women in the armed resistance, see: Ingrid Strobl, *Sag nie, du gehst den letzten Weg: Frauen im bewaffneten Widerstand gegen Faschismus und deutsche Besatzung* (Frankfurt am Main, 1989); Erpel, "Struggle," 397–414; Holzer and Wolff (01/247), Yad Vashem. Wolff worked with Dr. Gertrud Luckner of the Catholic Action.

36. Rothschild, LBI,131–32, 149, 157; for other German-Jewish women in the French resistance, see: Juliane Lepsius, "Widerstand in Südfrankreich. Charlotte Löwenthal," 1992, LBI, archives.
37. Fischer, *Aimée*. Elisabeth Wust had sheltered Felice Schragenheim, her lover, for one year before they were caught.
38. Irma Simon, tapes, LBI, and interview with Marianne Steiner, niece of Irma Simon, New York City, March 1994. See also: "Der Schmied von Lichterfelde," *Stern*, April 30, 1961. Thank you to Mrs. Steiner for providing this article as well as other details. Irma Simon was the daughter of Abraham Eisenstein, previously head of the Oranienburgerstrasse Synagogue.
39. All the information on Ruth Abraham is from her memoirs, LBI, 1–17. For her actions during the November Pogrom, see chapter 5.
40. All information on Becker-Kohen is from her diary, LBI. "Foreign" entered on Aug. 1942.
41. Primo Levi noted: "The need to tell our story . . . had taken on for us, before our liberation and after, the character of an immediate and violent impulse, to the point of competing with our other elementary needs." *Survival in Auschwitz*, trans. S. Woolf (New York, 1961), 5–6.
42. Aug. 1940.
43. Feb. 1942, March 1942.
44. The figure of 5,000 is too large according to Kwiet and Eschwege. *Widerstand*, 151. Berlin in Kwiet, *Widerstand*, 150–51.

CONCLUSION

1. "Earthquake" in Lyotard *Differend,* trans. Georges Van Den Abbeele (Minneapolis, 1988), 56 (as called to my attention in Saul Friedländer, ed. *Probing the Limits of Representation: Nazism and the "Final Solution"* [Cambridge, Mass., 1992]), 5). See introduction, note 2 on "social death" and Patterson, *Freedom*, 9–10, and *Slavery*.
2. Stefan Zweig, *The World of Yesterday: an Autobiography* (Lincoln, 1964), 363.
3. Trommler, "Normality," 119–38, quoting George Orwell's, "Catastrophic Gradualism," in *The Collected Essays, Journalism and Letters,* ed. Sonia Orwell and Ian Angus (New York, 1968), 4:15–16.
4. Cohn, *Breslau*, 38.
5. "[E]veryday" in Owings, *Frauen*, 108; "fairy-tale" in Klemperer, *Zeugnis*, II, 104.
6. Jacobson, *Selves*, 17.
7. Annemarie Tröger quoted by Martin, "Autobiography," 188–90.
8. Friedländer, "Trauma," 132.
9. Smith, *Train*, 190.
10. "Indifference" in Mommsen, "Reaction," 153; "ordinary" in Goldhagen, *Executioners.*
11. See chapter 7; Stern, *Whitewashing*, 220–237, and Scheer, *Ahawah*, 26–27, 121–22, 178, 184, 207, 232.
12. For minority responses to the majority's "disappearance" wish, see: Hugo Brettauer, *Stadt ohne Juden* (Vienna, 1922), for a Jewish response; Jeanne Wakatsuki Houston, *Farewell to Manzanar* (Boston, 1973), for a Japanese-American response; and William Melvin Kelley, *A Different Drummer* (New York, 1962), Douglas Turner Ward, *Day of Absence* (New York, 1966), Derrick Bell's parable, the "Space Traders," in his *Faces at the Bottom of the Well* (New York, 1992), Sidney Willhelm, *Who Needs the Negro?* (Cambridge, 1970), and Patricia Williams, *The Nation*, July 10, 1995, 63, for African-American responses.
13. In June 1933, there were 106,966 Jews under age twenty in Germany. In May 1939, there were 29,254 Jews under age twenty. Benz, *Juden*, 734. In July 1941, there were 20,669 Jewish people under age eighteen. Richarz, *Leben*, III, table, 61. I have estimated from these charts.
14. "[T]he end" in Ringelheim, "Reflections on Gender" (paper presented at the Women and the Holocaust Conference, Jerusalem, June 1995); "stations" in Felstiner, *Paint*, 204–7; "earth" in Arendt, *Eichmann*, 279.

Bibliography of Works Cited

BOOKS AND THESES

Abrams, Alan. *Special Treatment: The Untold Story of Hitler's Third Race.* Secaucus, N.J., 1985.

Akademie der Künste. *Geschlossene Vorstellung: Der jüdische Kulturbund in Deutschland 1933–1941.* Berlin, 1992.

Aly, Götz, Christian Pross, and Peter Chroust, eds. *Cleansing the Fatherland: Nazi Medicine and Racial Hygiene.* Trans. Belinda Cooper. Baltimore and London, 1994.

American Jewish Congress and World Jewish Congress. Institute of Jewish Affairs. *Hitler's Ten-Year War on the Jews.* New York, 1943.

Andreas-Friedrich, Ruth. *Berlin Underground, 1938-1945.* Trans. Barrows Mussey. New York, 1947.

———. *Der Schattenmann.* Berlin, 1947.

Angress, Werner T. *Between Fear and Hope: Jewish Youth in the Third Reich.* Trans. Werner T. Angress and Christine Granger. New York, 1988.

Arendt, Hannah. *Eichmann in Jerusalem: A Report on the Banality of Evil.* New York, 1965.

Backhaus-Lautenschläger, Christine. *... und standen ihre Frau: Das Schicksal deutschsprachiger Emigrantinnen in den USA nach 1933.* Pfaffenweiler, 1991.

Bajohr, Stefan. *Die Hälfte der Fabrik: Geschichte der Frauenarbeit in Deutschland 1914 bis 1945.* 2d ed. Marburg, 1984.

Baldwin, Peter, ed. *Reworking the Past: Hitler, the Holocaust, and the Historians' Debate.* Boston, 1990.

Bankier, David. *The Germans and the Final Solution: Public Opinion Under Nazism.* Oxford, 1992.

Barkai, Avraham. *From Boycott to Annihilation: The Economic Struggle of German Jews 1933-1945.* Trans. William Templer. Hanover and London, 1989.

Bauer, Yehuda. *Jews for Sale?* New Haven, Conn., 1994.

———. *My Brother's Keeper: A History of the American Jewish Joint Distribution Committee 1929-1939.* Philadelphia, 1974.

Baumann, Ulrich. "Die sozialen Beziehungen zwischen Christen und Juden in südbadischen Landgemeinden 1862-1940." Master's thesis, University of Freiburg, 1995.

Beck, Gad. *und gad ging zu david: die erinnerungen des gad beck.* Berlin, 1995.

Behrend-Rosenfeld, Else. *Ich stand nicht allein: Erlebnisse einer Jüdin in Deutschland 1933-45.* Munich, 1988.

BenGershom, Ezra. *David: The Testimony of a Holocaust Survivor.* Trans. J. A. Underwood. Oxford and New York, 1988.

Bentwich, Norman. *Jewish Youth Comes Home: The Story of the Youth Aliyah, 1933-1943.* London, 1944.

Benz, Wolfgang. *Herrschaft and Gesellschaft im nationalsozialistischen Staat.* Frankfurt am Main, 1990.

———, ed. *Die Juden in Deutschland 1933-1945.* Munich, 1988.

Bessel, Richard, ed. *Life in the Third Reich.* Oxford and New York, 1987.

Blau, Bruno. *Das Ausnahmerecht für Juden in Deutschland 1933-1945.* Düsseldorf, 1954.

Bock, Gisela. *Zwangssterilisation im Nationalsozialismus: Studien zur Rassenpolitik und Frauenpolitik.* Opladen, 1986.

Brenner, Michael. *Am Beispiel Weiden: Jüdischer Alltag im Nationalsozialismus.* Würzburg, 1983.

———. *The Renaissance of Jewish Culture in Weimar Germany.* New Haven, Conn., 1996.

Bridenthal, Renate, Atina Grossmann, and Marion Kaplan, eds. *When Biology became Destiny: Women in Weimar and Nazi Germany.* New York, 1984.

Broszat, Martin, et al., eds. *Bayern in der NS-Zeit.* 6 vols. Munich and Vienna, 1977–1983.

Burleigh, Michael, and Wolfgang Wippermann. *The Racial State: Germany 1933-1945.* Cambridge, 1991.

Büttner, Ursula, ed. *Die Deutschen und die Judenverfolgung im Dritten Reich.* Hamburg, 1992.

———. *Die Not der Juden teilen: Christlich-jüdische Familien im Dritten Reich.* Hamburg, 1988.

———. *Das Unrechtsregime: Internationale Forschung über den Nationalsozialismus.* Hamburg, 1986.

Cohn, Willy. *Als Jude in Breslau — 1941.* Ed. Joseph Walk. Jerusalem, 1975.

Colodner, Solomon. *Jewish Education in Germany Under the Nazis.* New York, 1964.

Czarnowski, Gabriele. *Das kontrollierte Paar: Ehe- und Sexualpolitik im Nationalsozialismus.* Weinheim, 1991.

Deutschkron, Inge. *Outcast: A Jewish Girl in Wartime Berlin.* Trans. Jean Steinberg. New York, 1989.

Deutschland-Berichte der Sozialdemokratischen Partei Deutschlands, 1934-1940. Frankfurt, 1980. [Cited as *Sopade.*]

Diner, Dan, ed. *Ist der Nationalsozialismus Geschichte? Zu Historisierung und Historikerstreit.* Frankfurt, 1987.

Dwork, Debórah. *Children with a Star: Jewish Youth in Nazi Europe.* New Haven, Conn., 1991.

Edel, Peter. *Wenn es ans Leben geht: Meine Geschichte.* 2 vols. Berlin, 1979.

Edvardson, Cordelia. *Gebranntes Kind sucht das Feuer.* Munich, 1986.

Ehre, Ida. *Gott hat einen grösseren Kopf, mein Kind.* Hamburg, 1985.

Eisner, Ruth. *Nicht Wir Allein: Aus dem Tagebuch einer Berliner Jüdin.* Berlin, 1971.

Elkin, Rivka. *Das jüdische Krankenhaus in Berlin zwischen 1933 und 1945.* Berlin, 1993.

Felstiner, Mary. *To Paint Her Life: Charlotte Salomon in the Nazi Era.* New York, 1994.

Fischer, Erica. *Aimée und Jaguar: Eine Liebesgeschichte, Berlin 1943.* Cologne, 1994.

Fogelman, Eva. *Conscience and Courage: Rescuers of Jews during the Holocaust.* New York, 1994.

Foster, John, ed. *Community of Fate: Memoirs of German Jews in Melbourne.* Sydney, 1986.

Fraenkel, Josef. *The Jews of Austria: Essays on Their Life, History, and Destruction.* London, 1967.

Frankemölle, Hubert, ed. *Opfer und Täter: Zum nationalsozialistischen und antijüdischen Alltag in Ostwestfalen-Lippe.* Bielefeld, 1990.

Freeden, Herbert. *Jüdisches Theater in Nazi Deutschland.* Frankfurt am Main, 1985.

Freund, Elisabeth. *Als Zwangsarbeiterin 1941 in Berlin.* Ed. Carola Sachse. Berlin, 1996.

Frevert, Ute. *Women in German History.* Oxford and Providence, R.I., 1989.

Friedländer, Saul. *Memory, History, and the Extermination of the Jews of Europe.* Bloomington, 1993.

———. *Nazi Germany and the Jews.* Vol. 1. New York, 1997.

Friedlander, Henry. *The Origins of Nazi Genocide: From Euthanasia to the Final Solution.* Chapel Hill, N.C., 1995.

Fromm, Bella. *Blood and Banquets: A Berlin Social Diary.* London, 1942.

Gay, Ruth. *The Jews of Germany.* New Haven, Conn., 1992.

Geisel, Eike. *Die Banalität der Guten: Deutsche Seelenwanderungen.* Berlin, 1992.

———and Henryk Broder, eds. *Premiere und Pogrom: Der jüdische Kulturbund 1933-1941.* Berlin, 1992.

Der Gelbe Fleck: Die Ausrottung von 500,000 deutschen Juden. Author unknown. Foreword by Lion Feuchtwanger. Paris, 1936.

Gellately, Robert. *The Gestapo and German Society: Enforcing Racial Policy 1933-1945.* Oxford, 1990.

Gemeinschaftsarbeit der Jüdischen Jugend: Aus der Arbeit des Reichsausschuss der jüdischen Jugendverbände, 1933-1936. Berlin, 1937.

Genger, Angela, ed. *Durch unsere Herzen ziehen die Jahrtausende: Briefe von Anna und Salomon Samuel, 1933-1942.* Düsseldorf, 1988.

Gerstenberger, Heide and Dorothea Schmidt, eds. *Normalität oder Normalisierung.* Münster, 1987.

Gillis-Carlebach, Miriam. *Jedes Kind ist mein Einziges: Lotte Carlebach-Preuss, Antlitz einer Mutter und Rabbiner-Frau.* Hamburg, 1992.

Goldhagen, Daniel J. *Hitler's Willing Executioners: Ordinary Germans and the Holocaust.* New York, 1996.

Gordon, Sarah. *Hitler, Germans and the "Jewish Question."* Princeton, 1984.

Grossmann, Kurt, and Herbert Strauss, eds. *Gegenwart im Rückblick.* Heidelberg, 1970.

Händler-Lachmann, Barbara, Harald Händler, and Ulrich Schütt. *Purim, Purim, ihr liebe Leut, wisst ihr was Purim bedeut? Jüdisches Leben im Landkreis Marburg im 20. Jahrhundert.* Marburg, 1995.

Hecht, Ingeborg. *Invisible Walls: A German Family under the Nuremberg Laws.* Orlando, Fla., 1985.

Heims, Steve J., ed. *Passages from Berlin.* South Berwick, Mass., 1987.

Henry, Francis. *Victims and Neighbors: A Small Town in Nazi Germany Remembered.* South Hadley, Mass., 1984.

Herbert, Ulrich. *Europa und der "Reichseinsatz": Ausländische Zivilarbeiter, Kriegsgefangene und KZ-Häftlinge in Deutschland 1938-1945.* Essen, 1991.

———. *A History of Foreign Labor in Germany, 1880-1980.* Ann Arbor, Mich., 1990.

Heuberger, Georg, ed. *Zedaka: Jüdische Sozialarbeit im Wandel der Zeit.* Frankfurt am Main, 1992.

Hilberg, Raul. *The Destruction of the European Jews.* 3 vols., Rev. ed. New York, 1985.

———. *Perpetrators, Victims and Bystanders.* New York, 1992.

Hildesheimer, Esriel. *Der Existenzkampf der Reichsvertretung und Reichsvereinigung der Juden in Deutschland.* Tübingen, 1994.

Jacobson, Kenneth. *Embattled Selves: An Investigation into the Nature of Identity Through Oral Histories of Holocaust Survivors.* New York, 1994.

Kaplan, Marion. *The Jewish Feminist Movement in Germany: The Campaigns of the Jüdischer Frauenbund, 1904-1938.* Westport, Conn., 1979.

———. *The Making of the Jewish Middle Class: Women, Family and Identity in Imperial Germany.* New York, 1991.

Kershaw, Ian. *Popular Opinion and Political Dissent in the Third Reich: Bavaria 1933-1945.* Oxford, 1983.

Kleiber, Lore and Eva-Maria Gömüsay. *Fremdgängerinnen: Zur Geschichte bi-nationaler Ehen in Berlin von der Weimarer Republik bis in die Anfänge der Bundesrepublik.* Bremen, 1990.

Klemperer, Victor. *Ich will Zeugnis ablegen bis zum letzten: Tagebücher.* 2 vols. Berlin, 1995.

———. *LTI (Lingua Tertii Imperii): Aus dem Notizbuch eines Philologen.* Munich, 1947.

Kliner-Fruck, Martina. *"Es ging ja ums Überleben": Jüdische Frauen zwischen Nazi-Deutschland, Emigration nach Palästina und ihrer Rückkehr.* Frankfurt am Main, 1995.

Kliner-Lintzen, Martina and Siegfried Pape, eds. *"vergessen kann man das nicht": Wittener Jüdinnen und Juden unter dem Nationalsozialismus.* Bochum, 1991.

Klüger, Ruth. *weiter leben: Eine Jugend.* Göttingen, 1992.

Kocka, Jürgen. *Sozialgeschichte: Begriff, Entwicklung, Probleme.* 2d ed. Göttingen, 1986.

Koehn, Ilse. *Mischling, Second Degree: My Childhood in Nazi Germany.* New York, 1977.

Koonz, Claudia. *Mothers in the Fatherland: Women, the Family, and Nazi Politics.* New York, 1987.

Krüger, Helmut. *Der halbe Stern: Leben als deutsch-jüdischer "Mischling" im Dritten Reich.* Berlin, 1993.

Kwiet, Konrad and Helmut Eschwege. *Selbstbehauptung und Widerstand: Deutsche Juden im Kampf um Existenz und Menschenwürde 1933-1945.* Hamburg, 1984.

Lange, Bernd-Lutz, ed. *Davidstern und Weihnachtsbaum: Erinnerungen von Überlebenden.* Leipzig, 1992.

Lauber, Heinz. *Judenpogrom: Reichskristallnacht November 1938 in Grossdeutschland.* Gerlingen, 1981.

Limberg, Margarete and Hubert Rübsaat, eds. *Sie Durften nicht mehr Deutsche sein: Jüdischer Alltag in Selbstzeugnissen 1933-1938.* Frankfurt and New York, 1990.

Lixl-Purcell, Andreas. *Women of Exile: German-Jewish Autobiographies Since 1933.* Westport, Conn., 1988.

Löhken, Wilfried and Werner Vathke, eds. *Juden im Widerstand.* Berlin, 1993.

Lustiger, Arno, ed. *Zum Kampf auf Leben und Tod! Das Buch vom Widerstand der Juden 1933-1945.* Cologne, 1994.

Mallmann, Klaus-Michael and Gerhard Paul. *Herrschaft und Alltag: Ein Industrierevier im Dritten Reich.* Bonn, 1991.

Manoschek, Walter, ed. *"Es gibt nur eines für das Judentum: Vernichtung." Das Judentum in deutschen Soldatenbriefen, 1939-1944.* Hamburg, 1995.

Marrus, Michael. *The Unwanted: European Refugees in the Twentieth Century.* New York, 1985.

Martin, Elaine, ed. *Gender, Patriarchy and Fascism in the Third Reich: The Response of Women Writers.* Detroit, 1992.

Milton, Sybil and Frederick Bogin, eds. *Archives of the Holocaust: An International Collection of Selected Documents.* Vol. X, *American Joint Distribution Committee, New York.* Part I. London and New York, 1995.

Mommsen, Hans, ed. *Herrschaftsalltag im Dritten Reich.* Düsseldorf, 1988.

Moritz, Klaus and Ernst Noam. *NS Verbrechen vor Gericht, 1945–1955.* Wiesbaden, 1978.

Morris, Douglas. "The Lives of Some Jewish Germans Who Lived in Nazi Germany and Live in Germany Today: An Oral History." B.A. thesis. Wesleyan University, 1976.

Mosse, George, L. *German Jews beyond Judaism.* Bloomington, Ind., 1985.

Müller, Ingo. *Furchtbare Juristen: Die unbewältigte Vergangenheit unserer Justiz.* Munich, 1987.

Nathorff, Hertha. *Das Tagebuch der Hertha Nathorff.* Ed. Wolfgang Benz. Munich, 1987.

Niethammer, Lutz, ed. *"Die Jahre weiss man nicht wo man die heute hinsetzen soll."* Bonn, 1983.

Niewyk, Donald. *The Jews in Weimar Germany.* Baton Rouge, La., 1980.

Noakes, Jeremy and Geoffrey Pridham, *Documents on Nazism, 1919-1945.* New York, 1975.

Noam, Ernst and Wolf-Arno Kropat. *Juden vor Gericht, 1933-1945.* Wiesbaden, 1975.

Nolan, Mary. *Visions of Modernity: American Business and the Modernization of Germany.* New York, 1994.

Ostow, Robin. *Jews in Contemporary East Germany.* New York, 1989.

Owings, Alison. *Frauen: German Women Recall the Third Reich.* New Brunswick, N.J., 1993.

Pätzold, Kurt. *Verfolgung, Vertreibung, Vernichtung.* Leipzig, 1983.

Patterson, Orlando. *Freedom: Freedom in the Making of Western Culture.* New York, 1991.

———. *Slavery and Social Death.* Cambridge, 1982.

Paucker, Arnold, ed. *The Jews in Nazi Germany, 1933-1945.* Tübingen, 1986.

———. *Standhalten und Widerstehen: Der Widerstand deutscher und österreichischer Juden gegen die Nationalsozialistische Diktatur.* Essen, 1995.

Pehle, Walter H., ed. *Der Judenpogrom 1938: Von der "Reichskristallnacht" zum Völkermord.* Frankfurt am Main, 1988.

————. *November 1938. From "Kristallnacht" to Genocide.* Trans. William Templer. New York, 1991.

Quack, Sibylle. *Zuflucht Amerika: Zur Sozialgeschichte der Emigration deutsch-jüdischer Frauen in die USA, 1933-1945.* Bonn, 1995.

————, ed. *Between Sorrow and Strength: Women Refugees of the Nazi Period.* Cambridge, 1995.

Rewald, Ilse. *Berliner, die uns halfen die Hitlerdiktatur zu überleben.* Berlin, 1975.

Richarz, Monika, ed. *Jewish Life in Germany: Memoirs from Three Centuries.* Trans. Stella Rosenfeld and Sidney Rosenfeld. Bloomington, 1991.

————. *Jüdisches Leben in Deutschland: Selbstzeugnisse zur Sozialgeschichte 1918-1945.* Vol. 3. Stuttgart, 1982.

Rittner, Carol and John Roth, eds. *Different Voices: Women and the Holocaust.* New York, 1993.

Röcher, Ruth. *Die jüdische Schule im nationalsozialistischen Deutschland, 1933-1942.* Frankfurt am Main, 1992.

Rosenberg, Blanca. *To Tell at Last: Survival under False Identity, 1941-45.* Urbana, 1993.

Rosenstrauch, Hazel. *Aus Nachbarn wurden Juden: Ausgrenzung und Selbstbehauptung 1933-1942.* Berlin, 1988.

Rothchild, Sylvia, ed. *Voices from the Holocaust.* New York, 1981.

Rürup, Reinhard, ed. *Jüdische Geschichte in Berlin: Bilder und Dokumente.* Berlin, 1995.

————. *Jüdische Geschichte in Berlin: Essays und Studien.* Berlin, 1995.

Runge, Irene. *Onkel Max ist jüdisch.* Berlin, 1991.

Sauer, Paul. *Dokumente über die Verfolgung der jüdischen Bürger in Baden-Württemberg, 1933-1945.* 2 vols. Stuttgart, 1966.

Scheer, Regina. *Ahawah: Das vergessene Haus.* Berlin and Weimar, 1992.

Scheurenberg, Klaus. *Ich will Leben.* Berlin, 1982.

Schleunes, Karl. *The Twisted Road to Auschwitz: Nazi Policy Toward German Jews, 1933-39.* Urbana, Ill., 1970.

Scholem, Gershom. *From Berlin to Jerusalem.* New York, 1980.

Schwarz, Gudrun. *Die nationalsozialistischen Lager.* Frankfurt am Main, 1990.

Sichel, Frieda H. *Challenge of the Past.* Johannesburg, 1975.

Silbergleit, Heinrich. *Die Bevölkerungs- und Berufsverhältnisse der Juden im Deutschen Reich.* Berlin, 1930.

Smith, Howard K. *Last Train from Berlin.* New York, 1942.

Sopade. See *Deutschland-Berichte.*

Spiegel, Marga. *Retter in der Nacht: Wie eine jüdische Familie überlebte.* 2d. ed. Cologne, 1987.

Stephenson, Jill. *Women in Nazi Society.* New York, 1975.

Stern, Frank. *The Whitewashing of the Yellow Badge: Antisemitism and Philosemitism in Postwar Germany.* Trans. William Templer. Oxford, 1992.

Stoltzfus, Nathan. *Resistance of the Heart: Intermarriage and the Rosenstrasse Protest in Germany.* New York, 1996.

Thalmann, Rita, and Emmanuel Feinermann. *Crystal Night.* New York, 1974.

Tramer, Hans, ed. *In zwei Welten.* Tel Aviv, 1962.

Vogel, Carole Garbuny, ed. *We Shall Not Forget! Memories of the Holocaust.* Lexington, Mass., 1994.

Wahrman, Shlomo. *Lest We Forget: Growing Up in Nazi Leipzig 1933–1939.* New York, 1991.

Walk, Joseph, ed. *Das Sonderrecht für die Juden im NS-Staat: Eine Sammlung der gesetzlichen Massnahmen und Richtlinien — Inhalt und Bedeutung.* Heidelberg, 1981.

Wyden, Peter. *Stella: One Woman's True Tale of Evil, Betrayal, and Survival in Hitler's Germany.* New York, 1992.

ARTICLES AND PAPERS

Allport, G. W., J. S. Bruner, and E. M. Jandorf. "Personality Under Social Catastrophe: Ninety Life-Histories of the Nazi Revolution." *Character and Personality: An International Psychological Quarterly* 10, no. 1 (Sept. 1941).

Angress, Werner T. "Erfahrungen jüdischer Jugendlicher und Kinder mit der nichtjüdischen Umwelt 1933-45." In *Deutschen.* Ed. Büttner.

———. "Jüdische Jugend zwischen nationalsozialistischer Verfolgung und jüdischer Wiedergeburt." In *Nazi Germany.* Ed. Paucker.

Baldwin, Peter. "The *Historikerstreit* in Context." In *Reworking.* Ed. Baldwin.

Barkai, Avraham. "Between East and West: Jews from Germany in the Lodz Ghetto." *Yad Vashem Studies* 16 (1984).

———. "Volksgemeinschaft, 'Aryanization' and the Holocaust." In *The Final Solution: Origins and Implementation.* Ed. David Cesarani. London and New York, 1994.

———. "Der wirtschaftliche Existenzkampf der Juden im Dritten Reich, 1933-38." In *Nazi Germany.* Ed. Paucker.

Baumann, Ulrich. "Jüdische Frauen auf dem Land." Unpublished paper, University of Freiburg, 1992.

Benz, Wolfgang. "The Relapse into Barbarism." In *November.* Ed. Pehle.

———. "Überleben im Untergrund." In *Juden.* Ed. Benz.

Bessel, Richard. "Political Violence and the Nazi Seizure of Power." In *Life.* Ed. Bessel.

Blau, Bruno. "The Jewish Population of Germany, 1939-1946." *Jewish Social Studies* 12 (1950).

———. "The Last Days of German Jewry in the Third Reich." *YIVO Annual of Jewish Social Science,* 1953.

———. "Mischehe im Nazi Reich." *Judaica: Beiträge zum Verständnis des jüdischen Schicksals in Vergangenheit und Gegenwart* 4 (1948).

Borscheid, Peter. "Plädoyer für eine Geschichte des Alltäglichen." In *Ehe, Liebe, Tod: Studien zur Geschichte des Alltags.* Ed. Peter Borscheid and Hans Teuteberg. Münster, 1983.

Büttner, Ursula. "The Persecution of Christian-Jewish Families." *LBIYB,* 1989.

Cahnmann, Werner. "Village and Small-Town Jews in Germany: A Typological Study." *LBIYB,* 1974.

Cohn, Benno. "Einige Bemerkungen über den deutschen Zionismus nach 1933." In *Welten.* Ed. Tramer.

Cohn, Werner. "Bearers of a Common Fate? The 'Non-Aryan' Christian 'Fate-Comrades' of the Paulus-Bund, 1933-1939." *LBIYB,* 1988.

Elkin, Rivka. "Kinder zur Aufbewahrung im jüdischen Krankenhaus." *Tel Aviv Jahrbuch,* 1994.

Enssle, Manfred J. "German Everyday Life after World War II." *Central European History* 26, no. 1 (1993).

Erpel, Simone. "Struggle and Survival: Jewish Women in the Anti- Fascist Resistance in Germany." *LBIYB,* 1992.

Freeden, Herbert. "Jüdischer Kulturbund ohne jüdische Kultur." In *Vorstellung.* Ed. Akademie der Künste.

———."Kultur 'nur für Juden': 'Kulturkampf' in der jüdischen Pressen in Nazideutschland." In *Nazi Germany.* Ed. Paucker.

Friedländer, Saul. "A Controversy about the Historicization of National Socialism." *New German Critique* 44 (1988).

———. "Trauma and Transference." In *Memory, History.* Ed. Friedländer.

Friedlander, Henry. "Deportation of German Jews: Postwar German Trials of Nazi Criminals." *LBIYB,* 1984.

———. "The Judiciary and Nazi Crimes in Postwar Germany." *Simon Wiesenthal Center Annual* I, 1984.

Fritzsche, Peter. "Where Did All the Nazis Go? Reflections on Resistance and Collaboration." *Tel Aviver Jahrbuch für deutsche Geschichte* 23 (1994).

Gay, Peter. "Epilogue: The First Sex." In *Sorrow*. Ed. Quack.

Geisel, Eike. "Störenfriede der Erinnerung." In *Widerstand*. Ed. Löhken.

Gellately, Robert. "The Gestapo and German Society: Political Denunciation in the Gestapo Case Files." *Journal of Modern History* 60, no. 4 (December 1988).

Geyer, Michael. "The Nazi State Reconsidered." In *Life*. Ed. Bessel.

———. "The State in National Socialist Germany." In *Statemaking and Social Movements*. Ed. Charles Bright and Susan Harding. Ann Arbor, Mich., 1984.

Grenville, John. "Die 'Endlösung' und die 'Judenmischlinge' im Dritten Reich." In *Unrechtsregime*. Ed. Büttner.

———. "Juden, 'Nichtarier' und 'Deutsche Ärzte': Die Anpassung der Ärzte im Dritten Reich." In *Deutschen*. Ed. Büttner.

Gruner, Wolf. "Die Reichshauptstadt und die Verfolgung der Berliner Juden 1933-1945." In *Berlin: Essays*. Ed. Rürup.

Helfand, Jonathan I. "*Halakhah* and the Holocaust: Historical Perspectives." In *Perspectives on the Holocaust*. Ed. Randolph L. Braham. Boston, 1983.

Henschel, Hildegard. "Aus der Arbeit der jüdischen Gemeinde in Berlin während der Jahre 1941-1943: Gemeindearbeit und Evakuierung von Berlin." *Zeitschrift für die Geschichte der Juden* 9 (1972).

Huerkamp, Claudia. "Jüdische Akademikerinnen in Deutschland, 1900–1938." *Geschichte und Gesellschaft* 19, no. 3 (1993).

Johnson, Eric. "German Women and Nazi Justice: Their Role in the Process from Denunciation to Death." *Historical Social Research* 20, no. 1 (1995).

Kater, Michael H. "Everyday Anti-Semitism in Prewar Nazi Germany: The Popular Bases." *Yad Vashem Studies* 16 (1984).

———. "Physicians in Crisis at the End of the Weimar Republic." In *Unemployment and the Great Depression in Weimar Germany*. Ed. Peter D. Stachura. London, 1986.

Koonz, Claudia. "Courage and Choice Among German-Jewish Women and Men." In *Nazi Germany*. Ed. Paucker.

Kramer, David. "Jewish Welfare Work Under the Impact of Pauperisation." In *Nazi Germany*. Ed. Paucker.

Krüger, Maren, et al. "Alltag im Berliner Untergrund 1943-45." In *Antisemitismus und Jüdische Geschichte: Studien zu Ehren von Herbert A. Strauss*. Ed. Rainer Erb and Michael Schmidt. Berlin, 1987.

Kwiet, Konrad. "Forced Labour of German Jews in Nazi Germany." *LBIYB*, 1991.

———. "Nach dem Pogrom: Stufen der Ausgrenzung." In *Juden*. Ed. Benz.

———. "The Ultimate Refuge: Suicide in the Jewish Community Under the Nazis." *LBIYB*, 1984.

Lüdtke, Alf. " 'Formierung der Massen' oder Mitmachen und Hinnehmen? 'Alltagsgeschichte' und Faschismusanalyse." In *Normalität*. Ed. Gerstenberger.

Martin, Elaine. "Autobiography, Gender, and the Third Reich." In *Gender*. Ed. Martin.

Mason, Tim. "Women in Germany, 1925-1940: Family, Welfare and Work." I and II. *History Workshop*, spring and autumn, 1976.

Maurer, Trude. "Abschiebung und Attentat: Die Ausweisung der polnischen Juden und der Vorwand für die 'Kristallnacht.' " In *Judenpogrom*. Ed. Pehle.

———. "Ausländische Juden in Deutschland, 1933-39." In *Nazi Germany*. Ed. Paucker.

Meynert, Joachim. " 'Das hat mir sehr weh getan!' Jüdische Jugend in Ostwestfalen-Lippe: Streiflichter 1933-1939." In *Opfer*. Ed. Frankemölle.

Milton, Sybil. "Women and the Holocaust." In *Biology*. Ed. Bridenthal.

Mommsen, Hans. "The Reaction of the German Population to Anti-Jewish Persecution and the Holocaust." In *Lessons and Legacies: The Meaning of the Holocaust in a Changing World*. Ed. Peter Hayes. Evanston, Ill., 1991.

————"What Did the Germans Know about the Genocide of the Jews?" In *November*. Ed. Pehle.

Mommsen, Hans, and Dieter Obst. "Die Reaktion der deutschen Bevölkerung auf die Verfolgung der Juden, 1933-1943." In *Herrschaftsalltag*. Ed. Mommsen.

Noakes, Jeremy. "The Development of Nazi Policy Towards the German-Jewish 'Mischlinge' 1933-1945." *LBIYB*, 1989.

Nolan, Mary. "The Historikerstreit and Social History." *New German Critique* 44 (Spring/Summer 1988).

————. "The Historikerstreit and Social History." In *Reworking*. Ed. Baldwin.

Nussbaum, Max. "Ministry Under Stress: A Rabbi's Recollection of Nazi Berlin, 1935-40." In *Gegenwart*. Ed. Grossmann.

Paucker, Arnold. "Jüdischer Widerstand in Deutschland." In *Kampf*. Ed. Lustiger.

————. "Resistance of German and Austrian Jews to the Nazi Regime, 1933-1945." *LBIYB*, 1995.

Peukert, Detlef. "Alltag und Barbarei: Zur Normalität des Dritten Reiches." In *Nationalsozialismus*. Ed. Diner.

Plum, Günter. "Wirtschaft und Erwerbsleben." In *Juden*. Ed. Benz.

Prinz, Joachim. "A Rabbi Under the Hitler Regime." In *Gegenwart*. Ed. Grossmann.

Quack, Sybille. "Changing Gender Roles and Emigration: The Example of German-Jewish Women and their Emigration to the United States." In *People in Transit: German Migrations in Comparative Perspective, 1829-1930*. Ed. Dirk Hoerder and Jörg Nagler. New York and Cambridge, 1995.

Reinharz, Jehuda. "Hashomer Hazair in Nazi Germany." In *Nazi Germany*. Ed. Paucker.

Ringelheim, Joan. "Women and the Holocaust: A Reconsideration of Research." In *Voices*. Ed. Rittner.

Rosenthal, Erich. "Trends of the Jewish Population in Germany, 1910-1939." *Jewish Social Studies* 6 (1944).

Rothe, Valentine. "Jüdinnen in Bonn, 1933-1945." In *Frauenleben im NS-Alltag*. Ed. Annette Kuhn. Pfaffenweiler, 1994.

Rovit, Rebecca. "Collaboration or Survival, 1933-1938: Reassessing the Role of the *Jüdischer Kulturbund*." In *Theatre in the Third Reich: The Prewar Years*. Ed. Glen W. Gadberry. Westport, Conn., 1995.

Rürup, Reinhard. "Das Ende der Emanzipation: Die antijüdischen Politik in Deutschland von der 'Machtergreifung' bis zum Zweiten Weltkrieg." In *Nazi Germany*. Ed. Paucker.

Schieb-Samizadeh, Barbara. "Die Gemeinschaft für Frieden und Aufbau." In *Widerstand*. Ed. Löhken.

Schmelz, Usiel O. "Die demographische Entwicklung der Juden in Deutschland von der Mitte des 19. Jahrhunderts bis 1933." *Zeitschrift für Bevölkerungswissenschaft* 8, no. 1 (1982).

Schorsch, Ismar. "German Judaism: From Confession to Culture." In *Nazi Germany*. Ed. Paucker.

Schwarz, Christina. "Tschaikowsky für die Seele, Brote für den Hunger: Die jüdische Winterhilfe." In *Zedaka*. Ed. Heuberger.

Seligmann, Avraham. "An Illegal Way of Life." *LBIYB*, 1992.

Strauss, Herbert. "Jewish Autonomy Within the Limits of National Socialist Policy: The Communities and the Reichsvertretung." In *Nazi Germany*. Ed. Paucker.

————. "Jewish Emigration from Germany, Part I." *LBIYB*, 1980.

Struve, Walter. "Entstehung und Herrschaft des nationalsozialismus in einer niedersächsischen Stadt." In *Terror, Herrschaft und Alltag im Nationalsozialismus*. Ed. Brigitte Berlekamp and Werner Röhr. Münster, 1995.

————. "The Wartime Economy: Foreign Workers, 'Half Jews,' and Other Prisoners in a German Town, 1939-1945." *German Studies Review* 16 (1993).

Thalmann, Rita. "Jüdische Frauen nach dem Pogrom 1938." In *Nazi Germany*. Ed. Paucker.

Trommler, Frank. "Between Normality and Resistance: Catastrophic Gradualism in Nazi

Germany." In *Resistance Against the Third Reich*. Ed. Michael Geyer and John Boyer. Chicago, 1992.

Vollnhals, Clemens. "Judische Selbsthilfe bis 1938." In *Juden*. Ed. Benz.

von Saldern, Adelheid. "Hillgrubers 'Zweierlei Untergang': Der Untergang historischer Erfahrungsanalyse?" In *Normalität*. Ed. Gerstenberger.

Wetzel, Juliane. "Auswanderung aus Deutschland." In *Juden*. Ed. Benz.

Wickert, Christl. "Sozialistin, Parlamentarierin, Jüdin." In *Juden und deutsche Arbeiterbewegung bis 1933*. Ed. Lüdger Heid and Arnold Paucker. Tübingen, 1992.

Zahn, Christine. "'Nicht mitgehen, sondern weggehen!' Chug Chaluzi — eine jüdische Jugendgruppe im Untergrund." In *Widerstand*. Ed. Löhken.

PERIODICALS (AND ABBREVIATIONS)

American Jewish Year Book (AJYB) (Philadelphia)

Blätter des jüdischen Frauenbundes (BJFB) (Berlin)

C-V Zeitung (CV) (Berlin)

Frankfurter Israelitisches Gemeindeblatt (FIG) (Frankfurt am Main)

Gemeindeblatt der jüdischen Gemeinde zu Berlin (GemBer) (Berlin)

Israelitisches Familienblatt (IF) (Hamburg)

Jüdische Rundschau (Rundschau) (Berlin)

Jüdische Wohlfahrtspflege und Sozial Politik (JWS) (Berlin)

Leo Baeck Institute Year Book (LBIYB) (London)

Statistisches Jahrbuch für das Deutsche Reich (Statistisches Jahrbuch) (Germany, Statistisches Amt)

Zeitschrift für Demographie und Statistik der Juden (ZDSJ) (Berlin)

ARCHIVES AND LIBRARIES

Only the most important archival file groups are mentioned. Full citations are given in the notes.

Brandenburgisches Landeshauptarchiv
PrBr Rep 12 B St Potsdam 80: "Rassenschande" in hiding.

Bundesarchiv Koblenz
R18 Reichsministerium des Innern
R22 Reichsjustizministerium
R58 Reichssicherheitshauptamt

Bundesarchiv Abteilung Potsdam
Jüdische Haushaltungsschule, Frankfurt am Main, 1925-39
Reichsministerium für Wissenschaft, Erziehung, und Volksbildung

Bundesarchiv Abteilung Potsdam-Coswig
75C Jüdischer Frauenbund
75C Prague: Coordinating Committee for Refugees

Harvard University: Houghton Library, Cambridge, Massachusetts
Memoirs in Collection BMS GER 91, written for contest: "Mein Leben in Deutschland vor und nach dem 30. Januar 1933." Publication of citations is by permission of the Houghton Library.
Memoirs of: Erna Albersheim, Elsie Axelrath, Alice Baerwald, Hanna Bernheim, Vera Deutsch (reader's comments), Maria Donath (summary of ms.), Mally Dienemann, Elisabeth Drexler (summary of ms.), Constance Hallgarten, Verena Hellwig, Hilde Honnet-Sichel, Maria Kahle, Berta Kamm (summary of ms.), Hilde Koch, Lily S. Krug, Helen Lang (pseudonym), Marthe Lewinsohn, Margot Littauer, Ida Fanny Lohr, Margaret Moses, Martha Neumann, Lotte Popper

Hauptstaatsarchiv Düsseldorf
RW 58 Gestapo-Personalakten

Leo Baeck Institute, New York. Publication of citations is by permission of the Leo Baeck Institute.
Memoirs of: Ruth Abraham, Anonymous ("Lest We Forget!"), Ruth Alton-Taubler, Elizabeth Bab,

Kurt Jacob Ball-Kaduri, Elisabeth Bamberger, Erna Becker-Kohen (diary), Kate Behnsch-Brower, Marianne Berel, Hanna Bergas, Lisa Brauer, Emily Braun-Melchior, Tilly Epstein, Manfred Fackenheim-Field, Elisabeth Freund (also see Books, above), Kate Freyhan, Rosy Geiger-Kullmann, Else Gerstel, Ruth (Sass) Glaser, Leo Gompertz, Lisa Grubel, Erika Guetermann, Julius Guggenheim, Charlotte Hamburger, Simon Hayum, Ida Jauffron-Frank, Liselotte Kahn, Helmut Kallmann, Helmut Krüger (also see Books, above), Toni Lessler, Joseph Benjamin Levy, Ann Lewis, Erich Leyens, Charles Marks, Senta Meyer-Gerstein, Mieke Monjau, Herta Nathorff (also see Books, above), Recha Rothschild, Erna Segal, Charlotte Stein-Pick, Gerdy Stoppleman, Ilse Strauss, Lilli Sussmann

Archival Collections of: Hedwig Burgheim, Klara Caro, Simon Gruenewald, Senta Meyer-Gerstein, Ottilie Schoenewald, Irma Simon (tapes), Luise Stern, Ella Werner

Research Foundation for Jewish Immigration, New York

Interviews with: Edith Bick (1972, born 1900), Marie Bloch (1971, born 1890), Alice Nauen (1971, born 1901)

Staatsarchiv Hamburg

522-1 Jüdische Gemeinden: 991–992, 297B, D38 (Familie Plaut)

Oberfinanzpräsident, 314-15

Yad Vashem Archives, Jerusalem

Ball Kaduri Collection: Frieda Cohn, Rudolf Demant, Ernst Gross, Charlotte Holzer, Edith Wolff (01/247 and 01/326)

Wiener Library Collection: Mrs. A. (02/29), Käthe Baronowitz, Siegfried Cohn, Ludwig Collm, Lotte Dixon, Olga Eisenstädt, Ursula Finke, Lisa Frank, Alice Goldstein, Leonie (Werner) Hall, Gertrud Hammerstein (letters), Marcella Herrmann, Charlotte Josephy, Irma Neumann, Herman Samter (letters), Annemarie Scherman, Rabbi Ernst Steckelmacher, Harry Sussmann

INDIVIDUAL INTERVIEWS BY AUTHOR

Anna Hamburger (from Nördlingen, born 1888), New Jersey, 1981

Elyse Reichenstein (from Nuremberg, child in 1938), New York, 1997.

Ruth von Bialy (from Hamburg, born 1908), Hamburg, 1990, 1992

PRIVATE COLLECTIONS

Atina Grossmann, New York, letters of Gertrud Grossmann

Index